MUSICAL CULTURE
OF
THE MUNDA TRIBE

About the Author

The author, himself a tribal and by training an anthropologist, has a long years of association and experience of working among communities of various tribes and castes of India. He keeps deep interest in the study of traditional cultures, and problems of the weaker sections of the societies. He has contributed a number of articles on the subjects and has published few books. He was associated with the Anthropological Survey of India, and the University Grants Commission in service life.

MUSICAL CULTURE OF THE MUNDA TRIBE

Sem Topno

CONCEPT PUBLISHING COMPANY PVT. LTD.
NEW DELHI-110059

ISBN : 978-81-8069-024-2

First Published 2004

Published and Printed by

Concept Since 1974

Concept Publishing Company Pvt. Ltd.
A/15-16, Commercial Block, Mohan Garden,
New Delhi-110059 (INDIA)
T : +91 11 25351460, +91 11 25351794
E : publishing@conceptpub.com, *W* : www.conceptpub.com

Cataloging in Publication Data--Courtesy: D.K. Agencies (P) Ltd. <docinfo@dkagencies.com>

Topano, Sema, author.
Musical culture of the Munda tribe / Sem Topno.
pages cm
Includes bibliographical references and index.
ISBN 9788180690242

1. Munda (Indic people)--Songs and music. 2. Chota Na?gpur (India)--Songs and music. I. Title.

LCC DS432.M8T67 2020 | DDC 780.89959 23

Reverently dedicated
to
My Parents, Late Gangi and Eliazar
who taught me to pay respect to the ancestors

"Scarcely ever one can find a mountain that looks the same from the north as it does from the south. Reality is like that; it has many aspects and can only be fully portrayed by views that are not identical nor even similar, because they are views from different points of the compass."

— **Dr. Allen Gregg**

FOREWORD

Sem Topno's work *Musical Culture of the Munda Tribe* is a welcome addition to the critical literature on the Mundas. This is an insider's view, who is both participant and observer.

While anthropologists and linguists have given considerable attention to this very important group, no enough attention has been paid to the interface of the Munda cosmogony, cosmology, world-view, life-function and the artistic expressions. One group of anthropologists have laid stress on the material culture and others to the value culture, and yet others only to the Mundari language, few have attempted to view the life of a cohesive group as a totality where there is an intrinsic inter-relationship between the cosmology, world-view, the life cycle and function and the seemingly simple and attractive music and dance traditions.

Dr. Sem Topno's monograph attempts to do precisely this. Painstakingly he contextualises the music and dance within the physical landscape, its flora and fauna, the life-cycle, life-style, daily function and the cosmology and mythology.

The book is neatly divided into six parts, viz. the Munda tradition of music and dance, journey through the stages of life, the environment and views on the cosmic universe, the philosophy of life and social world, and finally economic and political history. This undoubtedly is a comprehensive coverage of almost all facets of the group.

Most revealing is the perception of the universe, the myths of creation and the hierarchy of powers as reflected in the songs of the Mundas. Through them one learns of the awareness of a unified vision which conceives of the Sing Bonga and the consequent creation of the universe through a series of complimentary principles. Equally illuminating is the presence and communication with the flora and the fauna and all aspects of nature. This dialogue of Man-Nature is the great contemporary relevance as it points to a world view where there is no sense of a violent confrontation with nature.

Equally pertinent is the world view and the philosophy of life and the social organisation. A balance is made between the individual and the collective group. Often in our anxiety to assert the identity of only the individual, we forget that group cohesiveness is a source of emotional security and confidence rather than individual fear and aggression.

The life-cycle from birth to death is punctuated with a series of rites, which facilitate transition from one stage to the other, music and dance are essential markers of this journey. Each song and dance acquires special significance as it is intrinsically linked to life experience.

Music and dance and other artistic expressions, thus become an essential and indispensable part of everyday life and are not leisure time activities of entertainment and filling up vacuum. The compositions of the music and dance reflect both social structure as also gender relationships. Indeed they are indicators of understanding inter-relationships as also phases and stages of life. Dr. Sem Topno gives us a detailed account of the vast repertoire of the musical compositions of the songs and dances. The section on the musical instruments is informative and valuable. Students of Indian folk music and dance will have much to learn from this account.

Dr. Sem Topno does well to bring his account in the two concluding chapters on the recent economic and political history. These chapters make his readers aware of the multiple identities of the Mundas. As a cohesive group committed to a cosmology and world view they have one identity. As individuals and a group within a large democracy, they have the need to assert another identity. The question is, can they contain both, or must there be inner conflict and outer dissent? These chapters bring to fore the whole question of empowerment and disempowerment, the so called majority and minority questions and those of the debate of main stream and subsidiary streams. Dr. Sem Topno handles them with sensitivity and gentleness. An extensive bibliography is evidence of the author's having examined the writings of many distinguished anthropologists and writers.

All in all, I have enjoyed reading the monograph, have benefited a great deal.

It is my hope that other readers will find this monograph equally educative and illuminating.

New Delhi
March 17, 1999

KAPILA VATSYAYAN

Map. 1: Villages of Naguri Country

PREFACE

The Mundas are one of the widely studied tribes in India. There is an array of literature on this tribe which throw sufficient light on all aspects of the people's lives, that is, history, politics, society, economics, language and culture in general. Almost all the works, however, carry the outsiders view as the people and their culture was observed through the lance of other cultures. The views expressed in some of these works are laden with value judgement and suffer from attitudinal biases. It is natural that such study suffers from misconceptions and misrepresentation of people's culture. But there are also good works on the people and their culture which throw some light on their rich cultural heritage.

The present treatise is in the direction of presentation of self by the tribe themselves through the music of their own creation which is so clear and transparent that it reveals the whole society and culture in totality as well as its process and functions. The most important thing in any tribal society is that it is embedded in the eco-environment so deeply that conceptualization of their society and culture without it, is impossible. Music has an important role in human society and this has been perceived by the human beings since primordial times. But unlike the music of the developed society, tribal music has myriad functions. It is a feast not only for the eyes, ears and mind of the people but it is also a heritage of knowledge and wisdom of the tribal people. The theme of the music is derived from the eco-environment of the tribe, their society, economy, history and politics including their philosophy and world-views.

Change and development is the law of the nature and the tribal society and culture is no exception. The change from within the society is always for sound growth and development but change from outside which is thrust upon the people and particularly on the tribals, is not always healthy. Prof. Sachchidananda while studying the Munda tribe identified some basic factors responsible for unhealthy change in their society and culture. He has stated this in these words :

"Munda culture is fast changing because of contact with an alien people and alien ways of life. The process has been continuing for a very long time and as facilities for communication have increased, the isolation of the tribal villages has been broken. Constant living with non-tribal castes in villages, growth of education, the growth of townships in the interior of the tribal regions, the increasing industrialization of the area due to its wealth of mineral resources and the growth of new industries, the work of various missionaries as well as the growth of political consciousness have brought about a great deal of change in the life of the tribes in this area. Administrative agencies, forest officials, businessmen, contractors, and moneylenders have given further stimulus to culture change" (1979 : 14).

The study of musical culture and culture history of the Mundas was made among the autochthonous group who still uphold the traditional forms of culture though greatly reduced in number. Under great stress of change and strain of modernity and laden with psychological pressure of practising the outdated customs and practices, they may not be able to carry it over to the twenty-first century. A sure death is awaiting this great culture of unwritten tradition. Culture is an index of quality of life of the people and heritage of the mankind as traditions. It is the sum-total of achievement in excellence of the people over an unrecorded period of time. And so, the music in particular is taken as the common heritage of mankind.

The data on music and songs were collected from the Konkpat Mundas of the Naguri country who inhabit the south-western and southern parts of Ranchi district in Chhotanagpur plateau and areas covered by the police stations of Khunti, Torpa, Kamdara, Karra, Bero, Lapung, Sisai, Basia, Palkot, Bano, Kolebira, Rania, Manoharpur, Bandgaon, Murhu, etc. The Mundas of this area socially, linguistically and politically are well integrated people. They are girdled on the west by the Oraon tribe, the south-west by the Kharia tribe, south by the Ho tribe, the east by the Mundas of Hasada country and on the north by Oraon and other tribals as well as caste groups. A number of other minor tribes and castes are found settled among them like Turi, Kumhar, Mochi, Teli, Rautia, Ghasi, Chik-Baraik, Jogi, Badae or Lohara, Mallar, Jhora, Perain, Bhogta, Jolha, etc, and few other high castes like Brahmin, Rajput, Bania and Muslim. The presence of these social and ethnic groups have variously influenced the economy, society and to the musical culture of the Mundas.

I owe deep gratitude to the Mundas whose names are embedded in the music of their creation which lives on through countless throats like the sounds of winds and streams of the wilderness. Myself being a member of the culture group, I had the privilege of observing music in the making and its process of growth and development, intimately. The present work is the result of long years of association with them and sharing their experiences in everyday life.

I am thankful to my late teacher Prof. L.P. Vidyarthi, the then Head of the Department of Anthropology, Ranchi University, Ranchi and Deepak Tyagi, my dear colleague of the Anthropological Survey of India whose consistent persuasion and advice in writing this treatise, is unforgettable.

My thanks also to Prof. A.B. Saran, the former Head of the Department of Anthropology, Ranchi University, Ranchi, who has shown keen interest for its publication for the benefit of the students of Anthropology.

My sincere thanks of the Mundas who are engaged in action for the continuity of the musical culture of their ancestors and who have always been humiliated, looked down upon and exploited by all classes of people. In spite of this onslaught, they have preserved and given continuity to the musical culture which is a representative example of many tribal groups of India who lead the same way of life and are placed in similar situation and environment.

Also reverently acknowledged are to all writers and authors, the references of whose works have been made in this book for the sake of better understanding of the subject.

SEM TOPNO

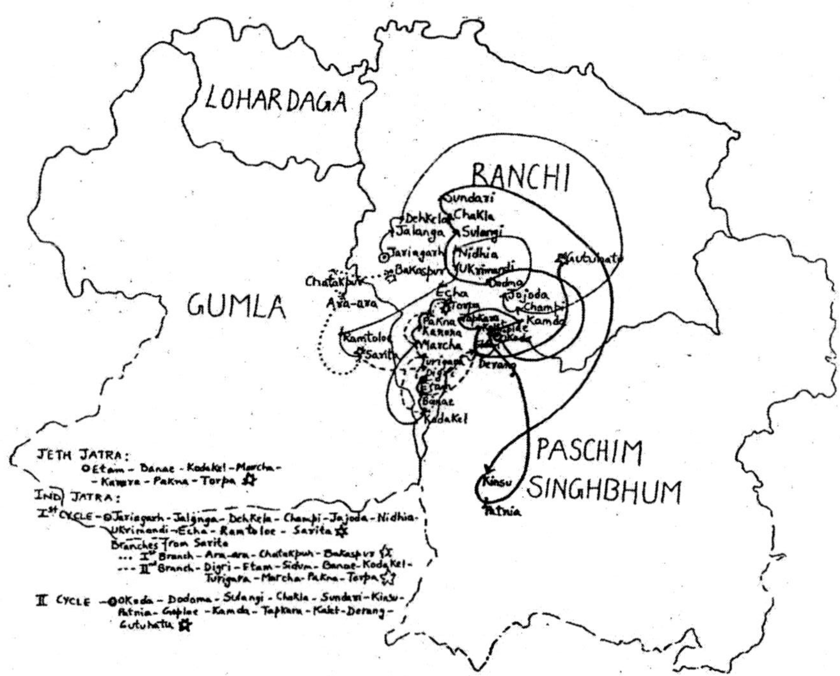

Map. 2: Villages of Hasada Country

CONTENTS

PART I

THE MUNDA TRADITION OF MUSIC AND DANCE

1

ANTHROPOLOGY OF MUNDA SONG

Among all the creatures of nature, it is only the human being who has been endowed with an active and creative mind. In developmental history, this has helped him in surpassing all others and enabled him to raise himself above the animal level of existence. The systematic utilization of body and mind and combination thereof resulted in an unexpected infinite outlet of progress in human history. A human level of existence not only necessitates a unique biological structure and a sociocultural mode of life, it necessitates a peculiar and a distinctive kind of psychological structuralization, characterized by a level of personal adjustment and experience in which a unique and complex integration occurs between responses to an 'outer world' of objects, events and responses to an 'inner world' of impulse, fantasy and creative imagination. Besides this, a human existence is one in which potentialities for adjustment, reorientation, change are constantly present (Hallowell, 1995). Above all, the constant social interaction of the people and sharing of each other's experience through communication makes the human life going.

"Man has physiologically been endowed with such sound speech organs, the articulation of which enables him to make communication easily with others. These organs in the human body are identified as lips, teeth, tongue, palate, bronchial tubes, nose, etc., which have specific geometrical forms. The respiratory organs as well as the speech organs regulate the volume of air in order to produce quality voice or sound. The quality of voice, however, is influenced by such social and cultural characteristics which results in the patterned identification of individuals as members of a societal group and persons of a certain sex, age, state of health, body build, rhythm state, position in a group, mood, bodily condition and location, etc.

Every culture develops and selects its own forms and style of expression and manners of articulation" (UNESCO, Vol. I).

Tribal song or music evolves through a process of oral transmission and continues to exist as tradition. It represents the cumulative expression of many ages and is not the product of particular period (Kuppuswamy and Hariharan, 1978:133). In itself, it contains the features of perpetual growth, variation, selection and continuity. As such, it is supposed to be the phenomenon of prolonged social growth—a culture and one of the means by which the culture has come to be, what it is and continues (Seager, 1967:148). The music is time made audible *(Ency. Britannica,* Vol. 12:62), has actually been defined keeping in view the socio-historical perspective of music for being its ability to associate what is happening in the present with what has happened in the past and what one expects will happen in the future. The music of each region or social group is the product or growth of a particular culture complex. It may or may not have meaning for another group 'who lives outside the culture zone' but it certainly has 'meaning' or 'appeal for the home group' (Chouhan, 1971:19). Tribal song is the cognitive and perceptive experience of the people of their objective as well as subjective world and is concerned with all aspects of their lives. It is based on the values and concern of life of the people and need to be understood in their historical, psychological and philosophical context as it faithfully reveals and records the thoughts, customs and habits of the people. It is the true and natural reflection of the ideas of the community and gives profound aesthetic satisfaction (Kuppuswamy and Hariharan, 1978:133).

In tribal society, everybody is a prospective music maker and practitioner and youthful age is the most suitable period for such activities. The actions and expressions of musical behaviour and its aesthetic beauty can be conveniently observed in their vocal and bodily expressions—melody, tone control, rhythm and style in dance. All these forms are, however, expressed within the set norms of tribal tradition. The dress and ornaments and musical instruments, which are indigenously produced and are the objective indicator of particular tribal identity, also are based on the aesthetic taste of the people.

Tribals everywhere are located in a specific geographical region and eco-environment and have developed their respective sociocultural environment which is dynamic in process. With the change in situation, the man-environment relationship go on changing. A change in natural environment, social organization, economic pursuit, rules of governance and beliefs and practices brings about changes in the whole system of relations in man, nature and spirits *vis-a-vis* the existing musical culture. Human beings, since time immemorial, are engaged in a constant process of cognition, classification and discerning of elements and systems of the entities in the total network of relations for better understanding and adjustment. In every society and culture, this is done in a most systematic way—formally and informally, through the process of socialization and enculturation. However, on the basis of experiences gained and knowledge acquired, a person constantly verifies, refines and reformulates his own ideas, actions and behaviours.

While, on the one hand, the tribal or Munda sense of perception, their feelings and emotional reactions are clearly visible in the words and phrases of songs, on the other, the underlying environmental features are brought to the level of perception and understanding through the process of cognition, conceptualization and articulation. This is in fact the man's inquisitiveness and search for qualities, values and unique features of nature. The environmental phenomena are, however, culturally interpreted which is not possible without having sufficient knowledge and experience of the culture and society as well as the nature of man. The latter, however, can best be perceived and conceptualized through the characteristic features of physical phenomenon. The understanding of either of the character is possible through the use of the medium of 'images' or 'symbols'. Images are the powerful instrument for interpretation and may manifest all conscious and voluntary aspect of human life. The symbols carry double or triple meaning or relations. For proper understanding of the meaning of symbols, it needs to be analysed against the context and situation of its reference. In tribal music these features are amply found.

The content of song is generally derived from the natural world as well as the social environment of man. Cognitive mapping of topographical features, weather and climatic environment, flora and fauna world as well as the sense and perception of colour, odour, shape, sizes, etc, are portrayed in tribal songs which provide us an understanding to their approach to nature.

The interaction with different entities of natural environment with members of the society and outside and with the spirit world generally affects and shapes the interpersonal and inter-ethnic relations. Ownership and control over assets, resources, customary laws, morals and etiquettes and ritual beliefs are the direct outcome of such interactions which reveals the nature and character of man as well as his philosophy of life.

The tribal songs and dances have versatility in itself. It is supposed to be a literature as well as the culture of the people. It is the only via-media through which people express themselves. The tribal music in its domain has endless characteristics. There is variety in its structure and texture, style of expression, conceptualization, flexibility and flow.

The song and dance have invaluable role to play in tribal life in creating and fostering congenial social atmosphere and feelings of oneness as human being. In itself, it combines arts, literature and music which are the essential assets of human beings and separates man from animal species. The knowledge and ideas of the society are preserved through songs.

Conceptualization in Tribal Music

Human beings, as the Munda tells, were created out of nature, that is, clay of the earth by the Supreme Being 'Singbonga'. He created everything and taught men how to live in this world. A Munda, thus, grows up in the lap of nature and receives support and sustenance from it. The knowledge about nature is, therefore, a must for a Munda to live in this world. Nature is perceived as dynamic and every element is supposed to be bubbling and thriving with life and activities like human beings.

In Munda songs we can decipher a set of themes in which one of them is nature itself and its environment. The description is made either objectively or symbolically. In the first case, we get no ornamentation in its presentation and its description is made in the same level as one sees, perceives and experiences it, while in the latter case, the elements of the natural world is conceptualized as living being and a replica of the human world full of activities. In natural world everywhere one can hear the sound of music which enthralls the mind and body. Every sound produced by nature adds up to this body of music in quality and values. Nature is the greatest teacher of mankind and the Munda, being a part and parcel of it, automatically learns and derives musical inspiration from it. And not only the Munda learns creating of sound systems from nature but the elements of the whole universe is the subject matter of his music.

Themes of Songs

In the context of nature and its environment, the content so selected indicate the cultural values of the elements of nature revealing attitudes, behaviour patterns and world views of the people. The portrayal of nature is usually made in relation to its quality, beauty, sacredness, economic value and social relationships.

Physical Features

One of the theme is based on physical features, that is, landscape of the country and place of habitation of the Mundas. In it we get the detailed description of hills and mountains, valleys, dales, lakes, streams, swampy lands, rivers, plains, rocky and grasslands, etc. The description is given either in conversational form or it is simply mentioned.

Climate and Seasons

Another theme is derived from eco-environment, that is, from weather and climatic environment of the country of their habitation. Chhotanagpur plateau falls in the zone of tropical climate. Here three main seasons are identified by the people: *Jete* (summer), *gama* (rainy season) and *rabang* (winter season). The contents which the song derives is the perception and feeling of expression of the individual Munda as he sees and bodily feels the climatic environment and weather conditions. As the experience differs from individual to individual according to the context and situation, there is difference in its expression or presentation also. When two individuals meet, they talk about on a number of subjects. Each one of them talks on the subject in his own way, on the basis of his cultural conditioning which is reflected in his way of expression and presentation. This is why, on the same subject or theme, we get number of songs, revealing a bit of the quality and feature of the subject. Each song, therefore, is the model in itself of experience of particular nature.

Flora and Fauna

Another theme is based on the floral environment that exists in the Munda country. Various species of flora find place in the song to express joy, beauty, and mood of an individual. The nature of man is best described through these mediums. On the other hand, the features of floral world is best understood only in relation to man and climate.

Fauna or animal world is an important theme in the Munda song. Animals personify human character. A wide reference is found in Munda songs on animals, birds and insects that are found in the region. While domestic animals have socio-economic and ritual values for the people, the wild ones are symbols of beauty, nuisance and terror. And it is on these aspects that they are referred most in the song.

The Cosmic World

References are also made of the cosmic world, that is, the sun, the moon and the stars in the songs. References of them are either made symbolically or are simply described as nature's wonder whom the creator has made for the benefit of human beings.

Socio-cultural Life Cycle

While nature and its environment provide support and sustenance to man in this world, he depends upon others of his species for security and continuity of his genera. For this he has created a social world—a web of network of relationships. While living in this world, a man passes through different stages of life—childhood, adulthood and old age and undergoes various institutionalized dogmatic processes in his life-cycle. Man has also developed a number of institutions and organizations for a good and peaceful life. He also keeps a record of every event of his life.

Man is a thinking being. He also looks himself from beyond this profane world. Life is not only for living, it has a purpose. Every society lays down its philosophy of life for its coming generation which acts as guide for them.

Man, not only lives in this world but he lives beyond. And he works for both the worlds during his lifetime. In his profane and sacred life he maintains a link between visible and invisible forces to achieve his desired goal in life.

The Mundas have composed a large number of songs of this social world. In this social context of music, the theme or content are varied and endless. The whole socio-cultural life are recorded in details covering life cycle, events, norms, ritual process, institutions and organizations. Any event which emanates from interpersonal relations often becomes the theme or content of the song. The experience derived during living together with fellow community people as well as others are stored in the forms of stories, legends and ballads. Besides, his philosophy of life, values and attitude are the theme of the song which directs social life in its true path as selected by the society. Education to new generation and social control as well as recreation in life are the widely derived themes in songs. The songs nicely record the behavioural attitude of the individual, his sentiments and emotions as well as his aesthetic taste. In tribal life, the institutions of fairs and festivals have a very important place. It is there that different facets of human interactions are seen which get a very prominent place in the song.

Mythological Heroes

The Mundas have also composed a large number of songs around the mythological, legendary and historical heroes and heroines. A detailed song-prayer has been composed on the life of Toro Kora of *Asur Kahani,* the hero of a Munda myth or legend. Similarly, a good number of songs have been composed on Ram, Sita and Hanuman of *Ramayana* stories and on Krishna and Gopies of *Mahabharata.* In historical period, a large number of songs are found on the events that happened during the days of the Nagbansi dynasties of the Munda kingdom.

The Colonial Past

The recent past had the British colonial rulers taking control of the

Munda country, which saw the end of the golden days of the tribals of this region. During this period, the tribals of the region received inhuman treatment by the Dikus who were all outsiders to their territory. The songs composed during this period depict the sufferings and struggles of the people. The names of Sidhu and Kannu in Santhal tribe and Birsa Munda in Munda tribe shine like the sun in the history of the region, who laid down their lives for the liberty, justice and peace of the people. Thousands of immortal songs have been composed on these great souls of uncomparable wisdom and dedication who cherished peace and human equality among all. The Mundas have also recorded faithfully in their songs about the good things which the British government did for the people and the country.

Post-independence

The contents of songs, after the attainment of freedom, have been on the process of modernization, new administrative machinery, its functions and modern technologies. The evils and benefits of these changes also have received suitable place in Munda songs.

Within the domain of the social world, musical tradition receives a major place in tribal life. From conceptualization and definition of music and dance, a whole gamut of it are included as the content of the songs. In it we get a wide range of aesthetic taste, subtlety of its expression and style of presentation and lyrical composition, etc. The style of personal decoration, making of music and musical instruments and its tuning, etc, also are found in the content of songs.

Economic Activities

Another major area which occupies the stuff of content in the song is the economy and economic activities of the people. Mundas are traditional agriculturists but supplementary activities such as hunting, gathering, fishing and earning through labour and services are also carried out in a small-scale. The livelihood, therefore, is basically based on nature and so the earning is solely dependent on the suitability of natural environment.

Nature, according to the Mundas, is controlled by the Supreme Being Singbonga. A Munda, therefore, remembers Him at the beginning of every activity and the first fruit of every harvest or labour is offered to Him as well as to the departed ancestral spirits who are supposed to oversee every activity of their people. Besides these, there are other supernatural forces and spirits who are also supposed to influence or affect the yields in their own way. A man's survival, according to the Mundas, therefore, depends on nature and on the help and support of the unforeseen forces. Besides economic organization and management, the song includes in its contents the knowledge of geography, botany, ecology, technology and the whole process of economic activities. It also includes the wide range of experiences of the people, their difficulties, happiness and joy which they pass through during the course of these activities.

Music, in tribal society, therefore, derives its contents from the whole life aspects and situation of man and his environments. Creation of music, therefore, requires a deep understanding of the organizational structures and function of the whole environment of man. Man's approach to the understanding of the natural environment is, not merely the observation of different phenomena, but it is also knowing and learning in which the objects and events are deciphered according to some definite characteristics on the basis of their relative context and situation. Learning becomes rapid on the basis of past experience of the fellow members of the community. But the individual encounters the world by his own way and what is seen is, as much a function of who is looking, how he is looking and what he is looking for, as it is of what is 'out there' or relevant to him (Worsley, 1970:342). Thus, the way something is seen depends upon the interest that one has and upon the knowledge, information and opportunity available to him (*Ibid,* p. 343). Every individual in the society misses something, rejects or ignores the past experience and learns something by himself objectively and intuitively. The external stimulants, the social, ritual and natural environments and internal stimulants, the drive, passion, anger, emotion, etc, which are meaningful to a person, become the objective of learning. This is why the individual perception of the environment of man and nature differs but there are some basic features in which uniformity of consensus exists largely because of a common cultural background. Thus, past knowledge and experience of society helps a person in rapid acquaintance of the environment of man and nature. In understanding these objective and subjective features of social and natural world in the time dimension, man approached it through the philosophical, mechanistic and mathematical concepts.

In Munda songs, an individual's interaction and perception is described either objectively or subjectively. In the former case, it is expressed in a most simplistic style and sometimes in idiomatic phrases.

The symbolic presentation, on the other hand, is an indication of progress of human knowledge and understanding about the social and natural environment. It is the cumulative experience of the community gained on the perception and cognition of the natural world *vis-a-vis* the social nature of the individual and his philosophy, the meaning of which is shared equally by all others in the group. This has helped in the development of the organismic concepts where an understanding of natural phenomena is sought in terms of analogies with the behaviours of animals and human beings. An individual's nature and his personality is best known through such symbols and concepts which are themselves a construction upon experience, a product of mind, an artifice or conventional product (Douglas, 1971:11). It is an abstract expression of the perceptual world which is always relative. A symbol only has meaning from its relation to other symbols in pattern. The pattern gives the meaning. Therefore, no one item in the pattern can carry meaning by itself isolated from the rest (*Ibid.*, p. 11). The existing socio-cultural condition, their personalities and philosophy and values and such other abstract features are reflected in symbols. Anything from tangible to intangible phenomena of the perceptual world furnishes for symbolization which comes into the concept of man limited only by his mode of expression. In other words, the perceptual world provides a limitless scope for symbolization. Understanding the meaning of symbols by the people set the limit of the domain of a culture. It is on this basis Geerz (1966:3) defines culture as "a historically transmitted pattern of meanings embodied in symbols, a system of inherited conceptions expressed in symbolic forms by means of which men communicate, perpetuate and develop their knowledge and attitude towards life". These concepts, images and symbols are thought provoking and mind titilating and a storehouse of wisdom. The human philosophy and psychology of happiness and sufferings find best expression through such concepts and symbols in songs.

Impact of Modernization

Modernization has now made inroads into the tribal belt of Chhotanagpur with the opening of modern communication systems and mines, setting up of factories and establishment of educational institutions. This has made a great impact on the existing prescriptions, prohibitions, the rites and ceremonies once regarded as essential for peaceful and successful life. The detailed economic pursuits, amenities that the modern world has brought, interaction with other community people, etc, are recorded in songs which have an educative value to the youngsters and acts as precepts and guidelines and gives directions to them during the hours of despair.

Mundas of today are, however, an alienated and a divided lot. They are fast losing their self-esteem and cultural identity. A good number of them have already discarded or dissociated themselves from cultural symbols which are supposed to be the indicator or which give continuity to tribal identity. The father figure of the society no longer exists. It is no longer the custodian of Munda culture and tradition. The result is the growth of individualism, group and sectorial interests. The Munda idealism is no more there. In day-to-day life, a Munda no more looks for his guidance to traditions, customs, norms and values, nor he follows and practises for its continuity. The social and cultural degeneration as well as crisis in confidence and clash of interests has led to great instability in the whole set-up of Munda life. The net result is the apathy and ignorance of the newer generation towards musical culture of the Mundas. The social pathology of this nature are also found recorded in Munda songs.

2

MUSIC OF THE MUNDAS

In almost all tribal society, song and dance are the most popular forms of amusement. For them, it is their life and culture. It is a peace time invention and an outcome of the happiest moment in life of a person or a society. Darwin, therefore, has rightly defined it as a "pleasurable outlet". Song and dance are the medium through which people express and share each other's feelings, emotions and experience. Song and dance are culture specific and an indicator of the state of the society, that is, its development and also an aesthetic taste of the people. It grows out of the style and quality of life of the people. The existence of song and dance in a particular culture and society is determined by "the economic resources, social cohesiveness, political structure, its relative isolation, its prevailing morality etc." (*Encyclopaedia of Social Sciences*, Vol. I : 39). In fine it is an indicator of an attainment of a sort of refinement and perfection in civilizational development of the society.

Music and Dance: A Way of Life

Amusement among the tribal people, in general, develops directly and with spontaneity as an integral part of their lives in everyday activities and social interaction which arises out under various life situations and experiences of the people in time dimension as well as of the needs, aspirations and interests and continues as traditions. As such, it reflects the whole behavioural lives of the people as well as their way of thinking and feelings.

Amusements, particularly of song and dance are integrated in all the life activities of the people. All auspicious occasions in life—social, economic, religious and political are celebrated with some sort of accompaniment of music and dance which involves the whole community or segment thereof. Entertainment at community level is mostly functional and is performed on the basis of the customs, morals and values of the society. Mass participation in such activities induces social life and brings harmony and unity among the people. All activities, in one way or the other, are related to sacred and secular aspects of life of the people and very rarely one can come across isolated from one another. The sacred and profane nature of activity can be understood only in relation to the context and situation. Ceremonies and festivals, without accompaniment of music and dance are dull and dreary affairs, particularly for the youngsters who usually are drawn away from the participation of such ritual activity unless their association and presence is ritually demanded. Ritual proceedings make the situation drab and dry and often loaded with emotions which the youngsters seldom like due to their immature acclimatization to the situation. Such a situation is boring and monotonous for the youths. For instance, during weeding and transplantation of crops which requires large participation of people, particularly women, to finish the job within a stipulated time, it is observed that there is a large participation of young girls in the work wherever some old ladies and known folklorists happen to participate or there is a likelihood of singing soirees while working. It indirectly points to the fact that work and entertainment go together in tribal society for it reduces the physical pressure and refreshes the energy. This is why music and dance are associated in both types of activities, that is, profane and sacred where its need is not at all felt, with the sole objective to lessen the morbidity of the situation as well as to involve the youths in good number. Besides the stated occasion of merriment, music and dance are the regular features of every tribal village where during evening hours, prior to retiring to bed, dance and songs are organized in the village *akhra*. And there is no denying the fact that as claimed by the Munda youth, the area of his habitation resounds with music all through the year.

In tribal society, music grows out of life and continues as traditions. Therefore, a wholistic life of the tribe is visible in their music tradition. However, total absence of this feature is found in other musical traditions. Besides its role as a means of amusement along with other mediums such as tales, legends, myths, riddles and proverbs, etc, it is the storehouse of knowledge, experience and wisdom of the community. In it we see the quality and style of life of the community. It brings them unity and solidarity as well as identity and pride.

Musical Activities

The Munda tribe have a very crude concept of music and dance. Its scope is too wide and involves every conversation and activity in its fold. And it is true to their concept as stated earlier that work and amusement go together in their lives. The three musical activities, dancing, singing and playing of musical instruments are conceptually expressed in the following phrase which in itself have been composed musically:

> *Kaji ge duraŋ*g (to speak is to sing),
> *S̃enge susun* (to walk is to dance),
> *Kumuni dumaŋ*g (fish traps is a musical instrument).

Kaji Ge Duraŋg

Song or music, according to the Mundas, is neither a deliberate construction nor a fanciful imagination of the composer but it is rooted to the fact of life and cultural tradition. Music making and rendering it into action is a continual process in which the perceived stable features of socially organized environment are continually created and sustained (Polner, 1974:27). The phrase *Kaji ge duraŋ* conveys the very concept of the Munda song. The songs for them is nothing but a dialogue or conversation with all seriousness with respect to everyday affairs of practical activities and concern of life of past, present and future in relation to nature, man and the supernaturals.

Conceptually, the song is *kaji* or dialogue for the Mundas and so is less imaginative and it rarely makes any makebelief statement. Song, being a conversation, whatever details can be talked about, are being conveyed in a nutshell in music. However, the Munda song is more than a mere conversation for whatever is talked about, is not of the nature of 'speak and forget' type but is rendered into timeless significance. It is a storehouse of experience and knowledge of the people. In music the experience of the perceptual world attains the status of a temporal character and its empirical feature mingle with perennial and eternal presence. It is in this form that music carries the deeper meaning or reality of life. A piece of music, however, is not an exhaustive one but it is only an exemplary and carries meaning only in relation to wider system in totality.

The Munda language, at the level of its sound systems does not seem to be too musical. Besides, neither the conversation between two Mundas ever attains differences in pitch or loudness, nor the rhythm. But one may find a little difference even in quarrel and conversation between them. One enjoys life in conversation and that is what the Munda call music. In details and depth there is not much difference in between the Munda concept of music and their perception and that of the modern literary concept. The *Encyclopaedia Britannica* defines the term from two angles. The first is defined from cultural point of view and that is "a sonic event can be called music if the people who use it, call it music, regardless of one's perception to it." Every community, however backward, has the notion of music and has some standard at their level to distinguish musical and non-musical sounds. Another definition is provided from structural or organizational point of view for the sake of comparison at the level of inter-cultural perspective. It has been defined in these words, "a sound event may be considered and studied as music if it constitutes the element of pitch, rhythm and loudness in such a way that they communicate emotionally, aesthetically and functionally on the levels that either transcend or are unrelated to social communication." All these musical features or elements are implied in the Mundas' notion of music. As the music falls under the domain of speaking language and their technology which the Munda concept of music rightly implies, its structural form is complex and expression artistic. Language is the best expressive device of emotions, feelings, as well as of human perception, experience, concept and ideas. So, it is the language expressed through various techniques and styles which is called music by the Mundas.

Senge Susun

In defining dance as *senge susun* (to walk is to dance), Munda means to say that as soon as he gets up from his bed or leaves his place, the very action can be called as dancing. There is style in walking or movement of the body also. So taking a step is the beginning of dance which accompanies movement of the whole body. Walking can be slow or rapid or hopping or jumping, it can be straight or zigzag or round, it can be in a sitting posture, or stooping or upright and forward or backward. The other parts of the body cannot remain static while walking, so movement of these are either automatic or are caused in style. In fine, the process of walking with stylish movement of the body has rightly been defined as dance by the Mundas.

Kumuni Dumaŋg

The phrase *kumuni dumaŋg,* that is, 'fish trap is *durnaŋg'* musical instrument, has a very deep meaning and cannot be explained easily. It has, however, explained in detail in another context later on in the book. Munda prepare musical instruments by themselves from local available materials. It involves technological and scientific approach in the selection of new materials, preparations and handling.

The Mundas have composed songs which describe forms, styles and rhythms of music, dance and playing of musical instruments besides, bodily decoration and ornaments. The songs in subsequent paragraphs reveal how ingenious are the Mundas in the fields of artistic expression and aesthetic presentation.

Musical Instruments

There are a variety of musical instruments of the Mundas which can be classified into (1) wind instruments, (2) string, and (3) percussion. While, *rutu, murli, bhennr, shehnai,* and *sakhoa* are of the class of wind instruments, *kendra, banam,* and *tuila* are string instruments. There are a variety of percussion instruments of various sizes and shapes. These are *dumaŋg, jhanj, ghanti, ghughura, damru, nagara* or *dama, dhulki, dhol, dhank, kartal, rabka, dafla, mridang* and *manjira,* etc. Most of these musical instruments are made by the Mundas themselves while some are procured from neighbouring communities who prepare it on order and some are purchased from fairs and markets. While wind and string instruments are used all the time besides the time of dance, the percussion instruments are used only during the dance. Every dance has its selective set of musical instruments. Among the Mundas, all the musical instruments are handled by the males. The exception being during *jani sikar,* that is, the women's hunting ceremony when the women act the role of men and get the chance to handle these instruments.

In Munda songs, we get the following contents with respect to musical instruments (1) materials made of, (2) place of availability, (3) technique of instruments making, (4) its handling and occasion, (5) sound or tune of the instrument and (6) players of these instruments. The song is not exclusive to one content but sometimes it contains more than one content. The theme or the subject matter of the song, moreover, does not go by the category of song, but the tune of the song and sound of the drum, that is, musical instruments go by the class of song and dance in which it is associated. The song not only describes the above mentioned themes but expresses the whole cultural features in a suitable way which would, otherwise, be missed in observation.

The song below belonging to Bala category, describes the materials from which the *dumaŋg* or *mandar is* made of. The lines of the song are as follows:

1. *Rarangi daru, Rarangi daru dore nayo*
   The Rarangi tree, mother
   Moriyo gela re, sario gela re
   Has died and is rotting
   Besia ke kawan puchhae re
   Who will care for the thing that emits bad smell?

2. *Koili pare Kochdega*
   Beyond the river Koel at Kochdega
   Jhalia mandar khelae re
   Dancing on the tune of decorated mandar
   Hare, Sunsunia Dhankuria, nunjhari, nunjhari re
   Hear the sound of *nunjhari, nunjhari O Dhankuria.*

The same lines are repeated in the following song too which belongs to Bala category of song except the first line, which are as follows:

Ne sargirạ daru do, ne sargira daru dore nayo
The tree by the side of waterfall, mother

Sario gelare, morio gelare
Has got rotten and died.
The rest of the lines are same as above.

These two songs indicate that *dumaŋg* or *mandar* is prepared from the dried up wood. The days are now gone when *dumaŋg* were made from dried up wood. It is now prepared from other materials which the song below indicates. The above song also indicates where the dance is going on. The couple are talking about the dance hearing the sound of *dumaŋg* who reside in the village which is just the opposite of village Kochdega beyond the river Koel. The sound of music and dance has broken the environment of sleepy night as it is travelling far and wide in the river valley. Materials used in making of *dumaŋg* other than wood, have been indicated in the following *jatra* category of song, the lines of which are as follows:

Karigara bhele kumbhara bhaiya
You are the skilled artist O brother potter
Mati ka kalesha banae debe
Make a clay jar for me
Mati ka kalesha bara rijhuwar
The jar made of clay instils rejoicing
Mati ka kalesha banae debe
Make a clay jar for me.

The *kalash* or jar mentioned in the song is no other than the musical instrument called *dumaŋg* which is made of clay. This clay jar is prepared by the potter community who have settled down in many tribal villages.

Nagara or *dama* is generally made of iron or bell metal. The following song belonging to *jatra* category indicates that the *nagara* made of iron and bell metal is beaten in the early morning and at the time of the rising moon. The lines of the song are as follows:

Biria nungiyate, kansa ka nagera thokae
With the rising sun, they beat up the bell metal *nagara*
Chando nungiyate kansa ka nagera thokae
With the rising moon, they beat up the bell metal *nagara*.

This song seems to have been taken from the neighbouring Oraon tribe who reside in the Western side of the Munda country as the words *biria, chando* and *nungiyate* belong to Kurukh language. The beating up of the drum, as mentioned in the song, is also not at the time of dance but most probably it is in the temple. Nevertheless, the song indicates that *nagara* are also made from bell metal.

Ghanti and *ghughr̄a* are also made of bronze. In the following song belonging to *jatra* category, we get this indication. The lines of the song are as follows:

> *Na janae bhainsur*
> Neither the brother-in-law knows
> *Na janae putau :*
> Nor the daughter-in-law
> *Pitar ka ghanti chutar mein tange*
> Bronze bell is hanging on the torso

Though in normal times a little social distance is maintained by brother-in-law and daughter-in-law but during dance, there is no such distance and both can share the same dancing ground. In this song, as mentioned, both the in-laws are participating in the same dance together quite forgetful of this taboo at the tingling sound of bronze bell hanging on the torso of the brother-in-law. The Munda, customarily, do not allow to mix up persons of prohibited degrees, but during dance such prohibition is overlooked at certain level of interaction.

The basic materials from which *tuila* and *kendra* are made, is *gourd.* It is a vegetable fruit which is cultivated by the Mundas. All the fruits are generally consumed but one or two are spared for the sake of seed from which *tuila* and *kendra* are made. The song below which belongs to *jadur* category, mentions the conversation of the friends in which one of them is asking of the fruit for making musical instrument. The lines of the song are as follows:

1. *Chetan tola re, Tuila suku chire*
   Is it the *tuila* making gourd in upper hemlet
   Miyad gatim re omaing me
   Let me have one my dear friend
   Latar tola re, kendra banam chire
   Is it *kendra* and *banam* in lower hemlet my dear

Miyad sangaiŋre chedain me
Pluck for me my dear friend

2. *Kare gatim re oma meya*
My dear friend I won't give you
Miyad giya Tuila suku
We have but only one *tuila* gourd
Kare sangaiŋ le, cheda meya
We won't pluck for you my dear friend
Miyad geya tale, kendra suku
We have but only one *kendra* gourd

3. *Tujila suku ho oma mere*
If we spare one *tuila* gourd for you
Engaiŋ-apuiŋ ko eranga
Parents mine will abuse me
Kendra Banam ko cheda mere
If we pluck *kendra banam* for you
Hagaiŋ-bareiŋ ko sigiding
Brothers and nephews mine will ill speak to me

The above song clearly indicates that *tuila, banam* and *kendra*— all string musical instruments— are made from gourd. The gourds best in size and shape are selected for the purpose and it is protected from being taken away by someone. Such gourd is not given away even to near and dear ones. In the song, as stated, a friend has come to the house with a request for the gourd for making musical instruments at the time when all the members of the family were out in the field except the boy or the girl. The boy or the girl is in no mood of parting with the gourd for fear of being abused by parents or elders.

The model of *dumaŋg* (most prominent percussion musical instrument of the Munda tribe) is normally prepared by the potter caste and its finalization is done by the *mochi* caste. The song below which belongs to Jadur category describes the materials with which *dumaŋg*, is prepared and also indicates the place where it is made. The lines of the song are as follows:

1. *Oko reko bai tana hende hasa muchi Dumaŋg*

Where the *Muchi-Dumaŋg* from black clay is being made
Chimae reko bai tana, jo suku dinḍa' Tuila
Where the *tuila is* made from maiden gourd

2. *Bunḍu reko bai tana, hende hasa Muchi-Dumaŋg*
Muchi-Dumaŋg from black clay is being made at Bunḍu
Tamaṛ reko bai tana, jo suku dinḍa Tuila
Tuila from maiden gourd is being made at *Tamaṛ*

Decorated *dumaŋg* with coloured threads cut into the shape of flower as well as coloured shawl made at Bundu, Murhu and Tamaṛ were once famous in western parts of Munda region. The following song belonging to Lahsua category indicates from where these objects come from. The lines of the song are as follows :

Kahaṇ kera jhalia Mandar
Decorated Mandar from where
Kahaṇ kera raŋgal gamchha
Coloured shawl from where
Muṛhu kera jhalia Mandar
Decorated Mandar from Murhu
Tamaṛ kera raŋgal gamchha
Coloured shawl from Tamaṛ

Small tinkling bell known as *ghughura* which is worn by the leg ankle and waist, add the rhythm during the dance. The following song which belongs to Lahsua category, appreciates the sound produced by it and also indicates the people who make these bells. The lines of the song are as follows:

1. *Ghughura re ghughura, nawa chandal ghughura*
The beautiful newly casted *ghughura*
Ho, hore bole re daiya, ghughura to bole runu-jhunu
How melodious the *ghughura* produces the sound
Gari dere sonera, nawa chandal ghughura.
Mould the ghughura O goldsmith, cast new one
Ho, hore bole daiya, Ghughura to bole run-jhunu
How melodious the *ghughura* produces the sound

Similarly, there is an addition to the sound of music by the ornaments worn by the ladies. The following song belonging to Lahsua category states how melodic is the sound of *jhuṭia* which is worn on the leg fingers by the ladies. The lines are as follows:

1. *Jhuṭia tor baje ram-jham, ham to sunalon*
   I hear the *ram-jham* sound of your *jhuṭia*
   Jhuṭia tor baje ram-jham
   The *jhuṭia* yours is producing *ram-jham* sound

2. *Na dekhu chuṇwaṇ ghaṭ, na dekhu dari ghaṭ*
   It neither cares *chuṇwaṇ ghat* nor *dari ghaṭ*
   Ham to sunaloṇ
   I heard the sound
   Jhuṭia tor baje ram-jham
   The *jhuṭia* yours is producing *ram-jham* sound

Therefore, it is not the beauty of musical instruments that matters, but it is the sound that it produces which is appreciated. Handling and producing of melodious sound from musical instruments requires a great skill which is achieved only by devotion, integrity and perseverance in learning and practice. Mastery over the handling technique is the first step of learning. People who constantly or regularly hear the sound produced by musical instruments can very well judge the quality of music played by any musician. And for that matter, it is not necessary that the commentator should himself be a good player as indicated in the following Jadur song, the lines of which are as follows:

1. *Chetan ṭola gongor salu*
   O gongor salu of upper hemlet
   Ride lekam oronge
   You are blowing like grinding
   Latar ṭola bareja piyuṛ
   O my *bareja piyur* of lower hemlet
   Takui lekam baname
   You play Banam like spinning

2. *Rideyachim orongeya*
   Are you grinding or blowing?
   Ride lekaiŋg ayum me

Hearing it like grinding
Takuyachim baname
Are you spinning or playing on *banam?*
Takui lekaiŋg atene
It sounds like spinning.

Flute is carried everywhere by the youths who play on it whenever they like. It is why they rightly call it friend. Flute as friend has been mentioned in the following Racha song, the lines of which are as follows:

1. *Chakonṭa pakonta ruṭu mor saheli*
   In bush or thorn, flute is my maiden friend
   Ruṭu ke rutu keŋsa re gatim samen
   Like head hair flute is my dear friend

2. *Mar hari hari me*
   Let you drive him off
   Mar tuŋji tuŋji me
   Let you shoot him down
   Ruṭu mor saheli do
   Flute is my dear friend everywhere
   Ruṭu ke ruṭu keŋsa re gatim samen
   Flute is like my head hair as friend

Flute is carried everywhere—towards the works, in the field while tending cattle or in the forest or rivers. It is carried on the head turban or on loin cloth in the waist. It is why, when someone takes it away or it gets lost, the owner becomes restless. The following Lahsua and Jadur songs mention the restlessness of the youth whose flute was taken away by someone without his knowledge. The lines of the Lahsua song are as follows:

1. *Ho, hore, mocho bhitar railo dada*
   Oh, it was in the mocho (fish trap), brother
   Aiŋga ruṭu okoe idi keda re
   Who did take away my flute
   Mocho bhitar railo dada
   Oh, it was in the fish trap, brother

2. *Amaga ruṭu saŋgim idi keda re*
Your 'saŋgi' (loving friend) took away your flute
Mocho bhitar railo dada
It was in the fish trap, brother

The lines of the Jadur song of the same theme as above are as follows:

1. *Mor baŋsi lei gelain*
Someone took away my flute
Dego mor baŋsi
Let me have my flute
Haere, ke baŋsi bajatau, ke baŋsi bajatau
Alas, who is playing on flute

2. *Baŋsi suni-suni prem chorae*
Stealing love, hearing the sound of the flute
Hae, ke banalau baŋsi mono bhulae
Oh, who invented the flute for entertainment?

In the above songs, while the youth is deeply feeling for the lost flute, he appreciates and expresses his gratitude for the person who invented it.

The youths keep variety of musical instruments and in good number. The following Jadur song indicates this in these lines:

1. *Mid koyoŋg-koyoŋg kuri ruṭu do*
A lap full of flute O damsel
Bar koyoŋg-koyoŋg kora Banam do
Two lap full of Banam O boy

2. *Da taing do ruṭu do*
Let me have mine flute
Da taing dore ḍinda Banam do
O dear, let me have a single Banam

3. *Haṛka reing manḍao kada rutu do*
I have kept the flute in Haṛka
Baksa reing doha kada Banam do
I have put up Banam in the box
Da taing to ruṭu do

Let me have mine flute
Da tain dore ḍinda Banam do
O dear, let me have a single Banam

The boy has kept his flute and Banam in the bamboo and wooden box in order to avoid from being stolen. The sound of flute resounds on the hills and valleys of Chhotanagpur plateau and when it breaks up, it hurts the feeling of the youth. The following song mentions that the velleys are vibrating with the sounds of flute and *banam*. Now the flute and *banam* have broken and only the cry of youth can be heard. The song belongs to Lahsua category and the lines are as follows :

1. *Chetan badi latar badi re*
Over the high and lowlands
Ruṭu teko sesen tan
Walk on the flute
Chetan badi latar badi re
Over the high and lowlands
Banam teko ṭunaŋ gen tan
Creeping through Banam

2. *Ruṭu teko sesen tan*
Walk on the flute
Ruṭu ḍanḍi doraŋg jan
The body of the Banam was broken
Banam tako tunaŋg gen tan
Creeping through Banam
Banam ḍanḍi doraŋg jan
The body of the Banam was broken

3. *Mahra koṛa ra-a tana re*
The shepherd boy is weeping
Kusudeken, kusudeken
Uninterruptedly sobbing
Chiṛia koṛa iyam tana re
The cattle tending boy is lamenting
Biriŋ ken, biriŋ ken
Incessantly shedding tears

How the melodious sound of musical instrument is being produced which attracts everybody, has been mentioned in the following Jadur song. The king is playing on *tuila* which is giving out melodious sounds like ebbs and flow of water. The lines of the song are as follows:

1. *Pani hile-hile chaoṇra dolae*
   Like waves of water the tuft of hair is being waved
   Pani tare raja tuila bajae
   Like waves of water the king plays the *tuila*

2. *Achha-achha chhokṛi gitamae gawalaiṇ*
   The beautiful girls sang the songs
   Panitare raja ṭuila bajae
   Like waves of water the king plays the *tuila*
   Achha-achha chhokṛa gitamae gawalaiṇ
   The handsome boys sang the songs
   Pani tare raja ṭuhila bajae
   Like waves of water the king plays the *tuila*

The sound of music is appreciated by all, and it is particularly the youths who hear the music attentively. The travellers, as stated in the following Jadur song, hearing the sound of music, became spellbound and are asking as to which musical instrument the sound is being produced. The lines of the song are as follows:

1. *Ne hatu tala re chikan baja saṛi tan*
   In this village which of the musical instrument is being played
   Chikan baja saṛi tan senogi sanaiŋa
   Which of the musical instrument is being played on I would like to go
   Hare, chikan baja saṛi tan senogi sanaiŋa
   Which of the musical instrument is being played on I would like to go

2. *Saṛi doga saṛi tan, gaja-baja saṛi tan*
   It is really the sound of some musical instrument
   Gaja-baja saṛi tan senogi sanaiŋa
   The sound of some musical instrument is being heard I

would like to go
Hare, gaja-baja saṛi tan senogi sanaiŋa
The sound of some musical instrument is being heard I would like to go

The sound of musical instrument is so enchanting that it thrills everybody. How the youths feel when they hear the sound of music, has been described in the following Jadur song, the lines of which are as follows:

1. *Koṭa, Kurumba Dumaŋg saṛi do*
The sound of Dumaŋg is humming in Kota and Kurumba village
Jige ho liṭib-liṭib
My heart thrills merrily
Baṛigaṛa kartal do
The sound of Kartal of Baṛigaṛa village

2. *Kuṛam ho dopol-dopol*
My bosom leaps-up off and on
Jege ho liṭib-liṭib
My heart thrills merrily
I cannot stop myself from going there
Kuṛam ho dopol-dopol
My bosom leaps-up off and on
Senogi sanaiŋa
I cannot stop myself from stepping out there

The youth whoever has composed this song, could not stop himself in telling the impact of music that he felt in his mind and heart. The musical environment that exists in Munda country has been described in the following Jadur song in which two friends are talking about the experience they have in their area of habitation with respect to music and dance. The lines are as follows:

1. *Ale disum, ale gamae do*
In my country and in my village
Piṛi-piṛi ruṭu saṛia
The fields resound with the sound of flutes
Ale disum, ale gamae do

In my country and in my village
Beṛa-beṛa Banam rumule
The sounds of *banam* hums at every valley

2. *Ale disum, ale gamae do*
In my country and in my village
Hatu-hatu dumaŋ datuŋge
The tune of *dumaŋ* is heard in every village
Ale disum, ale gamae do
In my country and in my village
Ṭola-ṭola rasika duraŋge
People sing merrily in every hamlet

The reality of musical environment has objectively been described in this song and there is no exaggeration at all in it. Happiness abounds in every hut, village and region and is shared by everybody through music and dance.

Music is enjoyed by everybody—the performer as well as the audience. The following song mentions that a boy who is out in the field for work and has no musical instrument with him, is hearing attentively the sound of music sitting under a tree during a summer mid-day. The song belongs to Lahasua category and the lines are as follows:

1. *Kuda suṛa, suṛa lena sagen lena*
The tender blackberry leaves, sprouted and laiden
Enderegi umbulre duba kanae Manibaha
My dear Manibaha is sitting under the shade of that tree
Okosate bajae ayum tan
Hearing the sound of music from nowhere

2. *Dub dogae duba kan kuda sura umbul re*
He is but sitting under the shade of blackberry tree
Tikin sate bajae ayum tan
Hearing the sound of music by mid-day

What is the sound of *dumaŋ* like, has been mentioned in the following Lahsua song. The melodious sound of *dumaŋ* become nice when the sound of bangles worn by the girls are rhythmically produced in unison with the sound of *dumaŋ*. The song also tells that the girls may enjoy dance and merriment till they remain unmarried. The lines of the song belonging to Jadur category are as follows:

1. *Nai gitil saka-saka, Dumaŋ saṛi tana re*
   Like the sound of floating river sand, the sound of *dumaŋ* is being heard
   Ayar te susun mai, sakom sek̜ saṛiya
   The leading girl in dance is producing 'sek' sound from her bangles

2. *Rasika ko metam re, chhaela ko metam re*
   If you are called *'rasika'* and *'chhaela'*
   Chimin dinam ḍinḍaya, imin dinam chhaela, ho hore
   As long you are single, so long you may enjoy merriment

It is not that dance is organized every night in a village. There is a routine for dance and some nights in a week no dance is organized. It is on this occasion, the youths visit other villages during night where dance is going on. They proceed to the village simply on hearing the sound of music. In the song which belongs to Lahsua category, the guest youths are apologetic to the host youths and mention them the trouble they received on the way while coming there. The lines of the song are as follows :

1. *Mandera sunate ham ali, pardesia*
   We strangers have come hearing the sound of *mander*
   Ali pardesia, mandera sunate ham ali
   Strangers as we, have come hearing the sound of *mander*
   Haere, haere hae, mandera sunate ham ali
   Oh, we have come, hearing the sound of *mander*
   Pardesia, mandera sunate ham ali
   We strangers, have come hearing the sound of *mander*

2. *Girte parte ham ali, pardesia*
   Stumbling down all the way, we strangers have come
   Ali pardesia, mandera sunate ham ali
   We strangers have come, hearing the sound of *mander*
   Haere, haere hae, mandera sunate ham ali
   Oh, hearing the sound of *mander,* we have come.

This indicates that even if there is no dance in the village, the youths cannot remain inside. The sound of music make them restless. The song below too which belongs to Lahsua category, describes that the girls are waiting for their friend to come out for dance. The girl is cooking food so she has become late. The lines of the song are as follows:

1. *Jojo buta nakeṛa*
   'Akhṛa' under the tamarind tree
   Juṛi dumaŋ saṛi tan
   The tune of a pair of *dumaŋ is* humming
   Delare rasika, chia mentere kame oḍongo
   O dear, why don't you come out?

2. *Diri chirem manḍi tan*
   O dear, are you cooking stones?
   Ruguṛi chirem utu tan
   Is it pebbles that you are cooking?
   Delare rasika, chia mentere kame oḍongo
   O dear, why don't you come out?

This song is a call to the girls who are hurrying up to finish their job of cooking and feeding the family members. Cooking and feeding is usually done by the girls. The boys are already out in the *akhra* and are playing on *dumaŋ* and also are singing songs giving out a call to every youth to come out in the *akhra.* As the dance is to be performed within the time schedule, that is, up to midnight, all should come out early.

Dress, Decoration and Ornaments

Munda celebrate almost all the auspicious occasions of life through songs and dances. Besides this, as stated above, music and dance are organized regularly in every village. There is also biannual dance fair which usually takes place after midnight and continues till morning. This dance fair is called *jatra* by the Mundas. This is the occasion when the youths are seen in their best and beautiful dresses and ornaments. In this dance festival, a variety of dances are organized in the same ground at a time without consideration of their being associated to a particular period of time. For this, the youths start making preparations at least three to four months before the festival. The musical instruments are made, repaired and purchased, so also dress and ornaments. It is generally stated that tattooing and ear piercing is done for the sake of decoration of the body, but it is a totally wrong concept. This is done on the belief that if left unpierced and un-tattooed, the departed souls of the ancestors will not allow to mingle in their company when one leaves this mortal world.

In the case of musical instruments, a detailed description is also found in songs with respect to dress and ornaments, that is, their design and pattern, material made of, its look, style of dressing, worn by whom and where and how and also in which part of the body and also the place of its availability. The Mundas of two regions are clearly distinguished through the styles and designs of their dress and ornaments which have also been recorded in songs.

The song below describes how a Koṇkpat Munda youth of Naguri country dresses and decorates himself. The song belongs to Jadur category and the lines are as follows:

1. *Koṇkpat Munda chigo laŋg-laŋg bondol*
   Is it the Koṇkpat Munda that has long sweeping loin cloth
   Hichir leka geing nele lia
   I saw him like lightning

2. *Rupa beṛa chigo sona mudam*
   Wearing silver armlets and gold rings
   Sasaɲ leka geing china lia
   I identified him like turmeric (golden colour)

Naguri youth with long sweeping loin cloth can be easily identified from non-Naguri youth. They also decorate themselves with armlets and wear rings on their fingers. They keep long floating hair on the head which they keep by knotting in one side but usually wear turban over it. This style of hairdressing by the youths have long been discontinued and now they keep short hair which touches the shoulder. It is kept tightened with brass or bamboo bands. They wear varieties of necklaces and bangles. There is a famous saying which, of course, indicates this feature of the Naguri youth. The lines are:

Tirki tiki-tiki, chi
Naguri jalab-jilib, chi
Bodra botor-botor

The lines *'Naguri jalab-jilib'* have the same meaning as 'I saw him like lightning'. The Naguri youth, particularly the girls wear ear ornaments with a piece of glass embossed in it which reflects light when the sun rays falls on it. While moving it glitters in the sun's rays like lightning.

While the above song described the style of dress of male Naguri youth, the song below describes the dressing style of the damsels of Naguri as well as Hasada country both in the following Jadur song, the lines of which are as follows:

1. *Naguri kuṛi dada, bo danda pundaya*
   Naguri girl has spotted head, brother
   Hasada kuṛi dada, senae hisạd hosod
   Hasada girl walks draggingly, brother

2. *Bo danḍa pundaya dada, naki kiriŋgai meya dada*
   Spotted head brother, buy combs for her
   Senae hisạd hosodeya dada, duli tolaime
   Walks draggingly brother, bring a palanquin for her

3. *Naguri kuṛiya daḍa, ji reiŋg sukuwaiya dada*
   The Naguri girl brother, I like her from all my hearts
   Hasada kuṛiya dada, kuṛam reyaṛ jan
   In Hasada girl brother, my, heart got peace

4. *Naguri kuṛiya dada, aute auwalaṇg me*
   Naguri girl brother, by hook or crook bring for me
   Hasada kuṛiya dada, tiyu seṭeralaṇg me
   Hasada girl brother, please send one for me

In this song, as stated the girl of the Naguri country has a spotted head because she has worn a number of colourful combs and hairpins. It was observed by the composer of this song that the girl of Hasada country walk very lazily and so a palanquin should be arranged for her. In Hasada country, palanquin is used during marriage to carry the bride.

While a number of personal decorative articles and ornaments are made by the youths themselves, some are purchased from the markets. In the following Jadur song some indication of this has been made. The lines are as follows:

1. *Okoe rakab led pital pudena*
   Who introduced brass flowers *pudena*
   Chimae upar led raŋga doriya
   Who brought golden *doriya*

2. *Bypari ko rakab led pital pudena*
   The traders introduced brass flowers *pudena*
   Ladna ko upar led raṇga doriya
   The pack animals brought golden *doriya*

3. *Kiriŋgaiŋ me ayaŋ re pital pudena*
   Buy for me brass flowers *pudena,* mother
   Khejaiŋ me apaŋ re raṇga doriya
   Obtain for me golden *doriya,* father

No Munda youth is to be seen without an ornament of one kind or another and everybody desires to wear as many as one can procure. The youth, particularly the girls, keep pressure on their parents to purchase ornaments from the markets. And if there is some delay in its procurement or are reluctant, they express their resentment through non-cooperation in work or even disobey the orders or advice of the elders. In the following Racha song the discontentment of the youths has been described. The lines are as follows:

1. *Ne hon do khori re duba kana*
   This child is sitting on the open field
   Chinae ra-a: tana goṛe, chinae ra-a: tana
   Why she is weeping, for what

2. *Hisir kiriŋgai metam, sakom kiriŋgai metam*
   Purchase necklace for her, purchase bangles
   Jhutia kiriŋgai metam, angutha kiriŋgai metam
   Purchase *jhutia* for her, purchase *Angutha*
   Tarpat kiriŋgai metam, Aṇdu kiriŋgai metam
   Purchase *Tarpat* for her, purchase *Andu*

Ṭad kiriŋgai metam
Purchase *Tad* for her
Chinae ra-a: tana goṛe, chinae ra-a: tana
Why she is weeping, for what
Ne hon do khori re duba kana
This child is sitting on the open field
Chinae ra-a: tana goṛe, chinae ra-ra: tana
Why is she crying, for what

Most of the ornaments worn by the girls have been mentioned in the above song. These ornaments are either purchased from the markets or are made to order to the silversmiths who usually visit the annual fairs in tribal region.

The youths decorate themselves and wear ornaments as per the prevailing cultural tradition of mode, types and styles. A distinct taste in colour and design is found among the youths tribe-wise. There is no borrowing or inter-mixture in pattern and styles. Ornaments are worn by the youths for self-satisfaction and not for a show to others. They are also aware that nobody is perfect in style and decoration and correct each other's style whenever they meet. This practice is, however, restricted to among the unisex only. The girls have variety of hairstyles but they follow the prevalent one only. A deviation also is found in exceptional cases. Some girls like to keep the end portion of the hair loose after making a knot which sways at the blow of winds. The ornaments of brass, bronze, silver, aluminium, etc, are always kept sparkling by rubbing with ash dust or by fine dust of clay. The following Racha song mentions how the hair is swaying by the wind and the ornaments are glittering while they rub each other. The lines of the song are as follows:

1. *Jhuṭia ṭasar-ṭasar baini*
   Jhuṭia yours are tussling to each other, sister
   Jhuṭia baṛa ritiyaela
   Jhuṭia are flashing bright

2. *Khoṇsawa dalar-dalar baini*
   Hair locks of yours are floating high, sister
   Khoṇsawa baṛa ritiyaela
   Hair locks of yours are shining bright

3. *Kongoso bijir-bijir baini*
Hairpins of yours are glittering bright, sister
Kongoso bara ritiyaela
Hairpins are flashing bright

How the leg ornaments which are non-musical materials, are producing musical sound when the girl walks, have been mentioned in the following Jadur song, the lines of which are as follows:

1. *Gaṛa gitil kuda umbul rena, maigo*
On the river sand under the shade of black-berry tree, daughter
Saka seke saṛi tana
Saka seke sound is being heard

2. *Baru buṭa sereṇg chetan rena, maigo*
Upon the rock under the Baru tree, daughter
Pola sitạb sotob
Pola are producing sitab sotob sound

3. *Saka seke saṛi tana, maigo*
Saka seke sound is being heard, daughter
Supid chetạn ba ekela tana
Flowers are swaying over the hair lock

4. *Pola sitạb sotob tana, maigo*
Pola are producing *sitab sotob* sound, daughter
Iṛi tayom paela tayur tana
Waist cloth is floating behind the heels

The above song describes the look and movement of a beautifully dressed girl. She is on the river side and sometimes walks on the sand and sometimes on the rocks. She has tucked flowers on her hair lock. She has worn toe rings and anklets on her legs are producing musical sound as she walks. Her waist cloth is floating behind her heels as she walks on sands and rocks. This scenery is exceptionally beautiful and the environment filled up with music.

The song below which belongs to *khemta* category also describes the melodious sound of the *pola* worn by a water fetching girl. The lines of the song are as follows:

1. *Kita binda sạb keyate*
   Holding a date pad on the hand
   Lenga tite hichi koṭa
   Swinging and shaking it with left hand
   Hare ḍinḍa chham-chham, kaṭare pola Chilka niral
   O damsel, how nice is the *chham-chham* sound of pola of your legs

2. *Kita binda sạb keyate*
   Holding a date pad on the hand
   Jom tite hichi koṭa
   Swinging and shaking it with right hand
   Hare ḍinḍa chham-chham, katare pola chilka niral
   O damsel, how nice is the *chham-chham* sound of *pola* of your legs

3. *Da-a chaṭu sạb keyate*
   Holding earthen pitcher on the hand
   Lenga tite hichi koṭa
   Swinging and shaking it with left hand
   Hare ḍinḍa chham-chham kaṭare pola chilka niral
   O' damsel, how nice is the chham-chham sound of *pola* of your legs

The water fetching girl, as mentioned in the above song, is walking hurriedly throwing her hand to and fro. As she has worn *pola* on her legs, it is producing melodious musical sound.

How in the normal times too, the youths remain in their best attire and ornaments, is to be found in the following Lahsua song, the lines of which are as follows:

1. *Bo tạm risi-risi*
   Head hair of yours are dishevelled
   Supid tạm raṇga rupa
   Hair lock of yours have zinc and silver ornaments
   Pindigire kitam galaŋ tana
   You are weaving mat on the portico
   Nelkete jido lo tana
   My heart is burning to see you

2. *Andu tamạ, sakom tamạ*
Your anklets and bangles
Liza tamạ raṇga saṛi
You have colourful saṛi
Pola tạm do chilka saṛi tana
How nice is the sound of pola of your legs
Nelkete jido lo tana
My heart is burning to see you
Pola tam do chilka saṛi tana
How nice is the sound of pola of your legs.

And how the bracelets are glittering, is to be found in the following song belonging to Racha category, the lines of which are as follows:

Na lage sona re, na lage rupa re
It is neither gold nor silver
Bhaiya ka pheta ka chhati ka, chaṇḍowa je lawakae re
It is but the bracelets tucked on the turban and hanging by the chest that is glittering.

There are various non-metallịc ornaments also with which the Munda youths adorn themselves. The following song belonging to Baroya category indicates that even the queen is wearing ordinary ornaments. The lines of the song are as follows:

1. *Kekara muṛe hardi raṇgạl phita re*
On whose head beautifies the turmeric coloured ribbon
Kekara muṛe jawa phul re-2
On whose head is the jawa flower

2. *Rani ka muṛe hardi raṇgạl phita re*
On the head of the queen lies the turmeric coloured ribbon
Raja ka muṛe jawa phul re-2
On king's head bloom the jawa flower

The ladies remain so busy in their works that they hardly get time for dressing. As most of the time they carry a load on their head, the hair remain dishevelled. Nevertheless, they keep the hair lock tight with hairpins and combs. They have their own style of making the hair lock. In the following song belonging to Lahsua, describes the hairstyle of the girl who is too busy to attend her work quite unmindful of her dishevelled hair. The lines of the song are as follows:

1. *Okosa:te hijũ lena*
   From where she came
   Okosa:te seno jana
   To where she proceeded
   Nirago maina, nirago maina
   O my *maina* dear
   Goṇje goṇjem supidakạn ama rasika
   Made hair lock on one side of the head, how glad you are

2. *Purab sa:te hiju len*
   She came from the east
   Pachhim sate seno jan
   And proceeded to the west
   Nirago maina, nirago maina
   O my *maina* dear
   Goṇje goṇjem supidakạn and raskia
   Made hair lock on one side of the head, how glad you are

One more style of hairdressing has been mentioned in yet another Jadur song in which two of the lines are worth noting in this connection:

Kapi chuṭi supida kada
Has made hair lock like the tip of the battle axe
Sar kapi-e daṇḍida kada
Has ear-spike of arrow-blades

The youths also make multicoloured thread flowers and feather flowers. The mention of these have been made in the following Jadur song, the lines of which are as follows:

1. *Phudena do phudena re, Marchi ba, ba phudena*
   The *Marchi ba* thread flower stands out among the flowers

Kalega do kalega re, sae murga diṇda kalega
Among feather flowers, single feather flower from hundreds cocks stands out

2. *Oko hoṛoe roye leda re*
Who did cultivate it
Marchi ba, ba phudeṇa
Marchi ba thread flower
Oko hoṛoe bai leda re
Who made it
Sae murga ḍinḍa kalega
Single *kalega* from feathers of hundreds cocks

3. *Munḍa hoṛoe roe lada re*
Munda had cultivated it
Marchi ba, ba phudena
Marchi had thread flower

4. *Santa hoṛoe bai leda re*
Santa had made it
Sae murga ḍinḍa kalega
Single *kalega* from feathers of hundred cocks

The following Jadur song mentions an incident in which the thread flower has caught fire while smoking. The lines of the song are as follows:

1. *Phudena do, phudena do*
The thread flower
Marchi ba, ba phudena
The Marchi *ba* thread flower
Dola tạbu nele lia re
Let us see it
Phudena do lo tana
The thread flower is burning
Phudena do phudena do re
The thread flower dear
Marchi ba, ba phudena
The Marchi ba thread flower

2. *Haṛam hoṛo hukae nu tana re*
   The old man is smoking on hubble-bubble
   Phudena do lo tana
   The thread flower is burning

The youths make variety of thread flowers of different sizes. *Marchi ba* is the small size thread flower like the flower of chilli plant. These thread flowers are made on the borders of loin cloth as well as on the borders of cloth worn as turban. Thread flowers are also fastened dangling on the ear as ornaments. Similarly, spike is weaved with thread flowers and used as decorative ornaments during dance.

The *'kalega'* made from birds' feathers of multicolour and *'phudena'* from multicoloured threads cut in the shape of flowers, look beautiful when the youths decorate with it while participating in dance. The following Racha song describes the beautiful scenery that is created during the Ind Jatra dance. The lines of the song are as follows:

1. *Ayur reyo baka baha*
   Cranes feather flowers on the lead, too
   Tayom reyo toṇyaṇ baha
   Feather flowers from toṇyaṇ bird on the rear, too
   Haere, Indi piṛi lodob kena
   The Ind field was turned lively

2. *Engateke diri teko thene kija re*
   Her mother was buried under the stone
   Aputeke janum teko rame kija re
   Her father's graveyard was covered with thorny plants.
   Haere, Indi piṛi lodob kena re
   The Ind field was turned lively, alas

The song describes the scene of *Ind Jatra* in which all the participants have decorated themselves with multicoloured feather flowers. The dance is lively. The song mentions that there is one person who is participating in the dance whose parents have died recently and still he is dancing. This is quite contrary to the customs, and the composer of the song deeply feels.

A person has decorated himself with crane's, feather flowers, white in colour and is walking down the path. This scene has been conceptualized by the composer of the song as 'crane's feather flowers floating away'. The following song belonging to Racha category describes the scene in these lines:

Hora-hora te bakula ba re atu tana
The crane's feather flowers are floating down the path
Kesed redo kesedem, taraṇ redo taraṇ gem
Stop it if you can, divert it if you can
Bakula ba re atu tana
The crane's feather flowers are floating down
Bakula ba re bual tana
The crane's feather flowers are floating with the current

The song below in which the youths are busy in making the ornaments and decoration, belongs to Jarga category and the lines are as follows:

Jhunur-jhunur ghughura ko tolen tana
They are wearing bell-metal ornament sounding *jhunur-jhunur*
Ghughura ko tolen tana
Wearing bell-metal ornaments
Dola rebu nele liare
Let us proceed to see him
Dola rebu china liare
Let us identify him
Lemko lekoṛ phundena ko hade tana
While in half slumber are making thread flowers
Phudena ko hade tana
They are making thread flowers

Songs describing Dances

In songs, we also get records of dance forms and its styles. A few songs also record the time and duration of a particular dance. The following Jadur song indicates the period of Karam and Jadur dances, the lines of which are as follows:

Asar Sawan re karam kodo ho
In Asar and Sawan month, Karam dance is organized
Magh Fagun re Jadur kodo ho
In Magh and Fagun month, Jadur dance is organized
Karam kodo ho liṭi lopoṇga
Karam dance is dust raising
Jadur kodo ho otoṇg koyoṇg
Jadur dancers follow and stoop
Dolabu senoa Karam susun te
Let us proceed for Karam dance
Dolabu birida Jadur susun te
Let us rise for *Jadur* dance
Ale dole sen kena karam susun te
We had been to Karam dance
Ale dole birid kena jadur susun te
We had been to *jadur* dance
Hiyatiṇg sanaiṇga karam kodo
I badly remember the Karam dance
Chakatiṇg mone iṇga Jadur kodo ho
I deeply feel for the Jadur dance

The above song not only mentions the occasion of Jadur and Karam dances but also indicates how it makes a deep imprint in the minds of the youths who participated in it. This event could be remembered throughout the life. And when one becomes old and shoulders the role of the elders in the family and society, he does appeal to the youths to organize dance regularly in the village *akhra*. Such appeal has been made in the following Jadur song, the lines of which are as follows:

1. *Smbharae pandey hale guchu pandu jana*
   Uncle Sambharae Pandey, beard ours have turned white
   Hatu kabu bagia marbu jadura
   We should not leave the village, let us dance

2. *Dasi nabu guti nabu*
   Even if we have to become the servant of others
   Hatu kabu bagia marbu jadura
   We should not leave the village, let us dance

In the above song, an appeal has been made to the youths by an elder himself who has now become old and cannot participate in dance. The youths of the village too, because of poverty are moving out to distant lands to earn a living. This is a very precarious situation for the continuity of music and dance—the old are not in a position for its regularity because of age and there are no youths in the village as they have gone out in search of a living. The continuity of music and dance is possible only by retaining the youths in the village and create jobs for them. In the following Jadur song a most fervent and philosophical appeal has been made to the youths, the lines of which are as follows:

1. *Isu duku tebu napa̭m tada*
   After a great hardship we have arrived at
   Sona leka̭n ba chaṇḍu muluakna
   Gold like Ba month have arrived
   Janao bu su-sunare soṇgoti gatim
   Friends dear, let us dance regularly
   Karebu bapagia piriti saṇgaiŋg
   Beloved friend, let us not leave each other

2. *Ne hatu tala rebu janama kana*
   We have taken our birth in this village
   Okoe jido, okoe gojo mena geya
   Life and death is there always for everybody
   Janao bu su-sunare soṇgoti gatim
   Friends dear, let us dance regularly
   Karebu bapagia piriti saṇgaiṇg
   Beloved friends, let us not leave each other
   Sona leka̭n Ba chaṇḍu seno: jan redo
   When the gold like Ba month passes away
   Karebu nameya re jadur susun
   There will be no more *Jadur* dance
   Janao bu su-suna soṇgoti gatim
   Friends dear, let us dance regularly
   Karebu bapagia piriti saṇgaiṇg
   Beloved friend, let us not leave each other

In every village, there is a fixed place where dance is held regularly. This place is known as *akhra.* After dinner, every night, in normal days, dance is organized there. Initially, few boys carry with them musical instruments like *dumaŋg* and assemble there playing on it till sufficient number of youths turn up. The dance then is started with a specific song—particularly in Jadur dance. This very song is sung in every Jadur dance prior to the formal starts of the dance. This song acts as spell to bring out the youths from their homes. The lines of the song are as follows:

1. *Posare bale golo*
   Let the single go on increasing
   Niṇdiyo bajari ke marae
   Let the sleepiness vanish with a lighting

2. *Hirpelo, pampelo*
   Like strayed butterfly assemble on the flower
   Posare bale goṭo
   Let the single go on increasing
   Niṇdiyo bajari ke marae
   Let the sleepiness vanish with a lighting

On hearing the sound of *dumaŋg* at *akhra,* the youths come out one after the other, and the old persons too. The following Lahsua song describes how the young couples are packing up all works hurriedly for dance. The lines of the song are as follows:

1. *Doti dolaṇg*
   Let us proceed
   Kita galaṇg bagi tạm susuŋg telaṇg
   Stop weaving mat, let us proceed for dance
   Doti dolaṇg
   Let us proceed

2. *Akhṛa re saṛi tana, juṛi Dumaŋg lodob leka*
   At *akhra* a pair of *dumaŋg* are resounding melodiously
   Ḳami udam bagi tam susunalaṇg
   Leave aside the work, let us participate in dance

3. *Haṭia tem seno re, doria nacha kiriṇgeya laṇg*

When visit to market, we shall purchase *doria nacha*
Niral gechiṇg supid ta: ba talaṇg
I will make hair beautiful with knot and flowers on it

Sometimes, girls do not get time to leave the household duties and sometimes they are not allowed to participate in dance. But as mentioned in the following Jadur song, there are so many excuses to befool the elders or wait for the opportunity for escape. The lines of the song are as follows:

1. *Lohor-lohor diya barela*
   The lamp is burning continuously
   Hạm kaese jab goi diya mor jagéla
   How shall I go out when lamp mine is awake

2. *Juta palita diya barela*
   In the shoelace the lamp burns
   Hạm kaese jab goi diya mor jagela
   How shall I go out when lamp mine is awake

The girl is not allowed to participate in dance. In the sleeping room of the girl, a lamp is burning. The girl is planning to escape stealthily but as the lamp is burning, there is no way out. Had there been darkness, she would have escaped. She is lamenting for this as her friends are waiting for her.

While dancing, everyone has the liberty to start a song. The song in some category of dance is normally started by the boys such as in Jadur dance. In Jadur song, the boys first start a song. As soon as the first line of the song is sung, girls repeat the same line. If the girls repeat the lines at least twice, the *dumaŋg* is sounded and they start keeping pace slowly. The boys again sing the line which is repeated by the girls and dance starts. But sometimes, it happens that the girls would not repeat the lines and the attempt goes in vain. The same song cannot be repeated again and a start must be given with a fresh song. It is to express this very situation that the following Jadur song has been composed, the lines of which are as follows:

1. *Akhṛa koiṇg sen kena*
   I had been to *akhṛa*
   Miyad geiṇg duraṇg leda

I had sung but one song
Aiṇg durang kako tela kena
Song mine was not repeated
Haere taiṇg samae seno yana
Alas, my chance did go waste

2. *Daṭa boraiṇg bora jan*
I lost all my teeth
Bo panduiṇg pandu jan
All my hair has turned white
Aiṇg duraṇg telae redo honaṇg
If my song would have been repeated
Aiṇg nutum tinoga honaṇg
My name would have remained forever

Why the song of the person was not repeated by the girls, have clearly been mentioned in the above song. He is an old person and has lost all his teeth. It is because of this the words are not clearly audible to the girls, so they fail to repeat. Though the person takes a deep interest in music and dance, he is physically handicapped because of his age.

If the dance is not organized for one reason or the other, the boys of the village, on that night proceed to the other neighbouring village to take part in the dance. The group of boys so comprised is called '*Pahi dal*'. We have number of songs relating to *Pahi* group. The *Pahi* boys on receiving permission from the boys of the host village, take part in the dance with the girls of the host village. As long as the Pahi boys stay in the *akhra*, no host boy participates in the dance. But sometimes the guest as well as host dance together. The songs are composed on variety of themes relating to *Pahi* group.

The *Pahi* boys usually narrate their experience of night travelling. One such night travelling have been mentioned in these words. We, the strangers, have arrived here hearing the sound of *mander,* staggering and tumbling many a time on the way. The following Lahsua song describes the experience of the *Pahi dal* which is as follows:

1. *Bar dur se awali*

We arrived from a distant village
Eko gito gawali
We sang but one song
Gito suni chupi na rahibo
Don't keep silent after hearing the song
Achha sunder gito jhuik lewa
Please repeat this nice song

2. *Toheṇ maiya khelauiya*
You yourself are the dancer
Toheṇ maiya gawaiya
You yourself are the singer
Gito suni chupi na rahibo
Don't keep silent after hearing the song
Achha sunder gito jhuik lewa
Please repeat the nice song

The *Pahi* boys beg apology to the host boys for any mistake they may have committed during the dance. The following Jadur song has been composed with this theme. The lines of one of the song are as follows:

1. *Ape doga hatu haga ko*
You are the native brothers of this village
Ale doga duraṇg pahi ko
We are the *Pahi* group of singers
Alo gape eger leya
Please don't abuse us
Alo gape seger leya
Please don't blame us

2. *Ape doga dhoti pindha ko*
You dress yourself with dhoti
Ale doga tonom botoe ko
We have but tattered loin cloth
Alo gape eger leya
Please don't abuse us
Alo gape seger leya
Please don't blame us

In the above song the guest party does not find himself comparable to host party economically. They have too poor a standard of living. In the name of dress they have only a tattered loin cloth while they, that is, the host are economically far better off. They have dhoti and shirts as dress. Therefore, they beg that they should be pardoned in case some mistakes may have been committed by them due to their ignorance. These lines have been composed satirically. The lines of the other Jadur song are as follows:

1. *Ape doga hatu kisan Munḍa ko*
   You are the native farmer Munda of the village
   Ale doga susun nala ko
   We are but earning livelihood by dancing
   Alo gape udur le, alo gape solka le
   Please don't push us, don't pound upon us

2. *Udur lere gape solka lere*
   If you push and pound upon us
   Udur lere dole sandangowa
   We may fall flat if you push us
   Udur lere dope solka lere
   If you push and pound upon us
   Solka lere dole tumbilowa
   We may tumble down, if you pound upon us

3. *Udur lere gape solka lere*
   If you push and pound upon us
   Udur lere dole chimin le nira
   If you push us, how long shall we run
   Udur lere gape solka lere
   If you push us and pound upon us
   Solka lere dole chimin le done
   If you pound upon us, how long shall we jump

The above song describes the dance scene in which the guest and the host, both are participating in the dance together. As described, the guests are hardly given chance for full participation in the dance for they are being pushed around by the host boys. So the guest boys request the host, not to do so for they will not be able to run and jump constantly.

The next Jadur song of the same theme is as follows:

1. *Ape do hatu kisan ko*
   You are the native of the village
   Ale do susun basa ko
   We are the nomads for dance
   Alo repe tega leya
   Please do not trample us
   Alo repe kuṇdusu leya
   Please do not kick us

2. *Ka hale jagar kena*
   We had no conversation
   Ka hale lapanda kena
   We had not cut jokes
   Alo repe tega leya
   Please don't trample us
   Alo repe kuṇdusu leya
   Please do not kick us

The Pahi dal boys are not allowed to talk with the girls with whom they danced. If they are seen talking, they receive harsh treatment from the host boys and are also not allowed to dance. The above song mentions the scene in which the guest boys are being trampled and kicked about while dancing. The guest boys beg to be pardoned for they had no talk with the girls.

If the Pahi boys belong to a separate clan they may cut some jokes with the girls as well as the boys. An indication of this is found in the following jarga song :

1. *Sen nala duraṇg nala*
   The wage of dance and singing
   Oko kuṛi gape oma leya
   Which of the girls will you give us

2. *Sen nala duraṇg nala*
   The wage of dance and singing
   Ayur te susun kuṛi gape oma leya
   You will give us the girl leading the dance

3. *Sen nala duraṇg nala*
The wage of dance and singing
Tayom ren susun kuṛi gape omá leya
You will give us the girl dancing in the rear

The above song indicates that the guest boys belong to separate clan and the two groups have the joking relationship. This is why the *Pahi dal* boys are requesting the host boys as to which of the girls they are offering them in marriage. Well, they have no objection in having any of the girl dancing from front to the rear in the dance row.

Now, it is the time for departure for the guest boys, but the dance is on and the youths are so mixed up that it was difficult to identify any of them. A youth is searching for his friend but he could not locate him. This problem has been described in the following Lahsua song. The lines of the song are as follows:

1. *Chhoṭe moṭe nakeṛa*
A small Akhra
Ghumaralaiṇ rasika ho kejạn
How many times my beloved has made round of, I do not know
Nai re dise, kejạn chhaela chhokṛia kejan
None is visible who the girl is, I do not know

2. *Danto raṇgạl chhokṛi*
Even the girl with coloured teeth
Mati raṇgạl gamchha
The shawl is brown colour too
Nai re dise, kejạn chhaela chhokṛia, kejan
None is visible who the girls is, I do not know

Similar to the above situation, the dancers also don't know as to what has made them so enchanting that they are moving around under the same tree continuously for hours. The lines of the Jadur song with this theme are as follows:

1. *Ranu bul jana chibu ili bul jana*
Whether by medicine or by rice beer, we are intoxicated.

Ne jojo suba rebu biyuren tana
We are making rounds under this tamarind tree
Ranu bul jana chibu ili bul jana
Whether by medicine or by rice beer, we are intoxicated
Ne uli suba rebu sekoren tana
We are making rounds under this mango tree

2. *Ranu bul kage ho ili bul kage*
It is neither the effect of medicine nor rice beer, the intoxication is
Biyuren gena bu biyuren tana
We are but simply moving around
Ranu bul kage ho ili bul kage
It is neither the effect of medicine nor rice beer, the intoxication is
Sekoren gena bu sekren tana
We are but simply making the rounds

At midnight, after the dance, all disperse and retire to their respective houses. In some villages, the youths sleep together and in such cases, they all retire to the sleeping place. The following Jadur song describes about the sleeping places of the boys and girls, the lines of which are as follows:

1. *Lalibu susun kedare, Lali bu karam keda*
O dear, merrily we danced and sang
Mạr dolabu senoga re
Let us now retire
Giti ọra dupuṛum te
To sleep in retiring rooms

2. *Ale giti ọra dore*
The retiring room of ours, dear
Bugi leka pundi gi
It is whitewaṣhed brightly
Ape giti ọra doṛe
Your retiring room, dear
Busu ọra ruduṛ-ruduṛ
Straw thatched and rugged

The girls and boys have separate sleeping house known as '*Giti Ora*'. In this song, the girls tell the boys that they have beautiful whitewashed *Giti Ora*, but their's (the boys) is straw thatched and rugged. It is natural that the boys have no expertise in maintenance of the house they live in and they cannot stand in comparison to the girls in this area.

Musical instruments can be played at any time and place besides the *akhra*. Similarly, a person can sing any song at any place. The Jatra category of song is sung even when one is out in journey. People usually sing songs when they are engaged in some work or are moving around leisurely. The following Khemta category of song indicates this in these lines:

Munga buṭa Jathṛiṇ buṭa
Under the *munga* tree and by the side of fence
Parkom bila kana re
A cot is lying
Horo kobu rasika jana
When we people are glad
Khemṭa kobu duraṇga
We shall sing Khemta song

This song indicates that people sing song when they are in happy mood. The song is sung to amuse oneself and not to entertain others.

On Style and Rhythm in Dance

Just as each category of song has its own *raga* or tune, each dance form has its own style of rhythm. While the style is reflected in pace and movement of the dancers, the rhythm is produced on the subtle movements of the parts of body. Mundas do identify the rhythm through various terms such as *lodob-lodob, tinang-nachang, heche-chere, cha-chandi, hojar,* or *hujul,* etc. We have a number of songs, though not very expressive, on the style and rhythm of dances. It may be noted that just as tune and style of singing differ from region to region, so also the style and rhythm of dance. The following Jadur category of song states the style of Jadur dance in these lines:

1. *Niku-niku gecha ruru kodo*
   Are these the players of musical instruments

Borojad leka geko boton Ja:-inga
They are frightening me as if I am afraid of
Niku-niku gecha susun kodo
Are these the dancers
Guna dos leka geko kudao ja:-inga
Driving me away, as if I have committed some mistakes

2. *Boro jad leka geko boton ja:-inga*
Frightening me, as if I am afraid of
Bu-akan dutu teko botong ja:-inga
Frightening me with a hollowed up wood
Guna dos leka geko kudao ja:-inga
Driving me as if I have committed some mistakes
Paela kichiri ko dondowaing tana
Raising waist cloth against me

3. *Bu-akan dutu teko botong ja:-inga*
Frightening me with a hollowed up wood
Bu-akan dutu teching botongoa
Shall I be afraid of, with a hollowed up wood
Paela kichiri ko dondowaing tana
Raising waist cloth against me
Paela kichiri ching boroa
Shall I fear from waist cloth

The above song describes the style in Jadur dance. Normally, there are two groups of youths in a dance—the boys and the girls. While dancing, the girls hold each other in a row or two and the boys, who play the musical instruments, remain in front of the girls. There are other boys in front of the girls who take the leading role in dancing and singing who either hold the sticks or cloth piece in their hands. The girl who leads the dance, also holds a cloth piece in her hand. The rhythmic movement of cloth and sticks create or add up to the style while dancing. And it is they who hold sticks and cloth and play on other musical instruments, while dancing, create rhythm by their concerted movements in unison. The girls too, exert their style by rhythmic movements and sounds. The following Jadur song describes the rhythm produced by the girls in these lines:

1. *Am do mai mundli gundi leka*
   Like hornless cow, you O girl
   Am do maim sur-sureya
   You produce sound of *sur-sur*
   Am do mai dopali sandi leka
   Like fighting cock you O girl
   Am do maim dopalin ge
   You jump off and on

2. *Am do mai oko reko idi meya*
   Where will you be married away O girl
   Am do maim sur-sureya
   You produce sound of *sur-sur*
   Am do mai chimae reko chala meya
   Where will you be taken away O girl
   Am do maim dopalin ge
   You jump off and on

The style and rhythm created during the Jadur dance through the sound of *sur-sur* and action of hopping add up the tempo and movement of dance. The comparison of this action with that of the jump of fighting cock and the sound of hornless cow while charging someone in anger, is funny and hilarious to the singers as well as to the audience which is enjoyed by everybody. While dancing in Jadur dance, the girls produce a sort of whistling sound and make a rapid pace all of a sudden which has been stated as jumping. Similar to the above song, the following song too, describes the style of Lahsua dance. The lines of the song are as follows:

1. *Amchi mai sauri muti leka*
   Like the bundle of *sauri* grass, you O girl
   Am chi maim soren ge
   You do slip yourself
   Am chi mai panada san leka
   Like splitted wood, you O girl
   Am chi maim tenderen ge
   You always seek supports

2. *Am chi mai susun Akhra re*

While dancing at Akhra
A̭m chi maim̭ soren ge
You do slip yourself
A̭m chi mai karam Akhṛa re
While dancing Karam dance you O girl
A̭m chi maim̭ tenderen ge
You always seek supports

3. *Aiṇg gecha engaiṇg ko bugin geya*
My mother is good therefore
Aiṇg gecha soren ge
I always go on slipping
Aiṇg gecha apuiṇg ko napae geya
My father is nice therefore
Aiṇg gecha tenderen ge
I always seek supports

4. *A̭m do mai jati chaela kuṛi ge*
You are by nature merry-go-girl, O girl
A̭m do maim̭ soren ge
You always go on slipping
A̭m do mai jati landiya era ge
You are by nature a lazy girl, O girl
A̭m do maim̭ tenderen ge
You always seek supports

The above song describes the style of Karam dance. While making movements they throw the whole body together in one direction and fall back again in the earlier position and bend backwards towards the right in support of each other. This style of dance has been illustrated through the action in daily activities of works and behaviour of the individuals. Giving a decription of style and rhythm in dance in words is very difficult. Something is missing in giving description of Lahsua dance style in the above song and the song below makes up these lacunae in the following lines. The song belongs to Jadur category of dance.

1. *Karam susun kuṛi hon ko*
The girls dancing the Karam dance

Kabu nire seneya ko meneya
We will not run but walk, they say

2. *Jadur susun kuṛi hon ko*
The girls dancing the Jadur dance
Kabu dub seneya ko meneya
We will not sit but walk, they say

As stated in the above song, the style of Karam dance is that the movement of the body remains in between the speed of running and walking, that is, it is like jogging. The dancers while dancing, sometimes pick up the speed of steps and sometimes walk on. In Jadur dance, they stoop like sitting and then walk on.

The dance is so enjoyable that even the old persons could not keep themselves aloof in participating in it. They participate in dance, holding sticks for support in their hands. The following Lahsua song describes how an old person is dancing with the support of the stick. The lines are as follows:

1. *Budạn sing timpu-tipur, banka ḍanḍae ṭunḍa: nare*
Lean and thin Budan sing, holds forked stick
Daina, rasika haṛam samae re
How deeply he enjoys the dance in old age, sister
Susun tanae daina, rasika
He is dancing merrily, sister

2. *Ḍanḍa te ṭunḍa tana*
He is measuring the pace with stick
Ku-u: keyate duraṇg tana
After coughing he is singing
Daina rasika haṛam samae re
How deeply he enjoys the dance in old age, sister
Susun tana daina rasika
He is dancing merrily, sister

Walking through with measured pace by the dancers and sticks in hands for support is in itself a style. The occasional coughing at interval while singing, though it does not form a part of the *raga* of the song but similar to a cry or shout during the dance, it also becomes a part of the music and is enjoyed by all.

3

DANCES OF THE MUNDAS

The Mundas have different categories of song and dance which are associated to a particular occasion, period of time and season. The youths, besides learning the song and dance, have also to learn and memorize the period and its sequence. Generally, every song is associated with a respective kind of dance with few exceptions. Jadur, Lahsua, Karam or Dubung, Jatra, Baroya, Khemta, Jarga or Jarapi or Japi, Racha and Bala are the main category and sub-category of song and dance. The Racha and Bala category of song-dance are sung without accompaniment of musical instruments. While *racha* is a song-dance, Bala is only a category of song which is sung during a series of marriage ceremonies. Jatra song, besides singing during the Jatra dance, are also sung individually or in group during work or journey. No other category of song has the popularity which the Jatra song has, and, it is due to the fact that this is sung beyond its particular period of time.

The Jadur category of song-dance has *Nir, Hojor* or *Gena* variety. The two sub-categories differ in all respects, that is, in tune of the song, style and rhythm of dance and in sound of music too. These two varieties are supplementary to each other and follow each other in alternate sequence during dance. The sequence normally is Jadur song-dance, followed by one or two Gena song-dance. The two varieties of Jadur, thus, share the same period. The Jadur songs are even sung during marriage along Bala song, but it is sung always in the tune of Bala category of song. Except Jatra, Bala and Racha category of song-dance, all other categories of song-dance are held in a particular spot of the village called *akhra* which happens to be the central place in the village.

Dances and its Calendar

The Munda follow the Gregorian calendar which is based on planetary month, and the lunar calendar. They know the approximate period or duration of the planet or *nakshatras* as well as of the lunar movement. The months, according to the Mundas are *Chait, Baisakh, Jeth, Asar, Sawan, Bhado, Kuar, Katik, Aghan, Pus, Magh* and *Fagun.* Rohini, Nirbisra and Hathia *nakshatras* are particularly known to the Mundas due to their association to seasonal changes The period or duration of any song-dance is counted with or is coterminous to the duration of the month or months as stated. However, the duration of any song-dance does not go strictly with the duration of the month as stated but begins or ends with the full moon or its disappearance. The duration of various song-dances are as follows :

Jadur :– Katik to Magh (roughly from October to April). There will be no Jadur dance as soon as the month of Fagun sets in.

Lahsua :– Chait to Sawan (March to September). Lahsua dance beings after Sohrai festival. Formerly there was no Lahsua dance and Jadur and Jarga dance with its variety of Jethua, Asaria, Sardia and Aghania continued to be danced during the period also.

Karam or Dubung:– Sawan and Bhado (August to September) with Garua, Hambal, Chhalkua (Rambal), Therua, Bhinsaria and Khemta variety.

Jatra:– This song-dance known as *phada jatra* takes place twice a year—once in the month of *Baisakh* and second in *Katik.* The *phada jatra* which takes place in the month of *Baisakh, is* called *jeth-jatra* when Jethua variety of song are sung. During *Katik jatra,* Ind flag is erected at the centre of the dance ground. No Jethua variety of song is to be sung in *Katik jatra.*

Katik Jatra:– Two Jatra dances at two different places and time are held within a period of less than 12 hours in which roughly the same dancers participate during the *Katik Jatra.* The distance of these two places does not go beyond two to three kilometres but never in the same village. The places happen to be in two adjoining villages. The dance which is held in the early hours of the evening or just prior to sunset, is called *jhanda jatra.* In the same night, at about eleven, another jatra dance is held in the adjoining village which is called *Ind jatra.* It is here that flag is pitched in the dance ground. These two jatra dances also differ in the number of participants. The participants of *jhanda jatra,* usually happen to be the youths and old persons of adjoining villages, while the participants of *Ind jatra* come from far-off villages.

In the month of Asar, when there is no rain till the end of this month and when people eagerly await for it for the sake of cultivation of crops, a ceremony is held by the village maidens around the *jitia* tree, preferably that stands in village Sarna. After returning their hemlets they break up the penance and organize a dance which turns into a big gathering and Jatra dance continues till mid-night and the youths of neighbouring villages too, participate in it. This Jatra dance is called *Chakonda Jhanda.* This dance has no link either to *Jeth Jatra* or *Katik Jatra* and may take place in any village whenever the ceremony is performed.

Jatras are held in some selected traditional villages where they are being held since generations. It begins from a particular village and on a particular day of a particular month and ends up in a particular village. People count the day from particular month and the village is identified on the basis of the traditional history when the time for Jatra dance arrives. There is no need of announcement in villages or markets about the day and name of the village where Jatra dance is to be held. But in case of organizing Jatra for the first time, announcement is made in a number of weekly markets. The villagers, who want to start Jatra in their own village, offer free drinks to the participants whatever be their numbers. Such Jatras often discontinue after few years.

Jeth jatra is traditionally held in the villages of Itam, Banae, Kodakel, Marcha, Karora, Pakṛa and Torpa. Formerly, Jatra was also held in the village Jathin Tola but later on discontinued. The Jatra now held there is a later addition. The *Katik jatra* begins just after the Dasai or Dussehra festival which was traditionally started from village Jariagarh, the erstwhile capital of Chhote Lal of the

Nagbansi dynasty of Chhotanagpur Maharaja. After Jaria, the villages where *Katik jatra* is successively held are Jalanga, Dehekela, Champi, Jajoda, Nisiyo, Ukrimandi, Icha, Ramtoloy, Sarita, Ara-ara, Chatakpur and ends up in Bakaspur.

Like the road, it branches, after Sarita. The *Katik jatra* successively held in villages—Digri, Itam, Sidum, Banay, Kodakel, Turigara, Marcha, Karora, Pakna and Torpa.

There is yet another cycle of *Katik jatra* which begins after Sohrai festival. It covers the villages which were excluded in any of the cycle mentioned above. It begins from the village Okoda and successively goes on the villages—Dodoma, Sulangi, Chakla, Sondari, Kinsu, Patniya, Goplae, Kamda, Tapkara, Kalet, Derang and ends up in Gutuhatu Koronjo tola.

Jatra, the dance festival, generally known as *phada jatra* or *leko karam*, is held for a night only in any village. The villages as mentioned above, are not adjoining ones but they are far off from each other in distance and rarely they happen to be adjoining villages. The entire Naguri country is, thus, covered in a series or cycle of *Jatras*. The youths attend even a very distantly located Jatra, sometimes carry food or other eatables or they stay with one of their relatives, however, distantly related they may be. When a youth or youths have no relative in the village where jatra is held or in any adjoining village, they stay in any Munda household for the day and from there they attend next Jatra during the night. Such youth guests are merrily welcomed by the host family.

The night journey is always hazardous in a hilly and forest clad country but the youths—both boys and girls of a village undertake the journey in groups equipped with battle weapons. In pre-independent days, it is told, the *jatra* used to be held for the whole night, that is, from sunset to sunrise. The timing has now been modified considerably. Now, the dance starts just after midnight. In such *jatras* tens of thousands of youths assemble and organize all sort of music and dance in an extravaganza of merriment. The night comes into alive in Munda country during the *Jatra* season.

The month of Pus and Magh are dedicated to the ancestors. During this period, the last rituals for the departed souls is held which is called *jang halang* or *jang topa* ceremony. It is during this period that *Bid-diri,* that is, memorial stones are erected for the departed souls and washing and annointing, that is, *Diri-dul*, ceremony is held. There is, however, no prohibition of dance during this period. Dance is prohibited for a month only when there is a death in the village, and partially prohibited when someone in the village is seriously ill.

The main song-dance have been allotted different and fixed periods in a year, however, few are in exception.

There is no fixed period for song and dance of Khemta. It is even held during the month of *Jeth*. The Khemta song-dance, which is a sub-category of Karam or Dubung dance, is an auxilliary to every song-dance. It has its own style and rhythm. When it is danced at interval along with other song-dance, it brings a temporary change and greatly reduces the monotone in music and style. It is why, there are Khemta song-dance even in *Jadur* and in its parent Dubung dance.

Racha song-dance is held in the month of *Jeth*, rather it starts in the month of *Chait* after the *Fagun* month and continues till *Jeth* month. It is often called '*Dhuria*' dance because it is danced on dusty ground. It is the only song-dance which is not held in *akhra*, that is, in traditional dance ground, but takes place anywhere in the open field in the village under the moonlit nights. No musical instrument is played upon during the dance.

Matha song-dance is held after the Jitia festival. During this dance, the youths decorate themselves with *rampa* a decorative ornament, specially made for this dance. During the dance, the youths also hold umbrella in their hands which serve as decorative ornaments. A mixture of style in dance, tune of song, and to some extent, in the sound of music, is found in Matha song-dance.

Baroya song-dance is held in the month of *Jeth* only.

Jarga, Japi or Jarapi, that is, the Mage sub-category of song-dance go hand-in-hand with Jadur dance. Hence, there is no separate period of song and dance for this song-dance.

The time is changing fast with respect to the traditional music and dance. And this change is visible clearly during Jatra dance. Nowadays, in *Katik jatra*, for instance, it is the Matha song-dance that occupy larger areas and also attracts bigger crowd.

As stated earlier, at the outset of any work and before eating and drinking, the Supreme God Singbonga along with one's departed ancestral spirits and other local presiding spirits are remembered by the Mundas. So also, before the start of song-dance, and particularly during Jatra dance, the *pahan* or the village priest ceremonially performs a ritual in the name of the God Singbonga and other local presiding spirits. The non-performance of such ritual, it is believed, invites misfortune for the village community.

The distribution of a particular song-dance is not uniformly found in the Munda country because of their dispersal in space and contiguity to other tribal communities. The major tribal communities such as Oraon, Kharia, Ho and Santhal, who surround the Munda tribe, have not much difference in social structure and share or have common sociocultural tradition. It is because of this, there is the commonality in conceptualization and in the thematic composition of songs, but the only difference that is found, is in styles, tunes and in language. Due to the development of Sadri as common dialect, diffusion of song texts have become easier which have crossed the ethnic boundary. Similarly, dance techniques, its styles and musical instruments too, have diffused in a wider space. A hetrogeneity in dance form and in style is thus, found in almost all tribal communities inhabiting the region. Under this situation, it is rather difficult to identify as to which dance technique and form is indigenous to a particular tribe. The music and dance of the Mundas, have thus, become enriched due to this influence and diffusion of traits. The process of incorporation of new dance technique, style of song, theme and discarding the traditional one as well as its revival, is continuous.

In Munda parlance, as stated in previous pages, 'to walk' is to dance. And this definition or cognition of dance is true to the fact that every Munda dance starts with steps of feet or pace of the dancers in unison to each other. Steps may be slow or rapid and often running or jumping. Movement of the body is closely linked with the speed of the footsteps. It is in dance that rhythm and style are quite understandable to all the audience.

Normally, dancers divide themselves into two groups on the basis of sex. Among the Mundas, there is no dance exclusive to a particular sex. No dance is possible in the absence of either of the sex. The musical instruments, during the dance, are however, exclusively handled by the male dancers. Each dance is associated with its specific song and *vice versa.*

As already stated, at the start of every dance, the boys and girls

1. Karma-Dancer in different style

2. Karma Dancer in slow action

3. Women readying situation to start the Dance

4. Japi-Dance in progress

5. Karma-Dancer in Progress

6. Tilguti games in progress author in sleeveless coat right side

7. Village priest and priestest with author's wife in the middle during the celebration of annual Ba (flower) festival

8. Musical instruments of every dance

9. Welcoming guests

10. Dancers of Jadur dance at *Akhra*

11. Gena dance in Progress

12. Jadur dance in Progress

13. Another variety of Jadur dance

14. Paik dancers in full dress

15. Musical instruments of the Paik dancers

16. Common style of male decoration

stand face to face singing few lines of the song. Normally, the boys initiate the song and the girls repeat the lines, and in the process walk as many steps around the *akhra* till all, particularly the girls set themselves for the dance in unison of the sound of musical instruments. The boys, who usually remain in front of the girls, dance individually but in group, while the girls hold each other by hands, waist or by shoulder with the girl or girls of one's immediate side or next to her. The detail formation of dancers, however, differ from one category of dance to the other. The Mundas, as stated earlier, have as many category of dances as there are classes of songs with only one exception of Bala category of song which is not associated to any dance. It is also notable that each category of dance has its specific style of the beat of drum. A dance can be easily classified hearing the style of sound of drum or *dumang* only. In every Munda dance, *dumang* is the main musical instrument. 'Kumuni Dumang' is the well-known phrase in Mundari which is said in connection of *dumang*. Kumuni is a bamboo made fishing implement through which fish in running water are caught. The implement is placed in running water by diverting it through an embankment. The fish get trapped in the Kumuni. The Kumuni and Dumang both serve the same purpose of drawing a crowd. Kumuni gathers stray fish at one place just as on hearing the sound of Dumang people gather in the *akhra*.

Each dance has its specific style and rhythm of expression. Some of the dance styles have been articulated by the Mundas in language which reveal the style of dance. Though, the style or rhythm of dance can seldom be described accurately through language, there are words which at least express or attempt to catch up the stylistic body movements of the dancers. The words are actually used to evaluate the performance of the dancers such as *'tinang-nachang'*, etc, which has already been referred in previous pages.

In the succeeding pages, a description has been given with respect to the organizational aspect of the dance and its process. The description has been given by the dancers themselves.

Organization and Process of Dance

Jadur Dance

It has *the Nir (Hojor)*, *Or-r* and *Gena* variety.

The girls stand side by side to each other in a row holding each other by the waist.

The boys stand in front of the girls in jumble. The position of the drummers is in the middle in between the girls and the boys.

As stated earlier, before the start of the dance, the players of drum or *dumang* go on playing the initial *khod* or *tal* such as *'dhetang' 'dhetang'*, etc. The boys sing the first line of the song with this sound of the *dumang* or the boys first sing the line of the song which is accompanied by the sound of the drum immediately. The girls, after repeating the line of the song, once or twice, walk as many steps before the move for the dance is set in. With the repetition of song once or twice, by the boys also, the players of *dumang* produce the sound such as *'teyang natang natang dhur, didang'tan, didang dhur,* etc, and the girls begin to dance.

At the start, the right feet after lifting it and moving it a step forward, touches the ground, followed by the left leg swiftly which is moved forward across the right leg. At the touching down of left feet on the ground, the right leg is brought at its side bringing the body to its balance. Then the left feet is lifted up a pace forward again, followed by the right feet in succession. The left feet, then, swiftly crosses the right leg, as in the start of the dance and successive steps and movement of the leg and body go on. During, this process of dance, the dancers make the circle in the *akhra*. While dancing in this process, the movement of the dancers become perfectly mechanical. When the girls repeat the song as soon as the line of song sung by the boys is over, they simply move on forward towards the right hand side. As soon as they sing the last line, the left feet is swiftly moved forward across the right leg and so on. Throughout the dance, a perfect combination of song, music and dance is maintained which automatically brings out styles and rhythm. The stage thus, reached during the dance is appreciated by the audience by saying: *'Susun do beṡ jamkut kana'* (the dance is perfect).

Gena Dance

It is a sub-category of Jadur dance. It has its own class of songs. The sound of the *dumang* too, differ from the Jadur dance. The sound of dumang in Gena dance is like this—'Daink *dhur,* dedang dhur....... dedang natang, taink-taink.' The tune is repeated twice and so on.

The formation and holding of hands are the same as in Jadur dance. Gena dance takes place at the end of two Jadur dances, that is, after one Nir or Hojor dance and one Or or two Jadur, dance.

While dancing, the left leg is first lifted up and brought forward swiftly, followed by right leg in the same speed. When the right feet touches the ground, immediately the left feet is thrown back three steps backward bringing with it the right leg for balance of the body. Then the dancers rhythmically, is called *hujul* in Mundari, which go on dancing and again the steps start as in the beginning of dance.

Lahsua Dance

In Lahsua dance, the second girl in the line crosses her right hand fingers with the left hand fingers of the leading girl in dance from the side below and holds it firmly. The rest of the girls in the line form themselves accordingly.

In this dance, girls and boys do not form separate party as in the case of Jadur dance in which they normally remain face to face. The boys form themselves as second line of dancers behind the girls row, but they hold each other's hand loosely and not in the pattern of the girls. The only other party in front of the girls are the drummers who play on *dumang*.

In this dance, the lead is given by the sound of *dumang*, but the girls all in all do sing and dance. The boys and girls, in this dance, sing together. While it is a stylistic dance, with much rhythm.

While paces are made towards the front for dance, the crossed up hands remain in elongated position. The dancers go on walking in a measured way several steps singing the song, also making rhythmic movements of crossed fists up and down. They continue the process till the finish of the first stanza of the song. As soon as they finish singing, they bend down frontward by the waist rhytmically moving the hands, particularly the crossed up palms, and one step forward and then one step backwards. Then in erect posture they make pace a little towards the right hand side, then again stoop down and make one step forward and one step backwards. After this they come in the same position as they were at the beginning of the dance and continue singing moving rhythmically their crossed up palms as usual.

Dubung (Karam)

The formation of the dancers in this dance is the same as in Jadur dance, that is, they hold each other by the waist. Like Lahsua dance, in this dance too, girls make one line and the boys behind them. The line of dancers are made in this pattern and there is no limit of this so far the dance ground, that is, *akhra* can accommodate them. The drummers, in this dance too, remain in front of the dancers facing them.

There are two varieties of Dubung dance which are as follows:

(a) The dancers go on walking frontward while singing and then at the end of the song, they jump a little immediately throwing their right feet a step forward and fall back swiftly stooping a little and successively they lift up their feet above the ground twice changing its place. Raising themselves upright, they go on walking and singing, *khelare,* and pick up next line of the song.

(b) Make three steps forward and in quick succession lift up and down their right feet twice. Then they fall two or three steps backwards stoopingly a little. Then keeping standstill on the left leg, the right feet is moved frontward once and backwards once, touching the ground. Then they move on frontward singing the song and repeat the dance as usual.

Jarga

Dancers hold each other by the waist from behind the back. Both legs remain in walking position. While starting the dance, the feet are taken frontward twice and in the same position towards the left. Then joggingly they walk two steps towards the right hand side. The dance continues in this process.

Racha

In this dance too, the position of hands remain like the Jadur dance.

Two parties of dancers are formed in this dance who stand facing each other. In Racha dance, no musical instrument is played on. There are two dance techniques of Racha dance:

(a) One party of dancers while singing, walk two steps frontward and the other party of dancers recedes backwards. At the end of the song, they fall back speedily and then jump forwards together, then they repeat the song sung by the other party. After the jump, the left feet is taken a step backwards and its place is taken by the right feet.

(b) They go on walking and then balancing on the right leg at the right side, it is moved to its left and backward once in each case, and then they raced back and again walk frontward. In this way they dance three to four times. Towards the end, they walk speedily like running and jump frontward. Then again they walk frontward and begin the dance afresh.

Baroya

Like Jadur, it also has two parties of dancers—boys and girls separately who stand facing each other at the beginning of the dance. The drummers remain in between the two. Holding of hands by the dancers, are the same as that of Jadur dance.

First, they prepare the move by walking around the *akhra.* At the start of the dance, the right and left feet are lifted alternately which they take backwards, then stoopingly move three steps frontward and then fall back swiftly. Then they move two steps towards the left, keeping right and left legs at their own sides. In this pattern, the dance is started again. It may be noted that while they fall backwards, the left leg goes a step backwards than the right and it is at this position that they move two steps towards the left.

Gena of Dubung and Baroya Dance

The dancers stand in line side by side and either cross hands with immediate neighbour without holding him or it is left loose without crossing it. When they dance, they clap with their own hands in crossed position. Before the start of dance, the position of right leg remains a step backwards than the left. Then while making a move towards the left, the right leg is taken to the place of left feet and then again taken backwards. And then they race back three or four steps and when they stop clapping, they hold each other by shoulder from behind and then they jog towards the right. At this moment, the right feet is taken to the side of left feet, and left feet to the right, once in each turn. The dance proceeds in this pattern.

Khemta

Like Lahsua dance, the fingers are crossed with the immediate neighbours of either side and keep it in elongated position bent by the elbow.

The position of feet at the start of the dance is like this—the right feet remains a step ahead than the left in walking position. They move rhythmically, in the same position two steps towards the left. Both the feet remain parallel to each other. Then they stop moving and stand rhythmically moving the hands and bodies in unison. Then, keeping the left feet a step ahead than the right in walking position, they walk a step towards the right in sitting posture and then again start the dance as in the beginning.

Japi or Jarapi

Similar to Dubung dance, the dancers hold each other. The dancers sit on the strength of the toes of their feet and it is in this position, they rhythmically make movement of their body and hands side by side and alternately, also clap their hands.

Jatra

This dance, as stated in previous pages, is held bi-annually in traditionally selected villages. The dance is held on an open space and not in traditional dancing ground, the *akhra*. It, thus, accommodates thousands of dancers at a time.

The dancers stand behind the other facing his or her back in a single file and so, there is no separate group for boys and girls. The dancers move in columns in a single file behind each other, and thus, make a number of circles in a centrifugal pattern. Sometimes, more than one such circles are also made by the dancers to facilitate the dance. The dancers move in anticlock-wise. They carry with them all sort of musical instruments and play on at intervals. No musical instrument is played on separately for this dance. But while the dance is on, the players of *dumang*, the main musical instrument which is used in all dance by the Mundas, who attend Jatra dance, assemble at one side of the dance and play on it. The sound, thus, produced is in such a great volume that it reaches 20 miles and even beyond that. And since youths gather there from very far off villages, crossing forests, hills and rivers, they carry with them heavy bamboo or wooden clubs and various shapes and sizes of battle axes, spears and other missile weapons for their safe journey. All these weapons in Jatra dance, become a part of decoration of the dance. The song sung during the dance is also known as Jatra song. There happens to be only one leader in this dance and from centre point of the circle, controls the multitudes. Such person must have the personality and quality of extraordinary leadership. He must have sufficient experience in this field. This person belongs to any village. Such a quality and reputation of dance and experience of the person keeps the multitudes together. Such quality is to be developed slowly in years and so the Jatra dance is conducted only by experienced mature persons. Before entering into the circle, the dancers natural inquisitiveness is to know the name and address of the leader.

When the first stanza of the song is over, the dancers halt at their own place and play on their respective musical instruments which they carry with them. In playing the musical instruments, there is no set tune or *tala* to follow and every one plays it according to his own sweet will. Then, after a minute or two, the leader from the centre, shouts loudly 'Hurra'. Hearing the word 'Hurra', the line expands backward in rapid succession so as to have sufficient space for making a jump. Before the jump, each dancer holds his or her immediate front person's left arm with his or her right hand firmly. With the cry of 'Hurra', the dancers in batches jump up three times in the same place where they stand shouting 'Hurre' with each jump. While thumping the ground and before lifting oneself for the next jump, they rhythm the body together and move a step towards the right side. In Jeth Jatra dance (held during summer) the singing of each song ends with 'Lekore' or repetition of few lines again which add up to the sweetness of the tune and at the end of the song, all play on their respective musical instrument.

The Jatra dance, as stated in the previous pages, always begins at the middle of the night and continues till the morning.

So, the Munda music and dance, though limited in number and variety, have very rich expressive tradition—in technique and style both. It shares many features and category of dance in nomenclatures with the neighbouring communities, but they differ in details in respect of language of the song, in tune, in instrumental music, in technique of dance and in style, etc. The limitation in number, however, has in no way affected the joyous life of the tribe for they have been well distributed in space covering the whole region of their habitation through well planned timetable and the sequence is strictly adhered to. Periodization of song and dances, in spite of their limitation and variety, maintain the taste of the tribe throughout the year.

The tradition of music and dance is embedded in time and its evolution and growth is associated with innumerable experiments. It is a peace time evolution and when the tribe did attain sufficient socio-economic stability. It is no denying the fact that nature is the greatest teacher of man. The Mundas, it seems, have derived their inspiration of singing and dance, on the one hand, from natural environment like physiography, that is, the high hills and undulating valleys and serpentine rivers, the sound of the flow of water and winds, the birds, animals and insects and plants, and on the other, from their own social environment. In music and dance, the qualities and features derived from these two areas of environment are absorbed in one way or the other. The body movements and activities, the sounds and tunes of music are all symbolic of various experiences derived from the socio-physical environment.

The Munda music and dance have become rich as they have imbibed many traits and features, though unidentified, in their music, dance and style of decoration from neighbouring communities—caste and tribe both. In fact, Jatra dance have become multi-community dance festival in which all the neighbouring communities, irrespective of caste and tribe differences participate and perform their respective dances. This is a unique gathering and a symbol of sociocultural integration of communities which fosters fellow feeling and brotherhood.

Music and dance is the living tradition of the tribal people which has integrated in itself all the values and knowledge that the community have inherited and acquired. The lack or absence of music and dance in a community is an indication of social or cultural degeneration and disintegration—a symptom of social pathology.

Music and dance reflect the social personality of the community as well as their history. Many communities have war dance or war like dance, while some have the techniques or style of dance which are akin to the course in physical exercise. These are but indicators whether the community was invader or defender. In dance technique, these two personality types are also reflective. While in case of the Mundas, the physical environment have the greater effect in their personality and musical life. Mundas are great conciliators and solicitors in a situation of feud and conflict and because of this, they have avoided and evaded a number of invasion on them. But their history has never revealed them as invaders. This is why, in their technique of dances, war like features are almost absent.

Last of all, contribution made by the Mundas in the field of music and dance, though small, is not negligible and cannot be overlooked. Music and dance are the human achievements in the sphere of social communication and artistic expression. To it, almost all communities have contributed from the ingenuity, knowledge and resources at their disposal. The contribution made to this human treasure, however small, is invaluable for the community itself as well as for the humanity at large. It is the only means at the disposal of human beings that sublimate the thinking and feeling of the people which obliterate all human differences and it is in this field that people can cooperate without thinking of any superiority or inferiority and bargain. Music and dance are an indication of human beings' ability to exist as well as his humaneness. So long as the community is active in the act of creation and recreation, his existence is secured in this universe.

The Song

'*Kaji ge durang*', which can be literally translated as 'to speak is to sing', is the operational definition of the song given by the Mundas themselves. For the Mundas, so far as the concept is concerned, this is true. When we go through the text, we find that the songs are either in the nature of description or of dialogue or in question-answer form. The statement or dialogue, which happen to be most simple and clear in form and content, while singing, it is suitably modified to suit the tune of the song. In other words, each category of song has its fixed tune, but this is not so in case of form or structure of song. The regular audience can easily decipher the tune and can differentiate the songs from each other. A song cannot be classified on the basis of song text. As each song has its fixed tune and melody, the form or structure follows accordingly. In other words, the syllables of words are transformed to suit the tune of the song. This is why, some songs of Jadur category can be easily sung in Bala category of song too.

The dance-song usually has its fixed measures, that is, it neither should be too short, nor too long. It would be of medium length, otherwise in either of the case, it may loose its rhythm and style. Normally, a dance-song happens to be of three to four stanzas, having two to four sentences in each stanza in which the initial two lines of the song are sung as *'labja'* or signal for getting prepared for dance. But the dance can only be started when the lines are repeated by the girls and again by the boys till the former are fully ready for making pace in consonance with the tune of the song and music.

Each song text is complete in itself so far as the meaning is concerned and conveys or depicts a total picture of an event or subject matter under reference in few concise sentences as stated above. Every song has its central theme or concern around which the whole narrative of song is based. From structural point of view, Munda songs normally consist of two varieties: (a) topic-comment or cause-effect, and (b) background-process—conclusion. Almost all dance-songs fall under the first category, while in the second, are Bala and Ballad songs.

Munda songs can be basically classified into two from the viewpoint of their own concept *kaji* (a) dialogue, and (b) descriptive or narrative, but they are not exclusive in itself, rather there is only one category, that is, dialogue song. Following forms are found in dialogue song:

Conversation Between Two or More Persons

(a) In the form of question-answer

(b) For consultation
(c) Asking for something

To Address or to Refer

(a) Advice
(b) Praise or abuse
(c) Narration of something

Communicational

(a) To convey message
(b) Advice

Descriptive

(a) Event (historical)
(b) Experience
(c) Myth, legend, stories

From the viewpoint of style of singing, two basic forms exist. While in some category of songs, initial few lines are repeated once or twice as the case may be, at the end of each stanza or at the end of the song. While, on the other, there are words or sentences which are suffixed at the end of each stanza. In the first case, the sentences so repeated in the first and last line of the song, carry double meaning. While in the case of words so suffixed, they act as progress of action and carry no other meaning. But in either of the case, they bear literary features. Rhymes are maintained in every song, and particularly in dance song in which suitable phrases or words transformed into poetical forms, are used to suit the tune of the song. For instance, the sentence 'oko *tem seno, tana'* in ordinary parlance is slightly transformed into *'okokotem seno tan'* in poem or song. Rhymes are similarly maintained with words like *tana* into *tan, leda* into *led,* etc. So rhymes are maintained according to the traditional tune of the song and have no fixed form by itself. "There is no true rhyme in traditional Mundari song, although there is often a great deal of repetition of last words or syllables (typically line-final vocative particles, and line-final sequences of identical verb suffixes)" so write Norman Zide and Ramdayal Munda, and further state that internal rhymes do not occur and are used with great skill as assonance and play on repeated vowels and consonants, and sequence of either or both of these. Each word and onomatopic forms (as in many languages of India) are common (Zide and Munda, 1969: 73-74).

As stated above, the first one or two sentences of dance-song except a few category of song, are repeated twice or thrice as per norm which is called *labja*. The progression from *labja* is called *tanab*. This is the main part of the song and may consist either one or two sentences or one or two stanzas as the case may be. When action is over or sentence made is complete, then the song is concluded by repeating the initial line of the song, which is sung as *labja*. To quote Norman Zide and Ramdayal Munda,"the line and half line repetition (either perfect or imperfect) is common in many of these songs. In almost all the songs—in all the traditional ones—each stanza consists of two-paired sentences which are usually synonymous or nearly synonymous with each other. For the purpose of our action and discourse analyses, we consider only one, the first, of a pair; but for each statement, action, question, comment, etc, mentioned below, there is always a second parallel but derivative, statement, action, etc, paired to the first. The paired sentence, if not synonymous or nearly synonymous may extend the first by adding a new metaphor to one in the first line of the pair, or specifying a new item in the context mentioned in the first line. This adds little to the action or discourse except for the formal reiteration required by the form" (*Ibid*, p. 247).

"The paired line is only rarely an identical repetition more usually, one or two words are replaced by associated lexical items, these being fixed and invariable for the most part. Typically, these second members of the pairs are synonymous of the first, usually less common (sometimes archaic or borrowed) words not used freely in ordinary Mundari prose discourse, sometimes they are not synonymous but words associated in song contexts and elsewhere with each other, for example, antonyms, 'former' and 'latter', 'top' and 'bottom', or pairs that are associated with other common semantic features, for example, 'twelve' and 'twenty-two'. In all (or almost all) of these cases the meaning of the second where it differs and does not plausibly extend it from the first is irrelevant to that of the first and not to be taken literally" (*Ibid*, pp. 274-75).

The analyses made by the two scholars as above about the structural features of songs which is in conformity to its tune, portrays the formal pattern of the Mundari songs.

A piece or song in action, can touch the heart of an individual through the contents of its text as well as through the sound or melody of the song. Through songs, human feelings like love, hate, despair, endurance, hope, anxiety, forbearance, loyalty, betrayal, anger, etc, can effectively be expressed and conveyed to others. Mundari song is full with these lyrical features.

As stated earlier, different categories of Munda songs have their respective tune. In some, the measure of pitch are short, some have medium and others long. It is observed that pace in dance and beat of musical instruments too, follow this pattern. For instance, the tone in Bala and Jatra category of song is long, but Jadur, Lahsua, Dubung, etc, has medium tone. While in one way, this feature of toning the song is to have variety and, on the other, an indication of optimum development of music in the sphere of aesthetic taste and styles. However, the innovative process is an intrinsic feature in any system. It is due to this vitality of innovation that the Mundas of today have invented quite a new set of music and dance which can very well be classed as 'modern'. It has musical instruments of its own kind and the song and dances too, have its own *ragas* style and rhythm which is distinctly separate from the classical one. The beat of the drums usually go by the pitch or *ragas* of the songs. This modern class of music is known as '*Bhajan*', a Hindi word used for prayer or hymn. It has two varieties: (a) *Dub bhajan* and (b) *Susun bhajan*.

In *Dub bhajan*, young boys and girls do a singing soiree by sitting on the ground, preferably in a room or courtyard. In sitting too, the girls and boys make separate rows, sometimes facing each other. While sitting, the girls stretch out their legs and the boys in *yoga* position bending legs by the knees. The musicians sit either in the centre or at the sides. The big musical instruments like *nagara* and *rabka* are not used in *Dub Bhajan*. The rhythm and style are produced by movement of the body clapping of hands. The contents of the songs are mostly derived from Biblical stories and moral lessons from it with the sole purpose of urging the believers on Christ for purity in action and behaviour as He likes and to have faith in His power of deliverance from all sorts of worldly woes and eternal peace. Though various facets of beauty of the world and human relations are also there as contents of songs which are of profane nature, they all praise, in one way or the other, to the God Almighty for His gift to mankind. The verses so composed are usually long and poetic. The composition does not follow one set of rules with respect to pitch or tune or number of stanzas.

In form and style, the *Susun bhajan* is one of the traditional dances. The holding each other during the dance is made either by the shoulders or by the waist as per convenience of the dancers. Sometimes during the course of the dance, the dancers often change the holding pattern to facilitate the rightward or leftward movement. The paces are often made long and movement swift or rapid, the steps go forward or backward with the same speed. The dance almost seems like running in some cases.

Nagara and *Rabka* are the two main musical instruments in this, dance. The size of *nagara* often vary from one and one and half metre in diameter and height and weight upto five kilograms. The player of this musical instrument carry it all through the dance slinging it on his shoulder. While beating, he makes stylistic movement, sometimes clockwise and anticlockwise and quite often jumping along with the *nagara*. *Rabka* is another percussion musical instrument which is played on in accompaniment of *nagara*. It is the lead musical instrument for *nagara* and is played on to create rhythm in dance.

The *bhajan* category of music and dance are very popular among the tribals who have embraced Christianity. This system of music developed during the course when the Christian tribal youths were prohibited from participation in traditional dance-music by the Church authorities. Though, the rigidity has now slackened down, it has already done an irreparable harm to the traditional music which the community may repent for the generations to come.

Paika is another variety of modern dance-music which is now located in the eastern part of the Munda country only. This music system developed during the British period when chiefs and petty kings were the rulers of Chhotanagpur plateau. '*Paika*' is particularly a class of warrior dance and equally practised by the tribals as well as non-tribals whose services were normally required by the rulers. This dance is performed during the festivals and on the occasion of social ceremonies like marriages. For dance, the dancers decorate themselves with all sorts of colourful dresses with tinkling bell metals on their waist and legs. Instead of helmet, they wear colourful turban wrapped round the heads as well as tight dress on the upper portion of the body. One of the important ornament for this dance is the tuft of hair obtained from the tail of the wild bison which is worn by the arms and waist. Besides this, the dancers hold sword, spear, battle axe and shield, etc, in their hands. The rhythm and the move in dance is created by the beat of the drums consisting of *nagara*, *dhank*, *sahnai*, and *bugle*, etc. All these musical instruments in unison create a war environment, enough to instil courage and inspiration even in the body of the weakest. The challenge, the marching and the actual fight during the war are all produced through the musical instruments and the dancers create the very warlike scene like well trained warriors.

The dance has no song and the dancers remain mute performers only through actions. The clarinet players, however, use the tune of any song they like. The main objective of this dance, nowadays, is to entertain the audience and so, generally their expertise in this dance in hired during social occasions by the well-to-do families.

Today, the tradition of music and dance is rapidly waning down to oblivion due to various reasons. Entertainment is becoming an individual affair which has no relation at all with people's life experience. This is weakening the social relationship and adversely affecting the traditionally accepted social norms and behaviour, that is, their ethics, etiquette and morality. Traditional music is the epitome of sharing of experience of life by the people of a particular society. Once this tradition is lost, it is lost forever. However, there is awakening in some groups and sporadic attempt of its revival is on the offing through various platforms.

PART II

JOURNEY THROUGH THE STAGES OF LIFE

4

MAKING THE LIFE

Role of the Family

Social life emanates from social relations or behavioural interactions of the people in a society. Individuals come into interactions with some expectations or to fulfil some basic human needs. The social life is possible in living together and under harmonious relations with mutual help and cooperation. The basic unit of any human society is the family consisting of husband, wife and their children who generally live under one roof. The relationship among them is the primary level of human social relations which extends and engulfs the whole community through the web of kinship systems. In tribal society, the individual and family relations are strengthened and harmonized through various institutions which make the social life going. It is these institutions that bring about a patterned social life in the society. It has its own ways or devices to satisfy the individual as well as the social needs of the members of the society. These devices or knowledge are acquired through the experience of the people who give it continuity through the customs and traditions of the community over the ages. The way in which these needs are satisfied differs substantially in different cultures. In socializing the child, each culture serves to organize the child's needs in such a way as to cause it to expect its satisfaction in a particular style and to fulfil its duties to others in a manner expected to it (Montague, 1961: 32). The process of socialization and acculturation in sociocultural life is best observed in the institution of family. Thus, the family not only meets the basic needs of the members but also gives continuity to values and philosophy as enshrined in customs and traditions of the society. The socialization process also differs from family to family because of difference in socio-cultural background or experiences of the elders. Children get influenced in their learning process by the presence or absence of old and skilled persons in the family. Moreover, the learners are also not equally susceptible to acquire the knowledge, habit and practice of the society. While there is a basic difference in individual urge, taste, mentality, personality, etc, which may present problems for smooth adjustment in interactional situation, this problem is solved through the ethical codes, and customary laws of the society. Thus, a constant process of conciliation or adjustment operates on the basis of sociocultural system among the members which facilitates in evolving a patterned social life.

In Munda society, the family has an important role to play for the perpetuation of culture and tradition of the people. In Mundari, there is no specific term for the family but generally the members of the family are known by the term *Hon-Hopon* which indicates the nuclear form of family consisting of husband-wife and children. But there are collaterals and affines also who live with them. This grouping is best known by the term *Ora-renko*, which means members of the household. Each member enjoys special status and privilege according to age, sex and position in the family. They are bound together by basic human qualities and sentiments of mutual trust, love, affection and respect. This closeness is knitted by kinship terms identifying parents, siblings and collaterals, etc. The most close and intimate relationship is, however, observed between mother and child. During the age of infancy of the child, the mother feeds, bathes and dresses the baby according to the custom, habit and taste of the society. When the baby grows up, its every need and activity is closely observed by the elders who help and guide it for the right conduct. In bringing up the child, the mother plays the leading role. She guides and teaches the child, if she is a female, in all feministic habits and practices of dressing, cleanliness, conversation, walking, sitting and in all other behavioural activities which the society recognizes as proper for the female sex. Thus, the girl while learning, assists her mother in all household and outside activities such as cleaning, cooking, weaving mat, and broomstick making, etc. The son, on the other hand, receives training and guidance from male members of the family in all sorts of economic activities such as ploughing, digging, load carrying, planting, harvesting, storing, rope making, weaving, making and repairing of various agricultural equipments, construction of houses, etc. The child's sphere of learning widens as she or he grows up, so also their interaction with members of the locality and society.

Normally, a village is settled by more than one lineage but it is the hamlets that are found with uni-lineages. In the case of settling the village by single lineage families, they act as joint family in all life activities and share the joy and trouble together. Socially and economically, they act as a corporate group and intimate kinship relations are found among them. It is this social environment that the child grows in learning and imbibing the family and social norms, skills, knowledge, ethics and morality.

Villages which are settled by the members of a uni-descent group, have the feature of uni-clanship also except the affines who come by marriage from other villages. The social interactions differ on the basis of uni- and multi-lineage or clan villages, particularly during social gatherings. The child gets maturity in all aspects of life in the social environment he or she grows up in.

The Age of Infancy

Babies are cherished by every couple and their birth is welcome with joy. The news of the birth of a child reaches every member of the *khunt* or lineage who usually reside in the same locality through the ladies, but formal news is circulated either by the father of the newborn or any member of the family on the day or two before the birth ceremony. The newborn is identified as '*pera*' or guest till her birth ceremony when it is ritually and socially accepted as member of the family and community. Its personal identity is established only when given a name.

To ensure easy birth, the Munda perform an offering to *Garasi bonga*—the guardian spirit of birth, a few days or a week before the birth. The offering of red cock and rice and beer is performed by the head of the household. The parent, brother or uncle of the mother are generally invited to attend this ceremony.

Normally, no pre-natal arrangement is made to receive the newborn but the couple as well as their parent and grandparent remain alert for the occasion and all essential preparations are slowly made as the time of birth approaches. The song below describes the condition of the would-be mother just before the delivery. The song belongs to Jadur category and the lines are as follows:

1. *Elare sarajom ba, elare kau-bau jan*
   O dear sarajom flower, you are full to the brim
   Bapare suṛa sagen, baparem ebe-tobe jan
   O dear tender leaf, you are at now and then

2. *Mar ho din munḍi hiju tan, mar hoiṇg kau-bau jan*
   The day is approaching dear, so I am full to the brim
   Ter ho bochor neḍa nachur tan, ter hoiṇg ebe-tobe jan
   The time is approaching dear, so I am becoming now and then

3. *Mar ho sim kaji tolipe, mar hoiṇg hiju geya*
   Fasten a cock I must come
   Ter ho riṇri kaji aguepe, ter hoiṇg nachur geya
   Get loan I must arrive
   Mar ho illi kaji kaṛipe, mar hoiṇg nosoren ge
   Borrow rice-beer, I must slip down

The first stanza of the song relates to the conversation between husband and wife regarding the condition of the latter just before the birth. The physical expression of labour is visible in the face and body of the would-be mother. The husband, who has neither seen nor encountered such a situation, is disturbed and does not know what to do. The economic condition of the couple is lean so he has to take loan to perform the birth ritual.

The birth of a baby, whether a male or female, is a matter of great joy as the song below mentions. The song belongs to the Bala category which brings out the Munda view of male and female child. The lines are as follows:

Munu-munu ren raja hon do
The first born prince of the king
Siṇgi leka chanḍu leka baraṇg-baraṇg, babure tur lena
Had risen shining bright like the sun and moon, O dear
Munu-munu ren rani hon do
The first born princess of the king

Chaṇḍu leka baraṇg-baraṇg
Like the shining bright moon
Ipil leka biriṇg-biriṇg
Like the twinkling stars
Babure tur lena
Had arisen, my dear

The age of the song is very much indicative in the lines. When the song was composed, the prestige of the prince and princess was considered to be very high in any society. The first born child, as described in this song, has the status of king's son or daughter though they themselves stand nowhere in comparison to him. The child, on the other hand, has been compared to the sun, moon and stars. In other words, the child has the qualities of the cosmic entities. The sun makes the day and gives energy to all living objects. The moon and stars, on the other hand, make the horrible dark night exceedingly beautiful and cool. The sun represents power and vitality, that is, energy, and so also the male child. The moon and stars, on the other hand are cool, refreshing and beautiful, so also the female child in the family and society whose presence make the life liveable. The male and female both have the respective role in the family and society like the sun and moon who play respective role to make the universe going. The male child, in the following song, therefore, has been compared with that of the rising sun and female child, of shining and twinkling moon and stars. So the birth of the child in Munda society, be he a male or female, has equal importance. The sex of the child has secondary importance but it is the function which he or she does when grown up which matters. The function of one is no less important than the other for the running of the family and society. The experience of the people tell that a household where there are only unisex persons, the life becomes miserable. Like the sun and moon, whose role and importance are well-known to the human beings, the male and female child, in the Munda society, have equal status and importance.

When the child starts walking staggeringly, it is a great joy for the parent. Every movement and cry of the child, at this age, is admired by everybody. How best the children are taken care of, has been described in the following Jadur song, the lines of which are as follows:

Towa telang asul lija sirja
We nurtured her with milk O sirja
Towa towae sowana sirja
She smells like milk
Dahi telaṇg jataṇ lija sirja
We protected her with curd sirja
Dahi dahie sowana
Emits smell like curd

The baby emits the scent of the food she takes. Nourished with milk and curd, there is healthy growth of the baby. The following Jadur song describes how the child appears at this age. The lines are as follows:

1. *Nete dugur dugur gatiṃ*
   Walks on measuringly with little steps dear
   Loyoṇg noṛe do
   The lowland bird
   Nete dugur dugur gatiṃ
   Walks on measuringly with little steps dear
   Piṛi gundari gatiṃ, loyoṇg noṛe do
   The field partridge dear, the lowland bird

2. *Towa telaṇg asul lija*
   We nurtured her with milk
   Loyoṇg noṛe do
   The lowland bird
   Dahi telaṇg jataṇ lija
   We protected her with curd
   Piri gundari gatiṃ, loyoṇg noṛe do
   The field partridge dear, the lowland bird

3. *Towa telaṇg asul lija*
   We nurtured her with milk
   Towa towae sowana, loyoṇg noṛe do
   Emits smell of milk, the lowland bird
   Dahi telaṇg jataṇ lija
   We protected her with curd

> *Dehi dahi-e sowana, piri gundari gatiṃ loyoṇg noṛe do*
> She emits smell of curd, the field partridge dear, the lowland bird

The walking of the child is like field *gundari* (partridge) the lowland bird. The steps of these birds are too small when they walk and look like rolling stones when they run. As the feet are small and the child is hardly able to balance herself, she walks with small steps staggeringly. The parent remembers how they looked after the child with the best food available at their disposal. And hence the growth of the child is not very bad. In short, children are looked after by the parent in the best possible way they know and through the means available with them.

Youthful Age

The Munda also differentiate in the age of the person through different terms as soon as he or she grows up. At the age of infancy, that is, when the child is in the lap, she is called *Bale hon* or *Dele Buchu.* When the child runs about and till the age of 10 or 12, he or she is called *sitia.* At adolescent age, the term *Dhangra* is used for a boy and *Dhangri* for a girl or the word *Chithor* to denote both the sex. The youthful or maturity of age is called *Samae.*

The above classification of age of a person is, however, not based on actual age of the person but indicates the behaviour of a specific age group of persons. The behaviour as such is not an individual characteristic but it is cultural, and it is not inborn but is cultivated. During the age of *Chithor* the boy or girl learn and practise the customs and traditions of the community.

The period of childhood to adolescence is the period of learning. Children at this age accompany their parents or elders everywhere and learn many things simply by hearing and observation. There is no institution for training and education in traditional customs, world-views, morals and etiquette except the now defunct institution of *Giti-Ora.* These are learnt from day-to-day life—in the household, in the field and forest, in the gatherings, in the company of elders and friends and by self-perception. Parents and other members of the family, however, play a major role in the education and training of the children through informal ways. The age of adolescence is supposed to be the most important period in an individual's life in learning and character building. It is also the most emotional period in the age of any youth.

It is during the age of adolescence that a boy or girl needs company for him or her to spend the leisure time. At this age such company is always unisex in nature. Sometimes, the companionship blossoms into friendship and often regularized through ritual performance in the presence of both the parents. The term for such friendship is *Sangi* for boys and *Sahiya* for girls. A less durable type of friendship is also established among the unisex of the same age group. It is called *flower friendship* for it is established making flower as medium in the presence of some witness. In this type of relationship, the two friends simply exchange a flower. Thereafter, the two friends never address each other by personal names but take the name of the flower with which the friendship was established. They henceforth, become very intimate friends and maintain it throughout the life. In both these types of friendship, the friends stand side by side during the days of trouble and share the joy of life together.

The flower friendship is normally established among the girls only. All these friendships are not restricted within the community only but can be established with a non-Munda or even with a non-tribal.

How the two friends bear sufferings for each other's sake has been described in the following Jadur song. The lines of the song are as follows:

1. *Ạm tingu tangi te saluing, rabang tanaya salu*
   While waiting for you, I am shivering with cold O *salu*
   Ạm taṇa-a: taṇa-a: te saluing reyaṛ tan
   While standing for you, I have become cold O *salu*

2. *Hisi muka Pagari salu, sisir janaya salu*
   Twenty feet long turban has become drenched with dew O *salu*
   Raṇgamaṭi gamecha salu, reyaṛ jan
   The red coloured shawl has become cold O *salu*

3. *Rabaṇg reya salu, uyu deṇga meyaya salu*

While you shiver, I am here to cover you O *salu*
Reyaṛ reya salu, dapal goṛoma me
While you feel cold, over covering I will make you warm

4. *Kuda suṛa te saluiṇg, uyu deṇga meya ya salu*
With tender leaves of blackberry, I will cover you
Baru suṛa te saluiṇg dapal goroṃ me
With tender leaves of Baru, over covering I will make you warm

As pre-planned, one of the friends (they have *salu* friendship) is waiting for the other somewhere in one winter night. May be the two had planned to visit a dance in some village. While waiting, as mentioned in the song, he was drenched with dew drops and was shivering with cold. When the other arrived, he tells his experience which he underwent under the open sky. The latter assures him that he will not allow him to feel cold for he will cover him with whatever cloth he has, even with tender leaves of the trees.

Below is another song in which one of the friends expresses his unbearable separation of the other. He remembers how the two had enjoyed each other's company when they were living together. The separation is now very deeply felt by him. But now they have met again. They are now enjoying each other's presence and conversation. The song belongs to Jadur category, and the lines are as follows:

1. *A̭m jagar lereya gatim̭*
When you talk O friend
Reyaṛ geiṇg tereya gatim̭
I feel calm in my heart
A̭m baṇkaṛ lereya gatim̭
When you speak O friend
Tutukun geiṇg adae
I feel excited

2. *Am̭ baṇg mereya sangaiṇg*
When you are not here O friend
Rohoṛ chaba janaiṇg ya sangaiṇg
I have become weak
A̭m ka̭m tain re sangaiṇg

When you are not here O friend
Goso chaba jan
I felt gloomy

3. *Alaṇg chalaṇg tai keṇ re gatim̭*
When we were together O friend
Taben potoma gatim̭
Bundles of beaten-rice we enjoyed
Alang chalaṇg tai ken re sangaiṇg
When we were together O friend
Toa mandi
We enjoyed milk food

After many years of separation, the two friends have met again and tell each other's feelings of joy when they are together and a painful life when they live apart. But the friendship of the two is as fresh as ever.

When two friends are likely to get separated for an unknown period, they exchange personal objects as a token of love and symbol of friendship. Before taking leave from each other, they confirm each other's love and exchange gifts. The following Jadur song describes the conversation of the two friends, the lines of which are:

1. *Amaga kanaji Sisiba iṇg ayum̭ ledaya Sisiba*
I heard the news about you O *Sisiba*
Amaga baṇkaṛ Hariba iṇg aten led
I heard the talk about you O *Hariba*

2. *Saṇgin disum̭ re Sisiba ko goṇ meyaya Sisiba*
You will be married away in a distant village O Sisiba
Jiliṇg gamae re Hariba ko chal me
In an unending path you will be taken away O *Hariba*

3. *Goṇ mereya ko Sisiba, tire mudam̭ kaji omaiṇ me*
If you will be married away, give me your finger-ring and a word of love
Chal mereya ko Hariba, hoto re kaṛe mala chedaiṇg me
If you will be taken away, give me the necklace in memory of your

The two girls have *Sisiba* and *Hariba* friendship. There is talk of marriage going on for one of the girls. The other girl on hearing this news, feels restive. So, she approaches her friend and tells her that if it is correct she very soon will be married away. She requests her that she must offer her ring and necklace in memory of her which will also be a symbol of her friendship. They not only exchange gifts but also make plans for their meeting in future. The following *Jadur* song describes how the two friends are making plans for their meeting where they can meet regularly. The lines of the songs are as follows:

1. *Deogami Korkoṭa saṇgin disuṃ, okorelaṇg nepela ho*
   Deogami and Korkota are separated in distance, where shall we meet
   Jiliṇg baramda jiliṇg gamae, chimae korelaṇg chipina
   The long portico and far off village, where shall we see each other

2. *Hasa buru ko buru jada, Hasa buru relaṇg nepela*
   In the fair at Hasa, we shall meet
   Bamni jatra ko jatra jada, Bamni jatra relaṇg chipina
   At Bamni Jatra, we shall see each other

3. *Hasa buru relaṇg nepel redo, tire mudaṃ kaji omaiṇg me*
   In case we meet at Hasa fair, give me the ring and words of assurance
   Bamni jatra relaṇg chipina redo, hoṭo re kaṛe mala kaji chedaing me
   By chance we see each other at Bamni Jatra, have me the necklace as token of love

4. *Tire mudaṃ going emaṃ redo, tire mudaṃ chi jagara meya*
   If I give you my ring, will it talk to you
   Kaṛe mala going cheḍam redo, kaṛe mala chi ho baṇkaṛa meya
   If I spare you my necklace, will it speak to you

Though gifts bear the memory of friend's affection to each other, they cannot replace their presence in person. This is why some friends do not get satisfaction through the exchange of gifts. And as stated in the song, one of the friends queries whether the gift will speak to him. So, instead of exchange of gifts, they should meet regularly in the fair or Jatra. Besides these, there are other meeting places too like forest, rivers and fields.

The song below which belongs to Jadur category, gives the description of a girl who meets her friend (male) at different places. The lines of the song are as follows:

1. *Tiril piṛi uli jom maina*
Eating mango at Tiril field O girl
Seno! duku geya do maina
You always take trouble in going
Maraṇg ior aṛa sid maina
Plucking vegetable leaves at big rivulet O girl
Birid duku geya do maina
You always take trouble of walking

2. *Okoe kaji te mainam*
Under whose request O girl
Seno! duku geya do maina
You always take trouble in going
Chimae baṇkaṛ te mainam
With whom to talk about O girl
Birid duku geya do maina
You always take trouble of walking

3. *Gatiṃ kaji te mainam*
It is at the request of your friend O girl
Seno! duku geya do maina
You always take trouble in going O girl
Saṇgam baṇkaṛ te maina
To talk with friend O girl
Birid duku geya do maina
You always take trouble of walking O girl

4. *Jige deraṇg suku jaṇ maina*
To feel happy at heart O girl
Seno! duku geya do maina

·You always take trouble in going
Kuṛạm deraṇg reyaṛ jạn maina
To feel solace in your heart O girl
Birid duku geya do maina
You always take trouble in walking

This song relates to friendship with opposite sex. The girl in the song, takes leave from the house under a number of pretexts—to collect mango fruits or plucking vegetable leaves, etc.

The friendship and love that develops among the youths of this age group are found in a number of songs. It is observed that the youths at this age care little for the real world and are found lost in their own world of merry making, in conversation, in singing and dance and in other exciting adventurous activities. By now they have understood the world and have learnt many sociocultural traditions of the society and participate in it as full members. They have now attained the marriageable age.

Munda feel happy when they share the food and drinks with friends and relatives. The practice of sharing or reciprocal exchange develops among the youths in their very early age. It begins with gifts to little children. When they grow up they share the things which they collect from the forest or fields. Gift giving or exchange is practised throughout the life. When a person visits his relatives, he takes with him some gifts and when he returns, he receives some. If one is unable to visit, he or she sends the gifts through someone. The song which follows belongs to the category of Jadur dance and is based on this very custom. The lines of the song are:

1. *Mide kotoyo sarajom ba*
   Even at least a twig of Sarajom flower
   De gatiṃ uyugaiṇg me
   Please drop down for me too O friend
   Bare kotoyo suṛa sagen
   At least a pair of twig of tender leaves
   De saṇgam nosoraiṇg me
   Please slip it down for me, O friend

2. *Mide kotoyo gatiṃ uyugaiṇg re*
   If you drop at least a twig

Gatim̭ keing idiyaiya
I shall carry it to the friend
Bare kotoyom nosoraiṇg re
If you slip it down at least a pair of twig
Barem keiṇg seteraiya
I shall take it to the nephew

3. *Mide kotoyo gatim̭ uyugam re*
If I drop a twig to you
Gatim̭ ko egera
Friends mine will abuse me
Bare kotoyo seṭeram re
If I carry a pair of twig to you
Sangam ko segera
Beloved mine will speak ill of me

The girls are in the forest and before getting back to their homes, they are collecting flowers for their friends. And as stated in the song there are not much flowers on the tree and the girl who is on the tree expresses her inability to spare even a twig or two to the other girl who is waiting under the tree. For, if she shares the flowers with the other girl, there will be no flowers for her friends and she fears, they will abuse her for not sparing at least a twig.

When one visits fair or markets, he or she never forgets to bring something for his or her friends. If the friend belongs to some other village, the gift is sent through somebody. The following Jadur and Lahsua category of songs are based on this subject. The lines of these two songs are almost the same. The lines of Jadur song run as follows:

Tara tite kaji nema̭m
With one hand I will give you words
Tara tite pan re
With the other hand, a bundle of beatle leaves
Haere hae, miyadaiṇg kaji kulame
Wait, I will send some message with you

The lines of the Lahsua song are as follows:

Noko sate hiju lena̭m

From where did you come
Goso-gosom hiju lena
You look pale
Nauri ho tiṇgun me, miyadaiṇg kaji kulame
Wait a little, I will send a message with you
Tara tite kaji nemạm
With one hand, I will give you words
Tara tite pan ho
With the other, a bundle of beatle leaves

In this song as indicated, a girl or a boy meets a friend of another village. The former has a very close friend in latter's village. Before parting with each other, they share beatle leaves and request the other to carry a message for his or her other friend. The message may be an invitation or some plan or simply a greeting. But sometimes exchange of gifts, particularly when it takes place between opposite sex is disliked by the elders. Parents, as stated in the following Jadur song express strong resentment against the girl who has passed her ornaments to her friend. The lines of the song are as follows:

Turku ghare suta ge mai
Thread is available at trader's house O girl
Malạr ghare mala ge mai
Necklace at goldsmith's house
Se mala kahaṇ ge mai
Where is that necklace O girl
Chhatiya me mala jhalke
The chain which was glittering on the chest

The girl who has passed the chain which she was wearing the other day to someone is taken to task. She is warned that such business is carried out in the trader's house only and should not be practised here.

When someone is in trouble, a word of sympathy or compassion is always expressed by friends. Below is one such song in Jadur category in which a boy or a girl is consoled by his or her friend. The lines of the song are as follows:

Ka dulu mulu re sarạjom ba
Why you look gloomy O sarajom ba

Ka jaka maka re sura sagen
What it is glittering O sura sagen
Aing hala jola re sarajom ba
You are of my age group O sarajom ba
Am dulu mulu re sura sagen
You look gloomy O sura sagen

'*Sarajom ba*' and '*sura sagen*' are the terms used in flower friendship. As stated in the song, one of the friend looks gloomy. He is consoled by his other friend that he should not be worried at this young age when life is there to enjoy. He gives him his own example stating that he does not give much importance to such happenings.

The causes of mental anxiety are many. Sometimes, the elders openly talk about the friendship of two friends which they do not like. In such cases, it is but natural to be worried for it becomes a hinderance in their regular meetings. As stated in the song, one of the friend is too worried but his or her friend consoles him or her saying that let the people speak of them, it will do no harm to their friendship. This subject matter has been composed in the following song which belongs to Jadur category, the lines of which are as follows:

1. *Hesa-tepel tepel chi bare kŏm-kŏm*
Under the Hesa tree or while in job
Alange gatim ko ukŭta tana
People are talking about us
Hesa tepel-tepel chi bare kŏm-kŏm
Under the Hesa tree or while in job
Alanga sangaing ko charcha tana
People are speaking of us

2. *Alanga gatim ko ukŭta tana*
People are talking about us
Nida singiko ukŭta tana
People are talking about us day and night
Alanga sangaing ko charcha tana
People are speaking of us

Singi saṭub ko charcha tana
Day long and day out people are speaking of us

Young boys and girls are often seen walking together holding each other's hands or arm in arm but, of course, with same sex. Below is one such song belonging to Jadur category in which it is stated that a girl is trying to hold the arm of another girl. The former is older in age than the latter and, therefore, she forbids the latter to do so. The lines of the song are as follows:

1. *De daigo, ocho daigo, hoṭore alom gatiṇg-a*
   Please sister, do not hold me by the shoulder
   De daigo ocho daigo, tire go alom sabiŋg-a
   Please sister do not hold me by the hand

2. *Tire going sabe megia, tire go gati piriti*
   I will hold you by the hand, holding by hand is friendship
   Hoṭore doing gati megia, hoṭore rupa maduli
   I will hold you by the shoulder for it is a silver necklace

Moving together and holding each other's hand indicates friendship and having arms on each other's shoulders denotes love and close friendship like silver necklace. Such behaviour are seen among the boys or girls of the same age group.

Friends help each other at all occasions and particularly during personal decoration and if something does not look nice, they draw the notice of the other and assist him or her in its rectification. In the following song, it is stated that two friends are dancing together in the *akhra*. While dancing, dress of one of the girl becomes loose and started unfurling. The other friend who saw this, immediately draws her friend's attention and requests her to get it tightened on the side of the *akhra*. The song belongs to Jadur category, and the lines are as follows:

1. *Delare kuda suṛa ḍinḍa sahiya*
   O sahiya, the young like tender blackberry leaves, please come
   Delare daorad me
   Come close to me

2. *Ochore mayaṇg lija lir-lir*

Move off dear, dress yours is flying
Ochore farekạn me
Please get away, dear

When friends see each other after a period of considerable gap, they lodge complain to each other for not making time for meeting. And when they take leave from each other, no one knows when they will meet again. So, as stated in the following song which belongs to Jadur category, the friends agree to meet in the forest when they go there for collection of wood. The lines of the song are as follows:

1. *Jau susun akhṛa re mai*
At the regular dancing ground O damsel
Fire-fire susun me
Dance like flying
Jau ruṛung selkuṭi re mai
While at regular pounding ground O damsel
Rile-rolob ruṛung me
Pound like ringing bell

2. *Musiṇgo re kabu nepela*
We never see each other any day
Sahạn au buru rebu nepela mai
We will meet in the hill while collecting firewoods, dear

The girls remain so busy in their household work as well as field duties that they do not meet even in the dancing ground. One of the friends gets annoyed of this situation and complains to the other jokingly that she should go on dancing at her own *akhra* and also do work at her own husking ground and spare no time for their meeting. In plain words, the girl wants her friend to visit her in her house or village during the work or dance, and if they do not get time, they should meet in the forest while they go for collecting woods.

As soon as the youths attain the marriageable age, they show inclination of friendship towards opposite sex. But such friendship always takes place beyond the prohibited degree of relationship. Sometimes, such friendship often blossoms into marriage. As stated in the song below, which belongs to Jadur category, a boy proposes for marriage to a girl. The girl it appears is reluctant to marry him but the boy says that he is the only suitable groom for her match and that if married with him, she will enjoy complete freedom as she is enjoying now in spinsterhood. The lines of the song are as follows:

Tor leke jori-jori mai
For the match of you girl
Hamar̯ leke jori nahiṇ
There is none like me
Jatra me jori-jori mai
Match made at Jatra dance O girl
Seṇdra me jori nahin
There is no match like me at Sendra dance
Ḍinḍa samae ker maya moh ke mat chhorbe
Don't leave behind the desires of spinsterhood

Below is another song of this theme in which a boy or a girl disagree with the other about the continuity of friendship. The song belongs to Jadur category and the lines are as follows:

Jeṭe samae jori nahiṇ jumae
No match is made during summer
Hamar̯ lek raja piriti
The king-like friendship like mine
Jeṭe siṇgi naṛa nahiṇ nagujae
Nothing grows during summer
Naṛa tore re baroya
Break off the twig O guard

The boy or girl, in this song say that his or her friendship is rare and not available to everybody. It is very difficult to establish friendship with the king or Baroya (the person who guards the crop and remains all alone throughout the day and night in the field). And so, their friendship are limited to few lucky ones. The boy or the girl proudly says that he or she is the one like a king or a Baroya with whom all people are interested to establish friendship, but only a few are lucky ones. So, he or she indirectly proposes that if she or he is interested to establish friendship with king-like person, he or she will consider it, but he or she himself or herself is not interested.

Friendship develops among all age group of people. The life becomes easy going with friends. Whether friendship can be established between unrelated persons only and whether the relation between husband and wife also fall in the category of friendship. These are but few thoughtful aspects of human relations where the literatures also are silent. In Mundari the word *Gati*, that is, friend, which is used for the relation between boys or girls, is also used for the relation between husband and wife. Friendship is based on equality, and mutual trust and respect. The husband-wife relation is based on this quality and so the married couple are friends to each other. Below is a song which reflects husband-wife friendship. The song belongs to Jadur category, and the lines are as follows:

1. *Gaṛa gena kadąm suba re*
   By the side of river under the *kadam* tree
   Tiri-riri rutum sari tan
   You are playing on flute
   Hare gatiṃ hare saṇgam re
   O my beloved friend
   Gota siṇgi kaṃe neloga
   You are not to be seen the whole day

2. *Tara tite medaiṇg gosona*
   I will wipe of tears with one hand
   Tara tite maṇding joma
   And take food with the other
   Hore gatiṃ hore saṇgam re
   O my beloved friend
   Gota siṇgi kame neloga
   You are not to be seen the whole day

The woman is waiting impatiently for the return of her husband. The sun has already gone down but her husband is still not to be seen. It is in this very lonely situation, while taking food she is weeping.

The same theme is also found in the following song belonging to *Jadur* category. It is the summer time. The wife is waiting in the house but her husband is not to be seen. So, she is thinking that her husband might be taking rest under some tree or he may be in the house of *mochi* in connection of repairing of *dumang*. The lines of the song are as follows:

1. *Kahaṇ se ale re chhaela*
   Where from are you coming O dear
   Mochi ghare ḍera re chhaela
   You did stop at the house of *mochi*,
   Chhaṇyari buda tare chhaṇyari le
   Or you, take rest under some shady tree

2. *Purbe re ale re chhaela*
   You did come from the east O dear
   Mochi ghare dera re chhaela
   You did stop at the house of *mochi*
   Chhaṇyari buda tare chhaṇyari le
   You took rest under some shady tree

The young boys and girls grow up under the watchful eyes of the parents and elders. They receive all the love, care, guidance and training from them. Adolescent age is the age of learning. Children from very early age are given education in tribal ways of life. The division of work according to age and sex, is the first step in this direction. The boys generally accompany their father to the field and forest while the girls stay back with their mothers or with other elder ladies in the household. The female children are usually assigned the job of looking after their younger brothers and sisters and in the absence, the male children do the same job. They also help their mother in cleaning the house, washing the plates, cooking food, fetch drinking water from the well or streams, watch and dry paddy, etc. The boys, on the other hand, tend cattle, collect grass, do ploughing, do hunting and fishing, help their father in making ropes and other agricultural implements and learn playing of various musical instruments. There are many other light works in which both the male and female children are engaged. In spite of this, the children are given ample time for play. One of the important fields of learning of girl children is personal decoration. In the early age, it is observed, children are so eager for learning that sometimes they themselves ask the elders to teach them. Below is one such song belonging to Jadur category, the lines of which are as follows:

1. *Bore binḍa tiire chaṭu*
   Pad on the head and pot in the hand
   Da-a: au kako jamaiṇga
   Do not allow me to mix up while fetching water
   Tiire soṭa mayaṇg rutu re
   While there is stick in hand and flute in the waist
   Uri gupire kako mesaiṇga
   Do not allow me to mix up while tending cattle

2. *Da-a: au re kako mesaiṇga*
   Do not allow me to mix up while fetching water
   Biṇdayo ko chagaṛ laṭije
   They tore apart my pad too
   Uri gupi re kako mesaiṇga
   Do not allow me to mix up while tending cattle
   Soṭayo reko peṭe thoje
   They break away my tending stick
   Rutuyo reko chagaṛ laṭije
   They split apart my flute too

The young boys and girls, though they are very eager to accompany the elders and learn something from them, are sometimes not allowed to mix by the latter. In this song, a little girl and a little boy, in separate incidents, got annoyed by the behaviour of the elders and complain to their parents. Grouping, according to age, takes place in the very childhood among the children and growing up with age, the grouping is again made on the basis of sex. In this song as mentioned, the elder group of boys and girls do not allow the younger ones to mix with them. And even if they dare to follow them they get strong reproachment. The song records a good example of how the younger ones are harassed by the elders—they do not allow to mix up in tending cattle and in fetching water from the streams and tore away their stick, pad and flute. When once the youngers get such treatment from the elders, they never accompany them in future.

The young boys and girls, often learn many things from the elders simply by watching them. They imitate the elders in their talk, in playing the musical instruments, in dance and in the manners of dressing and personal decoration. When, by repeated trials they fail to learn, they ask the elders to teach them. In the song below belonging to *Jadur* category, a little girl asks her sister to help her in dressing like herself. The lines of the song are as follows:

1. *Delaigo a̭m leka chuku-buru*
   Let me have elevation like yours O sister
   Delaigo supid taiṇg me
   Help me in making hair knot O sister
   Delaigo a̭m leka jhirpa jalaṇg
   Danglingly dressing like you O sister
   Delaigo paela taiṇg me
   Help me in dressing

2. *Haṛka reya paṛiya lija*
   With the *pariya* dress of the casket
   Delaigo paela taiṇg me
   Help me in dressing
   Delaigo ḍuba reya mani sunum
   With mustard oil of the cup O sister
   Delaigo supid taiṇg me
   Help me in making hair knot O sister

The young girl wants that like her elder sister she should also dress and decorate herself. But since she is only a novice in the art of dressing, she requests the help of her elder sister. She has a fascination of her sister's way of dressing.

At the adolescent age, the boys and girls usually spent most of their leisure time with friends, and they pay regular visit to each other. The elders become annoyed when work suffers. Below is one such song which belongs to Jadur category in which a boy is asked not to roam about with friends. The lines of the song are as follows:

1. *Neleka̭n samae re haṭia̭m honora*
   At this age you roam about in the village
   Neleka̭n oṇsaṛ re ḍare siṇgara
   With this figure you beautify the lanes

2. *Bale-bale re haṭia̭m honora*
   At this tender age you roam about in the village

Lindung-lindung re ḍarem singara
At this delicate age you beautify the lanes

3. *Haṭia honor do karem iuana*
Roaming about in the village you don't know
Ḍare singar do karem seria
Beautification of lanes you don't know

4. *Haṭia honor do ṭuila ko orongeya*
Tuila is played upon in roaming about in the village
Ḍare singar do paela ko jereya
Dress sweepingly to beautify the lanes

The boy is told that it is not his age to walk around in the village. He is too young to follow such habit. One should follow proper manner while walking around in the village. He is told that people wear proper dress and play on *tuila* while they walk around. For such manners to follow, he is a mere baby. Walking around in the village is not bad but that can only be undertaken by the grown up boys and girls who beautify the lanes through proper dressing and music. It is how the young tribal boys and girls are taught in the tribal manners and customs.

Youthful age is the carefree life of merry making and enjoyment. The song concerning the youthful age, therefore, has variety of themes. The nature, behaviour and psychology of the boys and girls are very much reflected in these songs. The songs also portray their feelings, emotions and tastes. The youths physically and mentally undergo constant change at this age and as such the songs also depict their mental condition. Interactions between youths and elders are common themes in these songs. It is in course of such interactions that the youths are given lessons of mannerism or on tribal etiquettes. The different stages of females growth is compared with different kinds of plants as well as its parts. The songs reveal each aspects of life and qualities. In one of the song below, she has been compared with tamarind leaves and banana trunk. This song is sung in Lahsua as well as in Jadur category. The lines of the song are as follows:

1. *Jojo sakam ribi-ribi*
Tamarind leaves falling down in succession
Namo maire ribi-ribi

You too walk in small paces quickly
Kadali sakạm kere bore
Banana leaves grow quickly
Namo maire kere bore
You too have grown quickly O daughter

2. *Natali sakạm goso jana*
Atali leaves have withered away
Namo mairem goso Jana
You too have faded away
Natali sakạm maela jan
Atali leaves have turned purple
Amo mairem maela jan
You too have lost your charm

It is a fact that the physical growth of the female child is rapid like banana leaves but like the Atali leaves, after few days, it withers away quickly.

Below is a song belonging to Lahsua category, in which a girl is compared with a flower. The lines of the song are as follows:

1. *Mainore chimin dinạm taina*
How long will you remain O girl
Jathriṇ ra: jhinga baha re goso jan
The *jhinga* flower of the fence has faded away
Mainore chimin dinạm taina
How long will you remain O girl

2. *Mainore samae bhairạm taina*
You will reamain till the youthful age O girl
Jathrin ra: jhinga baha re goso jan
The jhinga flower of the fence has faded away
Mainore emin dinạm taina
You too will remain so long O girl

In this song, the girl is reminded of the flying nature of the time and her youthful age. She is also reminded of the *jhinga* flower which blooms for a shortwhile and withers away. The youthful age of the girl is like the flower which does not last long.

The song below too, carry the same theme which belongs to Jadur category. The lines of the song are as follows:

1. *Chetan̂ ṭola suku naṛi mai*
   The pumpkin creeper of upper toli O girl
   Chimin sal taiṇa re suku naṛi
   How many years the pumpkin creeper will stay
   Latar̂ ṭola malan̂ ba mai
   The bean flower of the lower toli O girl
   Chimin sirma taina re malan̂ ba
   How many years will remain the bean flower

2. *Chetan̂ ṭola suku naṛi mai*
   The pumpkin creeper of upper toli O girl
   Mid sal taina suku naṛi
   Pumpkin creeper will stay a year O girl
   Latar̂ ṭola malan̂ ba mai
   The bean flower of the lower toli O girl
   Bare sal taina malan̂ ba
   The bean flower will stay for two years

The life of pumpkin creeper and bean flower are too short. The girl is indirectly reminded of her youthful age through the age of pumpkin creeper and bean flower. The youthful age, in short, is transitory and short.

In one of the song below which belongs to Jadur category, a boy tells a girl that though both are of the same age and are growing together, but her fate will be like Atali flower which blooms early and withers away soon. The lines of the song are as follows:

1. *Aiŋgo maina kere bore*
   I too have grown up quickly O girl
   Amo maina kere bore
   You too have grown up quickly

2. *Atali ba goso jana*
   The Atali flower have withered away
   Amo mairem goso jana
   You too have faded away O girl

3. *Atali ba maela jan*
   Atali flower has turned purple
   Amo mairem maela jan
   Your charm has also faded away

In the song below too, a boy tells the girl that though they grew together and even today she dresses and decorates herself like a youth in the same fashion, she, however, does not look like before. The song belongs to Lahsua category and the lines are as follows:

Misa telang hara len
We grew together
Misa telang ḍaṛi len
We attained the maturity together
Maire sida leka bara bari kame neloga, ho hore
But you do not look like as before, alas.

During youthful age, the boys and girls decorate themselves as beautifully as they can. The appearance of youths at this age has been described in the following song which belongs to Jarga category. The lines of the song are as follows:

1. *Dinda tan jarma tan*
   While remaining unmarried and participating in dance
   Bo chetan sunum, sunum joro tan
   From oily head drips down the oil

2. *Ḍinḍa tan jarma tan*
   While remaining unmarried and participating in dance
   Kaṭa laṭaṛ paela, paela nosor jan
   The dress behind the heels sweeping the ground

The unmarried boys and girls, at their youthful age are very careful about their dress and fashion. Everyone tries to keep oneself at the best of style. The boy, as mentioned in the song, has overoiled his head which is dropping down and his loincloth is sweeping the ground behind his feet.

How the youth look like, has been described in the song below belonging to Jadur category. The girl is so beautiful and frolicsome that she looks like a bird. The lines of the song are as follows:

1. *Chetan tola kuri hona dcda*
   The girl of upper *tola,* brother
   Lang chenre lekaya dada
   Is like a *lang* bird brother

2. *Latar tola kuri honă dada*
   The girl of lower tola, brother
   Bocho chenre lekae
   Is like a Bocho bird

3. *Lang chenre lekaya dada*
   Is like a Lang bird brother
   Okorebu gongia dada
   Where shall we give her in marriage

4. *Bocho chenre lekaya dada*
   She is like a Bocho bird brother
   Chimae rebu chalaiya
   Where shall we carry her

5. *Lang chenre lekaya dada*
   She is like a Lang bird brother
   Bundu rabu gongia dada
   We shall give her in marriage in Bundu

6. *Bocho cheŋre lekaya dada*
   She is like a Bocho bird brother
   Tamar rebu chalaiya
   We shall carry her to Tamar

Lang and Bocho are colourful birds with long beautiful tails. The girl of this song is slim and tall. She also dresses herself with colourful sari with long hanging ends. She is young and her two brothers are talking about her possible marriage either at Bundu or Tamar.

In the song below, it is stated that seeing a beautiful girl, the boys politely request her to give them a smile or a laugh and have a talk with them. In tribal way of life, everyone has the freedom to have conversation with each other irrespective of difference in age and sex and also with strangers. But the youths go even beyond that.

A youth has no strangers and no social boundary of interactions. They can have a conversation in normal way with any youth stranger also and enjoy each other's company. In this song, the boys openly express their desire that they would like to see her beauty while smiling or laughing. The song belongs to Jadur category and the lines are as follows:

1. *Mar̥ maina landa leme, chilkam̥, landaya*
   Dear girl, give us a laugh, how will you laugh
   Mar̥ maina jagar̥ leme, chilkam̥, jagara
   Dear girl, let us have a talk, how would you talk

2. *A̭m maina landa lere, kuṭi ba ribi-ribi*
   If you laugh O girl, Kuti flower may fall and spread all over
   A̭m maina jagar lere, Tarae ba tare taseya
   If you talk O girl, Tarae flowers may bloom

Girls are the symbols of happiness and joy. At their talk and smile, the flowers bloom and at their laugh the earth is covered with scented colourful beauty.

In the song below too, the boys want to see the laughing beauty of the girl who is sitting on a stool. The song belongs to Jadur category and the lines are as follows:

1. *Meṭe-meṭe hende kuṛi do*
   A jet-black damsel
   Machila re duba kana re
   Is sitting on a stool
   Terem resem landa tana
   Is smiling beautifully

2. *Dolabu nele lia re*
   Let us go to see her
   Marebu china lia re
   Let us identify her
   Machila re duba kana re
   She is sitting on a stool
   Terem resem landa tana
   Is smiling beautifully

3. *Nele dole nele lia re*
   We had seen her closely
   China dole china lia re
   We had identified her
   Machila re duba kana re
   She is sitting on a stool
   Terem resem landa tana
   Is smiling beautifully

Very often the boys and girls exchange abuses with each other in a mood of joke and enjoyment. This makes the social environment more lively. Below is one such song belonging to Jadur category, the lines of which are as follows:

1. *Ne kuṛi ko ruba tadiṇga*
   These girls did pinch me
   Hatna jo kope joa ko
   The girls of Hatna fruits like bulged cheeks

2. *Ne kuri ko ruchab tadiṇga*
   These girls did pull my hair
   Buru Lamă keyaṇ kaṭa ko
   Hill Lama fruit like legged girls

The girls, as mentioned in this song are, naughty and frolicsome. They get enjoyment in harassing a boy by pinching and pulling his hair. He in return abuses them in words which mention the appearance of wild fruits. The comparison which the boy makes of the girls evoke great laughter among them as the comparison is a strange one.

Though the girls are given in marriage early, the actual marriage does not take place till the attainment of physical maturity as well as acquiring of expertise in household activities. The most visible quality for a marriageable age girl is knowing—the weaving of mat, broomsticks, head-pads, is able to carry loads, knows social manners and etiquettes, etc. The youths often get acquainted when they attend marriage ceremonies of their relatives or pay visits to relative as guest with some friends. Thereafter they get ample opportunity to meet and talk when they visit markets and fairs. Such acquaintance often blossoms into friendship or develops into a liking for each other among the two of opposite sex, belong to two different clans of permissible category. The song below mentions that the boy admires the girl for her work, talk and style of dressing, etc. The song belongs to Jadur category and the lines are as follows:

1. *A̭m kaji dore mai*
   Your talk O girl
   Tee reyo *telae laka*
   It is like collecting in hand
   Ama baṇkaṛ dore mai
   Your conversation O girl
   Kaṇsa pital dale leka
   Sounds like Harp of Brass-Zinc

2. *Oko reko idi meya re*
   Where will you be married away O girl
   Tee reyo telae leka
   It is like collecting in hand
   Chimae reko chala meya mai
   Where will you be given away in marriage O girl
   Kaṇsa pita̭l dale leka
   Sounds like harp of Brass-Zinc

The boy was much impressed with the talk of the girl and says that if possible it is worth collecting in hand. The voice of the girl, it seems, is musical.

As above, in the song below too a boy admires a girl for her expertise in collecting and selection of firewood and leaves. The song belongs to Jadur category and the lines are as follows:

1. *A̭m au saha̭n dore mai*
   The wood brought by you O girl
   Diya leka juloga
   Burns like lamp
   A̭m heje saka̭m dore mai
   The leaves plucked by you O girl
   Ḍuva leka kalau baiyoga
   It is made up like cup

2. *Oko reko idi meya mai*
Where will you be married away O girl
Diya leka juloga
Burns like lamp
Chimae reko chala meya mai
Where will you be given away in marriage O girl
Ḍuva leka kalau baiyoga
It is made up like cup

In the song below, a boy tells a girl that wherever she will be married, it will be a distant village and meeting as usual will become difficult. The song belongs to Jadur category and the lines are as follows:

1. *Okote kote ga ko idi meya*
You were taken away O girl
Saṇgin gamari rem paṇdil jana
You were thrown off to a distant village
Chimae kore ga ko chala meya
Where will you be given away in marriage
Saṇgin gamari rem paṇdil jana
You were thrown off to a distant village

2. *Chimae kore ga ko chattạr meya*
Where will you be given shelter
Saṇgin gamari rem paṇdil jana
You were thrown off to a distant village

Sometimes, the boy and girl stop talking to each other when the sentiment of one is hurt by the behaviour of the other. The following song belonging to Jadur category, is based on this theme. The lines of the song are as follows:

1. *Hatu tala ṛe Ludạm ba*
Ludạm flower in the middle of the village
Jaugi chire kame kakala
Will you not talk forever
Disum tala re Kunduri ba
Kunduri flower in the middle of the country

Jaugi chire kame lapaṇda
Will you not share a joke forever

2. *Sasaṇg chire hade kedam*
Did you cut the turmeric forever
Jaugi chire kame kakala
Will you not talk forever
Sutạm chire ṭoṭa kedam
Did you break the thread
Jaugi chire kame lapaṇda
Will you not share a joke forever

The above song indicates that a boy cut a joke at a girl which the latter took very seriously as it hurts her sentiment or pride or dignity. And so, the girl stopped talking completely with the boy. *Sasang had* and *Sutam tota* are the two phrases which carry the meaning of taking an oath for a complete withdrawal. Below is yet another song on this theme of silence on the part of the girl. The song belongs to Jadur category and the lines are as follows:

1. *Dhuṭu rem duba kana re*
Sitting over on a log of wood
Chiyare kame kakala
Why don't you talk
Chiyare kame kakala
Why don't you talk
Kadal kuṇwari do
You plantain tree like damsel

2. *Icha baha leka*
Like the Icha flower
Samae seno tana re
The time is running away
Chiyare kame kakala
Why don't you talk
Murud baha leka
Like the Murud flower
Samae seno tana re
The time is running away

3. *Samae ruaṛ tana re*
The time is returning
Chiyare kame kakala
Why don't you talk
Kadal kuṇwari do
You plantain tree like damsel

The girl is sitting on a log of wood silent and thoughtful. A boy is standing before her trying to break her silence. The song does not give the reason of her silence. It may be that her proposed marriage may have broken or the boy himself has put a marriage proposal to the girl. The boy reminds her of the transitory nature of youthful age. He compares the youthful age of the girl with that of *Icha* and *Murud*—the two wild flowers that bloom only during the summer. The colours of these two flowers are red and the smile is an indication of love. Like plantain tree, the girl has got a very robust and healthy body. The boy, therefore, tells her that time has not gone or the time gone is returning if she agrees to his proposal of marriage. The girl is still sitting silently on the log of wood.

The young boys and girls are always guided by the elders in day-to-day life of the people according to the customs and traditions of the society as well as on the basis of practical situations that arise in everyday life. The youths like to spend most of their time in merry making and enjoyment and abstain themselves from assigned works. In such a situation, the elders tell the youths that such activity should not be made a habit. In the following song, a boy who instead of ploughing the field, is engaged in playing on the flute. He is soundly chided by his mother. The song belongs to Jadur category and the lines are as follows:

1. *Turi ko loyoṇg re boyo, turi gem oroṇga boyo*
On *turi* field O boy, you always play on flute
Japi ko badi re boyo, Japi gem sayad
On the valley of Japi, you always sing Japi

2. *Ama reya siyū hada boyo, tingua kan geyaya boyo*
Your plough bullocks O boy, are standing still
Ama reya nayal fal boyo tingua kan geyaya boyo
Your plough and ploughshare are lying idle there

3. *Ju siyū meta mere boyo, turi gem orongeya boyo*
When asked to plough, you always play on flute
Mar chalu meta mere boyo, jarapi gem sayad
When asked to dig, you always sing *Jarapi*

4. *Jati bondo-bondo ge boyo, turi gem oronga. boyo*
You are habitual idle, you always play on flute
Jati lang-chang-ge boyo, japi gem sayad
You are habitual playful, you always sing *Japi*

5. *Ne mandi meta mere boyo, lar-lar geyaya boyo*
When served food, you swallow up quickly
Ne utu meta mere boyo, sa:r-sa:r ge
When served gravy, you gulp it up quickly

This is the picture of an idle boy who avoids manual labour and devotes much time in merriment in playing on musical instrument and singing, but when he is served food, he finishes it quickly without any feeling of shyness. Below in another song belonging to Jadur category which depicts the picture of a lazy girl. The lines of the song are as follows:

1. *Nelekan samae re, chiahom tene-goneya*
At this young age, why are you so lazy
Nelekan onsar re, chia hom tanae-tunuya
With such healthy body, why are you so slow

2. *Tene-gone re chhadi ko meta meya*
If you are lazy, you will be called a divorcee
Chapu tunue re, buria ko kajia
If you work idly, you will be called an old person

Some girls, because of rapid physical growth and biological changes, become inactive and idle in work. Such girls are always advised by the elders to improve in their habit. They are warned if they continue behaving like an idle person, he or she will be nicknamed either a divorcee or an aged fellow. If a girl is so nicknamed, no boy will come to marry her.

An idle girl is a problem in the family. If she is given a piece of work, she may take long time to complete it. Below is a song of

Jadur category in which a girl is reproached for her laziness. The lines of the song are as follows:

1. *Tilasari baba chi mai tiril tuku*
   Tilasari paddy and mortar of *tiril*
   Ruṛuṇg-ruṛuṇg tegim tikir keda
   It became noon while pounding it
   Oṛeya haṭa chi mai leche-koche
   Is the winnowing fan in bad shape
   Gu-gum tegi mainam tarsing jan
   It is past noon while in cleaning

2. *Siyu kodo reko hiju kạṇa*
   The ploughmen have returned
   Ruṛuṇg-ruṛuṇg tegi mainạm tikin jana
   It became noon while pounding it
   Chalu kodo reko seṭer kana
   The diggers have come back
   Gu-gum tegi mainạm tarsing jan
   It is past noon while in cleaning

The process of making rice from paddy is a long and arduous one. As stated in the song, it became noon in pounding the paddy alone and in cleaning, it became afternoon. The family is big, as indicated in the song and the girl had to pound and clean a good quantity of paddy. It is, therefore, natural that cooking also took much time. The workers have come back from the field but the food is not ready. All are hungry and so the girl is being rebuked for taking much time in cooking. It is either the mother of the girl or her sisters who are taking to task to the girl.

The boy or girl of the above nature are disliked by all and are often reproached. The elders then cite their own example as precept which they did during their youthful age. They deliver a long lecture to such a boy or girl on the proper way of working. Below is a song belonging to Jadur category in which an old fellow is giving a sermon to a lazy girl. The lines of the song are as follows:

1. *Ạm lekaiṇg ḍiṇda tạn redo mai*
   When I was a damsel like you O girl

Ạm lekaiṇg ḍaṇgua tạn redo
While I was single like you
Nimtaṇg do ba suba riṇga mai
By this time I was under the flower tree
Nimtaṇg do dali suba riṇga
By this time I was under the branch of tree

2. *Nimtaṇg do ba suba riṇga mai*
By this time I was by the side of flower tree
Nimtaṇg do ba-iṇg gutu tan
By this time I was making garland of flowers
Nimtaṇg do dali suba riṇga mai
By this time I was under the branch of a tree
Nimtaṇg do dali-iṇg gutu tan
By this time I was weaving basket of branches

In this song, an old lady narrates her own story about her youthful age to a young girl as to how active she was. She is fed up with the idleness of the girl and tries to make her active by citing her own example and desires the girl to follow the same.

The boys and girls are always guided by the elders but it is the advice of the friends that counts most. Below is a song belonging to Jadur category in which a friend laments for the mistake of the girl. The lines of the song are as follows:

1. *Ạm dore gatim golem ayum jan*
You did follow the whistling O friend
Ạm dore saṇgaiṇg re riyuṛạm aten jan
You did listen the whistling

2. *Golem ayum jan, tukum tenḍer ked*
Following the whistling, you kept aside the mortar
Riyuṛạm aten jan, chatum rapud ked
Listening whistling, broke the pot

A friend of the girl reminds that it is nọt good to listen the whistling sound during work. The girl in this song stopped pounding paddy and went to meet the whistling boy and another time, when she was returning from the well at the sudden sound of whistling of the boy, stumbled and broke the pot at the diversion of her attention. Whistling is the communication language of the youths. Whistling is used in singing as well as in communication of message. Whistling by boys to girls is found in every society and the Munda youths are no exception.

A woman's life can be divided into different stages according to her role-status. A girl has a happy life so long she does not marry. After marriage, another life begins which is very rough and tough. The song below which belongs to Jarga category, describes the joy and happiness as well as sorrow and gloom in different stages of a woman's life. The lines of the song are as follows:

1. *Hara tanạm dari janạm mai re*
   You are growing up and attained maturity O girl
   Hatu tala pokhari re, lijạn sabun tana
   Washing clothes at the village pond

2. *Ọra: janạm, duar janạm mai re*
   When you are married and established own household
   Kita binḍạm ṣabeya, medạm joroya
   While holding pad you will shed tears

The girl is free from any responsibility before her marriage. The responsibility comes after the marriage and if the girl is inexperienced in running the household affairs, the life becomes hell for her. The song mentions that the girl was usually seen at the village pond cleaning her clothes and avoided other works, the result was that she did not learn anything. The composer of the song feels sorry for such girl, for her life will become miserable after marriage. *Kitabinda,* that is a pad made of date leaves indicates works and responsibility, in simple language it means carrying the load.

The avoidance or idleness in work is the theme of the song below which belongs to Jadur category, the lines of which are as follows:

1. *Ḍinḍa redo maina, daṇgua redo*
   During spinsterhood and being single
   Piṛi Budu lekạm limaṇg-lomoṇg
   You walk leisurely like field Budu fish

2. *Ḍinḍa redo mainạm, daṇgua redo*
During spinsterhood and being single
Jaraṇga silib lekạm richạd-rochod
Walk magnificently like matured wild goat

3. *Hebeyạn redo mainạm, hatarạn redo*
In carrying baby on your side and back
Eṇga seta lekam jundul-jundul
You walk like mother bitch

The song presents two contrasting pictures of a woman's life—the state of spinsterhood and after marriage. The physical features and movement of the body are just the opposite in the two stages of life. During youthful age, the girl, because of her excellent health and heaviness of her body, walks like a full grown wild goat whose walking steps are admired by all. But when the girl is married and babies dangle over her body, all the physical beauty vanishes and she becomes like a mother bitch after whom puppies run all the time for milk.

A girl has been compared with a tall and branchless tree. It is difficult to climb or reach to the top of such a tree. Similarly, a grown up girl, neither listens to the advice of the elders nor cares for them. The song below belonging to Jadur category is based on the theme of heedlessness of the youths. The lines of the song are as follows:

1. *Hora ra: sarajom ba*
The way-side *sarajom flowers*
Leseken-leseken
It is tall and straight
Hatu ren ḍinḍa dhaṇgoṛi
The damsel of the village
Mocho ken-mocho ken
Is beautiful and agile

2. *Baṇka tolaire*
Even when provided to forked pole
Baṇka teyo ka tebaga
Can't be reached out with forked pole

Kajiyo samujhai re
Even offered her advice
Kajiyo kae ayuma
Does not listen to advice even

The girls are generally stated to be very conscious of their beauty and style in dressing and usually run for merry making. But there are girls also who are unconcerned about it. It is a matter of anxiety for the elders for such girls who show aloofness in life even during the prime of their age when such activities are expected from everybody. The song below belonging to Jadur category is based on this theme. The lines of the song are as follows:

1. *Marna mai ḍinḍa sunum,*
Use the oil of spinsterhood O girl
Marna mai sunuman me
Use the oil O girl
Marna mai ḍinḍa osaṇṛ
Have the spinsterhood body O girl
Marna mai karaman me
Enjoy yourself in dance with youthful body

2. *Marna mai ko goṇ kem re*
In case you were married away
Jaṭi japa: tem nel koyo ya
You will peep through the folded mat
Marna mai ko chal kem re
In case you are given away O girl
Karae muchri te atenam
You will listen to from distance

The girl is advised to take full advantage of the youthful age and participate in merry making and in styling. After marriage when all household responsibilities will be upon her, she will not get time either for dressing or participation in dance. Then, she will have to satisfy herself by listening to music from distance or peep the dance through some hole, for the girl will not get time for these activities. It is observed that after marriage and when she has children and household chores to attend, she seldom finds herself free.

Excess of anything is disliked in all societies. In youthful age excessive indulgence in merry making and styling is criticized by the elders, for they have seen the world and know the reality of life. They say that beauty and charm are but transitory in life. In the following song belonging to Jadur category, it has been mentioned that everything will go away one day from an individual's life. The lines of the song are as follows:

1. *Chetạn ṭolạm rakạb re maina*
   When you visit upper hamlet O girl
   Supid gem chapu rakaba
   You touch up and down the hairlock
   Latạr ṭolạm aṛgun re maina
   When you come down to lower hamlet
   Paela gem jir aṛgu
   You manage your dress around

2. *Samae barige supid gem chapu rakaba*
   While there is time, you touch up and down your hairlock
   Oṇsaṛ barige paelạm jir argu
   As long as you are young, you will press down your dress
   Samae seno jan, supid raṛa jan
   When time flown away, the hairlocks become loosened
   Oṇsaṛ birid jan, paela checha jan
   When young age passed, the dress becomes tattered

In this song, as stated, a girl is being observed by the elders. She is very particular about her dressing whenever she goes out from the house. She touches her hairlock a number of times, so also sets her dress. The elders are unhappy for all these for they know the transitory nature of life. The girl will do such activities as long as her age and health permits.

Similar to the above, a boy is also advised to enjoy the life as long as his parents are alive. When parents are gone from this world, he will not get the time even to visit the dancing ground. The song belongs to Lahsua category and the lines are as follows:

1. *Eṇgạm-apum paṛia, raṇga saṛi paṛia*
   During the days of parents, dress colourful dresses

Babure nida-siṇgi rutum saṛia
You play on flute day and night, O dear boy

2. *Eṇgạm-apum goe jan, ranga saṛi maela jan*
At the death of parents, colourful dress becomes dirty
Babure jatra sendra hoko utạr jan
Participation in dance has stopped abruptly, O dear boy

Below is another song which also mentions that style and fashion is there till the youthful age and when old age comes, everything vanishes. The song belongs to Jadur category and the lines are as follows:

1. *Ne naki supid do samae bari*
Caring for hairstyle is only during youthful age
Ne boṇdol botoe do oṇsaṛ bari
The long loincloth suits but in healthy body

2. *Ne naki supid do tur tukaya*
Caring for hairlock will turn into squirrel's nest
Ne boṇdol botoe do sagae aṭede
The long loincloth will be used in kite's nest

3. *Chuṭi koto re tur tukaya*
Squirrel will make nest on the top of the branch
Suba tarae re sagae aṭede
Kite will make nest on the branches of tree

When the youthful age passes away and when one is unable to manage things properly, it decays slowly. A person who uses the available things extravagantly, he will suffer in his old age. This message has been conveyed in the following *Jadur* category of song, the lines of which are as follows:

1. *Samae bole taiken redo*
At the young age
Pitạl ṭaṭi rego mani sunum
Mustard oil brimmed in the brass bowl
Oṇsaṛi bole taiken redo
When there was health

Pachon paṛia re taben poṭom
Bundle of beaten-rice dangled in colourful *paṛia*

2. *Samae bole notaṇg jan redo*
At the passing away of youthful age
Pitạl ṭaṭi dore rochod jana
Brass bowl also broke
Oṇsaṛing bole otaṇg jan redo
When health gone
Pachon paṛia do doraṇg jana
Colourful *paria* became tattered

With the passing away of time, everything goes away with it—the health, the wealth and the beauty. The old age is meant for living in perpetual want and sufferings. So, one must be careful and use his time properly.

5

MARRIAGE AND SOCIAL LIFE

Like all other human societies, the Mundas too, have an elaborate custom of marriage. The change of stage at the prime of any youth's life, that is, from unmarried to married, is celebrated by involving all kins as well as the whole village community. This is an extraordinarily happy occasion and the happiness of the two youths of opposite sex are shared by all wellwishers. On the whole, this aspect of life of changing stage presents a very peculiar situation among two groups of people in which the donor group, that is, the bride party, plays the role of loser, and the receiver, that is, the bridegroom party, the gainer. The whole marriage process proceeds towards culmination slowly and slowly, ritual by ritual until the two unmarried fellows are united in one with the completion of last ritual. Each ritual stage has wonderful emotional bearings on the near and dear ones of the would-be couple. These have nicely been described by the composers of the songs. And kudos to the composers of these songs, who, besides the portrayal of the emotional life of the people involved, also have described the social necessity of marriage related to morals, philosophy and psychology of the people of the society. Sending away of daughters through the custom of marriage, on the one hand, has severely been criticized by the female youths, on the other, the elders have looked upon the custom as an obligation of the society which they must fulfil. The dilemma of the daughter as well as of the parents have nicely been portrayed in the songs that follow.

Early marriage is not the practice in Munda society. It is only when the youth attains the physical maturity, his or her parents and relatives talk of marriage. Besides physical maturity, a youth must qualify for the marriage. Character building and work experience are the two basic qualities for any Munda youth for eligibility for marriage. A boy will not be married unless he gets the expertise in ploughing techniques, in making and repairing of ploughs and various other agricultural equipments, preparation of fields and preservation of grains, etc. Similarly, a girl is supposed to have attained the marriageable age when she knows how to weave mat, broomsticks, making of leaf cups, cooking of food and preparation of rice-beer. These basic and primary qualifications must be encultured by the youths before their marriage. But while making selection of marriage mate, other qualities such as character, behaviour and physical appearance as well as background of the family are equally taken into consideration.

A boy or girl who have developed bad character according to the Munda standard of morality, find it hard to get married. A girl who is lazy or absconds from work, does not know the manners of behaviour with the elders, has bad habit of eating, drinking and stealing or is greedy and short tempered or mentally irritative, however, healthy and beautiful physically she cannot get life partner easily. So is the standard for the boy also. A strict social discipline, therefore, is maintained for the children by the elders from the very beginning to avoid any embarrassment in life. Marriage takes place only after a thorough investigation of the background of the family as well as of the character of the youth.

The following song of *Jadur* category mentions that the girl has developed bad habit of greed and stealing:

1. *Ne dai do kakru kumbṛu keda*
   This sister has stolen the gourd
   Ne dai do jiliṇg lacho jan
   This sister has developed greedy lip
   Ne dai do ṭuṭki jono kumbṛu keda
   This sister has stolen blunt broomstick
   Ne dai do maina kaṭa jan
   This sister's leg has turned forked like Maina bird

2. *Ne dai do okorebu goṇ gia*
   Where shall we give her in marriage
   Ne dai doe jiliṇg lacho jan
   This sister has developed greedy lip
   Ne dai do chimae rebu chalaiya
   Where shall we arrange her marriage

Ne dai doe Maina kaṭa jan
This sister's leg has turned fork like Maina bird

3. *Ne dai doe Bunḍu rebu goṇgia*
We shall give her in marriage in Bundu
Ne dai doe jiliṇg lacho jan
This sister has developed greedy lip
Ne dai doe Tamaṛ rebu chalaiya
We shall arrange her marriage in Tamar
Ne dai doe Maina kaṭa jan
This sister's leg has turned fork like Maina bird

The height and physical features of the youths are also taken into consideration while discussing and deciding the proposal. In the following song which belongs to Jadur category, a boy tells the girl about her stature. The lines of the song are as follows:

1. *Salaṇgi dom dungui geya mai*
In height you are small O girl
Supid tem salaṇgin jana
You are tall due to your hairlock
Hoṛmo dom nana geya mai
Bodily you are slim O girl
Paela tem moṭon jana
You are fatty due to your dress

2. *Supid tem salaṇgin jana mai*
You are tall due to your hairlock
Oko kore mainale goṇge meya
Where shall we give you in marriage
Paela tem moṭon jana mai
You are fatty due to your dress O girl
Chimae kore mai nale chala meya
Where shall we arrange your marriage

3. *Bunḍu kore mai nale goṇge meya*
We shall give in marriage in Bundu
Tamaṛ kore mai nale chala meya
We shall arrange your marriage at Tamar

While making choice, the boys generally exclude the girl who is either slim or dwarf. The girls also dislike such boys whose heights are much lower than herself. But in case of arranged marriage, persons of two extreme heights have no problem at all in the belief that the issue born out of such wedlock may attain the average height.

As stated above, marriageable age is not determined by the actual age of the boy or girl but it is the other criteria, which count most. It is, generally, observed that at around 20 years of age, a boy or girl acquires the qualities and expertise in all domestic as well as outside chores that make him or her to face the reality of life successfully. And it is at this age or a little before, that talk about marriage starts. There are other factors which affect the marriage, such as economic condition of the family or lack of guardian in case of orphaned boy or girl. However, there are always some exceptions and the following song which belongs to Jatra category, refers to a marriage which was celebrated for a boy whose age was only 12 years. And because of this exception the song was composed. The lines of the song are as follows:

1. *Ka janạm dele ge nayo*
   Mother, in which sex did you give me birth
   Baro bachhare mandowa chhaṇdae
   You arranged marriage at the age of twelve years

2. *Beṭa janạm dele ge nayo*
   You gave me birth in male sex
   Baro bachhare mandowa chhaṇdae
   You arranged marriage at the age of twelve years

The song states that it is because of male child, the marriage has taken place and so, it can safely be presumed that the age of the bride may be much lower than the groom. It may also be that the song may be referring not to the marriage of the Munda boy but to a non-Munda for such communities have also long settled down in the midst of the Mundas.

Forms of Marriage

Enthnographers of Munda tribes have mentioned various methods of acquiring mate that exist in the society. These forms are:

Raji-Khushi, that is, love marriage; *Oppor-tipi* or *Atangir,* that is, marriage by elopement; *Dhuku* or *Nir-Bolo,* that is, intrusion and *Dutam-Dari* or arranged marriage. Though clan exogamy is the rule of the marriage, cases of its breach is but natural. Clan endogamy is considered incestuous and the violators are either killed or banished from the society. Such couples are known by the term *Mago* which means to be killed by hacking. It is told that persons caught with incestuous relations were either killed at the boundary of the village or banished from the community. Formerly, inter-tribal marriages were strongly discouraged and marriage with non-tribal was unthinkable. These rules are still in vogue in the community. Such persons are generally excommunicated from the society. The reference of such illegal relations are also found in Munda songs. Such relations are never the *Raji-Khusi form.* In *Raji-Khusi* form, the pair belong to two different clans and though the society recognizes it but the boys and girls are strongly discouraged to establish such relations because marriage is a social affair and not the individual. It is told among the Mundas that if girls are not given in marriage at right time they may bring humiliation to the family and society. Below is a song belonging to Jadur category which states that if the girl is not given in marriage, she may forcibly enter into the boy's house. The lines of the song are as follows:

1. *Ne leka samae re chia ho kape goṇgia*
   At the prime age of youthfulness, why don't you give her in marriage
   Ne leka oṇsaṛ re, chia ho kape chalaiya
   Having such beautiful figure, why don't you arrange marriage

2. *Ne kalom kape goṇgi re, baba leka baṇdi taipe*
   This year if you don't give her in marriage, store her like paddy
   Ne kalom kape chalai re, saru leka ripa taipe
   This year if you don't arrange her marriage, dry and preserve her like Saru

3. *Ne kalom kape goṇgi re, Bunḍu re bolo soṛoa*
   This year if you don't give her in marriage, she may intrude in Bundu

Ne kalom kape chalai re, Tamaṛ re bolo soṛoa
This year if you don't arrange her marriage, she may intrude in Tamar

The above song mentions that delay in marriage may take wrong turn. She may either take forcible entry in someone's house or may run away with some boy of her liking. This is a great humiliation for the family. It is therefore advised that she may either be married at a right time or in case if it is not possible she may be kept in strict control like preserving of grains.

Below is another song belonging to Jarga category based on the same theme, the lines of which are as follows:

1. *Chia tetenga, chia giriṇi*
   O lizard, O chamelion
   Duar rem rosod-rosod
   Making cracking sound at the door

2. *Name lekaiṇg ḍinḍa tan re*
   If I would be young like you
   Maṛi-maṛi teiṇg kepad aderena
   I would creep into slowly

In this song an aged woman, most probably the sister-in-law of the girl, suggests the unmarried girl that had she been in her place, she would have made forcible entry by now like a lizard.

On the same theme as above, the song below belonging to Racha category, mentions how the two young girls are making plan for forcible entry into their lovers' houses. The lines of the song are as follows:

1. *Buchi ḍari re, dhaṇgora kore laṇg taina*
   At the broken wall well-spring, we will live with the lads
   Hare ḍinḍa, dhaṇgora kore laṇg taina
   O spinster, we will live with the lads

2. *Rai jang, mani jang*
   With mustard seeds
   Dhaṇgora kore laṇg taina
   We will live with the lads

Hare ḍinḍa dhaṇgora kore laṇg taina
O spinster, we will live with the lads

The two girls are planning to make forcible entry into their lovers' houses. The two have gone to the spring to fetch drinking water. There is nobody besides the two at the site. *Rai* and *Mani*—the two types of mustard seeds carry double meaning. In one case, it means deep love for the lovers. The two seeds cannot be distinguished so far as their colour is concerned. Whatever difference is their, it is the size. In another case, *rai* and *mani* seeds are used to ward off the evil spirits. So the girls are using these seeds to ward off the evil spirits who may create obstacle in their objective.

Dhuku or forcible entry is made by the girl when the boy's proposal of marriage is not accepted by the parents of either side. Sometimes, the pair run away to a distant place and live as husband and wife. The girl's guardian, in such case, cannot demand bride-price from the boy's parent.

Regular meeting with strangers, sometimes matures into intimacy. Below is a song which makes such reference of intimacy of a fishing boy with a cloth washing girl. They met usually near the river and fell in love. The song belongs to the Baa category and the lines are as follows:

Chhoṭe-moṭe ḍir jojang bancsi khelaere
They are fishing in a deep narrow pool
Hare, neṭo dhobin kapuṛ kachha chhitakalain sita re pani
The cloth washing girl, while washing sprinkled ice cold water
Chhoṛ-chhoṛ raja beṭa hamar nachera
Leave of my waist cloth O prince
Hare, neṭo dhobin kapuṛ kachha chhitakalain sita re pani
The cloth washing girl, while washing sprinkled ice cold water

In this song, as described, a boy is fishing in the river with his fishing rod where a girl is also washing clothes. As the girl is thrashing the clothes on the river stone, water sprinkled on the boy who was sitting on a stone nearby. The girl may be doing such activity purposely, so the boy caught hold of the girl's waist cloth. The girl requests the boy to let her cloth loose and also allow her to wash the clothes. Such meeting in isolated place by the boys and girls of opposite clan, often develop into intimacy which leads to marriage.

Sometimes, such meetings even with boys and girls of opposite community or even with non-tribals, develop into intimacy. Below is a song in which it is mentioned that a potter's girl and a Birhor's boy have fallen in love. The song belongs to Jadur category and the lines are as follows:

1. *Kunkăl-Munkăl dada, Kumbhar kuria dada*
   The potter's girl O brother
   Biyur, nachura dada, Birhoṛ koṛa
   The Birhor boy is making a round for her, brother

2. *Kumbhaṛ kuṛi honă dada, knoeyan jana dada*
   The potter's girl became bride, O brother
   Birhoṛ koṛa honă dada, boren jana
   The Birhor boy became the bridegroom, O brother

3. *Chetaṇ ṭola reya dada, koneyan janaya dada*
   In uppar tola, she became the bride, brother
   Lataṛ ṭola reya dada, boren jan
   In lower hamlet, he became the bridegroom, brother

As stated earlier other caste people also reside in Munda villages and there is close interaction among them. This has helped them in culture sharing. The result is that youths get ample opportunity for mixing with each other and sometimes cases of elopement or bringing the girl as wife is also reported. In such case the offenders are severely punished as per the tribal customary law. The above song is based on one such case in which a Birhor boy weds a potter's girl. Birhor is a distinct tribe other than Munda who belongs to Munda family. Kumhar or potter belong to low caste people.

Below in another song belonging to Lahsua category which also refers to love affairs between a tribal girl and a Jogi boy. The lines of the song are:

1. *Laṇg-laṇg dhotia, nirmala pichhora*
   Long sweeping dhoti with clean white pichhora
   Ho, hore, aisan buid nahiṇ janaloṇ re bhai
   Alas, I did not know such tricks, brother

Jogia sang piriti jorae
Developed friendship with a Jogi

2. *Hathe lelaiṇ gamechha, kandhe lelain sanduka*
Did hold shawl on the hand and box on their shoulder
Ho hore, aisan buid nahiṇ janaloṇ re bhai
Alas, I did not know such tricks
Jogia saṇg piriti jorae
Developed friendship with a Jogi

This song states a Munda girl's fancy for a *Jogi* boy. Like other Hindu castes in general, *Jogi*, a lower caste Hindu wears *dhoti* as loincloth. As stated, the *Jogi* boy always move about in his best dress with long sweeping *dhoti* with white shawl on his body. This way of dressing attracted the Munda girl and they may have run away one day. This became a burning topic for talk and someone composed the above song on the theme as stated.

A girl has made a forcible entry in a boy's house who she dearly loved. As stated in the song below, both were attracted towards each other by sheer fashion, otherwise they are a mismatch. People criticized this mismatch which became the talk of the day. This has been mentioned in the following Lahsua song, the lines of which are:

1. *Ka dekhi rijhale, ka dekhi lovale*
What took you fancy, what did attract you
Ho, hore, jhalari pati khosare baṇdhale
Alas, you made hair knot like horse tail
Ka dekhi jati ke dubale
What did you make to desert your tribe

2. *Toloṇg dekhi rijhale, khosa dekhi jati ke dubale*
Is it the sweeping loincloth? Or horse tailed fashion that made you desert the tribe
Ho, hore, jhalari paṭi khosare baṇdhale
Alas, you made hair knot like horse tail
Ka dekhi jati ke dubale
What did you make to desert your tribe

The boy and girl, mentioned in this song are highly fashionable. And it is this fashion that the two were attracted towards each other, otherwise the match was totally disliked by others. The criteria of making a match for marriage is not the fashion but something else. The fashion or dressing and style as mentioned in the song relates to the eastern part of the Munda country.

Cases of marriage by capture takes place when the proposal made by the boy's guardian is not accepted by the girl's guardian. In such a situation the people of the boy's party, in some market day or in some fair, forcibly carry away the girl to boy's house. The girl's guardian have ultimately to accept this relation and bride-price is demanded by the girl's guardian as per the custom. On some appointed day the marriage takes place and the matter is settled amicably.

Though the boys are not allowed to select the girl of their choice, but sometimes they do so and the choice later got approved by the elders. A go-between called *'dutam dari'* is sent later on the girl's house with the proposal so as to initiate the proper procedure of marriage. If the proposal is accepted by the girl's guardians, then the matter proceeds further otherwise it ends there. When the girl is pinpointed after the search, the would-be bridegroom makes his final decision when he sees the would-be bride at some convenient place, say some market place or fair. But observation is always done secretly. Below is one such song belonging to Jadur category in which a girl is reminded that she could not be selected though the fair is over. The lines of the song are as follows:

1. *Buru doko buru chaba keda mai*
   The fair is over O girl
   Ka na mai kam̥ juṛi jan
   You could not be selected
   Jatra doko Jatra ṭundu keda mai
   The Jatra fair is over O girl
   Ka na mai kam̥ joka jan
   You could not get your partner

2. *Ka na mai kam̥ juṛi jan*
   You could not be got selected

Sakam lekạm sala sare jana
You were set aside like discarded leaves
Ka na ma kạm joka jan
You could not get your partner
Chari lekạm piti bage jan
You were left like spare stitching pins

The fair is over and the girl could not be selected as bride. This situation of the girl has been compared with work of the people. Leaves are plucked from the forest for leaf cups or leaf plates. While plucking, they select the best one only. Similarly, while making leaf cups and plates, they select the fine bamboo splits as pins for stitching. In both cases, leaves and pins which are not good, are discarded. In the song, as stated, someone tells the girl that though the fair is over, she could not be selected for bride which is a matter of concern for the friends.

In the song below, a boy tells his mother about the girl he saw while going somewhere. He tells his mother about the personality of the girl whom he came across and heard about her. The song belongs to Bala category and the lines are:

Dahạr chalte-chalte dekhalo moe dumạri ka phool
While in journey, I saw a fig flower
Dumạri ka phool nayo
The fig flower, O mother
Daso kose gamakae nayo, biso kose gamakae
It has spread up its scent beyond ten to twenty *kos*

The delicious ripened fig fruit is liked by the people very much. When the fig flower, that is, fruit ripens, it spreads its scent in the environment. Similarly, when the girl attains the age of youthfulness, she is known by the youths of the neighbouring villages. In this song as stated, the boy was on his journey when he heard about the girl and was much impressed by her qualities. He tells his mother about the girl not directly but in a round about way because of shyness which is but natural for the youth of young age.

Though selection of girl is made by the elders, such selection are not always approved by the boy. The youths would generally like to select the girls of their own choice. This view of the youths has been described in the song below which belongs to *Jadur* category. The lines of the song run as follows:

1. *Kerkeṭa dutamo kain-a: dichuwa-a: daraṇ-o kaiṇ-o*
   I will not accept the selection of the go-between
   Aiṇg geiṇg sala joma, aiṇg geiṇg piti joma
   I myself will make selection and choice

2. *Dugu-mugu chaudol O kaiṇ-a, gaja-baja bajuṛio, kaiṇ-a*
   I will neither require palanquin nor band party
   Aiṇg geiṇg sala joma, aiṇg geiṇg piti joma
   I myself will make selection and choice

3. *Aiṇg geiṇg sala joma datraṇga joma kuṛi*
   I myself will make selection of a beautiful girl
   Aiṇg geiṇg piti joma, rola misi nela kuṛi
   I myself will choose the tinkling bell ornamented girl

Kerketa and Dichuwa are the two local birds who do shepherding to other small birds and usually depend upon their catch of insects, etc, for their food. Reference of these two birds are made in lieu of go-between for selection of brides whose help are normally taken by the parent of the boys. As mentioned, the boy refuses to accept the selection made by the go-between and goes by his own choice. He also refuses to engage band party as well as use of palanquin.

Disapproving of selection of marriage proposal occurs in cases when the boy or the girl has secret love affairs with someone. In the song below taken from Bala category, a situation has been mentioned when the regular meeting of the boy and girl will, most probably, develop into intimacy and love. Such relations are generally criticized by the elders. The girl, obsessed of such criticism tells them that had she been a boy, she would have carried out the job of ploughing and digging during the rains and would have cultivated the crops. The lines of the song are as follows:

1. *Jhbir-jhibir da-e gama led*
   It showered gently
   Bapahole kuṛi koṛae, har jotae, har jotae re
   I would have ploughed the fields had I been a boy
   Piṭ piṛi horare, raṇgaini baha lena
   On the way side of the market, Rangaini flower bloomed
   Nida mairem Jadur, susun kena
   You had song and dance during the night

2. *Kode holoṇg lăd leda re*
Baked bread from millets
Harạm teke tonka hora paromaja
She passed it through a hole to her husband
Piṭ piṛi hora re Raṇgaini baha lena
On the way side of the market, Rangaini flower bloomed
Nida mairem Jadur susun kena
You had song and dance during the night

The song carries another meaning also. It relates to illicit relations of the girl. Ploughing and cultivation, baking of bread and small hole are all symbolic to sexual organs and act of intercourse. These symbols and the meanings thereof are understood only by Mundas.

Marriage is a social obligation and like rule of nature it cannot be overlooked. The beauty of the person as well as the honour and dignity of the society is enhanced when the person is married. In other words, a person looks most beautiful only when he or she gets married. This view of the people have been expressed in the following Bala category of song, the line of which are as follows:

Hạm to dekhali Miṇjura ka jat re
I saw the species of peacock
Minjura ka jat baba jhail binu re sobhalaiṇ re
The specie of peacock looks beautiful without its tail
Hạm to dekhali raja beṭa jat re
I saw the prince of the king, specie
Raja beṭa jat baba rani binu re sobhalaiṇ re
The prince of king's specie looks beautiful without the queen
Hạm to dekhali haṇsa raja gora re
I saw the swan king all white
Haṇsa raja gora baba lil binu re sobhalaiṇ re
The king of swan looks beautiful without the hue of blue

In this song a person tells the other that there is beauty in being single or unmarried. The friend enumerates a number of examples who look beautiful in remaining unmarried. Having fun with opposite sex and enjoying each other's company through regular visits has beauty only after one marries the person with whom he has such relations. This idea is found in the following *Bala* category of song:

> *Raji-raji bulale falna, dese-dese bulale*
> You toured country after country O falna
> *Falna sadi binu sasurari sobhae*
> There is beauty only in having the *sasurari*

The above lines are the views of the girl who advises the boy to get settled in life by marrying a girl.

How to identify good and bad boy in the selection of bridegroom by the girl. These criteria have been mentioned in the following song. The elders warn the girl who generally dislikes fashionable boy. The song belongs to *Jadur* category and the lines are as follows:

1. *Laṇg-laṇg bondol chigo, tonom botoe*
   Would it be the long tailed loincloth or tattered dressed one
   Okoni mai regam sukuwai tana
   Which one of them you like O girl
   Laṇg-laṇg bondol chigo tonom botoe
   Would it be the long tailed loincloth or tattered dressed one

2. *Laṇg-laṇg bondol am sukuwai redo*
   If you like the long tailed loincloth one
   Ini do maire tạm kuṛi bage koṛa
   Such a boy may divorce his wife
   Tonom botoe mai rem napai redo
   If you choose a boy of tattered loincloth one
   Ini do mai re tạm ora-duar ni
   Such a boy is a family person

The above song indicates the index of the youth who would be the best husband. The experience of the elders tells that generally, fashion crazy boys fail to show themselves as good husband, for they have insatiable desire of fashion. A fashionable boy may like a girl who, in his eye is most fashionable and may marry him. But the facts in real life indicate that such marriage which is based on the consideration of fashion, does not last long and ends in divorce. On the other, the poorly dressed youth proves to be a faithful husband. The Munda give ample opportunity to their youths for making proper choice and decision in the selection of their life partner. The girls are specially advised to make right decision when the marriage proposal comes before her.

In case of wrong decision in matters of selection, the married life becomes troublesome. Mundas allow divorce to both the party equally. They also allow levirate and sorrorate marriages in the case of death of any member of the couple. Below is a song which states that a person is arranging his or her own marriage in old age. The children of the person have no knowledge of it. It is the neighbour who conveys this message to the children. The song belongs to Jadur category and the lines run as follows:

1. *Eṇgam mai budi dilare, eṇgam mai koneyan tan*
   Mother yours in old age is becoming bride O girl
   Apum mai bo chade re, apum mai boren tan
   Father yours at baldhead age is becoming bridegroom

2. *Eṇgam mai kajiai tabupe, eṇgam mai koneyan tan*
   Mother yours be told is becoming bride O girl
   Apum mai baṇkaṛai tabupe, apum mai boren tan
   Father yours be told, is becoming bridegroom

3. *Budi dilare koneyan tan, jati-jatige kajiaipe*
   Becoming bride at old age, tell her in strong words
   Bo chadere boren tan, kili nalaṇge baṇkaṛaipe
   Becoming bridegroom at baldhead age, be warned sternly

In case of death of any member of the couple, as stated above, the person alive is allowed to get married again, if young in age, he or she may even have children. But marriages in old age with grown up children are strongly opposed though it is not prohibited. The Mundas have extended family forms and a person has no problem in life even if he or she has no children and so marriage in old age does not serve any purpose in the family. Marriage in old age, therefore, attracts strong criticism from the people and may become their laughing stock.

Establishment of family by various ways such as *Raji-Khusi, Opor-tipi*, that is, by capture, Elopement, *dhuku* or *nir-bolo. Mago*, that is, by incestuous relation, are rare. Such relations are strongly denounced by the society and such couples are normally looked down upon. Public opinions against such practices are prepared through gossip, songs, phrases and short stories. Marriage by arrangement is the prevalent custom of the Mundas and many cognative tribes.

The Sequence of Arandi

Clan exogamy is the prevalent rule of marriage in Munda society. In case a person marries in his mother's clan or his or her cross-cousin's clans he or she can do so with the exclusion of the lineages of close blood relatives. The avoidance or exclusion of these immediate close relatives, is based on the ideas that they are the brothers and sisters in relation. Though as a rule, it is not a taboo but is discouraged.

Mundas are a patrilineal community for the sake of heredity and they practise patrilocal residence. And so in *Arandi* or arranged marriage, initiative is taken by the boy's guardians and never by the girl's. In case the latter takes initiative, something wrong is presumed with respect to the girl about such move.

Early or late marriage depends on the economic condition of the guardian or due to some social problems. Munda pay bride-price to the parents or guardian of the girl. The prevalent amount of bride-price is four heads of cattle. This ceiling has further gone down to three or even two. In some cases, even no bride price is paid, it depends on the mutual understanding of the party. It is due to this custom, often boy or girl remains unmarried. The custom of bride-price is denounced by the youths and songs with this theme have been composed by them.

Before placing proposal, the boy's guardians study all pros and cons of the girl's nature and that of her family's social background. Similarly, before accepting the proposal, the girl's guardians consider the boy's nature and character, his socio-economic condition and among other things, the diseases that the family inherits. All vital informations are collected and analysed before finalization of the agreement.

Search for suitable girl is undertaken by the lineage members as well as by the maternal uncle. It is the married women of the village who come from different clans and villages who bring proposal for the boy and girl of either of the village. They are the potential go-betweens.

Arranged marriages, better known as *Arandi* have several stages of ceremonies and to complete all the stages, it takes at least two to three years. After the acceptance of the proposal, each ceremony is performed under the guidance of *Dutam,* or *Agua* or *Dhechua,* that is, go-between. The different stages of ceremonies are (1) *Dutam-dari* or *Kurinel,* (2) *Da argu,* (3) *Ora nel,* (4) *Marang pera,* and (5) *Arandi.* It is rarely that the two stages are ever completed within a year's time. The various stages are described as follows:

Kurinel

Its literal meaning is to see the girl. The girl is first spotted by the kinsmen or other relatives of the boy. Sometimes, the *Agua* himself or herself brings the news or proposes before the boy's parents about the girl he or she has seen for the match. In other cases, the intending parent either send out some kinsmen or asks someone to find out a girl for the match of their boy. This activity is called *'Sangar'* in Mundari the literal meaning of which is hunting. Searching of girl is always kept secret among the few close relatives. If a relative of some distant village informs that there are few girls in his village of marriageable age and the boy should see and choose himself the girl of his likings, then the boy's parents send someone along with the boy with his few close friends to see the girl. They stay in the relative's house who later manages to show them the girls from a distance. If the boy likes any one of the girls, then they collect some more informations of the girl about her character and behaviour. If everything seems satisfactory, they return back and get someone who knows the girl's parents to act as go-between. This process is called *Dutam-dari* or *Kurinel* or *Sangar.*

Da-argu

This is the first formal stage in the long process of marriage. When the boy has chosen the girl or when there is possibility of accepting of the proposal of marriage then some close relatives, along with the boy and sometimes with the *agua,* visit the girl's house. Sometimes, prior information about the visit is communicated through somebody or they arrive at the girl's house all of a sudden. The purpose of their visit is then told and the proposal is then discussed with the girl's parents and their colaterals. The boy's party narrates every detail of their network of relationship and other vital information. If everything is normal and is agreeable to the proposal, then the guests are formally received by offering them water for washing and drinking, otherwise they are given nothing and return back to their village or somebody's house to stay with who happen to be their relative, however, distant he may be. If all agree on different aspects of the discussion, and parents of the girl agree for the relationship, then the date of *'Da-argu'* ceremony is fixed. In this rice-beer is served by the girl and the boy's father offer her few coins in confirmation which is known as *Baena*. Before this, feet of the guest are washed by the girl which indicates formal welcome to them. But *Baena* ceremony is performed only when the boy, that is, the would-be bridegroom is not present there. In case when the groom is present then after the acceptance of the proposal *'Da-argu'* ceremony is performed. In this ceremony, the girl, along with one or two close friends and also the boy with same number of friends, are made to stand or sit face to face. The girl is given a brass pot of water and both, the would-be bride and bridegroom are asked to exchange the pot. But before this, the girl is asked whether she agrees to the relationship. She is given enough time to discuss the matter with her friends who are present there, before she arrives at the decision and expresses it to the elders. There is no binding that the girl should agree to the proposal which might have been agreed by her parents. The girl has every liberty either to accept or reject. In case of latter situation, the *Da-argu* ceremony cannot be performed. But if the girl agrees in specific word of 'yes', then they exchange the brass pots of water and also exchange greeting saying *'Johar'* to each other as well as to all present there. The girl then washes the feet of the guests, serves rice-beer to them, and it is at this occasion that the boy's parents offer few coins to the would-be bride which is called '*Baena*'. The Haprom, that is, ancestor spirits are then worshipped with the water of the brass pot. If after the acceptance of the proposal, *Da-argu* ceremony could not be performed due to one reason or the other, in that case, a suitable date is fixed for the ceremony.

Ora Nel

This is 'to see the house ceremony performed at the boy's house after the *Da-argu* ceremony. A suitable date is fixed for the visit of the girl's guardians to the boy's house with the sole purpose to see the house of the boy and acertain the genuineness of the boy as well as his socio-economic condition. In this ceremony, only the female relatives, consisting of five to ten members participate. They normally happen to be the mother of the girl, her aunties and all her grandmothers.

Hora Pari or Chenre Uri

It is the ceremony in which the omens are consulted, read and scrutinized. On an appointed day, the boy's guardians, along with lineage members and other relatives, proceed to the girl's village after offering *Tapan* (rice-beer) to their ancestral spirits. The party observes various events and keeps its records in their memory from the very start of their journey till they cross their own village boundary. Similarly, when the party arrives at the girl's village boundary and enters into it, similar records are made of the events. The events which occur beyond these two village boundaries of either of the boy or the girl are however ignored for they have no meaning for the sake of the omen. When the party reaches the girl's house, they are received and are offered seats on the courtyard. The *agua* then describes the whole details of their journey and also their observation of omen. The various aspects of the omen, their good and bad implications are then discussed. If the omen does not indicate any bad implications, the business proceeds, otherwise the party returns with no further negotiation, however, they are given dinner for the night. If the result of the omen is favourable, the feet of the guests are washed and are entertained with rice-beer and feast. Seeing or reading of omen is not the consulting of supernatural spirits but they are natural events, the reading of which is based on the past experience of the people. It is believed and accepted by the people that Supreme God Singbonga through nature directs and foretells the future happenings of events. It is the Singbonga, who regulates and directs the universe, speaks with people through nature. The activity of human beings, birds, animals, reptiles or insects and happening with plants and other material objects all indicate the events that may occur in future. These events are read at every occasion of importance. N.C. Choudhury (1978:83) has mentioned few of these omens in these words: Some of the good omens are: a fox or a cock calling out, a cow and her calf calling each other, a girl carrying a pitcher full of water. Bad omens are: a snake or fox crossing the path, a cow bellowing, a crow coughing but not calling out in the usual way, a girl carrying an empty pitcher and so on. The events that carry omens are not concealed at the time of its narration. If, at the start of the journey, one sees a bad omen, the journey is abandoned and they take the journey afresh later on. They, at least, try three times but if all the time they get bad omen, no attempt is made any more and the programme is abandoned. This is how the nature keeps the secret of life to which the Mundas are aware of and seek meanings from every event.

Hora-pari ceremony is, however, not the final reading of omens. At every ceremony, till the marriage is over, omen is scrutinized.

As stated earlier, if the *Da-argu* ceremony could not be performed in the course of searching the girl, it is performed after the *Hora pari* ceremony.

Marang-pera

During this ceremony, *Gonong*, that is, bride-price is received by the guardians of the girl. As scheduled, during this ceremony, the bride relatives are invited at the boy house. The date of visit is settled earlier by the *agua* with the consultation of both the parties. In this ceremony, only the male members of the girl's relatives and close neighbours participate. They are led by the *agua* and omen is again recorded during the journey. On arrival to the boy's house, they are received and are offered seats in the courtyard already arranged for them. The omen is then deciphered. The feet of the guests are then washed and are entertained with rice-beer and feast. The guest and the host both participate in night long singing. Next day early in the morning, *Urij-taping* ceremony is performed. The guests are led to the field where cattle have been taken for grazing. The guests and hosts sit separately from each other. The *agua* brings the cattle before them and the guests are shown which one's the boy's parents have chosen for payment of bride-price. The guests may reject any of the cattle shown to them. In that case they are shown another cattle if there is any, or they are assured of sending the cattle later on but before the marriage. If the cattle is acceptable, the grandparents or the maternal uncle of the girl, strikes pebbles on each of the selected cattle to seal the acceptance. All then return to the house and *neg* or ceremonial rice-beer are given to the guests which is known as *Urij-taping tapan*. After this a series of ceremonies are performed, such as (a) *Da-argu*—the water is ceremonially taken by the parents of the girl from the boy, (b) *Bala-haprom*—in laws—meet ceremonially, (c) *Sunum-goso*—anointing of oil to the guest by the ladies, (d) *Bidauti*—giving the farewell to the guest. During all these ceremonies, separate set of rice-beer is served which is known as *Tapan*. The guests are then entertained with a sumptuous feast in which all the invitees of the boy also participate. At the time of farewell, the guests are once again served rice-beer known as *Bidauti Tapan*. The cattle are then led by the youths towards the girl's village and are handed over later to the bride's party at the boundary of the village. It is during the *Marang Pera* ceremony that all the relatives—agnates and affinals of the groom are introduced to the bride's party and *vice versa*.

Marriage can take place in any month except *Fagun* and *Chait*, that is, February and March respectively. Marriage cannot be celebrated on Tuesday, Thursday and Saturday for they are considered *khar din*, that is, strong or bad days. The birthday of the would-be bridegroom and bride are also avoided. If there is death in the family, its *Jang Topa* or last rite ceremony must be performed before the marriage. No marriage generally takes place during the rainy season as well as during the busy working months. This is, of course, not the rule but a convenience.

There is a sequence of ceremonies in marriage. These are: (a) *Kuarbar Argu* or *Charn Argu*, (b) *Mandba Dul*, (c) *Kalsa-Galang*, (d) *Mergharai* or *Bala Daparom*, (e) *Uli or Madkam Arandi*, that is, tree marriage, (f) *Samdia Hipirchi or Bala Haparub*, (g) *Bor-Ageya*, (h) *Sasang Goso*, (i) *Jang Da*, (j) *Sinduri Rakab*, (k) *Da-Au*, (1) *Chauli Heper*, (m) *Samdhi Bhent*, (n) *Chuman*, (o) *Baba Her Tuka*, (p) *Lota Uku Inung*, (q) *Jima and* (r) *Gati Bage*, etc.

Chem or *Kuarbar Argu* and *Kalsa Galang* ceremonies are performed much earlier than the actual day of marriage. The former rite is performed, in case the girl or the boy has been tied skin by the blacksmith at the time of their birth to protect and save the life of the child. Fastening of skin to the infant is believed to protect the baby from the evil spirit. It is done only in case when one or two babies earlier to the existing one have died after few days of their birth. The latter ceremony is performed in the name of the boy or girl who is to be married during the year. During rainy season, when transplantation of paddy takes place in the field of the family, the paddy stalks in bundles are pitched at the centre of the field. All the persons involved in the transplantation of paddy, smear clay to each other in the name of the boy or the girl. At the end when the day's work is over, all the participants are invited for the feast. Again, on an appointed day, breads are baked from rice flour and all the participants are invited. They are served rice-beer and bread. This custom is observed by every family where the marriage of any of their boy or girl takes place during the year.

Lagan Tol is, of course, the first step in the sequence of whole marriage process. It is the fixation of marriage date by the *agua* which is done in consultation of both the parties. Two more ceremonies are observed after the marriage when the bride settles down in her new home with her husband. The ceremonies are: (a) *Heta Ruar,* and (b) *Bahurat.*

Marriage is a biological as well as social necessity for the continuity of society. Arranged marriage is the only socially approved form and all must follow it for the honour and dignity of the individual as well as of the society. Through marriage new social relations are established and the existing ones are strengthened. These relations are authenticated by the Supreme God Singbonga as well as by the ones ancestral spirits for they are invoked at every stage and sequence of marriage and are guided by them. The relations thus, established are permanent and sacred. This feature of marriage as well as its socio-psychological implications and various cultural features have been described through the songs composed by the youths themselves.

When the proposal comes from the sources other than the would-be bridegroom himself, the girl is asked of her choice, whether to accept it or not. In the following song, the girl is being asked of her choice. The song belongs to Jadur category and the lines are as follows:

1. *Chanḍu kore chanḍuyo dada*
   Among all moons brother

Chanḍu birang barang
The moon shines sparkle brightest
Ipil kore ipilyo dada
Among all stars brother
Ipil biring-biring
The brightest twinkling star

2. *Chanḍu kore chal tạm re*
If you are given away to the moon
Napaya chi kagi
Would you like it or not
Ipil kore goṇg tạm re
If you are married away to the star
Sukua chi banogi
Will you agree or not

3. *Suku doreṇg sukuya dada*
I will agree, but brother
Pokhari pinḍa kora baha
The flowers of the ponds
Okoe bahaya
Who will decorate thereafter.

The moon and star implies two meanings in the above song. In one it means that the bridegroom is one of the best, and in other, he comes from a far off land. The girl agrees to be married away in the land of the moon and stars but she feels too much to leave behind the joy and happiness which she has so far enjoyed in decorating herself with the lotus flowers of the ponds.

But in the song which follows, the girl is aware that she cannot escape from the marriage bond and requests her parents and brothers that if she is given in marriage at all, she should not be given in a distant village and poor family. The song belongs to the Jadur category and the lines are as follows:

1. *Saṇgin disum re eṇgam apum*
In distant country, O dear parents
Alore gatiṃ rem kaji kule
Don't send words of relationship O friend

Jiling gamae re hagam barem
Brothers and sisters in far off village behind
Alore sangain rem bankar chale
Don't talk of marriage O friend,

2. *Alore gatim rem kaji kule*
Don't send words of relationship friend
Engam apum ko renge tana
Parent there are poor
Alore sangain rem bankar chale
Don't talk of marriage, friend
Hagam barem ko tetang tan
Brothers and sisters are living in scarcity

Distant village and poor family, both are disliked by the girls for their future household. The reason is that they would like to see their parents and brothers and sisters off and on and during all occasions, and if they are given in distant villages, such visits are not possible. Similarly, the poor family and particularly those who have small quantity of agricultural lands are also not liked by the girls. For such family may live in condition of perpetual starvation.

Marriageable girls generally talk among themselves about the geographical regions whare they would like to be get married, the kind of prospective husbands and the types of houses, etc. In the song below which belongs to Jadur category, the girl asks her brother not to give her in marriage in areas where Madkam and Sarjom trees are available, for the basic reasons which the song mentions in the following lines:

1. *Madkam raji reya dada, alom gong-inya dada*
Don't give me in marriage in country where Madkam tree grows
Sarjom gamae re dada, alom chala-inya
Don't give me in villages where Sarjom tree grows, brother

2. *Madkam raji reya dada, nida duru-durua dada*
There is night long walking in country where Madkam tree grows

Sarjom gamae re dada, singi laya-koya
In villages where Sarjom tree grows, there is stooping all the day

The above kind of desires are found among the girls whose parents are in the region where there is no forest. The girls of forestless regions are not habituated in the collection of Madkam and Sarjom flowers which are taken as food. While the girls of the forest regions do not like to be get married in treeless regions for they have their own likes and dislikes.

In Search of the Bride

When the boy or girl attains the marriageable age, it is the obligation of the parents, lineage members and maternal uncles to search the bride and arrange the marriage. When the boy or the girl has no parent, then the lineage members and the maternal uncle do the duty of the parents and help the boy or the girl in all respects. In the song below which belongs to Bala category, the boy's maternal uncle is out in search of bride for the nephew. The lines of the song are as follows:

Mami ho mama to hamar kahaṇ gel
Mami where did my mama go
Bhagina ho, mama Biru Pargana miṇjur marek gelaiṇ
Dear nephew, mama yours been to Biru Pargana to hunt peacock
Mama ho miṇjur tora baṛa chalitaṛ pani piyae
Dear mama, peacock yours drinks water very cautiously

Children develop great attachment to their maternal uncle and aunt and usually spend much of their childhood days with them. As stated in the song, the boy is living with his maternal uncle and the latter is searching bride for him. The boy has already seen the girl and the maternal uncle has gone to settle the proposal. The boy is in apprehension that the girl's parents may not accept the proposal. The song is in conversational form between the boy and her aunt.

In the song below, the go-between is called Ravana—the villain of great epic *Ramayana*. The song belongs to *Bala* category and the lines are as follows:

Kahaṇ se alaiṇ sahjala mahajan
From where did come the shameless creditor
Raja Ramchander se saṇge saj maṇgae
Asks friendship with king Ramchander
Sitá saṇge tal maṇgae
Asks the hand of Sita
Pacchim se alaiṇ raja Ravana
From the west did the king Ravana come
Raja Ramchander se saṇge saj maṇgae
Asks friendship with the king Ramchander
Sita saṇge tal maṇgae
Asks the hand of Sita

In this song, the go-between has either been identified with the creditor, that is, *mahajan* or with Ravana, as such both are not welcomed by the girls. They are the symbols of evil doers, for in case the proposal is accepted, the girl will be separated from her parents after the marriage when she is carried away like the Sita by the Ravana-husband.

The following song too, is based on the same theme. It belongs to Bala category and the lines are:

Kahaṇ se ale re Suya bhai
From where did you come O brother searcher
Suya bhai jaṇgal bhitare, suya bhai gaṇga jal jorae
Within the dense forest, you are establishing friendship O brother searcher
Purbe se ale re suya bhai
You did come from the east O brother searcher
Suya bhai jaṇgal bhitare, suya bhai gaṇga jal jorae
Within the dense forest, you are eastablishing friendship O brother searcher
Pachhim se alere suya bhai
You did come from the west O brother searcher
Suya bhai jaṇgal bhitare, suya bhai gaṇga jal jorae
Within the dense forest, establishing friendship O brother searcher

The go-between through which marriage relations are established, are given various terms such as, *Suya*, *Kerketta*, *Dhechua*, and *Agua*, etc. From selection of bride to final ceremony of marriage, the go-between takes up the leadership. He, besides knowing the detailed process of marriage and ritual, must possess the quality of a leader who tackles all intricacies and handles with tact and intelligence the unprecedented situation that arises in the whole course of marriage ceremony. He should be a shrewd and clever person. He plays the role of a guide, an adviser and consultant besides a friend and relative of both the parties. When the proposal is accepted, he, in consultation of both the parties, fixes the dates of visits for the completion of each stage of marriage. He helps the parties in arriving at the acceptable condition of bride-price. He keeps records of the good and bad omens throughout the marriage process. Service of the go-between is a selfless service, but when the marriage is over, he as well as his wife receive a piece of cloth and the best portion of the meat at each ceremony.

The song mentions that the *Suya* or go-between brings the two unknown families into relationship of permanent friendship. Ganga *jal,* literally means the water of the Ganga, has the meaning of friendship in Mundari.

Another song belonging to Bala category describes the go-between as a Brahmin who asks alms from door to door. The lines of the song are as follows:

> *Kahere bamaṇ beṭa dura-dura baisae, piṇḍa-piṇḍa baisae*
> Why O son of the Brahmin, sit door to door and portico to portico
> *Na dege kisanin aroa ka chaur, hia muṇgia dal*
> Don't offer him unboiled rice and cleaned up pulse
> *Eato ahe kaneya ka love*
> He has come but for the sake of bride

When the proposal is placed before the parents of the girl, the matter is discussed among the lineage members for its acceptance or rejection. The subjects of discussion are usually the boys age, his character, social and economic status of the parents and presence and absence of inherited diseases, etc. If the boy and his family background is good, the matter is left for the girl who takes the final decision. She also tries to know at her own level, through her friends about the boy. If the proposal is unacceptable, the girl's guardians do not reject the proposal outright or flatly, but make a number of pretensions. The most often excuses are their own poverty and girl's unwillingness to marry so early. This is done in good faith instead of flat rejection which may harm the future proposal of the boy or girl. The main reason of dislikes, are thus, kept secret by both the parties. The path of marriage is kept open for both.

As stated in the song the go-between visits every prospective bride's house with the proposal or merely to assess the willingness or otherwise. A would-be bridegroom who goes on seeing the girls only is also disliked and it may be difficult to get him married. As mentioned in the song, such persons should not be attended to.

It is the boy's guardian and not the girl's, as custom and a rule that initiate the talk of proposal for their wards. It is where there are marriageable girls, the bride seekers from all directions arrive to the girl's house with their proposals. The song below describes this scene in the following lines which belongs to the Bala category.

> *Hariyaro dhana nayo, hariyaro dhana re*
> The green paddy mother, the green paddy
> *Hariyaro dhana nayo sugawa heil parae re*
> Parrots alight on the green paddy, mother
> *Kekaṛ beṭi nayo, baṛhal beṭi kuṇwar re*
> In the house where there is grown up unmarried girl
> *Sekara ghare nayo manowa heil parae re*
> In his house people make crowd, mother

It is generally observed that where there is standing crop in the field, parrots come down there in good number. Similarly, in houses with grown up unmarried girls, people with marriage proposals arrive from all directions.

In marriage proposals, both the parties—boys as well as girls, want that they should find the best match for their wards. This is why some families receive proposals from a number of prospective bridegrooms and go on to study their detailed personal and economic background and then accept the suitable proposal. But since bride as well as bridegroom both are of floating nature at this age and cannot wait for long time, such families often fall in trouble, for sometimes, no one would like to establish the match with such families. So, some prefer first come first serve approach and settle the match early. They usually say that if the first proposal is rejected, who knows, people of what background would come next. So, it is thought better by them to accept the first proposal. The song below which belongs to Bala category has this theme, the lines of which run as follows:

> *Kekara beti nayo kera aisan boṛe re*
> Whose daughter has grown up like a banana tree, mother
> *Jait alaiṇ, kuṭumb alaiṇ, aṇgena khuṇḍalaiṇ,*
> When people of own tribe and affinal relatives arrive and touch down the courtyard
> *Kaise phirab nawa re gotia*
> How shall one send back the new affinal relatives
> *Raja ker beṭi nayo kera aisan boṛe re*
> It is the king's daughter, mother has grown up like banana tree, mother
> *Jait alaiṇ kuṭum alaiṇ aṇgena khuṇḍalaiṇ*
> When people of own tribe and affinal relatives arrive and touch down the courtyard
> *Kaise phirab nawa re gotia*
> How shall one send back the new affinal relatives

The first precondition for the proposal to be accepted is that the proposer should belong to one's own tribe and second from a clan other than one's own. So, when such relatives come with proposal, if it is acceptable keeping in view the other criteria, they are never sent back. The song also mentions that girls generally attain the physical maturity much earlier than the boys of the same age group. It is due to this fact that the girl is said to have grown up like a banana tree. It is observed that banana tree grows up rapidly in short period of time, so also the girls.

Marriage proposal creates a psychological disturbance for the girl. She never would have seriously thought of marriage and bidding farewell to her loving parents and friends. But when the proposal of marriage comes and is accepted by the parents, she finds herself in a precarious situation. Marriage will force her to leave the parent's house as well as her childhood friends and take her to a stranger's house and among the strangers. The thought of living with an unknown person, with apprehensions of his behaviour as well as his parents and the economic condition of the family there, all make her mind much disturbed. Such psychological disturbances are observed in any Munda life on occasions of birth, separation, marriage and death. The latter situation is psychologically more disturbing. When the marriage proposal comes, from the very moment the girl feels uprooted from the family. The song below belonging to Jadur category describes the state of mind of the girl. The lines of the song are as follows:

1. *Niku dore eṇgaiṇg oko horo ko*
   Who are these people, mother
   Niku dore apuiṇg chimae hoṛo ko
   To where these people belong to, father

2. *Niku dore ho maina am̂ dutam̂ ko*
   These people are asking of you O daughter
   Niku dore ho maina am̂ daraṇ ko
   These people are in search of you, daughter

3. *Sim kusuli rega eṇgaing uku taiṇg me*
   Hide me in the fowl's den, O mother
   Mara dopali rega apuiṇg danaŋg taiṇg me
   Put me at a distance of peacock's flight, O father

4. *Âm ge china ko nam̂ tana risa bo dae-dae*
   Are they searching you, O dishevelled head
   Âm ge china ko nam̂ tana chala bo dui-dui
   Have they come for you, O dust covered head

The girl has come back from the fields work as the song indicates that still she has dishevelled head with dust. She finds that some people are sitting in the house who are totally strangers to her. When she comes to know that they have come to see her, she feels shy and wants to hide herself but her mother tells her that they have not come for her for she still is a child. This very theme is told in the following song too, which belongs to *Jadur* category, the lines of which are as follows:

1. *Sen dulū-dulū reko nel led ma*
   They saw you first when you were walking staggeringly
   Supid barai-burui reko china led ma
   They had identified you when you had a small hair knot

2. *Nel-nelma tegena maim suku jumbar jan*
   In a twinkling of time you did attain a sturdy growth
   Chiname-chiname tegena maim lamka-landir jan
   You have grown up voluminously unrecognizably in a short time

3. *Uku taing meya engaing sim kusuli re*
   Hide me in the fowl's den, mother
   Danang taing meya apuing merom gudri re
   Conceal me in goat's shed, father

4. *Am gena ko nam tana risa bo dae-dae*
   Are they searching you, O dishevelled head
   Am gena ko daran tana chala bo dui-dui
   Have they come for you, O dust covered head

Persons who have seen the girl in her childhood age, are now hardly able to recognize her for she has now grown up into a young lady. But in the eyes of her parents, she still is a child and she has all the childhood simplicity and is quite ignorant of her age and physical growth. When people comment on her physical growth, she feels shy and wants to hide herself.

All these songs indicate that marriage proposal is made to the girl's parents when she is in the adolescent age. But by the time of marriage, she attains adulthood, as we will see in subsequent pages that the actual marriage takes place in about three years period after the proposal is accepted.

The boys and girls, both have equal rights in accepting and rejecting the proposals. The song below states one such case in which the girl has rejected the proposal though it was accepted by her guardians. The song belongs to Jadur category, the lines of which are as follows:

1. *Chia kore sida suku kaji do, chia korem, giri keda*
   Why did you reject the first good news

Chia kore tayom napae baṇkaṛ do, chia korem riring keda
Why did you forget the last best advice

2. *Chia deraŋ kajiam tana do, chia deraŋ kạm ayume*
Why don't you pay heed to the talk
Chia deraŋ alo-alo mente, chia deraŋ iṇg asdi jana
I have been fed up in advising you
Chia deraŋ ocho-ocho mente, chia deraŋ iṇg mukuiṇg jana
I have become sick of forbidding you

As mentioned in this song, the girl rejected the proposal which the parents had accepted. Thus, there is no guarantee that when the proposal is accepted by the parents it would also be accepted by the girl or the boy. This situation arises during *Da-argu* ceremony. The proposal, as mentioned in the song, was accepted by the guardians and they were too glad for the relation. On an appointed day the bridegroom along with the go-between and other kin members were invited in the bride's house to perform the *Da-argu* ceremony. The girl was advised to say 'yes' to the proposal. In this ceremony, the boy and the girl along with a friend each, stand or sit face to face and are asked whether they agree to the relationship. If they agree, they perform the ceremony of exchanging the brass-pot of water and greet each other and all present there. If not, no ceremony will be performed and the party returns back without any further talk on the matter. It is at this time, as mentioned in the song, the girl disagreed with the proposal. This made the parents disturbed as they had repeatedly advised her to accept the proposal. It is now too late and the proposal cannot be negotiated further.

The guests who come with proposal to the girl's house, are given warm welcome. Following are few songs which indicate how warmly they are received. The guest who come to see the girl turn up to the latter's house without prior intimation. The songs which belong to Lahsua category describes the awkward situation of the girl's guardians at the sudden arrival of the guest. The lines of the song are as follows:

1. *Siṇgi hasur nudum-nudum*

At the twilight after the sunset
Kupul kodo ko hiju akna
The guest have arrived
O hore maina, gaṇdu bano pati bila kom
There is no stool, spread up mat for them, O daughter

2. *Kupul kodo ko hiju âkna*
The guest have arrived
Maṇdi tabu banoa
We have no food
Maina, maṇdi bano, maṇdi auwa kom
We have no food, bring food for them, O daughter

3. *Kupul kodo ko hiju ǎkna*
The guest have arrived
Maina, hai baṇko, hai auwa kom
We have no fish, bring fish for them, O daughter

As mentioned in this song, the host was surprised as there was no arrangement at all to receive the guests. The girl is guided by the father or mother to make some arrangements hurriedly. It is told that there was no sitting arrangement in the house and the girl is asked to spread the mat instead of chairs or stools as there is none in the house. Similarly, the food which was available served the needs of the household members only. As there was no extra rice, the girl was asked to bring it from the neighbour's house. The guests are generally entertained with best of food and drinks. Fish, chicken and meat are considered special food for the guests by the Mundas. And as stated in the song, even fish are not available in the house, so the girl is asked to manage it from the neighbours. This is humiliating affair for the family but there are kinsmen all the time to help each other.

The song which follows belongs to Bala category and mentions the condition of extreme poverty of the host party. The lines are as follows:

Siṇgi doe dubui jan, kupul ko hiju tan
The Sun has set in and the guest are coming
Saona regi paṭi bila kom

Spread up mat on the portico itself
Ganḍuyo bano jan, paṭiyo bano jan
Neither there is stool, nor mat
Marya ote regi duba rika kom
Make them sit on the floor itself
Kocha-kochaiṇg honor keda, basao kaiṇg nam keda
Searched every household of the village, but resting place there is none
Helaya kupul ko, paṭiyo bano jan, basayo bano jan
Neither there is mat nor resting place. O dear guest
Samage ko gitika
Let them sleep without it

For poor family, even one or two guests are a big problem. The family has no mat to sit upon nor even resting place. The guests are told frankly that they have none to offer and were requested to sleep on the open ground. The host tried their best to find a resting place for the guests by visiting other kin members but as no one has house big enough to accommodate even one or two members of the guests, he returned helplessly.

On the other hand, the families whose economic conditions are better, entertain their guests decently. A song belonging to Bala category mentions this theme. The lines of the song are as follows:

Kohan kera eest kuṭum ai gelaiṇ—ai gelaiṇ
The guest from where have arrived
Dekhu-dekhu baba murgi guṛa
Look out into the fowl's den
Kahaṇ kera eest kuṭum ai gelaiṇ-ai gelaiṇ
The guest from where have arrived
Dekhu-dekhu baba chhagri guṛa
Look out into the goat's shed
Kahaṇ kera eest kutum ai gelaiṇ-ai gelaiṇ
The guest from where have arrived
Dekhu-dekhu-dekhu baba suwari guṛa
Look out into the pig's shed

The guests are not given any chance to complain about the food or their comfort. As mentioned in this song, the hosts are trying their best to entertain the guests with best food.

Sometimes all the marriage plans and programmes are foiled when the would-be bride or bridegroom run away with their sweetheart. A song belonging to Jadur category describes this phenomenon. The lines of the song are as follows:

1. *Aṛandi mente hoiṇg chauli leda*
   I husked rice for the purpose of marriage
   Kupul ta-ai kuṛi honae koneyan jana
   The would-be bride got herself married

2. *Koṛandi mente hoiṇg dali leda*
   I prepared pulse for the sake of marriage feast
   Boren koṛa honae agu aderana
   The would-be bridegroom has brought in his wife

3. *Hiatiṇg moneiṇga, chakatiṇg sanaiṇga*
   I am worried and deeply upset
   Kaji ta-ai kuṛi honae koneyan jana
   The proposed bride got married

4. *Hiatiṇg moneiṇga, chakatiṇg sanaiṇga*
   I am worried and deeply upset
   Boren koṛa honae agu aderana
   The would-be bridegroom has brought in his wife

The situation as mentioned above, is not a strange one among the Mundas but it creates a lot of problems for the guardians and is strongly disliked. The song mentions that everything is ready for the celibration of marriage but, in the mean time, the girl or the boy got her or his partner and have started living as husband and wife. In such a situation, if the girl finds another boy as her husband, all the bride-price which the girl's parents have collected from the would-be bridegroom, would have to be returned. They cannot keep even a single item. But if the boy takes another girl as his wife, he cannot claim back the bride-price which he has given to the girl's parents. The preparation of marriage becomes a wastage.

As stated earlier, when the proposal is accepted and *'Da-argu'* ceremony is over, an all women party pay a visit to the boy's house to ascertain and assess the actual condition of his socio-economic background. This ceremony is called *'Ora nel.'* Below is a song belonging to Bala category which says that the mothers have come to see the house. The song describes as to how a Munda constructs his house. The would-be bridegroom tells the details of house construction to the honourable mothers in the lines as follows:

> *Ghar dekhi nale nayoge*
> You have come to see the house, mother
> *Ghar tora ringi-chingi, ghar tora bana-china re*
> The house has been colourfully built
> *Dharti nupare gaṛha moe koṛalo*
> I dug up a hole on the ground
> *Gaṛha nupare khuṇta moe gaṛalo*
> I pitched a post on the hole
> *Khuṇta nupare maloa moe chaṛalo*
> I placed a *Maloa* on the post
> *Moloa upare dharna moe chaṛalo*
> I placed a *dharna* on the *maloa*
> *Dharna upare maniktham moe chaṛalo*
> I placed *maniktham* on the *dharna*
> *Maniktham upare kaṇd moe chaṛalo*
> I placed *kaṇd* upon the *maniktham*
> *Kaṇd upare Bata moe chaṛalo*
> Upon *kaṇd I* placed *Bata*
> *Bata upare khapṛa moe chaṛalo*
> I placed *khapṛa* upon the *Bata*
> *Khapṛa upare pani nai barisae*
> There is no rainfall on the tiles
> *Ghar dekhi nale nayoge*
> You came to see the house, mother
> *Ghar tora ringi-chingi, ghar tora bana-china re*
> The house has been colourfully built

The would-be bridegroom tells his mother-in-law how he constructed the house from different items. He also tells them that since the completion of the house, there is no rain. In short, it is a fine description of how the Mundas construct their houses.

Bride-price

Among the Mundas and many other neighbouring tribes, there is the custom of bride-price. Each member is an economic value for the family. Economic prosperity depends upon the number of able-bodied working members in the family. This is why, when a person's services are obtained from another person as one's family member on permanent basis or for a fixed period of time, they have to pay some stipulated amount in kind or fixed number of cattle heads in lieu of the services to the guardian of the person. This is why, when the girl is married away in another family, the boy who has married the girl, has to pay the bride-price to the parents of the girl. The custom has both good and bad aspects. The custom of bride-price and the views of the people with respect to it, have not remained constant in the culture history of the people. The girls who are subjected to bride-price, also look at the custom differently. Below are given few songs which reveal the views of the people on the custom of the bride-price. The birth of male and female child, is therefore, an indication of either an economic prosperity or poverty. The song below, which belongs to Bala category, describes this viewpoint of the people. The lines of the song are as follows:

> *Chaṇḍu doe muli lena numa*
> At the appearance of new moon, mother
> *Kuṛi hon doe janam̭ lena*
> The baby girl was born
> *Siṇgi doe tur lena numa*
> At the rising Sun, mother
> *Koṛa hon doe janam̭ len*
> The baby boy was born
> *Kuṛi hon doe janam̭ lena numa*
> The baby girl was born, mother
> *Goraṇ do perej jana*
> The cattle-shed was filled up
> *Koṛa hon doe janam̭ lena numa*
> The baby boy was born, mother
> *Goraṇ do ujaṛ jana*
> The cattle-shed became empty

On the very theme as above, below is another song which belongs to Bala category, the lines of which are as follows:

1. *Koṟa hon do janạm lena umana*
The baby boy was born, O mother
Goraṇ do suna jana umana
The cattle-shed became desolate, O mother
Goraṇ do suna jana
The cattle-shed became desolate

2. *Kuṛi hon doe janạm lena umana*
The baby girl was born, O mother
Goraṇ do pere jana umana
The cattle-shed was filled up, O mother
Goraṇ do pere jana
The cattle-shed was filled up

3. *Goraṇ do pere jana umana*
The cattle-shed was filled up, O mother
Hagate, hilite guri-racha jo: jo:te landa tana
While cleaning cattle-shed and courtyard, her brother and sister-in-law are laughing merrily

The above two songs indicate that the birth of the girl and the boy is a symbol of economic prosperity and poverty. There is peace and happiness at the appearance of new moon, so also the birth of the baby girl in the family. The birth of the boy, on the other hand, is compared with the sunrise which makes the day. Because of patriarchal system of inheritance, the male child is considered to be the light of the family like the sun. But economically, the birth of male child brings poverty in the family. This very fact has been explained through the songs.

Mundas have the custom of bride-price and cattle is the only medium for such exchanges. Since Mundas are the settled agricultural tribe, land and cattle are the most important factors of production. Cultivation is carried out through plough technology and cattle are the primary source of energy as the ploughs are drawn by the cattle only. Land requires manuring and the cattle dung is the only source of fertilizer. As residence after marriage is patrilocal, the girl moves into the house of her husband and in lieu of this, her parents receive back a number of cattle heads. So, a family may become rich or poor on the basis of presence and absence of cattle in the family and not on the basis of quantity and quality of land. The absence of cattle in the family is usually made up through the presence of working force, that is, the number of able bodied workers in the family. In short, economic prosperity depends on the number of baby girls in the family. Each girl fetches four heads of cattle in the family according to the custom. So, if a family has more number of girls than boys, there will be an economic boom in the family. On the other hand, if the family has more male children or only boys, such families have to face poverty. There are two reasons for it, (a) land will be divided among the brothers and, as such, its economic holding goes on reducing which affects the production, and (b) when the boys get married four heads of cattle against each boy will be given away to the bride's guardians, this reduces the number of ploughs as well as the quantity of manure. The result is obvious. In short, as mentioned in the song, the cattle-shed is filled up at the birth of girls and becomes empty at the birth of boys. And as mentioned in the second song, the girl's brother and her sister-in-law (brother's wife) will be the happiest persons at the marriage of the sister for they will get a good number of cattle heads.

Due to the prevalence of the custom of bride-price, sometimes, there arises a grave problem before the boy's parents, particularly when they have no extra cattle or when they are unable to manage it from somewhere. As mentioned in the subsequent song which belongs to Bala category, besides bride-price, the other items of demands can be reduced through discussion by the parties. This fact has been mentioned in the following song:

Ka me kinạb nayo, ka me kinạb re
With which we shall purchase mother, with which
Ka me kinạb nayo, rae muli sundạr kaneya
With which shall we purchase, mother, the beautiful bride
Bat me kinạb nayo, lali charaiya bulare
We shall purchase with sweet voice of our talk like brids
Jabana me kinạb nayo, rae muli sundạr kaneya
We shall purchase with words that bind, the beautiful bride

Kachia me kinab nayo, dhebua me kheja karab re
We shall bargain with money, mother
Jabana me kinab nayo, rae muli sundar kaneya
We shall purchase with words that bind, the beautiful bride

The song is in the form of conversation between the mother and son. The latter is worried because the family has no extra heads of cattle for bride-price. The mother tells the boy that bride can be brought by mutual understanding and discussion. The number of heads of cattle to be offered to the girl's guardian are in the case, either reduced or the boy's parents are given more time for the procurement of cattle. This concession is arrived at through discussion only.

To receive the bride-price, a special ceremony is observed by the Mundas which is called *Marang Pera*. During this ceremony, bride's relatives are invited by the boy's party. The boy's parent at this occasion, ceremoniously hand over the heads of cattle as bride-price to the girls' guardian. No female member, however, is allowed to accompany the girl's relatives to the groom's house The girl's guardians try their best to get the healthy and young cattle, but sometimes not all the cattle belonging to the boy's parent, are shown for selection. In such case, the girl's guardians have to select from the available cattle or may defer their choice if the cattle of their choice are not available. The boy's party must consider the demand of the girl's guardians, if they have to marry the girl, otherwise the latter may refuse to abide by the agreement of marriage proposal. Below is a song belonging to Jadur category in which the would-be bride has expressed her unhappiness over the selection of cattle brought from the house of her would-be husband. She complains against the selection to her brother. The lines of the song are as follows:

Gonraete chia bareng ko niad meya
Did they hand you over from the cattleshed, O brother
Teba te chia bareng ko songad meya
Did they measure from Teba, O brother
Chor-chor gundia bareng ko omad meya
They gave you slim-skeletoned cow, brother
Karan-karan dokra bareng ko chedad meya
They offered you a single quarter of paisa, O brother

The would-be bride is not at all happy at the quality and quantity of bride-price, which her brother has brought from her would-be husband's house. This indicates that there exists a warm affection between the brother and sister. She complains to her brother that the cow he has brought is old and unhealthy and the amount of money is also too small. She wants that her brother may get healthy cattle.

Sometimes, the parents as well as kinsmen dissolve the agreement of marriage on the ground of distant location of the groom's village. Below is a song belonging to Bala category on this theme, the lines of which are as follows:

> *Kahaṇ kera kuṭum kera beṭi ho dularo*
> The relative from where for our beloved daughter
> *Hare, toyeṇ beṭi rahbe kuṇwar*
> Oh, let our daughter remain unmarried
> *Kakai-pitia sarai laisan dialo*
> Both the brothers have kept her in loving care
> *Ore-ore-ore Gaṇga pare Jamuna*
> Far beyond Ganga and across Jamuna
> *Ore khijur, baitho khijur, lali maṇdoa*
> Far and near the date trees, the canopy of green leaves
> *Saraipure Nagpure*
> At Saraipur and Nagpur
> *Hare, toyeṇ beti rahbe kuṇwar*
> Oh, let our daughter remain unmarried.

No one is ready to marry away his daughter in a distant village. The reason is simple—the visiting would be difficult if one is in trouble. The means of modern communication system were not there when this song was composed. The people used to travel on foot only and long distance travelling was just impossible. At every auspicious occasion, the close relatives are invited and message is communicated orally through someone when one is in trouble. If the girl is in a distant village, such invitation or sending message in time is not possible. As the old persons and children cannot visit her, they dislike to give the girl in distant lands. This is why, the proposal which comes from distant villages are generally not accepted. N.C. Choudury, in his book, *Munda Social Structure* (1977:78), has indicated the radius of marriage. He states that most marriages were within the radius of 12 miles. There are very few cases of villages beyond this limit and in no case does the distance exceed 20 miles. However, he was unable to give the reason of spatial limitation of marriage relations.

Preparation and Marriage Scene

'Marang pera' and *'Arandi'* are the two major stages of marriage. When the date of marriage is fixed through the *Lagan Tol* ceremony, all the relatives—consanguines and affines, are informed about the date and day with a request to attend it. Each invitee is given a piece or full arecanut with turmeric coloured un-boiled rice wrapped in a *sal* leaf. The full arecanut symbolizes a request of financial assistance while piece, simply a participation. The despatcher also tells the invitee about the day and date of marriage. Arrangement starts at least six months prior to the actual date of marriage. The items of feast and other essential things are procured and stored. The rice, pulse, vegetables, goats, fowls, etc, are either purchased or borrowed from others if the family has no sufficient stock of these items. The preparation comes into full swing a week or two prior to the marriage date. The repairing and cleaning of the house is completed much earlier. Such activities are not only carried out in the house where marriage is to take place, but the houses of all the lineage members as well as neighbours are also properly cleaned by the respective householders. A week or two before the marriage, rice along with medicines are distributed to each family of the lineage for preparation of rice-beer. The arrangement of firewood are similarly made much earlier. *Sarjom* leaves for making leaf plates and cups and its twigs for toothbrush are collected by the ladies from the village forests week before. When the day of marriage comes closer, the young boys and girls assemble in the house where marriage is to take place at night and sing marriage songs, while the aged women engage themselves in the preparation of leaf plates and cups. A day or two before the marriage, *'Mandoa'*, that is, canopy from branches and leaves of *Sarjom* trees collected from the village forest is erected on the courtyard where marriage is to be performed.

Below is a song belonging to Bala category which describes the beauty of the *'Mandoa'*. The lines of the song are as follows:

Maṇdoa je sovae
The beauty of the Mandoa rests
Mahua gachha, baṇsa gachha, sidha maṇdoa sovae
With Mahua and bamboo trees, the straight canopy looks beautiful
Beṭi kuṇwari sadi, beṭa kuṇwar biyah
For the marriage of unmarried girl and the boy
Tabe junu aṇgena lila jhamḍa sovae
Then only the green canopy looks beautiful
Tabe junu aṇgena achha gita gawae
Then only melodious songs will be sung on the courtyard
Ghoṛa hathi sathe sath
The horse and elephant all together
Mahua gachha, baṇsa gachha sidha maṇdoa sovae
With Mahua and bamboo trees, the straight canopy looks beautiful

The resting place for the guests is prepared on the courtyard where a big shed from the *Sarjom* is erected. This shed is made up of branches of trees like *Mahua*, *Sarjom* and bamboo. At the centre of the shed, branches of bamboo, *Mahua* and *Soso* trees are pitched, and it is here that marriage ceremony is performed. All these trees have sacred significance—*Madkam* or *Mahua* stands for economic prosperity, *Soso* and *Secrej* trees for protection and security and *Mad* or bamboo for continuity of the generation. The *jhamda is* erected straight and rectangular covered with green leaves of *Sarjom* tree. Such a *jhamda* has beauty only when marriage is celebrated under it for the unmarried boy or girl. There takes no such arrangement in other forms of marriage or status of persons other than unmarried. The reference of horse, elephant, palanquin, band party, etc, have been made only to show the grandeur of the occasion and it has no relation with marriage ceremony, for the Munda do not employ them. The horse, palanquin and band party, etc, are employed by the local chiefs and kings during their marriage and not by the Mundas.

When the *Jhamda* or canopy is ready, the *Pahan,* that is, the priest or any elderly person performs ceremonial worshipping under the shed to ancestor spirits and the *Singbonga*—the Supreme God of the Mundas. The ceremony is called *Mandoa Dul* and rice-beer known as *Tapan* is shared by the lineage members. All those who had participated in the erection of *Jhamda*, are also given the rice-beer. In the mean time de-maidenhood and de-bachelorhood ceremony is performed in respect of would-be bride and bridegroom in their respective parental house and village. The ceremony is called *Kunwarbar argu.* A *kalsa galang* ceremony is performed in the bridegroom's house before they proceed to bride's house for marriage. The old cooking pots of the *Ading*, that is, kitchen are changed by the new ones. The bride and bridegroom also, in their house and village, are anointed with turmeric paste by the sisters-in-law, a night before the departure for marriage. When *Kalsa Galang* and *Sasang Goso* ceremony are over, the party is ready for the journey. Below is a song belonging to Bala category in which the bridegroom's party are making preparations for the journey. The lines of the song are as follows:

Chhaka-chhakiyo ḍiṇḍa pagaria
The bachelor is being crowned with beautiful turban
Hare, tisiṇgo nawa kalesa gaṛae
Today a new earthen pot is being preserved
Chalare, Ram, Lachman bhaiya ko sadi re
Let us proceed in brother's marriage, O Ram and Lachman
Hathi khuṇdalaiṇ, hathi piyae
Elephant treading and drinking
Ghoṛa khuṇdalaiṇ, ghoṛa piyae
Horse treading and drinking
Bhaiṇsa khuṇdalaiṇ, bhaiṇsa piyae
Buffalo treading and drinking
Ore piyae, pare piyae
All are drinking here and there
Chaiṇyaṇ dekhu, chhataṛ dekhu
Under the shade of trees and umbrellas
Hare, chalare Ram-Lachhman, bhaiya ko sadi re
Let us proceed in brother's marriage, O Ram and Lachhman

Kalsa Galang is actually the preparation of marriage when all get ready themselves for the journey. The marriage party consists of male, female and children, young and old. Besides, as mentioned in the song, elephants, horses and buffaloes are in the marriage procession. These are, but employed by the local chiefs and kings, not by the Mundas. Mention of these have been made only to show the grandness of the marriage party who is proceeding for marriage. Similarly, the reference of Ram and Lachhman, the epic hero of the *Ramayana,* have been made to indicate how important and sacred is the occasion of marriage.

When the auspicious day arrives, the host anxiously awaits for the arrival of the guests. The following song belonging to Bala category mentions this theme. The lines of the song are as follows:

> *Gaṛa nutrae dhipa chaṛae re*
> Travelling through hills and valleys
> *Ketai ghalạn nabaiṇ baratiya, nadho rati re*
> It is past midnight, when the marriage party will arrive
> *Diya baru toge nayo, bati baru toge nayo*
> Please, light the lamps and wicks, mother
> *Ketai ghalạn nabaiṇ baratiya, nadho rati re*
> It is past midnight, when the marriage party will arrive

Being a hilly region, the marriage party has to cross the hills, valleys, rivers, rivulets and forests. It, therefore, takes much time to reach the destination. The host, as mentioned in this song, are waiting for them anxiously. At last, the guests have arrived at past midnight and womenfolk are shouting at each other for lamps.

As the marriage party generally arrives at night, light arrangement is a must. Song belonging to Bala category which mentions that lamp was burning for long time and when the marriage party arrived, it went out. The oil and wicks, both have burned out. The women are running about and asking to get it from the oilmen's house. The lines of the song are as follows:

> *Lalten me diya baru, bati baru re*
> Light on the wicks of the lanterns
> *Pardesia dia niṇjhi gela*
> Light has gone off, O strangers
> *Kahaṇ kera nawal gotia, nawal gotia re*

From where the guests have arrived
Lalten me dia baru, bati baru re
Light on the wicks of the lanterns
Lalten me bati baru re
Put the wicks on the lanterns
Telin ghare tela, telin ghare bati
Oil and wicks are available in oil-women's house
Pardesia dia ninjhi gela
The light has gone off, O strangers
Pardesia bati ninjhi gela
The wicks have burned out, O strangers

Somehow the host manages the light and the guests are received. The song below describes how the guests are being received. The song belongs to Racha category and the lines are as follows:

1. *Gel ḍinḍa koṛa-kuṛi ko*
The ten maiden and bachelor youths
Bala darom teko seno tana
Proceeding to receive the marriage party
Gel ḍinḍa koṛa-kuṛi ko
The ten maiden and bachelor youths

2. *Bo chetạn binḍa mena re*
There are pads on the heads
Binḍa chetạn thaṛa mena re
There are plates on the pads
Thaṛa chetạn loṭa mena re
There are brass-pots on the plates
Loṭa bhitạr da-a: mena re
The brass-pot contains water
Da-a: chetạn nuli patera
Mango leaves dipped-in in water
Bala darom teko seno tana re
Proceeding to receive the marriage party

The song mentions how the youths are proceeding to receive the marriage party. The girls are carrying plates with brass-pot of water which contains mango twigs with leaves. The guest in-laws are sprinkled water with mango twigs. Mango is considered to be a sacred tree and its use during reception to guest on the one hand, cleans them ritually and accords them the highest honour that the community can give. How the in-laws are receiving each other, has been described in the following Bala category of song, the lines of which are as follows:

Saiṇyaṇ re saiṇyaṇ
The in-laws
Duyo saiṇyaṇ dahra me batiyae
Both the in-laws are talking on the way
Loṭa me pani, kheoncha me chiuṛa
Carrying water in the brass-pot and beaten-rice on the saree's fold
Hare, nămba ḍaura lele saiṇyaṇ jorae
Making friendship taking mango twigs

The in-laws welcome each other by taking brass-pot of water with mango twigs as well as beaten-rice on the saree's fold. The song below of the Bala category, also is based on the same theme. The lines of the song are as follows:

Saiṇyaṇ re saiṇyaṇ
The in-laws
Duyo saiṇyaṇ dahra me batiyae-haere-haere
Both the in-laws are talking on the way
Bo chetạn biṇḍa mena
Carrying pads on the heads
Biṇḍa chetạn thaṛa mena
Plates are there on the pads
Thaṛa chetạn loṭa mena
Brass-pot is there on the plate
Loṭa re da mena
The brass-pot contains water
Da chetạn uli patṛa
Mango twigs dip-in in the water
Saiṇyaṇ re saiṇyaṇ
The in-laws

Duyo saiṇyaṇ dahra me batiyae
Both the in-laws are talking on the way

The songs above indicate how the guests are being welcomed during the marriage ceremony. Though it is a custom to welcome the guests through the manner as mentioned in the song, the guests also take it as a privilege and sometimes claim as right to be welcomed and unless given such reception, they refuse to enter the host's house. The ceremony of welcoming the guest is known as *Bala-dapa-rom* in Mundari. The reception to marriage party is performed outside the hamlets on the open space where the guests remain waiting for the host for such ceremony. To perform the ceremony, both parties select at least three lady in-laws from each side who happen to be the knowledgeable women in the custom and in the art of welcome. The in-laws hold plates with brass-pots on their heads, which contain water and mango twigs. They also hold beaten-rice with piece of molasses in their saree's fold. On the reception ground, they stand face-to-face with the in-laws and sprinkle water with mango twigs on each other. Thereafter, they feed beaten-rice and molasses. When the ritual is over, they exchange greetings and hug each other. These women happen to be real in-laws of the bride and bridegroom. While *Balc-Daparom* ceremony is in progress the youths of the either side engage themselves in ceremonial joking with each other through songs which relate to the praise of one's brother or sister, that is, the bridegroom or the bride and also abuse the opposite party. Later on, they mix up and dance and sing together and are led to the house and are accommodated in the *Jhamda.*

The song below which belongs to the Jadur category, mentions how the music is being heard from a distance as the people are engaged in singing and dance. The lines of the song are:

1. *Oko kore ho ko araṇdi tana*
Where the marriage is being celebrated
Lowajo nagera ko giṛim-giṛim
The sound of the pair of drums is being heard
Chimae kore ho ko korandi tana
Where the marriage is being celebrated
Sukua pereṇ-ṛed toro-roro
The melodious sound of clarinet is being heard

2. *Hasada reko arandi tana*
In Hasada, marriage is being celebrated
Lowajo nagera girim-girim
The sound of the pair of drums is being heard
Tala Naguri reko korandi tana
In the middle of the Naguri country, marriage is being celebrated
Sukua peren-red toro-roro
The melodious sound of clarinet is being heard

As mentioned in the song, some elitist Munda of the Hasada country engage drummers and musicians during the marriage who generally belong to the Ghasi caste.

Duet Songs sung by the Youths of Bride and Bridegroom's Side

When the in-laws, as mentioned in the above song, are engaged in welcome ceremony, the maidens who are sisters of respective bride and groom and have joking relations among themselves, stand a little apart from the crowd and engage themselves in duet songs. It is a fine example of humour mixed up with satirical composition which seems to be slang or obscene and abusive in tone but the objective is to impart a moral lesson to the would-be bride and bridegroom. It is the girls of the bride side who start the song in praise of their sister, that is, the would-be bride, and sing the song of abuse against the bridegroom. The girls of the bridegroom's side, on the other hand, sing songs of praise in favour of their brother, that is, the would-be groom. Besides, the brothers and sisters of either of the two are also not spared. The singers, however, keep no ill-will among themselves but through these songs, the fact of life is conveyed and it carries meanings for the would-be couple who is to start a new life and have to bear the social burden henceforth. The couple must observe and maintain the social obligations and morals of the society. They should set good example by obeying the customary rules. The pair should not betray each other nor should indulge in unsocial and unnatural activities. The objective of the song is to offer moral teaching to the would-be couple through these songs though they seem to be obscene and abusive. Below are given a number of songs, each convey particular teaching and unfolds the reality of life. Almost all the songs belong to the Bala category. The songs which are sung by the girls of bride side, tauntingly pass a remark that seem very abusive to the groom. The lines of the song are as follows:

Daroming kako, daroming kakom meneya 'Falna'
Accord me welcome you say, O falna'
Amgia ko darom tana falna
Are we to accord welcome to you, O falna
Diri chol-chol, sadom chia dodocho
You sharp pointed stone, standing like a horse

As mentioned in this song, the bridegroom considers himself a honourable guest and wants that he should be given a warm welcome. The girls of the bride side tell the groom flatly that they have not come to welcome him as he is not worth that. They tell him that he is an ugly fellow who looks like a sharp pointed stone and stands like a horse.

The girls of the groom's side too, who sing song in defence of and in praise of the brother, reply it through the song and sometimes, often repeating the same lines of the songs replacing only the name of the brother to that of the bride.

In the song below which belongs to Bala category, the girls of the groom's side express doubt about the actual age of the bride and tell her that she is aged girl old enough for the marriage. The lines of the song are as follows:

Daroming kako, daroming kakom meneya falni
Accord me welcome you say, O falni
Amgia ko darom tana
Are we to accord welcome to you
Gaṛa genara kuṭi sakạm paṇḍu len rem janạm lena
Your birth was when *kuti* leaves of the stream side had turned purple

The last line of song have been expressed symbolically. The leaves of the *Kuti* plant do not follow the rule of autumn but they fall one by one on attaining maturity. No one knows which leaf of which branch may turn purple and may fall first. Similarly the age of the girl cannot be perceived by her appearance. Besides, the stream and leaf turning purple depict sexual organs in this song.

In reply to the above song, the girls of the bride's party go a little ahead by singing abusive song against the groom. The song belongs to *Bala* category and the lines are as follows:

Bale giaiṇg-bale giaiṇg am meneya falna
I am an infant you say *falna*
Ka ja falna bale tema, ka ja falna dulu tema
You are neither an infant nor a baby
Sauṛi buru ra soso nelau lem
Go and see Soso fruit of the grass field
Soso lekạm ripu tana
You are wrinkling like Soso fruit
Gaṛa gena ra: kuṭi sakạm paṇḍu len rem janama kana
Your birth was when the *kuti* leaves by the stream had turned purple

At the time of matchmaking, not only the physique and height are taken into consideration, but the age of the boy and the girl too. The consideration of age is not made on the basis of actual date of birth, but on the basis of physical built, for the Munda rarely keep the record of birth. It is why, in some cases, age disparity is clearly visible. The girls generally dislike such match. This theme has been taken up in the song and the girls of the bride's party make a sarcastic reference against the groom who is stated to be of comparatively older age. The girls tell him that you are not. an infant, you are an aged person as the wrinkles of your face indicate. They ask him to see the Soso (wild cashew) fruit which wrinkles after its ripening. In this song the phrase '*Sauri buru ra soso*' is a symbolic to female sex organ—grass represent the pubic hair and Soso fruit that of clitoris. So the girls indirectly mention female sexual part. Through these statements, the girls want to tell the groom that he is not ignorant of sex life. The objective of such *lewd* songs during this occasion, is, however, not very clear. But one of the objective is to drive out the shyness of the boy or girl to their reference. Below is another song on this theme which describes more realistically the facts of sex life. The song belongs to Bala category, and the lines are as follows:

Bale giaiṇg-bale giaiṇg ạm meneya falna
I am an infant you say, falna

Nạm jom me budi ruji metai mere mai
May you get an old vagina, tell him O girl
Huriṇg giaiṇg-huriṇg giaiṇg ae mene redo mai
If he says I am a child, O girl
Nạm jom me budi ruji metai mere mai
May you get an old vagina, tell him, O girl

Slowly the tempo of the verbal duel goes up higher and higher and the girls become more hypercritical to the would-be bride and bridegroom and attack the other party with forcefully composed songs. The age of the boy is concealed sometimes, but ultimately the reality is revealed. The girls do not allow this opportunity to pass without making comment against the statements of the groom's guardians. They tell the boy that you are lucky to get a young girl otherwise you would have got an old woman. The girls instigate their sister, that is, the would-be bride to tell the boy, that is, the groom that if he pretends to be young which he is not, he will get an old woman in case he refuses to marry her.

This song derives the subject matter from the fact of life and it is in anticipation that the boy may divorce the girl after marriage. Munda permit separation or divorce till the couple has no issue. But after marriage, the couple themselves control each other with respect to relationship with other girls and boys. If the boy or the girl maintains his or her relationship with previous friends, one may resent it by his or her behaviour. If the boy keeps on continuing his relationship with the girl which he used to before marriage, the bride may go away to her parent's house. By doing so, the attention of the elders can be easily drawn and the boy will be brought to task.

The following song describes the changes that may take place in the life of the girl. The song belongs to Bala category and the lines are as follows:

Namin din dore falni
For so long years, O *falni*
Chauṇria huni lekạm tai kena falní
You were like field mouse, O *falni*
Na·dore falni
But now, O *falni*

Ghongora choka lekam nelo tana falni
You look like wrinkled *Ghongora* fruit

The girls of the groom's party remind the bride that she is wrinkling now ever since the marriage proposal was accepted. They tell her that she has enjoyed a very nice time and freedom in her early life like field mouse who during night run about in the field without fear or care. The fact is that the field rat known as *Chaunira,* when the crops ripen, enjoy the most happy life for they get enough grain to eat or to store. They play and dance about in the field overrunning the crops. Wherever the field rats live, there remains only straw and no grains in the field. As they move out and in constantly, a clean path is made in every field. The presence of path in the field is an indication of the habitation of rats there. Seeing the clean path on the crops field, the Munda say that *Chaunria* rats had danced there. From this reference, it is inferred that girls too, in their parents' house enjoy such freedom. But after marriage such freedom is lost. The would-be bride is on the threshold of freedom and captivity and the mere thought of the situation has made the girl gloomy and physically wrinkled. The reality of the situation which is to occur very soon after the marriage, naturally affects the girl psychologically which gets its reflection on her body. The joy, which usually flashed on her face, has now vanished which has affected the girl adversely on her health. She now looks like an old woman with wrinkled face. The physical condition of the would-be bride has been compared with that of *Ghongora*—a vegetable fruit which grows up in good size but after maturity, it slowly dries up and wrinkles. The females, thus, have to undergo various life situations which affect them psychologically resulting in decay of their health.

In the following song, the girls of the bride's party tell the groom that the journey of life is full of troubles and miseries. It is like travelling through hills and valleys where rocks, pebbles and thorny shrubs would trouble his feet everywhere. They advise the groom that he must face it boldly for there is no escape. The song belongs to Bala category and the lines are as follows:

Buru-buru tem seno redo falna
If you travel through the mountains, O *falna*

Buru ruguṛi roroga
The sharp mountain pebbles may pierce on your feet
Beṛa-beṛa tem seno redo falna
If you travel through the valleys, O *falna*
Beṛa chiru roroga
The valley shrubs may pinch

The lines of the song are repeated by the girls of the bridegroom's side also referring the name of the bride.

And so the girls of the groom's party also remind the bride that married life is not at all rosy but it is full of problems and difficulties. Hence the couple should travel together in life and face the troubles boldly.

In the following song belonging to Bala category, an attack on the personal life of the bridegroom has been made. The lines of the song are as follows:

Jiliṇg buru redo
On the long mountain range
Aiṇg bhair, aiṇg bhair a̭m meneya
I am all alone you say
Bura̭m meko raka̭b tana tipa-taṛe
Your sweethearts are crawling up staggeringly
Jathriṇ gena-gena te
By the side of fences
Ghorṇa gena-gena te
By the side of boundary
Kaṭeya ko palad-pulude
The mice are hopping about
Na̭m jom me falna
Be careful, O *falna*
Luṛa ta̭m ko gereya, gereya falna
They may bite your penis, O *falna*
Bura̭m meko raka̭b tana tipa-taṛe
Your sweethearts are crawling up staggeringly

The lines of the song are repeated again.

The girls of the bride's party now keep on constant attack on the bridegroom. There is nothing which is secret from the knowledge of the girls. Though the song is not directly based on the real event, but it relates to the general situation that commonly exists about the relations of boys and girls before their marriage. It is not a serious allegation against the bridegroom but rather a warning as if there was such relationship which the groom had. The bridegroom tells the girls that while he used to go to the forest for collection of wood, etc, he used to go alone. But the girls tell him that there is nothing hidden and that is all lie. He was not alone. Look how his sweethearts are creeping up the hill. They are like mice who always play about by the side of fences or on the compound of the crops field and live on the grains of others. The girls tell the groom that he should be careful about his penis for the mice may bite it while playing. That is, keeping sex relations with those girls may destroy his social prestige. The message is that the bridegroom should abstain himself from such relations after marriage and he should avoid the girls who may be hovering around him.

Below is another song belonging to Bala category in which the girls ask the groom about the necklace he is wearing as to where he got it. The groom tells them that he got it by the wayside lost by someone. The girls do not believe on this statement of the groom. The lines of the song are as follows:

Puṇḍi hisir genej-genej
The ornaments of white beeds in rows
Heṇde hisir genej-genej
The ornaments of black beads in rows
Halaṇganaiṇg tumbalanaiṇg am meneya falna
I have picked it up you say, *falna*
Kaja falnam̂ halaṇgana, kaja falnam̂ tumbalana
You may not have picked it up, O *falna*
Sida-sida buram̂ meko omad̂ mete
Your previous lady love may have given you
Halaṇganaiṇg tumbalanaiṇg am meneya falna
I have picked it up you say, O falna
Seṇgel da: doe gama leda
It rained fire
Chatom falna sabe jom me
Hold an umbrella, O *falna*

Kachi falnạm sari leda
Did you not know, O *falna*
Kachi falnạm urum leda
Did you not understand, O *falna*
Seṇgel da: doe gama leda
It rained fire

The Munda use many blanket terms which are symbolic, particularly where sex organs or sexual behaviour are referred to as mentioned in the songs above. In the song, the girl means sex life of males and females but they do not mention it directly. Instead, they use the word '*sengel da*' which means knowledge about sexual intercourse. They indirectly tell the groom that the bride is the symbol of sex desire like fire and he should be ready to face it.

The song below belonging to Bala category also has reference of sexual organs, the lines of the song are as follows:

Horia kode holong
Hail to millet bread
Horia baba holong
Hail to rice bread
Horia chuduria ki kuda fau-fau
Hail to swollen vagina
Horia laoṛa ki kuda fau-fau
Hail to swollen penis

The girls sing the above song jointly hailing the conjugal life of the bride and bridegroom which the couple is entering into.

Many of the marriage welcome songs, including the above may be taken as obscene because of its reference to sexual organs or sexual intercourse. Such references are also found in songs of many tribal communities and castes of Chhotanagpur plateau who almost share the same culture with their own distinctive features. The significance of marriage and sex life of the couple is paramount in married life and they should not remain ignorant of it. Marriage without sex is not at all thought of by the Mundas. And reference in songs during marriage indicate how important is sex in married life. The reference of sex, therefore, has a contextual significance and it conveys more serious meanings than what it apparently seems.

The statement made through the reference of sex is both instructive and warning. The would-be bride and bridegroom are expected that the couple should not be ignorant about sex and its functional significance. The tribal elders have long felt the necessity of sex education among young boys and girls and for their training established the institutions like *Giti-ora* and *Dhumkuria,* etc. This is why many of the malaise of so-called advanced society is totally absent in tribal society. The meaning of the song is obvious. The millet bread in the song signifies the female organs which can only be shared by the couple after their marriage. Sex organs are hailed for the continuity of the generation which is depended upon its right use and proper function.

The brothers and sisters of the bride and bridegroom have *Goi* relations which permit them to exchange jokes with each other. During reception ceremony joking songs are also sung by the girls. For the purpose, the number and names of the brothers and sisters are collected by the youths of either party before the actual date of marriage. The song below derives its theme from the menstrual cycle of the females. Though the song is directed against the bridegroom's sister with regard to cleanliness during such periods, it indirectly gives out instructions to the bride that she should not be careless in such periods. She should clean the dress after boiling it in the ash. The usual methods of cleaning the clothes by the Mundas is by boiling it with ash. The song belongs to Bala category and the lines are as follows:

Likaiṇg nel me lika gadhila
Saw you yesterday in stained cloth
Gapaiṇg nel me gapa gadhila
See you tomorrow in stained cloth
Soso buru re soso torej
Ash of cashew tree from cashew hill
Kachi mairem tiki pundina
Why don't you clean yourself, O daughter
Soso buru re soso torej
Ash of cashew tree from cashew hill
Kachi falnim tiki puṇdina
Why don't you clean yourself, O *falni*

The song on the above theme have been composed differently in the song below belonging to Bala category, the lines of which are as follows:

Falni doe meneya
Falni says
Mayom tanaiṇg, mayom tanaiṇg ae meneya
I am bleeding, she says
Hadai me falna
Cut for her, O *falna*
More muka botejente
Five hand length loincloth

The bridegroom's sister, as the song mentions, says that she is bleeding. At this, the bridegroom is requested to provide her cloth for the use of underwear. This indirectly directs that whenever there is menstrual cycle, the bride should use cloth for underwear to protect the dress from being stained. The bride should know this precaution.

When the wife becomes pregnant, it is the duty of the husband to look after the needs of the wife. The song below belonging to Bala category, is based on this theme. The lines of the song are as follows:

Falni doe meneya
Falni says
Sui tuka, sui tukae meneya
Make a nest, she says
Baiai me falna chachandi
Hang a nest for her, O *falna*

Though the song is directed against the bridegroom's sister, it actually gives instruction to both bride and bridegroom. When a hen is about to lay eggs, she makes cackling sound which is an indication that the time of laying eggs has come. Similarly, when the bride tells about her pregnancy, it indicates that the birth of a baby is to take place soon. The bridegroom is, therefore, requested to make proper arrangement beforehand to avoid inconvenience during the birth.

Selection of bride by the boy himself is strongly resented by the parents as well as by the kinsmen. The bridegroom is abused by his sisters themselves in the following song, for he himself selected the girl for his wife. The song belongs to Bala category and the lines are as follows:

> *Cycle chetanete falna*
> Upon the bicycle, O *falna*
> *Kuṛim sala kena falna*
> You did select the girl, O *falna*
> *Laṭkij-paṭkij kuṛi falnam ramana*
> You got a very ugly girl, O *falna*
> *Chhoṭkim aderi redo falna*
> If you marry a second wife, O *falna*
> *Kuda suṛa leka kuṛi falna nam jom me*
> May you get a bride like black berry saplings

In this song, the girls abuse the bridegroom for his wrong selection of bride. This song is sung by the girls of the bridegroom's party themselves in which they have made some suggestions to him. If one stresses on too much selection of girls, he may not get good and beautiful girl. The song mentions that the boy made the selection while riding on bicycle, that is, did select the girl at first look and, of course, in one glance and so the mistake. Similar to the above song, in the song below too, the girls request the groom that since he has gone too much about selecting he should now settle down in life. There is no beauty in living alone and travelling around from place to place for the sake of seeing the country. Beauty is there in married life only. The song belongs to Bala category and the lines are as follows:

> *Raji-raji bulale falna, dese-dese bulale*
> You travelled country after country, O *falna*
> *Falna sadi binu sasusari sovae*
> There is no beauty without marriage, O *falna*

The girls dislike illicit relations before marriage and the boy who flirts gets strong resentment. Marriage is a must for it checks illicit relations between the boy and the girl.

Below is another song belonging to Bala category, the lines of which are as follows:

Ham to dekhali minjura ka jat re
I saw the species of peacock
Minjura ka jat baba jhail binu re sobhalain re
Does the species of peacock carry beauty without its tail
Ham to dekhali raja beta jat re
I have seen the king's generation
Raja beta jat baba rani binu re sovalain re
The king has no beauty without the queen
Ham to dekhali hansa raja gora re
I saw the king of white swan
Hansa raja gora baba lil binu re sovalain re
The white swan king looks beautiful without its blue colour

A person's beauty lies in remaining in pair. A number of examples can be cited as above justifying the notion that an adult person has beauty only when he or she is with his male or her female partner. So marriage for the Munda is rule of nature as well as sociocultural necessity.

Below is a song belonging to Bala category in which the girls of the bride's party admire her sister, that is, the would be bride. The lines of the song are as follows:

Apeya babu tape do
The boy yours
Gangayae horo kena kakaya-kukuyu
Did guard over maize crops till he became crooked
Aleya mai tale do
The girl of ours
Jhika babae horo kena jilabe-joloba
Did watch over *jhika* paddy shining bright

In the song above, the girls of the bride's party admire their sister for the works she did from her childhood to this day. Taking only one example of work say guarding of crops. Crops require guarding from sowing to harvesting in which every member of the family can be assigned this job. As mentioned in the song at one time, the bridegroom as well as the bride also did this duty. Maize is normally sown on upland and generally on hill sloping so the job of guarding of crops on this field is an arduous one. It was natural, therefore, that the bridegroom who guarded maize crops became crooked. The paddy of the lowland variety is sown on the plain land and the bride who guarded the plainland crops was as fresh and smart as ever. The girls want to tell the groom that their sister too is an experienced person who did her duty with ease.

The song below mentions that the bride's parents are economically better than the groom's and so he should not think that the bride is coming from a poor economic background. The song belongs to Bala category and the lines are as follows:

> *Apeya babu tape do*
> The boy yours
> *Thaṛa re jom kena thaṛa leṭkej*
> He ate food on broken plate
> *Aleya mai tale do*
> The girl ours
> *Chipa re jom kena chipa chem-chem*
> She ate food on shining and musically sounding bowl

Besides leaf-cups and dish, the Munda use brass dish and plates also. As mentioned in the song *thara* is a big size plate while *chipa* is small bowl. The girls say that their sister did eat food in a bright shining bowl while the bridegroom had broken plate only. So she has enjoyed better life than he and that status of her be maintained.

The song of jokes and satires as mentioned above, though most of them appear to be obscene have in reality a functional importance. These types of songs are found among almost all tribes of Chhotanagpur.

Hospitality and a Series of Ceremonies

When the *bala daparom* or *mergarai* ceremony is over, the guests are led to the leafy shed called *jhamda,* specially prepared for their camping and rest. The wooden clubs and other weapons carried by the guests are collected by the host and are kept at a suitable place. The feet of the guests are then washed by the village maidens. The guests are then seated in the *jhamda* and are offered drinking water.

The number of persons in the marriage party vary from 20 to

100 and more. Sometimes it so happens that the guests cannot be accommodated in the *jhamda*. Below is a song belonging to *Bala* category which mentions that the number of guests is so large that they are not getting place in the *jhamda*. The lines of the song are as follows:

Kuṭi paṭal paṭera
The shed thatched with *kuti* leaves
Kuṭi paṭal patera ge nayo
The shed thatched with *kuti* leaves, O mother
Hare, nai nagujae nai palarae
Neither it sprouts nor grows
Hare, kuṭi paṭal patera ge nayo
The shed thatched with *kuti* leaves, O mother
Bari kuṭum aṇgena
Guests abound beyond the courtyards and in the compounds
Hare, nai sambarae nai palarae
They are beyond the control and management
Kuṭi paṭal patera ge nayo
The shed thatched with *kuti* leaves, O mother

Marriage is an occasion of joy and merriment. It is why, a good number of persons attend the ceremony. Such big gatherings create a hospitality problem for the host. The above song mentions that the number of guests are so large that they are not getting place in the shed erected for the purpose.

When the guests settle down, the omen, are consulted. After this, the hosts and the guests ask each other's welfare. This has been mentioned in the following Bala category of song, the lines of which are as follows:

Ae gelaiṇ gotiya, dais delaiṇ patia
At the arrival of guests, the mat was spread up
Hare, dukhaṃ-sukhaṃ puche lagal gotiya
The guests are being enquired about of their welfare
Na mile goṇdli, na mile maṛua
Neither *goṇdli* nor *marua is* available
Hare, hamar gotiya upase sutalaiṇ hamar gotiya
Guest ours slept without taking anything

When the custom of asking each other's welfare is over, the guests are served food. But as stated in the song, as the hosts are poor, there is nothing in the house to feed them. The guests go to bed without taking anything.

Below is a song belonging to Bala category in which the girl is being asked to prepare everything for the comforts of the guests. The lines of the song are as follows:

> *Gaṛa-gaṛa, jola-jola, peṛe doko hiju lena re*
> Through the ravine and mountainous terrains, the guests have arrived
> *Mai re gaṇḍu bano, jaṭi ailakom*
> Daughter dear, there is no wooden pad, spread up mat for them
> *Hiju doko hiju lena re*
> They have arrived and
> *Dube doko dube jana re*
> They occupied their seats but
> *Mai re mid mocha jabaṉ ema kom,*
> Have a talk with them, O dear daughter

The guests who have come covering the ravines and ditches feel comfortable when they are received warmly by the village maidens. And as mentioned in the song, the would-be bride is requested to talk with the guests. But in reality, the would-be bride never reveals her identity and always moves about along with her friends till the time of marriage. However, it is only the expectation of the guests that if the would-be bride has spoken to them, they feel most happy and honourable.

Before taking dinner, the guests are served rice-beer and then they go on singing all the night. But prior to this, thanks and prayer is offered to the Supreme God Singbonga and to the ancestral spirits of the family for making the journey of the guests safe and for the smooth completion of the next day's works.

Next day in the morning, the guests are taken out by the go-between towards the river for freshening up. Sometimes, a pot of rice-beer is also taken. When the guests are back from the river, they are served morning breakfast or rice-beer. A series of ceremonies are then performed during the day including the marriage. At every ceremony, a pot of rice-beer is brought out and offered to the ancestral spirit and to God Singbonga before it is taken. A very tight schedule is maintained for the observance of each ceremony. However, even during a busy schedule, people have time for singing and merry making.

The song below mentions that for the guest a goat was killed who is boneless. The goat in this song symbolizes the rice-beer. The song belongs to Bala category and the lines are as follows:

> *Kahaṇ se awae gotiya*
> From where the guest have come
> *Hare, khasi kaṭi delaiṇ re*
> A he-goat has been killed
> *Hare, khasi ke haṛ nakhe, khawaiya ke daṇt nakhe re*
> The he-goat has no bone, and the takers have no teeth
> *Purbe se alaiṇ re nawa gotiya*
> From the east have come the new relatives
> *Hare khasi kati delaiṇ re*
> A he-goat has been killed
> *Hare khasi ke haṛ nakhe, khawaiya ke daṇt nakhe re*
> The he-goat has no bone and the takers have no teeth

Language is the means of communication of ideas and views. We get language excellence in every culture where even a single fact is expressed in symbolic term making it difficult to perceive the same even to the speakers of the language themselves. Parables and riddles are some such expressions where the fact is described in a simple language in symbolic terms. In the above song too, the boneless he-goat and teethless eaters are such expressions which evoke automatic laughters among the audience.

The rice-beer has, as in the above, got another symbolic expression in the following Bala category of song, the lines of which are as follows:

> *Ne dheṇki kocha re*
> At the corner room of husking machine
> *Seta chinae goya ṛana*
> Is it that dog has died there
> *Dhamchura-dhamchurae sowana*

It is emitting very strong smell
Kachi mairem nelana
Did you not see, O daughter
Kachi mairem chinana
Did you not identify, O daughter
Seta chinae soya tana
Is it that a dog is rotting
Dhamchura-dhamchurae sowana
It is emitting very strong smell

Illi or rice-beer pot has been kept in a husking room. The rice-beer is ready for use and so is emitting a strong scent. Everybody whoever comes near the room gets the smell and enquires the girl there whether a dog has died which is emitting bad smell though knowing full well that it is rice-beer. This is the way of asking someone of the thing he wants but in a lyrical way. When someone goes out in search of rice-beer, he goes on asking it but never takes its real name, instead takes fictitious name such as *Hende bahanda, Bucha chatu, Pundi da* and *Marchi,* etc.

As stated in previous pages, when the guests return from the river after freshening up, they are served rice-beer. The children are given light refreshment. At the end of the session *Bala haprub* ceremony is performed in which *Bor ageya* and *Da au* are the main ceremonies. The rice-beer is again brought out for each ceremony. In this ceremony, the priests of the respective villages—the host and the guest, along with one or two persons from each group, sit on the spread up mat facing each other. One or two *Lama sakam* leaves are placed before them. Each priest then, worships the respective ancestral spirits. The two priests then, taking a leaf cup of rice-beer each exchange it three times in the name of ancestral spirits and the Singbonga and the rest of the respective group also do the same. Few drops of rice-beer are then dropped on the heap of rice placed on the *Lama sakam* and then the cup of rice-beer is drunk. The two persons of each party, who represent the in-laws of each respective side, stand face-to-face and exchange rice-beer three times and then drink it. The two then, lift up each other one by one, three times from above the ground and shake the *Leafy shed,* that is, the *jhamda.* This confirms the formal approval of relationship of the two families.

It should be noted that the ancestral spirits of each family of the party, are also brought into confidence through the priest as stated above.

The details of the marriage ceremony, however, differ from village to village and marriage to marriage. In some areas, tree marriage of mango and *Mahua* is performed before or after the marriage ceremony which is called *Uli saki* ceremony as witness. The bride and bridegroom are also annointed oil and turmeric paste by the in-laws of the respective village before the marriage. The marriage is performed at the centre of the *jhamda* which is specially cleaned with cow dung slurry where bamboo, *mahua* and *sarjom* trees have been planted. The bride and bridegroom are either taken round the *jhamda* three times or simply taken out from the room on lap or on baskets at the centre of the *jhamda*. There they are made to sit side by side. In some villages, the bride and bridegroom sit on the respective laps of their maternal uncles. The *Pahan* (priest) of the village or some elder member of the lineage performs the marriage ceremony. A prayer to ancestral spirits and to the supreme God Singbonga is offered for the blessings and welfare of the off-springs. At the end of the ceremony, the bride and bridegroom are asked to exchange flower garlands. They are then asked to greet or offer *Johar* to everybody present in the ceremony. At the end, the two are then shut up in a secluded room for some-time. In the afternoon, *Da-ma* or *Lota uku inung* ceremony is performed in the river or pond in which the girls and other women participate. The two girls carry water pots on their heads, followed by two other girls with bows and arrows and act as if the two will break the pots. A basket of beaten-rice with an arrow on it and a pot of rice-beer are also carried towards the river. The rice-beer, is consumed by the participants on performance of the ceremony. On return from the river, *Sunum goso* and *Chuman* ceremony is held. The ancestors are again worshipped. The bride and bridegroom are made to sit on the middle of the *jhamda*. The relatives of both the bride and bridegroom occupy seats on the *jhamda*. The girls of the bride side annoint oil on the hair of all the guests and dress them with comb. Each one is then decked with a bunch of flowers. This follows the *chuman* ceremony.

The bride and bridegroom either remain seated or are made to sit again in the *Jhamda*. The *agua* then introduces the in-laws of both the parties and they exchange gifts to each other. During *Sunum Goso* ceremony all the relatives of the bride present gifts to her. At the end of *Chuman* ceremony, the guest and all the invitees participate in the grand feast, specially arranged for them.

The *Bidauti* or farewell ceremony to the bride is organized late at night or in the morning next day. During the ceremony, a pot of rice-beer is brought out and given to the guest as farewell drinks. The handing over of bride to the bridegroom is performed by the eldest of the lineage member or maternal uncle of the bride who gives a long sermon to the bride and bridegroom about the relationship which has now been established between them and the life that the two henceforth have to lead. The rights, duties and obligations to each other and to the family and society as well as moral values and traditions of the ancestors they have to follow and maintain, are narrated in details to the newly wed. The two are reminded that the two are now responsible individuals and should not do anything which may defile the family prestige and the society. The bride is then ceremonially handed over to the bridegroom and all responsibilities towards her welfare is made to him. The farewell ceremony takes place at an open space beyond the house of the bride's father where all kinsmen, relatives and villagers assemble to give a warm send-off to the bride.

After returning from the farewell ceremony, the bride's parents and relatives worship the ancestoral sprits and the supreme God Singbonga and offer rice-beer as a token of gratitude for uninterrupted completion of the marriage ceremony of their daughter.

Though a detailed description of marriage ceremony cannot be given in these pages, for no such details are available in the Munda songs, yet we get a very first-hand description of it from the mouths of the Mundas themselves in their songs. A vivid picture of culture in action is described in these songs. The Munda pay utmost respect and honour to the guest through behaviour and by other means. Feast is always arranged in honour of the guest in all marriage ceremonies but there are other things also that carry social prestige and dignity of the individuals such as rice-beer, tobacco, and items of smoking like *hookah* that is, hubble-bubble. If a person offers delicious food and all comforts but offers no tobacco or *hookah*, he is liable to receive criticisms for disobeying the customs of the society. So, if a guest has come in someone's house and the host has no habit to take any of those mentioned things, he has to tender his apology for his inability to manage those things. In marriage, rice-beer has a ceremonial importance but tobacco and hubble-bubble carry a social value. The song below belonging to Bala category takes a reference of the hubble-bubble which the in-laws during the marriage are sharing. The lines of the song are as follows:

> *Leo samdhin Hukḳa*
> Please have the hubble-bubble *samdhi*
> *Hukka je baje samdhin, baje khunur-khunur*
> The hubble-bubble is making sound of *khunur-khunur,* *O samdhi*
> *Hukka chetạn da: mena*
> There is water in the *hookah*
> *Da chetạn naṛa mena*
> The pipe is in the water
> *Naṛa chetạn chilạm mena*
> The pipe holds the fire container
> *Chilạm chetạn guṛhai mena*
> The fire container contains tobacco
> *Guṛhai chetạn angor mena*
> Fire is there on the tobacco
> *Angor chetạn khapṭi mena*
> There is earthen lid upon the fire
> *Khapṭi chetạn sukul mena*
> Smoke hovers over the lid
> *Leo samdhin Hukka*
> Please have the *hookah samdhi*
> *Hukka je baje samdhi baje khunur-khunur*
> The *hookah* is making sound of *khunur-khunur,* O *samdhi*

The song describes the hubble-bubble of the Mundas. It is well-ornamented with rings and metal bells, beads and colourful thread flowers. The *hookah* produces sounds whenever it changes hands. The lower portion of the *hookah* contains water in the hollow coconut fruit. It has two holes-one for smoking and another for supporting the pipe which holds fire container with tobacco. The fire is covered with earthen lid. While smoking, the smoke comes out from the side of the lid. The hubble-bubble, thus, goes round and round among the in-laws.

Below is another song belonging to Bala category which also describes the beauty of the *hookah* of the Mundas. The lines of the song are as follows:

> *Guṛ-guṛiya nariyara hukka dani re*
> The beautiful *hookah* of round coconut fruit
> *Dani maṇge chitaranga kamela ka dani re*
> The multicoloured coconut of the *hookah* is beautiful like lotus flower
> *Hukka chetan da: mena*
> The *hookah* contains water
> *Da: chetan naṛa mena*
> The pipe is in the water
> *Nara chetan chilam mena*
> The pipe holds the fire container
> *Chilam chetan gaṭi mena*
> The fire container has a pebble
> *Gaṭi chetan guṛhai mena*
> The tobacco is there over the pebble
> *Guṛhai chetan aṇgor mena*
> There is fire on the tobacco
> *Aṇgor chetan khapti mena*
> The earthen lid covers the fire
> *Khapti chetan sukul mena*
> Smoke is there over the lid
> *Guṛ-guṛiya nariyara hukka dani re*
> The beautiful *hookah* of round coconut fruit
> *Dani maṇge chitaranga kamela ka dani re*
> The multicoloured coconut fruit is beautiful like lotus flower

The song describes different portion of the *hookah*. The lower portion of the *hookah* which contains water in made up of wood, fruit and clay. The song mentions that the most beautiful one is that which is made up of clay. The clay water container of the *hookah* is coloured with multicolours in different designs. Nowadays coconut fruit container is most common which is called *hookah-dani* in Mundari.

The rice-beer and *hookah* both have high social significance among the tribal people. In the song below which belongs to Bala category, describes how the in-laws and others are sharing on the occasion of marriage ceremony. The lines of the song are as follows:

Saiṇya je jorae
The relations are established
Piṇḍe-piṇḍe hookah je piyae
They are smoking *hookah* from portico to portico
Saiṇya je jorae
The relations are established
Piṇḍe-piṇḍe haṇṛi je piyae
Drinking rice-beer from portico to portico

The Munda generally construct raised platform on the portico of the front portion of the house which is used as drawing room. The song describes how the in-laws are confirming their relation by sharing the *hookah* and rice-beer on the raised platform of the house. When the main marriage ceremony is over, the ladies of the groom's party are taken round the houses of the kins of the bride. This indicates that relations are established, not between the couple only but all the lineage members of both the parties henceforth become permanent relatives.

The song below belonging to Bala category describe the scene of marriage ceremony. It is observed that during such ceremonies, rice-beer is consumed heavily. During every ritual a rice-beer pot of one or two is needed for offering to the ancestor spirits and to the supreme God Singbonga. Besides ritual requirements, more and more rice-beer pots are brought out for the guests according to their number. The lines of the song are as follows:

Biriṇḍa bone kera koenara patai
The *koenara* leaves of Brindaban forest
Hare, hamạr thuchku doṇa, hare, hamạr dabl dona re
How nice are small and double cups of mine

Chipauya je chipe lagal choto-choto
The squeezers are pressing continuously to its last drop
Bantauya je bante lagal chira-choto
Distributors are dropping here and there continuously
Piyauya je piye lagal sak-saka sat dona re
The drinkers are gulping down at a stretch up to seven cups
Birinda bone kera koenara patai
The *koenara* leaves of Brindaban forest
Hare hamar thuchku dona, hare hamar dabl dona re
How nice are small and double cups of mine

As has been mentioned in previous pages that rice-beer is prepared from before the actual date of marriage in which the whole lineage members are involved. At the day of marriage, these pots are brought out one after the other as the ceremony proceeds. Sometimes, five to six pots are brought out at a time and juice are produced through the help of hands by pressing the fermented rice. The juice thus, collected, is distributed among the drinkers. While distributing to the drinkers, the juice is dripping from the cups here and there.

The *Bala-haprub* ceremony as described in previous pages, the in-laws sit together or stand face to face to each other. After a ritual performance, they exchange the cups of rice-beer and drink it. The song below belonging to Bala category describes this scene in the following lines:

Miyad jati miyad parkom re
In one mat and in one cot
Balaya-sakaya kin duba kana
Both the in-laws are sitting together
Ranga chari-chari tikina
Both are holding the colourful tin spikes
Pital puru-puru tikina
Both are holding the brass cups
Balaya-sakaya kin duba kana
Both the in-laws are sitting together

In *Bala-haprub* ceremony, the individual who act as a leader in the ceremony, prepares his own leaf cup at the spot. The leaf cups are made by stitching together of leaves with the help of thin bamboo spikes. The thin bamboo spikes are mentioned in the song as *ranga* and leaf cup as *pital*, that is, brass. *Ranga* and brass were once the valuable metal for the Mundas in their developmental history which still has place in their songs. The thin bamboo spikes and leaf cups are not the ordinary things and also the actions of the two in-laws, who are sitting together and are engaged in making of leaf cups. By sitting together the in-laws are confirming their relationship which cannot be broken. The song below which belongs to Bala category mentions this in the following lines:

> *Balare haṇsa jori*
> Hail to the beautiful pair of swan
> *Balare perowaṇ jorae*
> Hail to the beautiful pair of pigeon
> *Jorala kūtumb kaese chhutâl piriti lagi gelaiṇ*
> How the established relationship will break when there is love between the in-laws

The relationship between Balaya that is, the host party and Sakaya, that is, the guest party have been established and confirmed through *Bala-haprub* ceremony. This relationship of the in-laws will never break. The pair of swan and pigeon do not separate, so also the relationship of the in-laws who confirm it amidst the relatives and kinsfolk of the bride and bridegroom, who are the witness of this ceremony, will never break. We thus see that through marriage not only the couple are socially and ritually bound together for each other but their whole lineage members and relatives too are similarly committed to maintain the relationship through ritual and other customary performances. In future, in case of development of uncongenial relations between them, the persons involved, that is, the whole lineage members are called upon for explanation. And it will be a matter of disgrace for them. During the *Bala-haprub* ceremony the individuals performing the ceremony are asked by the people present there as to what the two are doing. They reply that they are establishing relationship, that is, *Bala tana ling* in Mundari.

Below is a song belonging to Bala category in which the in-laws are talking about the agreement which they have arrived at and confirm the same lifelong. The lines of the song are as follows:

Ore baitho re samdhin, pare baitho re
Sit close by and face to face, O *samdhi*
Duyo kane re samdhin, sona re laokela
In both the ears, the gold is glittering
Baṛhal beṭi re samdhin, ghare nahin sovae
The grown daughter has no beauty in the home, O *samdhi*
Jorala kuṭumb re samdhin, kaese re chhuṭala
How the established relationship will break, O *samdhi*

During *Bala-haprub* ceremony when the two in-laws perform ritual of confirmation of agreement, they assure each other of its lifelong maintenance. As mentioned in this song, both the in-laws are facing each other. They are in their best dress and ornament. The ear ornaments are glittering. By the by, the in-laws of the groom's side tell the in-laws of the bride side that there is no beauty if the grown up daughter remains unmarried in the house. So he should not hold back his agreement. The relationship has now been established and its breaking will bring disgrace to both the families.

The bride is being asked to get ready for marriage by the parent as mentioned in the following song of Bala category:

Kauwa je bolae, kala lala, kala lala kauwa je bolae
The crow speaks kala lala, kala lala
Kauwa je baisae machia me baisae
The crow is sitting on the stool
Awa beṭi sona singar, rupa singar pahirawa
Come and get dressed with gold and silver ornament, O daughter
Tabe junu bida debain
Then only you will be given farewell

The father of the bride is talking and singing continuously like a crow under the influence of rice-beer. He is sitting on the stool and asking his daughter to dress herself for the marriage.

Marriage of the daughter creates a disturbing situation for the bride as well as for the parents. The song below belonging to Bala category describes this situation in the following lines:

Hariyaro manḍowa me baisal ge nayo

You are sitting under the green leafy canopy, O mother
Dulu-mulu re
Look worried and gloomy
Kahena rakhal ge nayo
Keep words, O mother
Dulu-mulu re
Look worried and gloomy
Hare hariyaro maṇḍowa ge nayo
The green leafy canopy, O mother
Dulu-mulu re
Look worried and gloomy
Hare rakhal ge nayo
Keep words, O mother
Dudha ka molae, dudha ka molae
For the sake of milk mother
Hare, hiri-jhiri pahirab ge nayo
Let us wear marriage dress, O mother
Dulu-mulu re
Look worried and gloomy
Kahena rakhal ge nayo
Keep words, O mother
Dudha ka molae, dudha ka molae
For the sake of milk mother

The bride is being decorated for marriage. The father of the bride, as mentioned in the previous song, has ordered her daughter to dress up for marriage ceremony, but her mother looks gloomy for it is the last day for her daughter to be with her in the house to whom she nursed her with her breast milk. The mother is in awkward situation for if she has to keep her words to maintain the social custom, she must have to give her daughter in marriage. There stands personal attachment, on the one hand, and social obligation, on the other. The mother is being resquested to be cheerful and keep honour of the green leafy canopy as well as the breast milk and allow her daughter to dress herself for the marriage.

No detailed description of marriage ceremony is found in songs. The song below belonging to Bala category, however, gives a glimpse of the same in the following lines :

Rimi-jhimi, rimi-jhimi, pani nai barisae
There is no rain but a scanty of it
Bhaiya ka lal pheṭa bhinjat ahe
The red turban of the brother is getting wet
Chhatar dharu, chhatar dharu
Please hasten to hold the umbrella

The marriage ceremony is in progress. At this moment it started raining and his sisters ran out for umbrella to protect from getting wet. The spread up umbrella is also held up over the bride and bridegroom when marriage ceremony is performed besides the moment as stated.

Marriage also separates childhood friends. At the time of marriage, the bride remembers the happiness and enjoyment of her childhood days which she spent with her friends. The following Jadur category of song describes the mood of the bride in the lines as follows:

Ạm dore gatim re tur lekam onol jan
You were dressed like a squirrel, O friend
Ạm dore sangaing re mara: lekạm singaren jan
You were decorated like peacock, O friend
Tuṛ lekạm onol jan, am dorem juṛin jan
You were dressed like squirrel, you got your partner
Mara: lekạm singaren jan, am dorem jotạn jan
You were decorated like peacock, you got paired
Ạm dorem juṛin jan, susun gem hiating tan
You got your partner but you are thinking of dance
Ạm dorem jotạn jan, karam gem chakating tan
You were paired but thinking of *Karam* dance

Friends see the bride being decorated beautifully like squirrel and peacock. Marriage takes away the freedom of movement of the girl and so the bride is thoughtful of dance in which she had participated freely.

The girl is supposed to be the light of the house. So, when she is married away, she leaves behind darkness in the house of her parents, but the house where there is darkness, gets the light. This has been described in the following Baha category of song in the following lines:

Jul tana diya jul tana re
The lamp is burning bright
Saṇgin rege diya jul tana re
The light is burning in a distant
Maskal jana diya maskal jana re
It has lightened bright
Nuba disum rege diya maskal jana re
The lamp has lightened the dark country
Nuba jana oṛa: diya tama re
The lamp of your house has gone off leaving deep darkness behind
Goṇṛa oṛa: duar diya eṛinj jana re
The door lamp of the catttle shed has gone off

How important is the place of the girl in any house has been indicated in the song. It is the girl who does every household work, from cleaning to cooking and looking after the comfort of the members of the house. She takes care of the guests and visitors whenever any of them turn up in the house. She is the light of the cattle shed for she cleans it daily and so also tends the cattle when needed. This light has now gone away to distant village and is burning in another's house. In another song below in which only two lines are worth quoting, it indicates how happy is the family who receive her as bride. The lines are as under:

Siṇgi tur hora re, saṇdaka baiyo tana numa
Road is being constructed in the east mother
Saṇdaka baiyo tana
Road is being constructed

The bride leaves the house of the parents and her natal village through a very simple ritual, that is, application of a tip of vermilion on the forehead. This has been mentioned in the following Jadur song, the lines of which are as follows:

Hatu mairem dugu-mugu, hatu mairem bagi keda
With slow paces you left the village, O daughter
Disum mairem liyar-koyor, disum mairem raṛa keda
With strides you relinquished the country

Hatu mairem bagi keda, mid kiwa siṇduri te
You left the village with a tiny cup of vermilion
Disum mairem raṛa keda, bar kiwa kajora te
You relinquished the country with two tiny cups of *kajal*

This song has been sung by the friends of the girl at the time of her farewell. She leaves the house, taking small paces towards her new home, and thus, relinquishing all her previous relationships with parents, kinsmen and friends. The application of a tip of vermilion has made all this difference at a fraction of time. While this action, on the one hand, brought beauty in a stranger's house, it has left behind eternal darkness at her parent's house.

The following song belonging to Bala category describes this theme clearly. The lines of the song are:

Hatu go sona muni re, hatu gom singạr tada
You decorated the village, O my golden dear
Disum go rupa muni re, disum gom patạr tada
You made the country desolate O my silver dear
Hatu gom singạr tada, hatu gom bage jada
You decorated the village while leaving behind it
Disum gom patạr tada, disum gom rara jad
You made the country, desolate by relinquishing it
Mid kiwa siṇduri te, hatu gom bage jad
With a tiny cup of vermilion you are leaving behind the village
Bar taṛi sasaṇg te, disum gom raṛa jad
With two plates turmeric, you relinquished the country

The song may have been composed by the girls. It decorates the village where the girl is given in marriage. She, by entering into the marriage bond, not only adds beauty to the village, but to the whole country of the Mundas. In other words, the honour of the country and the community is maintained by following the customary rules of the society.

Someone has rightly said about the marrying girls as 'circulating cunnubium' who move from one clan group to another. Circulation of girls has been described in the following Bala category of song, the lines of which are as follows:

Bono bhitare juṛi tirio rana birana bhela, haere
In the forest a pair of friends were separated, alas
Apan beti biran bhelaiṇ
One's own daughter became daughter of the others
Biran beṭi apan bhelaiṇ
Other's daughter became one's own
Juṛi tirio rana birana bhela, haere
The pair of friends were separated, alas

The song mentions that in marriage, one's own daughter becomes the daughter of others and the other's one's own. Due to the rule of clan exogamy, girls as wife are brought from other clans and one's clan daughters are given away to others. In traditional Munda society marrying within the clan is strictly prohibited and is considered *sotra* or defilement. Such couple's identified by the term *mago* and normally excommunicated for life from the society. While establishing marriage relations, rules of clan exogamy is strictly followed. So, when a daughter is married away, the parents as well as the girl are fulfilling the society's custom and are praiseworthy.

The idea of marrying away the daughters into another's clan as beauty and fulfilment of tradition, is also evident in the following song which derives example from the objective world. The action is considered just and essential for the continuity of life. The song belongs to Bala category and the lines are as follows:

1. *Ghara je sobhae*
The beauty of the house lies
Kutumb sathe-sathe beṭi uthi gelare
When the daughter departs along with the guest
Aisana suṇdara re
Such beauty is beyond explanation
Ghara suna bhela re
The house became desolate
2. *Gachha je sobhae*
The beauty of the tree lies
Lale-lale charaiya binu re sobhae
It looks beautiful devoid of red coloured birds
Najar chalate ṭuṭi chali gelare

With twinkle of an eye when the arrow leaves the bow
Lagi gelare giri gelare
It hit the target and fell down
Gachha suna bhela re
The tree became desolate

3. *Dova je sobhae*
The beauty of the pool lies
Pothi machhari binu re sobhae
It looks beautiful devoid of *pothi* fish
Bhaṇwar jal fekate machhari faṇsi gelare
Fish were caught with the throw of net
Aisana suṇdara re
The beauty of the scene is beyond explanation
Dova suna bhela re
The pool became desolate

Everything is right when it goes well according to the laws of nature. The tree looks beautiful with colourful birds, so also the pool full of fish. At a certain extent the house looks beautiful with grown-up daughters. But hunting and fishing is essential for continuity of individual life and one has to take a very harsh step even for destroying the most beautiful one for this cause. It is moral duty of the parents to give away their beloved daughters in marriage to community people as per the clan rules. The custom of marriage enables the continuity of social life of the community. It is a disgrace if the girl does not go away along with the guest after marriage. The beauty of the house is retained when the daughter accompanies her husband to his village.

Attitude of Girls towards Marriage

The demands of the society of marrying away of daughters creates a situation of separation among the near and dear ones which is generally disliked, and particularly by the women. The ideal marriage as mentioned in earlier pages have been taken differently by the girls. For them, it is a hypocrisy of the people to follow traditional custom of marriage. Such views of the girls are reflected in many songs of the Mundas.

In the following song, the girls raise the voice of disagreement with the people in general and with the parents in particular. The song belongs to Bala category and the lines are as follows:

Budu leke rahloṇ nayoge
When I was like a Budu fish, O mother
Hare, keyo nahiṇ puchhae
No one ever enquired of me
Bhaṇḍa pani bheloṇ nayoge
When I was able to carry a pot of water, O mother
Hare daso kutumb baisae nayoge
Ten guests came to ask hand
Hare, biso kutumb baisae
Twenty guests came

The girl is critical of the behaviour of the people. She says that when she was a small child, no one ever looked towards her, nor anyone enquired of her. She was neglected rather looked down upon by the people. But when she grew up and was able enough to carry pots of water, there was a line of people to see her. The girl is critical of the double mentality of the people and does not expect such behaviour from them.

The girl, in the following song complains against her mother about the treatment she received during her childhood days and the position now she is having when she is given away in marriage. The song belongs to Bala category and the lines are as follows:

Aiṇg numa dulu chi pampelad̂
Am I a dragon or butterfly, mother
Aiṇg do numa raji notaṇg tan
I am flying over the country, mother
Aiṇg do numa dese notaṇg tan
I am flying over the continent, mother
Aiṇg do numa seta chi pusi
Am I a dog or a cat, mother
Aiṇg do numa fada lagaiṇgā
I am being kicked about, mother
Aiṇg do numa tika lagaiṇgā
I am being trampled upon, mother

Almost all the parents keep some sort of control over their sons and daughters. The control is always in the form of guide and advice. Daughters are particularly kept busy in household and other works, however light it may be. The mother or elder sisters always keep a watch on the activities of the daughters or younger sisters and criticize or rebuke them whenever they see wrong. In this song, the girl assesses the behaviour of the people as well as of their parents from childhood days and finds that she was always neglected and illtreated by them. Now when she is leaving her parents house after the marriage, she gets courage to tell her mother about their behaviours.

The song below is also based on the complaint to the mother who always was unhappy over the number of members in the family. The song belongs to *Bala* category and the lines are as follows:

> *Emin din do nuṃa*
> So long so far, mother
> *Kae kamia kae kamiam metaiṇgā*
> You do not work, you used to say, mother
> *Na dore umana*
> But now, O mother
> *Nir odoṇg nir bolo kami kete jomeme*
> By running in and out, you do work and eat
> *Emin din dore umana*
> So long so far, mother
> *Rasi khalgi, rasi purum meneya umana*
> Too many plates and cups, you say mother
> *Na dore umana*
> But now, O mother
> *Haṭiṇg lere, churu lere miyad khalgi miyad puṛu banoga*
> While serving, you will get one plate and one cup less

All parents take work from their sons and daughters and every child is assigned some kind of job everyday. But all the children are not equally obedient or laborious. Some are idle or lazy or escape from work. Such a child is generally rebuked at the time of evening meal. As mentioned in the song, the girl was always rebuked for one reason or the other. The mother would usually pass a remark that there are a good number of individuals at the time of meal but very few are available for work. The girl reminds her mother of the illtreatment she received from her and tells her that now she will get one set of plate and cup missing while serving meal and that she will get no chance to comment upon one another's work as she would have to handle all work alone by herself. The friends of the bride also take side of her in abusing her mother. The girls express strong resentment against the custom of bride-price and entertainment to guests and relatives by arranging a lavish feast for them by the parents. In the following song belonging to Bala category the girls have raised strong voice against these customs, the lines of the song are as follows:

> *Beṭi keto bechale nayo*
> You sold your daughter, O mother
> *Ketai chatekana gaṛale*
> How many stores did you make
> *Khasi kaṭale, Baṇḍa marale*
> You killed goat and boar
> *Nayoge, beṭi keto katai marjadi karale*
> Mother dear, what a lavish feast you arranged in honour of your daughter

The sarcastic remark made on the bride-price and on the arrangement of feast for the guests, present the general attitude of the girls towards such customs. The feast, in reality, is arranged not for the honour and respect of the daughter but it is for the guests. The daughter's value is not at all felt by the parent even at the time of her marriage. To store grains, the Mundas make bamboo or wooden barracks which they call *chhatka*. The girls in angry tone, ask the mother of the bride as to how many *chhatka* did she make out of the bride-price after selling away her daughter. Women in general are supposed to be the meek followers of the traditional customs in any human society and for that very reason they suffer inhuman torture and humiliation. The so-called self-proclaimed advanced societies in India have coded down the irrelevant customs and behavours in scriptures so as to justify their practice, which, in reality go against the dignity and honour of the females. The women of these societies follow the practice silently. But protest songs as above influenced the traditional ideology of the leaders of the tribal community resulting in total discontinuity of the custom of bride price.

The song below also reveals the general feelings of the girls against the marrying away of girls by the parents. The girls feel neglected who have no place and status in the society. They feel as if they are commodity or an object of lowest value. The song belongs to Bala category, the lines of which are as follows:

Seṇra kijam numana, eṇda kija re
You made her intelligent and then threw away
Khalgi puṛu lekam eṇda kija re
Like leaf cups and plates, you threw away
Tela kijam falna, tela kija re
You received her O *falna* (name of the bridegroom)
Sona rupa lekam tela kija re
Like gold and silver, you received her

The girls' hearts are sore over the customs of the society. She is given all sorts of wordly knowledge that may be beneficial to her in her future life. In spite of all these love and labour for the daughter, she is thrown out of the house like an unwanted leaf cup which is thrown away after its use. The parents, it is complained that they do not feel the necessity of the girl when she attains the youthful age. So, parents are accused of their double standard of behaviour. Separation with near kinsmen always hurts the feeling, but forcible separation as in marriage, creates the feeling of love and hate as is evident in the present song. The girls speak ill against the mother who turned out her daughter after the marriage but they admire the bridegroom who receives her like gold and silver, that is, the most precious possession. It may be noted that all the above songs of protest have been composed by the womenfolk themselves.

Leaving aside ritual processes, marriage is a big gathering of people who interact closely during the occasion. It becomes the platform for numerous social experience. The young and the old, all mutually interact and enjoy the occasion.

In the song belonging to Jadur category, a boy narrates his experience of the marriage in which he had participated. The lines of the song are as follows:

Saṇgiṇ disum jate hiju lena
I came from a distant country
Sadom chapri ga ko uduba diṇga
They showed me a stable to stay there
Jiliṇg gama jate seṭer lena
I came after travelling a long distance
Busu guyu ga ko chundula diṇga
They directed me to a straw-thatched hut to stay there
Sadom chhapri ga ko nuduba diṇga
They showed me a stable to stay there
Sadom tiṇgu mai goiṇg tiṇgu kena
I remained standing the horse's way
Busu guyu ga ko chundula diṇga
Directed me to a straw-thatched hut to stay there
Seta kucha mai goiṇg kucha kena
I coiled round myself the dog's way
Sadom tiṇgu mai goiṇg tingu kena
I remained standing the horse's way
Rabaṇg tena mai goiṇg ekela jana
I shivered from biting cold, O dear girl
Seta kucha mai goiṇg kucha kena
I coiled round myself the dog's way
Rabang tena mai goiṇg tayur jana
I was freezed by the chilly cold

Marriage is performed in winter as well as in summer. Both the seasons have good as well as bad aspects so far as the marriage ceremony is concerned. In summer, there is the scarcity of water which is most needed during the occasion. People do not get water even for drinking and even if it is available, it is found undrinkable. In winter, people cannot carry enough clothes with them, so they suffer from cold. And as mentioned in the song, a boy tells his experience to a girl, that they were put up in a horse stable and second time in a straw-thatched hut where they either remained standing like horse or coiled their body like a dog. In winter, to beat back the cold, the marriage party are provided enough firewood. It keeps them warm the whole night. Straw thatched hut remains air-tight and warm. This experience is told not as a complaint but as a joy of experience of adventure.

It is observed that during the marriage, the parent of the bride had to spend in hospitality more than the parents of the bridegroom. For, the bridegroom brings the marriage party to the bride's house, the number of which varies from 50 to 200 and more. The parent of the bride have their own relatives besides the lineage members and other friends of neighbouring villages. Nowadays the expenditure has gone up on almost all the items. The song below belonging to Bala category states how the ladies are busy in the preparation of rice, etc, as the date of marriage is nearing. It also describes how the marriage party of a chief or an elite Munda are proceeding to the bride's village. The lines of the song are as follows:

Jhandi-jhandi-jhandi nipil turakan
The flag star has appeared in the sky
Hare, nane-nane taṇgera me kuṭi lelaiṇ
They pounded on the flat rocks
Aba Iswar saṇkaṭ boṛe re niranka
The trouble is typical O God
Hare nane-nane tangera me kuṭi lelaiṇ
They pounded on the flat rocks
Aba Iswar saṇkaṭ boṛe re niranka
The trouble is typical O God
Hariyaro bagicha me khariyan je chholaloṇ
At the green grove I cleared for a barn
Hare, khariyan upar hathi charae
Alas, elephants rested on the barn
Hathi upar ghughur dolae
The bell swings upon the elephants
Ghughur upare chaṇwar dolae
The tuft of hair swings on the bell
Chaṇwar upre gaja-baja
Musicians play on with the swings of tuft of hair
Gaja-baja bari bajena
Band party is with scores of musical instruments
Bari bajena ban barud
Bomb and crackers with scores of musical instruments
Raja beṭa duyo re sadi bhelain
Both the princes were married at a time

This song does not describe the marriage scene of an ordinary Munda. It either describes the marriage ceremony of an elite Munda or of a Hindu chief or of a prince of the local king. For, it is the local chiefs or kings who only employ band party and musicians as well as drive horses or elephants in the marriage party and explode bomb and crackers. The reference of '*Jhandi epil*' or the evening star in the context of marriage is an indication of the symbol curse. The elephants as described in the song were camped on the barn of a poor man and trampled down the stored up grain. The song belongs to the period when *Jagirdars*, *Zamindars* and local kings were exploiting the indigenous tribal people at will.

The song, though refers to the marriage of the two princes of the local king and sung by the Mundas, is meant to show the grandeur of marriage ceremony. Though nothing of the sort of bomb and crackers are exploded or musicians employed. The marriage ceremony even of an ordinary Munda is nonetheless grand than the marriage of the prince or princess.

The Farewell after Marriage

The boy and girl till their marriage remain strangers to each other and it is only when the two start living together that love blossoms between them. The bridegroom may love his wife immensely as the following song belonging to Lahsua category indicates. The lines of the song are as follows:

> *Piriti janama kan boṇga chaṇḍu leka ho*
> Love has taken birth like the full moon
> *Ṭura kanae ama kiriya kaiṇg bagi meya*
> I swear in your name, I wili not divorce you
> *Nila kila inuṇg alaṇg*
> We will play all along
> *Ama kiriya kaiṇg bagi meya*
> I swear in your name, I will not divorce you
> *Cheṛeṇ leka juṛiya kana*
> Like birds we have been paired
> *Ba leka daliya kana*
> Like flower it has blossomed

Ama kiriya kaiṇg bagi meya
I swear in your name I will not divorce you
Gojo alaṇg mod te
We will die together
Ama kiriya kaiṇg bagi meya
I swear in your name I will not divorce you

At the time of farewell after marriage, the bridegroom is asked to give assurance by the village elders that he will not illtreat her nor he will divorce her. The above song is perhaps the part of the same swearing-in ceremony.

At the marriage of the daughter, the girls have spoken against the parents and of the community as heartless fellows. But it should not be taken that the parents do not feel the separation of their daughter. The following song which belongs to Bala category, describes the agony of the parents at the departure of their daughter and remember how they helped her in becoming a grown up lady, but now the stranger has taken away their daughter. The lines of the song are as follows:

1. *Nasul kijaiṇg, nasul kijaiṇg*
I brought her up
Towate nasul kijaiṇg
I brought her up with milk
Nasul kijaiṇg, nasul kijaiṇg
I brought her up
Khudi te nasul kijaiṇg
I brought her up with small pieces of grain
2. *Hiju lenae, seṭer lenae*
He came and arrived
Buru ren richi
The mountain hawk
Seṭer lenae, leba lenae
He arrived and alighted
Beṛa ren besra
The valley raven
3. *Hayur kijae, edi kijae*
It collected and carried away

Buru ren richi do
The mountain hawk
Hayur kijae, edi kijae
It collected and carried away
Bera ren besra
The valley raven

When the bride is given farewell, her mother feels too much for the separation of her daughter. She remembers how she nourished her with breast milk when she was a mere infant and later with food of broken rice pieces. Now, she has attained adulthood and is sharing her hand in household work, the hunting bird of the mountain and valley all of a sudden alighted in her house and collected her daughter and carried away. This is an unfortunate and sad affair in the life of the mother who sacrificed all her happiness and comfort of life for the well-being of her daughter. The bridegroom, in this song is looked upon like a hawk who generally pounces upon the carefree and innocent birds.

Below is another song in which too, the bridegroom has been compared with that of the epic villain Ravana and vulture. The song belongs to Bala category and the lines are as follows:

Kahaṇ se ale re Ravana gidi
From where did you come, O Ravaṇ vulture
Paiṇkh tor jhanar-jhunur
Wings yours are making sound of *jhanar* and *jhunur*
Hare Ravana gidi
O Ravan vulture
Purbe se ale re Ravana gidi
You came from the east, O Ravan vulture
Paiṇkh tor jhanar-jhunur
Wings yours are making sound of *jhanar* and *jhunur*
Hare Ravana gidi
O Ravan vulture

The bridegroom is like a raven, hawk, vulture and Ravan. They are all heartless creatures. They do not show any compassion in the misery of others but they enjoy it. When the vulture flies, its wings produce some sound. So also the bridegroom comes like Ravan and vulture and takes away the bride from her parents.

Below is yet another song in which the bridegroom is described as *besra* or hawk. The song belongs to Bala category, the lines of which are as follows:

> *Kono dahar̯ gele baba*
> On which way you did go father
> *Kono dahar̯ gele ho*
> On which way you did go
> *Bono dahar̯ ekela, haere*
> On the path of forest alone, alas
> *Tongori ko tare-tare baisalaiṇ re runia*
> Runia took rest by the side of the hill
> *Runia ke lokiyo lelaiṇ re besera*
> Runia was collected by the hawk

The way to the bridegroom's village is hilly and forest clad. The bride does not know on which way to go. The hills are in all along the route and the path is lonely. The wild hawk, that is, the bridegroom kinapped the *runia*, that is, the bride through this zig-zag path of the hills and forest.

The song below describes the fate of the girl after her marriage. The girl is like a domesticated bird after her marriage who is kept in the cage all the time. The song belongs to Bala category and the lines are as follows:

> *Nayo ghare posala paṇṛki*
> The domesticated dove at the mother's house
> *Sasuri uri gela*
> Flew away to her in-laws house
> *Pinjra men rahi gela*
> Remained in the cage
> *Janam juga rahi gela*
> Remained there forever

The content of the song is packed with emotions. The girl is like a domesticated dove who was looked after by her mother from the very infancy. The wings of the dove are now strong enough to fly out from the nest and it is at this moment she was caught by someone and was kept in a cage there. The custom of marriage for the girl is like a cage for she will not be allowed to move freely in her husband's house. This is the fate of every girl whoever is given away in marriage.

During the feast, the in-laws of both the sides sit opposite to each other face to face. The bride and bridegroom are also made to sit side by side.

After the feast, the guests are allowed to take rest for two to three hours or as the time permits them, for farewell is always given to them in the early hours of the next morning. The girl is again decorated with marriage dress and all her gifts are packed up in some baskets or boxes. She also is given a basketful of beaten rice along with molasses and one or two arrows. All the kinsfolk assemble and after worshipping to the supreme God Singbonga and ancestral spirits at the courtyard by the *pahan,* that is, village priest *bidauti illi,* that is, farewell drinks are served to the guests. The bride is then bodily lifted out from the house by the younger brother of the bridegroom and is carried to the open space of the settlement, a practice remnant of the ancient *atangir* form of marriage, that is, marriage by forcible kidnapping. The bride is then ceremonially handed over to the bridegroom, the details of which have already been mentioned in previous pages. When the sermon is over, the newly weds greet all the persons one by one who are present there. It is at this time that the bride asks her father about the house of her new abode. The song belonging to Bala category, describes the conversation between father and daughter. The lines of the song are as follows:

Baba ho baba, kaisana jaga me diale
Father dear, how is the new place
Ho kaisana jaga me diale
How is the place (let me know)
Beṭi ho beṭi
My daughter dear
Eke loṭa pani lagin
For a brass-pot of water
Muhạk jabạn lagin
And to keep words
Taisana jaga me dialoṇ beti

I gave you in such a place, my daughter dear
Hare, taisana jaga me dirion
I gave you in such a place

In personality and behaviour people differ from each other. The bribe does not know about the family members of her new abode. The bride is doubtful about the treatment she will receive from them. the father tells her that he has fulfilled the custom of the society by giving her in marriage. The brass pot of water means honour, and to keep words means to abide by the agreement which he entered into while accepting the marriage proposal. It is to maintain the honour and dignity of the society as well as of the individuals that he has given her in marriage. Except this, he has no idea about the family members and their behaviour.

The bride is given farewell by her parents and relatives but she does not know her destination as to where to go. So, she finds here self alone among the strangers like the bird who flies over in the sky aimlessly knowing not where to go. The bride is under the grip of psychological loneliness. This situation of the bride has been described in the following Jadur category of song, the line of which are as follows :

1. *Hare engaing hare apuing*
   O my dear mother and father
   Cheren lekaing otang tana
   I am flying like a bird
   Chika meyaing beti re, neka gia ama dasa
   What shall I do for you my dear daughter, this is your fate
2. *Cheren lekaing otang tana, lipi-lipi, lupu-lupu ge*
   I am flying like a bird up and down slowly
   Chika meyaing beti re, neka gia ama dasa
   What shall I do for you my dear daughter, this is your fate
3. *Alom maina hiatinga, ama geya ora: duar*
   Don't worry my daughter, yours is the household
   Alom maina chakatinga, ama geya chatu lundi
   Don't be depressed my daughter, yours is the kitchen

The bride feels homelessness and lonely. She tells her parents that she is like a bird who has no permanent abode. The girl is given words of compassion by her parents saying that she need not worry for she will be the queen of the household where everything will be at her command.

The bride finds herself among the strangers. For her, they are like travellers or traders. In course of their journey, they occasionally visit the villages, stay for few days and again move on. The marriage party is like these people. The song below describes this theme which belongs to Bala category, the lines of which are as follows:

Aiṇg do numaiṇg seno tana numa
I am going away my mother dear
Ladani kolo basari koloiṇg seno tana
I am going away with the load carriers and nomads
Ladani kolo seno tan redo numa
If I am going away with the load carriers
Ladani hiram̂ metaiṇga
You will call me diamond load carrier
Basari koloiṇg seno tan redo numa
If I am going away with the nomads
Basari hiram̂ metaiṇgā
You will call me diamond nomads

The girl is in desperate position. She now has come to the conclusion that no request will be granted and that she must accompany the load carriers and nomads. Even if she is going away with such strangers, their parents will not abuse her but they will feel extremely glad and admire her for accompanying the strangers.

Before bidding farewell to all near and dear ones, her friends surround her and would not allow the husband to take her with him unless they are given some token amount for the last rite called '*sang chhoraouni*,' that is, separation from friends. The girls then sing the farewell song. The song belongs to Bala category and the lines are as follows:

Seno tanam̂ mairem seno tana re
You are going away dear daughter, you are going away
Falna hatu (name of the village) *tegim seno tana*
You are going away to *falna* village

Bagi kedam mairem bagi keda re
You have left behind, dear daughter, you have left behind
Falna hatu mairem bagi keda re
You have left behind the *falna* village

The bride is given warm send off by the relatives, friends and villagers. The song as cited above clearly mentions that now she has left her natal village and is going to her husband's village. The content of the song as well as its tune touches everyone's heart. But the separation is inevitable and she accepts it with heavy heart. It is observed that most of the brides at such occasion, break down to tears.

The functional participation of the lineage members as well as the village people in marriage ceremony from the beginning to end, never allow the parents to think that they by themselves performed the marriage of their daughter single handed. The song below belonging to Jatra category mentions that it is the village people who gave farewell to their daughter and not they, that is, the parent of the daughter alone. The lines of the song are as follows:

Pancho bhaiya
The five brothers
Pancho bhaiya re baini ke bida delain
The five brothers gave farewell to the sister
Adho rati pahar rati re, baini ke bida delain
At midnight they gave farewell to the sister

The five brothers are the village community who conduct the whole marriage procedure. It is actually the obligation of the females of the lineage to perform the *samdhi bhent* ceremony. Thus, the girl is either the sister or the daughter of the whole village. It is the *panch*, that is, the village community who take all the responsibility of marriage. This is why, it is stated in the song that the *panch* brothers gave away the daughter in marriage.

The vacuum thus, created in marrying away the daughter is not only felt by the parents but the sisters-in-law of the house feel the absence in the same intensity. The song below belonging to Bala category describes this state of the situation in the following words:

Chit pahạr bhelaiṇ hariyara
The land beyond the mountain has become green
Uch pahạr pạt diya hariyara
The high mountain was brought to the level turning it green
Nanadi ke lei gelaiṇ chora daiya
The sister-in-law was carried away by the thieves
Hare, hamạr niṇdwa
Alas, I have no sleep
Sasur sute piṇda-piṇda
The father-in-law sleeps on the platform of the portico
Nanaṇdi sute khiṛki dura men
The sister-in-law would sleep on the door close to the window
Nanaṇdi ke lei gelaiṇ chora daiya
The sister-in-law was carried away by the thieves
Hare hamạr niṇdwa
Alas, I have no sleep

When the husband's sister is married away, his wife becomes restless. So long her sister-in-law was there in her parents' house, she was of great help to the brother's wife in all sort of women's work. She has now been left alone and so has to attend all the works by herself. The girl as wife is now rendering the same service to her husband's family members. This very upside down affair has been stated in the song 'the other side of the mountain has now become green'. The girl's natal family, so long she was there, had attained great height of prosperity like mountain. Nevertheless, the brother's wife has to bear this responsibility by herself and has to turn the flat mountain into green. In short, the girl's brother's wife is now thoughtful of the situation created out by marrying away of her sister-in-law, for she has now lost her rest and freedom. It is why she is accusing the bridegroom as thief.

With the farewell of the daughter, the marriage ceremony at the bride's parent's village is over. The next stage of ceremony will now be held at the bridegroom's village. But, let us see how the marriage party is returning to their village with the bride. The song belongs to Bala category, and the lines are as follows:

Jojo ko chuṭi re
On the top of the tamarind tree
Dhichuwa bhale re sobhae
The watch-bird looks beautiful
Bajania bajate awae
The drummers are returning playing on drums
Nachania nachate awae
Dancers are returning dancing
Dulha dulate awae
The bridegroom is returning sleepily
Kaneya kandate awae
Bride is coming weeping
Lukudina lukate awae
Bride's escorts are coming hiding
Baratiya barate awae
The marriage party is returning murmuring
Jojo ko choṭi re
On the top of the tamarind tree
Dhichuwa bhale re sobhae
The watch-bird looks beautiful

The *Dhichuwa* in this song means the *agua,* that is, the go-between who is returning along with the marriage party. He is happy as he has accomplished the marriage successfully and looks beautiful. The return journey is long and arduous. Traditionally the Mundas did not employ the drummers and musicians nor the dancers. In the Munda region, as stated earlier caste people also reside who employ the professional drummers and dancers during all life cycle rituals. Their services are required by the Mundas only during the last rite, that is, when memorial stones are erected in the name of the departed souls. With the passing of time, sometimes, few elite Mundas influenced by Hindu manners and customs, also employ these professional musicians during some life cycle rituals. The song mentions two contrasting scenes—while the bridegroom and the marriage party looked tired, they are being welcomed by the villagers merrily with all fanfare of music and dance. The other scene is that the bride is weeping. The escorts who happen to be the friends of the bride, are feeling shy among the strangers and are hiding themselves. The escorting girls usually belong to the flowers friends like *sahia* or *sangi*. They stay with the bride till latter feels homely in the new place.

On Reaching the Bridegroom's Home

When the newly weds set their feet on the courtyard of the husband's house, the bride is carried into the house. The mother of the bridegroom or any lady belonging to the lineage, then washes the feet of the bride with *Illi-rasi*, that is, undiluted rice-beer juice. The washed off juice is collected on a plate and every room of the house and roof beginning with cow-shed, is sprinkled with juice. The juice is supposed to be sacred and believed to bring happiness in the family. The bride is then asked to wash her clothes as well as that of the husband's which she does after boiling it in ash water as usually the Munda do. The ancestral spirits are then worshipped by offering them rice-beer, and if, necessary, chicken of required colour is also sacrificed. When the bride returns after washing clothes, she is asked to cook rice-bread in new utensil. This is again offered to the ancestral spirits. During mid-day meal, she has to serve rice-beer and food to the household and lineage members. On the same or next day, all the invitees assemble in the house. Along with them they bring rice, pulse and other vegetables for the feast and gift for the newly weds. The feet of the invitees are ceremonially washed by the girls of the lineage and are led into the house. The women, while drinking rice-beer and singing marriage songs, prepare leaf plates and cups for the feast. At this moment, the bride distributes flattened rice which she has brought from her natal home to everybody, those who are not present are also given at some other time.

The *chuman* ceremony is again performed at the bridegroom's house when the gifts are presented to the new couple. In the evening all the invitees participate in the feast.

When night sets in the couple are set up in the kitchen. The young boys kill a chicken and hang its intestine at the door and indulge themselves in gossipping in obscene language but they seldom refer to the new couple. The objective is to remove the shyness between the two and bring in closeness in them physically and mentally. The boys are given a fowl and rice-beer to enjoy it for their function. They go to sleep late at night.

Post-wedding Ceremonies

The '*hera ruar*' ceremony is performed by the bride's parents two days after the marriage. In this ceremony, the bride's parents with other lineage members accompanied by maternal uncle pay a visit to their daughter. They carry with them two pots of rice-beer. The purpose of the visit is to ascertain and see whether their daughter has arrived safely in her husband's house and how she is living in her new home, is she happy or not? How is she being treated? etc. The main objective of the visit is to assure the daughter that they have not left her alone and are equally worried of her well-being. When they arrive at the bridegroom's house, they are welcomed warmly and their feet are washed as usual. They are then seated in a room and enquire each other's welfare. They ask their daughter, how she is feeling in the new home, with new family members and the local environment. Then offering of rice-beer is made to the ancestral spirits and is later served to all the individuals present there, except the non-lineage members. A number of rice-beer pots are then brought out. At night they are entertained with a sumptuous dinner. Next morning, after taking rice-beer again, the guests return to their village. The *lukdins* or escorts also either return along with the guests or stay few days more.

Visit to In-laws

There is yet another ceremony known as *bahurat*. Eight days after the *hera ruar* ceremony, the bride and the bridegroom pay a return visit to the bride's parents, village. One or two boys and girls also accompany the couple who carry a pot or two of rice-beer and a basketful of flattened rice to be distributed in the bride's village.

Below is a song belonging to Bala category in which it is stated that the bridegroom is making preparations for the visit to his bride's village during *bahurat* ceremony. The lines of the song are as follows:

> *Chacheṛa ghaṭ re baṛa re bijkaṭia*
> The mountain pass of Chacheṛa is most difficult one
> *Hare ladna bareda aṭaṭ nahiṇ hobaiṇ*
> The pack bullocks are unable to pass through it
> *Moeṇ kaise jabo sasurair*

How shall I go to my in-laws' house
Dal ke kaṭa̤t jamu
I shall pass through by chopping off the branches
Daura ke feka̤t jamu
I shall pass by throwing away the branches
Laraṇg ke kaṭa̤t jamu
I shall pass through by chopping off the creepers
Dhela ke pasa̤t jamu
I shall pass through by thrashing the lump of clay
Pakhena ke kucha̤t jamu
I shall pass through by crushing the stones
Tabe junu jahaj mora chalae
Then only my palanquin will pass on
Hare ladna bareda aṭa̤t nahiṇ hobaiṇ
Alas, the pack bullocks are unable to pass through it
Moen kaise jabo sasurair
How shall I go to my in-laws' house

The way to in-laws' house, that village is through the dense forest and rockey valleys. It is not the regular one and so is covered with tree branches, shrubs and serpentine creepers. The bridegroom wants to carry gifts on animals and he himself would travel in palanquin. He is aware of the difficulties that neither the beast nor the palanquin will pass through the valley. And so he decides to clear the path by cutting the branches and creepers. There are hills and rocks on the path to his in-laws' village but he will take his pack animals and palanquin by crushing the rocks and making the hills plain. Before the Britishers set their feet in Chhotanagpur plateau, the region was covered with dense forest and there was not a single regular path. People would generally travel in groups clearing the path as mentioned above.

Munda do not use palanquin as a means of travel neither they ever take the services of the animals for carrying the burden on their backs. These things were employed by the *jagirdars* and local kings only.

When the bride and bridegroom come for the first time to the bride's parent's house and after staying for some months there when they express their intention for returning to their home, they are requested to stay there for few days more. This has been mentioned in the following Jadur song, the lines of which are as follows:

1. *Kuhuṛ-kuhuṛ guṛia kuṭae re*
   The rice is being pounded into flour
   Chengen-mengen roṭia pakae
   And bread would be baked
   Ajuk dina rahi lebe gotia
   Stay for today; O guest
   Kail-kail jabe sasurair
   Proceed tomorrow to your in-laws' house

2. *Ek* dona *hanṛi pee* lere
   Drink at least a cup of rice-beer
   Ek khanda roṭi khae le
   And take at least a piece of bread
   Ajuk dina rahi lere gotia
   Stay for today, O guest
   Kail-kail jabe sasurair
   Proceed tomorrow to your in-laws' house

The bride and bridegroom as described in this song are requested to stay back for at least a day or two, for rice flour for baking the bread is being pounded. The bride, when she returns to her in-laws' house, besides rice-beer and flattened rice is also given a basketful of baked bread for distribution at her in-laws' village.

Yet another song belonging to Jadur category which has the same theme as above, the lines of which are as follows:

Nayo pisal khudiwa ge nayo
The broken rice floured by the mother
Ghiwa me chhanal roṭi lei jabo re sasurair
I will take bread to my in-laws' house baked in clarified butter
Najuk dina rahile, kail baṭe jabe sasurair
Stay for today, proceed tomorrow to your in-laws house

When the days pass, the bride slowly settles down in her in-laws' house but she visits her parent's house occasionally, sometimes alone and other times with her husband. In their in-laws' house, they receive love and care and hospitality as mentioned in the above two songs. Among the Munda, it is customary to carry some gifts for the host and in reciprocity while they return they are also given something as a token of love. In this song, as mentioned, the bride is given specially prepared bread to be carried to her in-laws' village. The guests are also requested to defer the journey for a day or two. Such is the courtesy request which usually is made by the host Munda to the guests.

At the time when the bride returns to her in-laws, house from *bahurat* her parents offer her valuable advice with respect to works and family life. The song below belongs to Bala category is based on one such theme. The song and the lines are as follows:

> *Babure dularo dameda*
> O beloved son-in-law
> *Hare, chhati bara-bari paena, dhuri nuṛae re*
> Alas, the chest length stick makes dust-storm
> *Na maru re dameda, na dharu re dameda*
> Dear son-in-law, don't strike her and don't catch hold of her
> *Hare, chhati bara-bari paena dhuri nuṛae re*
> Alas, the chest-length stick makes dust-storm

The couple are now ready to undertake the return journey. The mother of the bride advises the groom that he should not mistreat his bride. Such instructions are always given by every mother-in-law to the bridegroom. The bride also advise to obey her husband's advice. The Munda, whenever they undertake long journey, they carry with them weapons like *lathi,* battle axe and bow and arrows, etc, to protect oneself from any impending danger, particularly from wild beast.

In the song below which also belongs to Bala category, the girl is advised to carry any sort of weapons whenever she undertakes the journey. The lines of the song are as follows:

> *Hoṛa-hora tem seno redo maina*
> If you travel on the way, O daughter
> *Hatheyara sabeme maina, hatheyara sabeme*

Carry weapons, O daughter, carry weapons
Hatheyara sabeme maina
Carry weapons, O daughter
Hora redo pandu biṇg fenae Joṛao kada
Cobra has spread up its hood on the path
Hare, maina, biyura sekora najari chalae me
Cast your eyes all around, O daughter

In the present song as described, the girl has visited her parents' house and after staying for few days or months, she is now returning to her husband's village. Nobody is accompanying her, so she is advised to take precaution of the danger on the path. She is told that at one place, a cobra lives who generally attacks the people, so she must hold some weapons. In hilly and forest clad area, during journey, such dangers are encountered at every step.

The song below which also belongs to Bala category, the girl is given some advice. The lines of the song are as follows:

1. *Siŋgi tur hora redo numa*
   To the way of rising sun, mother
   Rohoṛ daru raṛaṇg ken raṛaṇg ken numa
   A dried up tree rattles ferociously, mother

2. *Kachi mairem boroya, kachi marirem chiriya*
   Would you not be afraid, O daughter
   Ka numaiṇg boroya, ka numaiṇg chiriya
   I have no fear, mother
   Hora redo rohoṛ daru raṛaṇg ken raṛaṇg ken
   A dried up tree rattles ferociously on the way
   Hora redo banḍu naṛi lodob ken lodob ken
   The *bandu* creeper sways beautifully on the path

In this song as mentioned, the girl is bold enough to undertake the journey alone. She is well acquainted with the path. A dried up tree on the way gives out strange sound all the time due to strong wind. The girl tells that she is not afraid of it. It is a mere tree and there are *Bandu* creepers swaying beautifully all the way. It indicates that the girl has become homely in her husband's house and wants to return there as early as possible.

As stated in previous pages, the bride and bridegroom sometimes visit the in-laws' house separately. In the song below as described, the groom wants to visit his in-laws' house and so asks some money from his mother. The song belongs to Bala category and the lines are as follows:

> *Detoge nayo tumba ka dhibua*
> Mother, let me have *dhibua* from pumpkin container
> *Moe to jamu chali Jamu sasurair*
> I would like to go to in-laws' house
> *Ka karbe babu tumba ka dhibua*
> What will you do from *dhibua* of pumpkin container
> *Dahar me to leda domari*
> On the path you will get ripened fig fruits
> *Luga kachhe bini bichi*
> Collect it on your cloth
> *Khate pite pani pite, chali jabe sasurair*
> Eating and drinking you proceed to your in-laws' house

The bride may have returned to her parents' village. The bridegroom wants to bring her back. So, he asks his mother, some money from the pumpkin container. The boy wants to purchase some eatables on the way. But his mother tells him that there is no need of money for there are fig fruits available on the way which he should collect on his cloth. He can eat the fruits when he feels hungry. People usually carry beaten or perched rice along with some piece of molasses whenever they proceed on journey which they eat on the way near some streams. Nowadays as mentioned in this song, money is taken and eatables are purchased from some shops on the way. But it was not so when the area was covered with forest with variety of fruit trees. Moreover, buying and selling of things was unknown to the region in those days.

After the marriage, the couple usually visit their in-laws' and relatives as and when they like. The song below mentions this theme which belongs to Bala category. The lines of the song are as follows:

> *Nayoge sutala ki jagala*
> Mother, are you awake or sleeping
> *Ham baba newari, ham baba pechhora*

I myself have the cot and cloth
Sute keto sutali, jage keto jagali
We are only half asleep
Hạm baba newari hạm baba pechhora
I myself have the cot and cloth

The boy arrived one winter night at his in-laws' house. It was midnight and the inmates of the house were sleeping. The boy was aware of the condition of their in-laws. There was no sufficient sleeping space and clothes to cover any additional individual. Therefore, the boy tells them that he himself has brought cot and cloth and that they need not worry for that. They tell him that they were half asleep.

The song below belonging to Jadur category also relates to the theme of visiting together of the couple to their in-laws, house. The lines of the song are as follows:

Rarangi daru re, eeti kanki rana do
I hear the cries of *kanki* bird upon the *rarangi* tree
Binga-bange sereng re, eeti dundu generang
I hear owl's moan upon the stripped rock
Otong redo otoging me, otong girem jagare
Follow me if you would like as you always talk of accompanying me
Panyar redo panyaring me, panyar girem bankara
Accompany if you would like, you always talk of walking together

The bride, whenever she talks of visiting her parents, her husband tells her that she should not go alone, for on the wayside *rarangi* tree and on the stripped rock *kanki* and Dundu bird, wail strangely. The bride is frightened at such talks and at last agrees to take her husband also.

It is not only the couple who visit the bride's parents' house, but sometimes other family members too. In the song below, the father of the bride visits his daughter. The song belongs to Bala category and the lines are as follows:

Bono dahạr gele baba, bono dahạr ekela

You all alone went through the forest path, father
Charailo chungunia manoa ko heki re
The chirping birds on the path are but human beings
Bono dahar gele baba, bono dahar ekela
You all alone went through the forest path, father

The father visited his married daughter. He now wants to return to his village. The daughter tells him, since he is going alone in the forest path which is infested with dangers, he should not go alone. The father tells her that the path is not lonely for there are chirping birds all along the path who are no other than but human beings and there is nothing to fear.

The song below describes the visits of the brother to his sister. The song belongs to Bala category and the lines are as follows:

Hare, hare chhagri charoa
O goat shepherd boys
Hare hare, bhegri charoa, bheri charoa re
O the shephered of sheep
Kono desa re bhaiya, bahin ko raji
O brothers, which is the country of the sister
Kono desa re bhaiya, bahin ko desa
O brothers, which is the land of the sister
Hine ho songolpure, hune ho ratanpure
This side Songolpur, that side Ratanpur
Seo majhe re bhaiya, bahin ko raji
In between lies the country of the sister, O brother
Seo majhe re bhaiya, bahin ko desa
In between lies the land of the sister, O brother

After the marriage, the girl is visited by almost all the family members and relatives. As mentioned in this song, one of the brothers of the girl visits her for the first time. Prior to this, he had never been to that part of the country and so he does not know the village of his sister. In spite of this, he sets out for the village. It was agricultural season and there were people all along the route. He asks the shepherds about the direction and path leading to the village. He is told that the village is located somewhere in between the two well-known villages—Songolpur and Ratanpur. On the basis of the location told by the shepherds he proceeds to the brother-in-law's village to see his sister.

During the days of trouble as well as happy occasions the daughter is always remembered by the parent as mentioned in the song below. The song belongs to Bala category and the lines are as follows:

Eko goṭo beṭi nadi pare dialo
I gave my only daughter beyond the river
Hare, naai dekhi-dekhi nando nahiṇ awae
Seeing the spating river my sleep has gone away
Pani upar doṇga
The boat is on the water
Doṇga upar manoa
People are on the boat
Hare jhora beṭa rijhe doṇga chalae
The boatman is merrily steering the boat across

The daughter is invited during all important occasions such as marriage, festivals and fairs. But during rainy season, it is very difficult to visit each other as all the rivers and rivulets are inundated. In this song the parent, and particularly the father is anxious for his daughter who has been married beyond the river. It has inundated the banks but people still are crossing it through the boat. They have overcrowded the boat and the boatman is happy and is rowing merrily for, he is earning a lot. Sometimes the boat capsizes due to strong currents or due to overcrowding of people. This kind of happening has created anxiety among the parents.

6

THE MARITAL LIFE

Life with In-laws

The bride is now living with her husband in his village. The new bride is received by the villagers cordially. The theme of the song below is the same as stated in one of the earlier songs, that is, one's own daughter becomes the daughter of others; and other one's own. The lines of the song which belongs to Bala category, are as follows :

> *Booṭ khete masuri khete*
> On the field of gram and lentil crops
> *Kekara suga liyar koyor*
> Whose parrots are loitering about
> *Gharak suga jane kane*
> One's domesticated parrots are elsewhere
> *Aṇkar suga liyar koyor*
> Other's parrots are loitering about

The song describes the beauty of the birde in parents in-laws' house. The bride, besides the household works, goes out in the field along with other members of the family. She is a stranger to the villagers. So, when she is moving around in the fields, people of other hamlets who were not present in the marriage ceremony, enquire about the girl as to who she is. When told that she is the daughter-in-law of such family of the village, they say that one's own daughters are beautifying the household of others in other villages and that other's daughters are adding beauty to our own. The brides are like the beautiful parrots. The beauty of the house as well as of the village, is thus, preserved through the custom of marriage.

Below is another song which also describes the beauty of the bride. The song belongs to Bala category and the lines are follows :

Jotala khete
One the ploughed up field
Harina chhauwa dega-degi khelae, haere
The calf of the doe are hopping around
Na lage harina, na Jage kotena
They are neither the deer nor the wild goat
Eto heke bhaiya kinal dhumal dhusa kaneya
She is but a beautiful bride brought by the brother

In this song, the bride looks like a beautiful deer or a wild goat from a distance. Both these animals are playful and frolicsome, so also the bride is playful and beautiful. She is working in the ploughed up field running here and there. The girls or the boys from distance hardly recognize her. At last they identify her as the wife of their brother.

There exists a very cordial relation in between the bride and her brother-in-law, that is, husband's younger brother. So also between the husband and her own sisters and brothers. The relationship is so intimate that sometimes they exchange jokes but the youngsters always pay regards to the sister-in-law or brother-in-law. The wife of the younger brother gives high regards to the elder brother and his wife. She maintains avoidance relationship with the elder brother of the husband. The wife of the elder brother is a *hili* for the younger brothers and sisters and they are *iril* for her. But elder brothers and sisters are *bau-honjar* and *aji-hanar* of the status of father and mother for the wife of younger brother. For them she is *kimin,* that is, the daughter-in-law. Such avoidance and joking relationship are maintained even with other lineage members and affinals who happen to be the brothers and sisters of the husband.

Below is a song which describes the relationship of the bride with that of the younger brother of the husband. The song belongs to Bala category and the lines are as follows:

Jugte jugal re keora re rasa bhaonra
Humming bird makes rounds on the *keora* flower
Sur se alain re chhot deora

The brother-in-law came all of a sudden
Lali bunab nayo merali jabo re ṭeṭu ghoṛa
We shall weave of love to control the obstinate horse
Sur se alaiṇ re chhoṭ deora
The brother-in-law came all of a sudden

The younger brother of the husband is very frolicsome and always makes fun with this sister-in-law while running in and out like the humming bird who hovers over the flowers all the time. He is obstinate like an indisciplined horse who strides off in a slight provocation.

The song below too, which belongs to Bala category has the same theme as above. The lines of the song are as follows :

Keora re rasa bhaoṇra (re)
The humming bird of the *keora* flower
Sur se ghar mor mati keora re
Don't make round of my room like *keora* flower
Lali bunab daiya
We will spread love, O sister
Merali jabo re ṭeṭu ghoṛa
To control the obstinate horse
Sur se ghar more mati keora re
Don't make round of my room like *keora* flower
Keora re rasa bhaoṇra
The humming bird of the *keora* flower
Sur se ghar mor mati keora re
Don't make round of my room like *keora* flower

There are few songs below which describe disharmonious relationship of the bride with that of her husband's family members. In these songs the bride lodges a complaint to her husband, against the parents-in-laws or against the overall environment of the family.

Below is a song belonging to Bala category in which the bride describes as to how the members of her parents-in-laws house misbehaved with her. The lines of the songs are as follows :

Hanariṇga chenta do, hanariṇga chenta do
The jealousy of my other-in-law

Buru jola jharia re, hel'a peteje metainga
Asks me to collect bamboo offshoots from the valley by the stream
Hanaringa chenta do, hanaringa chenta do
The jealousy of my mother-in-law
Buru jola jharia re, dhuru kuṭamae metaiṇga
Asks me to collect firewood from the hill valley by the stream
Teṇja koṛa chenta do, teṇja koṛa chenta do
The jealousy of my brother-in-law
Buru jola jharia re jara chopae metaiṇga
Asks me to clear the forest patch by the stream of the valley
Teṇja kuṛi-a chenta do, teṇja kuṛi-a chenta do
The jealousy of my sister-in-law
Buru jola jharia re haku crejae metaiṇga
Asks me to catch fish in the stream by the valley

This song mentions that everyone of the household wants to take work from the bride. She is sent alone to do the work in the forest valley and hill stream. The loneliness in work is a boredom. She feels that she is asked to do the job merely because of jealousy and nothing else. It is one of the situation that the brides are forced to run away from their husbands house.

Below is another song in which the bride is critical of her mother-in-law's behaviour. The song belongs to Bala category, the lines of which are as follows :

Goiṇtha je bichhae
The cow dung is being collected
Eko khaṇchi duyo khaṇchi re bichhae
It is collected on one or two big sized baskets
Sais je kahela chuṇwa ghaṭe
The mother-in-law speaks ill at the stream
Didi ge moen to nahiṇ re rahbo
O sister, I will not stay there any more

The bride in this song tells her eldest sister about the treatment she received from her mother-in-law. She had to collect cow dung one or two basketful daily, yet her mother-in-law speaks ill against her at the stream among the ladies of the village who hapen to be there while collecting drinking water. The bride recounts her experience and tells her elder sister that she will not stay in her parents-in-laws' house any more. This is one of the serious situations which leads to separation if not intervened by the elders.

The cow dung is collected for two purposes—for using it like firewood and for manuring the fields. In areas where they have been denuded, cow dung is used like firewood. The women go out for collecting the same in the fields. After the harvest is over, the cattle are let loose from morning to evening. In areas, however, where there are forests, no cow dung collection is done. And the bride who comes from forest region to forestless areas, naturally finds herself in an awkward situation. The mother-in-law who expects from the bride to carry out the work and when she does not find it to her satisfaction, she calls the name of her daughter-in-law, behind her back, before the village women. The bride could not bear such humiliation and decided to leave her husband.

In the song below too, which belongs to Jadur category of song, the bride complains to her brother against the condition of her parents-in-laws' house. The lines of the song are as follows:

1. *Buru-buru hau koṭa bareṇg ko goṇga kaadiṇga bareṇg*
   I have been married for collecting insect's larvae from
   Buru-beṛa lama poṭa-a bareṇg ko chala-a kadiṇga bareṇg
   I have been married for collecting *lama* rope from the valley brother

2. *Buru-buṛu hau kota bereṇg iṇg ekela tanaya bareṇg*
   I am trembling collecting insect's larvae from the hills brother
   Buru-beṛa lama pota-a bareṇg iṇg tayur janaya bareṇg
   I am tired of colleçting *lama* rope from the valley brother

The bride tells her brother about the works she did at her parents-in-laws' house. The economic condition of the family does not seem to be good, so they spent most of their time in collecting the larvae of tree ant which is taken as food and *lama* rope from the forest. Lama rope is collected from the *Bandu or Gungu* creepers for making different kinds of rope implements, they are sold in the local market or are supplied to other persons in lieu of grain or money. The bride's parents, it appears, are economically better than her husband's and the activities she is now doing is quite an embarrassing one for her. She has to go out in the forest daily to collect the things as mentioned. She does not like the work at all and finds the life unenjoyable.

Below is a song belonging to Karam category in which the bride states that her husband is a hot tempered person and at slight provocation, hits out at her. The girls is making a complaint to her father. The lines of the song are as follows :

> *Abaga kaiṇg taina*
> Father dear, I will not stay there
> *Kula jomi setha, gopoe geyae*
> He always resorts to killing, the dog like person, deserves of a tiger's dish
> *Biṇg or-e orr kiṇga*
> Dragged me for long like a snake pace
> *Sukuri dalae dal kiṇga*
> Thrashed me like the way boars are bitten
> *Abaga kaiṇg taina*
> Father dear, I will not stay there
> *Kula jomi setha, gopoe giyae*
> He always resorts to killing, the dog like person, deserves of tiger's dish

The girl is fed up with inhuman treatment of her husband. So she emphatically tells her father that she will not live in the house any longer for he always resorts to thrashing, biting and killing. She tells her father that he (husband) dragged and thrashed her mercilessly just as snakes or boars. She further tells him that he is a dog who always quarrels and fights. May tigers eat him up. In short, the girl hates her husband so much that in her eye he is no better than a dog and she will be glad if he is eaten away by the tiger. The husband-wife relations as stated in the song have worsened to the stage of irrepairable stituation. The girls has taken the decision that she will not go back to her husband's house.

In the song below too, the girl lodges a complaint to her parent. The song belongs to Bala category and the lines are as follows :

Dure gandure sembi moen ropaloṇ
I sowed been seed on the distance garbage
Hare, nane-nane dari me jhabarae
The slender creeper became laden with fruits
Toraloṇ, bhapaloṇ, randhaloṇ, bataloṇ
I plucked, steamed, cooked and served
Hare sasur mor ke diyaloṇ
I served to my father-in-law
Seo sasur ana-dhana gari delaiṇ re
The father-in-law mine abused me at will

As mentioned in this song, the bride is abused though she did the work assigned to her. She planted bean seed in the garbage which gave abundant fruits. The bride plucked the fruits and cooked it. She served it to all the family members. The song indicates that the father-in-law of the bride did not like the taste of the cooked beans. He may have abused the bride for her method of cooking which rendered the food tasteless. But women in general, may not agree to this statement. For they say that there is taste in the food when variety of spices are used during the preparation. And most of the families, it is observed, do not add spice while cooking the vegetables, as described in the song, the girl first cooked the bean by steaming, then added oil and cooked again. The taste of the food may differ in preparation, which may depend upon the length of the time of steaming and cooking. It is a fact that over-steamed or over-boiled food becomes tasteless even if spices are added to it. The bride may have over steamed the bean. So, it is natural for the father-in-law to be angry. However, this situation is not very serious and with the passing of time, the bride may learn the preparation of food according to the likings of the family members. But some brides take the matter seriously and get an excuse of divorce from her husband.

As the bride is new in her husband's family who has been brought up in another family environment, difference in likings and behaviour with the new members is but natural. One such situation of discord has been described in the following Bala category of song. The lines of the song are as follows:

Jiling-jiling-jiling bakaṛi
A long garden

Dunguj-dunguj-dunguj bakari
A short garden
Sasang numa ko roe leda
Turmeric was cultivated, mother
Sida-sida-sida burate sasang sarej
Earlier lady love memory is like a left over turmeric in his life
Sasang numa ko roe leda
Turmeric was cultivated, mother

The bride and bridegroom's premarital connections or love affairs sometimes become the bone of contention of discontent among the married couple. As mentioned in this song, the bride complains to her mother that her husband still maintains relations with his previous girl. This situation is like the leftover turmeric in the field which sprouts again whenever it gets water. This relation of the husband is being observed by the wife silently. She says that however small the turmeric may be, its pigmentation cannot be concealed. And she fears that like leftover turmeric, the relationship of her husband may spoil their married life. The mother is in a fix. She is unable to take a decision whether to send back her daughter to her husband's house or ask her for divorce.

The separation or divorce also takes place when the husband takes another woman as his wife. In this case he may not be able to pay equal attention to both the wives and either of them may feel neglected due to jealousy as is natural in such situation. The song below which belongs to Bala category mentions this situation. The lines of the song are as follows:

Sonpur ke chhoralain
Sonpur was divorced
Nagpur ke kahe puchhae re
Why much attention is paid to Nagpur
Hare daiya, Basia ko dure hanka nagae re
Alas sister, the Basia was driven off
Borki ke chhoralain
They divorced the eldest

Chhoṭki ke puchhae re
They are giving much attention for the youngest
Hare daiya, Basia ko dure haṇka nagae re
Alas sister, the Basia was drive-off

Marriage with more then one wife is not prohibited among the Mundas, as indicated in the song. But nowadays such cases are rarely found. As stated in the song the wife from Sonpur, the first one, is totally neglected and the second one too, who belongs to Nagpur, receives the same treatment, while the third one who comes from Basia Pargana of the Munda country, has been driven off from the house by the husband. He now has brought another wife, the youngest and the fourth one and pays exclusive care to her. Sometimes, such wives who have *hirum* relationship among them, also quarrel forcing one or two of them to leave the husband. The latter situation is a serious one for no mediation can bring the wives into compromise unless they themselves settle the dispute. Customarily, the first wife, claims a privileged treatment from her husband. But, as mentioned, in this song, the first wife is being neglected by the husband. In such a situation, the eldest one, if she has no issue of her own leaves the husband and goes back to her natal home.

The brides are always addressed or referred to by the names of the village they come from and never by personal names. In this song too, though Sonpur, Nagpur and Basia are not the names of the villages but Parganas (an administrative region having number of villages), have been referred to in place of bride's names. If the bride is, brought from another pargana, she will be addressed to by the name of the pargana to which she originally belongs. In case of the people too, when they happen to visit the area or region of another pargana or country, they carry the identity there of the pargana or the country, such as Sonpur, Nagpur, Naguri and Hasada, etc, and are addressed there as such. This indicates the importance of the social geography by the Mundas in their tradition. The identification of the individuals are also made on the basis of the clan they belong to in reference. such as *Surin horoko, Baṛla ko,* etc.

The co-wives or *hirumia* relationship have been described in the following Lahsua category of song. The lines of the song are as follows:

Chhoṭki ke har-pair
Ornaments and fine dresses for the youngest wife
Baṛki ke re sada luga
And plain dress for the eldest wife
Kalau re dada baṛa daga dele
Why did you cheat her brother
Chhoṭki ke nawa saṛi
New dress for the youngest wife
Boṛki ke re purna luga
But old cloths to the eldest
Kalau re dada baṛa daga dele
Why did you cheat her brother

In this song as stated, it is the sister who makes complaints to her brother against the discriminatory treatment he makes between his two wives in which the second wife gets the best treatment than the first in matters of dress and ornaments. During the marriage, the husband had promised before the kinsfolk and relatives that he will provide her every good thing she will need in her life, but with the marriage of second wife, he bypassed all those promises. He is, therefore, a lier and cheat. Such misconduct, generally, leads to a very strained relation in life.

The co-wives, sometimes become very troublesome in the family, particularly when they develop jealousy and hatred among them. In case of quarrel among such wives, no arbitrator usually turns up to settle the enmity. In case of second marriage, often the second wife is not consulted by the husband or the second wife herself makes forcible entry in her lover's house. In such case, the first wife receives the public support. The song below which belongs to Jadur category indicates that wives coming by second marriage, are always disliked by the general public with some exceptions. The lines of the song are as follows:

Ne merai dondo meral
This ignorant *meral* fruit
Sakam re jowa kana
Is hanging on the leaves
Ne kuṛi ḍinḍa kuṛi
This unmarried damsel

Hirum re boloa kana
Has intruded into as co-wife
Koto ko banō leka
As if there are no branches
Sakạm re jowa kana
It is hanging on the leaves
Ḍiṇḍa koṛa ko baṇko leka
As if there are no unmarried boys
Hirum re boloa kana
Has intruded into as co-wife

Meral is a wild fruit which bears no leaf-stalks. The leaves remain on the tree for some time, that is, it is seasonal and if the leaves fall, it is but natural for the fruits also to fall down along with the leaves. In the song it is asked whether there is the scarcity of branches on the tree that the fruits are hanging on the leaves. Similarly, girls who agree to be as co-wife, are silly as there is no permanency in such marriages. There is no dearth of unmarried boys in the society. Such relationships usually do not last long for there develops tension among the co-wives due to jealousy.

The girls before marriage usually enjoy lives in their parents' house but no one is certain about it after the marriage. It is the uncertainty that makes the girl weep when she takes leave after marriage from parents and friends. If the girl gets difficulty in adjusting herself in her parents-in-laws' house then her life becomes miserable. The song below belonging to Bala category describes the sad plight of the girl in the parents-in-laws' house. The lines of the song are as follows:

Baini re baini, baini re baini
Sister, O dear sister
Ghar bhitare khiṛki me
Inside the house by the window
Achera me lora pani girale
You shed tears on the borders of the dress
Sais-sasur ghare gele baini
Since you left for your parents-in-laws' house

Ghar bhitare khiṛki me
Inside the house by the window
Achera me lora pani girale
You shed tears on the borders of the dress

The elder sister is worried over pitiable plight of her younger sister in her parents-in-laws' house. She is not treated well by her husband's kin. She does not raise voice against such behaviour instead sheds tears silently. Her elder sister is watching the changes that have developed in her younger sister ever since she was married away.

Below in another song belonging to Bala category in which it is stated that the brother of the married sister also weeps looking at the sad condition of her sister in her parents-in-laws' house. The lines of the song are as follows:

Eko kose pani
A *kos* long water belt
Biso kose jaṇgal bhitarege nayo
And within twenty *kos* widespread forest, mother
Duyo bhaiya-bahina kandae ge nayo
Both brother and sister are weeping, mother
Age nai lage, bajạra pahar ge nayo
Let catch fire and let lightning strike on them, mother
Duyo bhaiya-bahina kandae ge nayo
Both brother and sister are weeping, mother
Aisana jana to, aisana buja toge nayo
It has neither been known nor ever perceived, mother
Jahaṇ jina tahaṇ marna ge nayo
Where one is destined to live, the end of life is there too.

The girl has been married away in a distant village which lies in the midst of forest surrounded by wide lakes. The girl is not happy there for she is unable to see her parent as often as she would like. This may be one of the reasons of divorce. But the girl, as stated in the song, compromises with the situation as she follows what has been said by the elders he or she should accept to live gladly where the life has been destined and lead the life till end comes. Such precept of the elders give courage to one in distress.

The first year of married life of the girl is a test of her patience in her parents-in-laws' house. As her husband is a stranger, her companionship with him may be cordial or she may get bored. Sometimes the family members fill the gap otherwise the girl may feel lonely and neglected. If the girl does not receive good treatment from the family members, instead of developing attachment with them, the feeling of isolation and homesickness may disturb her life and if she is not allowed to visit her natal home, she may run away without informing the in-laws. Below is a song belonging to Lahsua category which is based on such a theme. The lines of the song are as follows:

> *Nai gena-gena te keda yako seno tan*
> The water buffaloes are walking away by the side of the river
> *Dada ho dolaṇg dada keda gupi te*
> Brother, let us go for tending the water buffaloes
> *Kaiṇg sena dada ho, kaiṇg sena bacha ho*
> I cannot accompany you my dear brother
> *Dada ho toraiṇg, hora hiliṇg nir tana*
> Brother dear, my sister-in-law is running away

The bride finds an opportunity when her husband and younger brother were proceeding for tending the water buffaloes which were heading towards the river. No one was in the house except the brothers. As the two brothers were busy, the bride silently leaves the house and heads for the parents' house. The younger brother, however, sensed the plan of his sister-in-law and asks his elder brother to accompany the water buffaloes who were already out towards the river and further tells that he himself is going to bring back his sister-in-law who is running away. It is generally the husband who brings back the fleeing wife, but in case he is absent or busy in other jobs, the younger brother does the job as mentioned in the song.

The following song too, belonging to Bala category which also is based on this theme, states that the husband is out in search of his wife who is running away. The lines of the song are as follows:

> *Hare-hare chhagri charoa*
> O goat tending boys

Hare-hare bheṛi charoa, bheṛi charoa re
Listen O sheep tending boys
Hare, dekhala ki nahiṇ, chinala ki nahiṇ
Had you seen and recognized
Dekhe keto deikh rahli
Yes, we had seen
Chine keto chin rahli
We had recognized her
Eri me paṇyari ahe
She is wearing leg ornaments
Ḍanḍa me saṛi ahe
And she is wearing sari
Chhati me jhula ahe
She is wearing blouse on her body
Gheṇcha me chandoa ahe
She is wearing silver locket on her neck
Muṛe me mota-jhota
She is carrying a bundle on her head
Maṛu re tero soṭa
Strike her with stick as many as thirteen times
Tabe junu sasurari sobhalaiṇ re
Then only there is beauty in in-laws' house
Tabe junu sasurari sobhae
Then only there is beauty in in-laws' house

The bride is running away and the husband is out in search of her. The cattle tending boys are in the field. He asks them about the girl who might have passed through that route. The boys tell him that they had seen a girl who is in such and such dress and ornaments and that she is also carrying a bundle of clothes on her head. The husband is convinced hearing the identity and proceeds on the same route hurriedly. The cattle tending boys advised him to beat his fleeing wife otherwise there is no beauty in staying in in-laws house. The cattle tending boys are enjoying the event and tell him that if there is no quarrel and wife beating after marriage then there is no beauty of *sasuṛair*. The event is like the play of hide and seek for the new couple and both enjoy it. The wives are never beaten by the husbands with some exception, otherwise it may invite the wrath of the lineage members who may take such husband to task.

It is the obligation of the parents or the elders to give counsel to their sons and daughters in matters of personal behaviours, social customs and values. The bride being new to the family may not be aware of the likings and dislikings of the family members which may create mistrust and strained relations. But the bride also, after all is their daughter and she is to be guided in all matters. It is, in course of advice that she, sometimes, is reprimanded for the negligence in duty. The song below which belongs to Jadur category states that after marriage the bride must learn the practice and behaviour pattern of the in-laws. The lines of the song are as follows:

> *Sais ghare newan ge mai*
> It is the manners that matter in the mother-in-law's house
> *Sasur ghare chalạn ge mai*
> It is the conduct in father-in-law's house, daughter
> *Bhaṇṭa tiyạn lamba-lamba ge mai*
> There are full size brinjals in the curry, daughter
> *Hae tor newạn ge mai*
> Damn to your knowledge, O daughter
> *Hae tor chalạn ge mai*
> Damn to your conduct, O daughter
> *Bhaṇṭa tiyạn lamba-lamba ge mai*
> There are full size brinjals in the curry, daughter

The girl in general enjoy great liberty in their parents house, but it varies from family to family. It is why, some girls remain ignorant even of elementary knowledge of works of day-to-day activities. But as stated earlier, taste and ways of doing things differ from person to person and family to family. The knowledge acquired at one's parents' house, sometimes, helps very little in parents-in-laws' house. If the family members are not of conservative nature, they would like a change very much and the bride may receive appreciation from them, otherwise the life of the bride becomes miserable. As in the song above, the mother-in-law, strictly tells the bride that it is the parents-in-laws' house and the habit and practice developed in her natal home will not do, it is the manners and ways of doing things of the parents-in-laws' house that must be followed and practised henceforth. The girl cooked the brinjal curry in which she left the brinjal in its full size.

As in cooking, so also in other activities, the bride may invite criticism from their parents-in-laws. The song below belonging to Khemta category mentions that the bride is greedy. The lines of the song are as follows:

Bakṛi bhitar muṇga suba
Inside the garden under the *munga* tree
Parkom bila kana
A cot has been spread up
Ne kimin neka chalan kae bagia
The bride will not forsake this habit
Gum tan-gum tan chaulie kapaya
Eats up rice while cleaning
Ne kimin bagi taime
Divorce this bride
Tawaete utue luya
Takes out curry from the pan
Am bolem bagi-iṇg redo kora
If you divorce me, O boy
Lutur japa sae sunupid lingi tana
Oil will drip down to the side of the ear from my hairdo
Am lekan kuṛiko
The women like you
Disum reko jaltiṇg tana
Are hovering over the country disappointed
Am teyo kaiṇg haya tana
I have no attraction towards you

The song describes the causes that lead to divorce of the couple. There is a kitchen garden where at one side of the fence a *munga* tree stands. It is under this tree, on a cot the father-in-law of the bride is resting. The bride is busy in cleaning the rice. While cleaning, she would eat some grains of rice also. She is also cooking pulse which she takes out in a cup and goes on eating. The father-in-law is watching her from the kitchen garden. When the bridegroom comes from the field, he makes a complaint against the bride and also advises him to get her divorced. The bride is an outspoken one. She will not be cowed down by the criticism. She boldly replies to her husband that if he divorces her, she will walk around in best dress and fashion. The bridegroom also retaliates in the same tone and tells her that there are so many girls like her who are hovering over the country restlessly. He also tells her in harsh words that he has no attraction for her. Such exchange of words between husband and wife spoils the relationship and leads to separation.

There are various grounds of dislikings of the bride's working habits. The song below describes that the bride does household duties without taking consultation from her parents-in-laws. She, thus, becomes the target of criticism. The song below belonging to Jadur category, has this theme, the lines of which are as follows:

Ne kuṛi do khudi maṇḍi re ranu keda
This girl did apply medicine in the food of broken rice
Ne kuṛi do adwa chauli re jiṇyaṛ keda
This girl made unboiled rice sour
Ne kuṛi do eṇgate apute banko leka
This girl did as if she is an orphan
Ne kuṛi do ranu keda
This girl did apply medicine
Ne kuṛi do hagate barete baṇko leka
This girl did as if she has no brother and sister
Ne kuṛi do jiṇyaṛ keda
This girl made sour

The girl without asking her parents-in-laws brought out paddy, thrashed it in the mortar and cleaned it. She then, after half cooking applied medicine so as to make the rice-beer. The song states that this rice would have been cooked for food for the family members instead of rice-beer. The bride did the work without prior consultation from her parents-in-laws. Such activities generally invite criticism from the elders.

Besides, those who are careless in their work also get criticism. The following song. belonging to Jadur category is based on this theme. The lines of the song are as follows:

1. *Dahar-dahar gele ge mai*
   you walked along the path, O daughter
   Dahar meto lahar lagele
   The path burns for you

2. *Kapas khete gele ge mai*
   You went to the cotton field, O daughter
   Kapas khete jhuṭia hiraile
   You lost the toe ring in the cotton field

3. *Luga kachhe gele ge mai*
   You went to wash the clothes
   Luga keto jhaṇḍa garaile
   You pitched flags of the clothes

4. *Khoir bule gele ge mai*
   You went for walking on the lawn
   Chhauwa keto sutae rakhele
   You left the baby sleeping.

In this song, a number of improper activities of the bride have been mentioned. The mother-in-law is critical of her activities, though they are very trivial. When the bride goes somewhere, she never adopts the usual path. The mother-in law asks her, whether the path was burning that you did not go by the path. When the bride was in the cotton field, she lost the toe ring there and when she went to the stream to wash the clothes, she pitched all the clothes like flags. One serious allegation is that the bride never takes the baby along with her whenever she goes out for walking. Such improper activities did greatly annoy the mother-in-law.

As mentioned above, some brides do not care for the words of the parents and confront them when criticized. The song below which belongs to *Jarga* category, mentions one such confrontation. The lines of the song are as follows:

> *Am doga era, marang diri gara koeteng sala ked meya*
> I selected you girl, from among the pebbles of big stony river
> *Lowa ge chowa gem eranga*
> You abuse us at random

Amdo era, marang diri gara koe teng sala led meya
I selected you girl from among the pebbles of big stony river
Lasur ge badur gem segeda
You scold us all the time

The song indicates that it is the bride who is playing the upper hand in the family affairs. It is the bride who controls the family members and takes them to task all the time. So, not all the brides are alike, The fact is that as the days pass, the bride takes control of the household affairs and particularly so when the husband also does not speak against her. All have become cows before the bride except the mother-in-law who is obsessed of hearing the abuse of the bride and faces her boldly. The mother-in-law tells the bride that she selected her from among the scores of girls like selecting the pebbles from the river bed. While selecting her as bride, she had not expected such behaviour from her.

As stated in earlier pages, a girl must learn some basic work essential in day-to-day life. It will be difficult for the bride to run the household if she does not know the elementary things considered essential. If she shows ignorance she may attract criticism from all. The following song is based on this theme which belongs to Jadur category, the lines of which are as follows:

1. *Bale ga bale reko gong tad meya*
You were given in marriage in infancy
Lindung-lindung reko chal tad meya
You were given away when you walked staggeringly

2. *Puru tukui ho kam ituana*
You don't know how to stitch leaf cups
Chari chata ho kam saria
You don't know how to split fine sticks

3. *Ju maina ruar me engam ko ora: te*
Get back to your mother's house, O daughter
Ju maina nachur me apum to rosom te
Return to your father's residence, O daughter
Engam ora: re tukui enung me
Better play stitching at your mother's house

Apum rosom re chaṭa: sarin me
Better learn making fine sticks at the father's residence

In this song as mentioned, the mother-in-law finds her daughter-in-law too ignorant to do any work. The bride does not know how to prepare leaf cups and making fine sticks for stitching. She, therefore, tells her to get back to her parents' house and learn all work, first. The husband's house is not the place of learning but it is for serious works. Life after marriage cannot be spent in learning. It is a serious part of human life and one must be ready to face it and learn everything before one's marriage.

Sometimes it happens that the boy and the girl are not ready for marriage but due to compulsion of the parents, they agree for the relationship. The couple under such relationship often do not get along together. The bride in this situation, may feel loneliness. And when once the bride gets back to her parents' house, she is reluctant to return again to her husband's house. This leads to separation. Below is the song belonging to Jarga category in which the bridegroom complains that he has been cheated. The lines of the song are as follows:

Hae numa aba buṛia
Alas, mother and father, the old woman
Kuṛi rem beda keḍiṇga
You cheated me in girl
Buṛia kuṛi rem beda keḍiṇga
Cheated me in old girl
Hae numa naba-saba
Alas, mother assured me fresh but got me tasteless one
Mayaṇg rem beda keḍiṇga
You cheated me by the waist
Saba, mayaṇg rem beda keḍiṇga
You cheated me in tasteless waist

The boy in this song complains that he was cheated into an old or aged woman. The match is not liked by the bridegroom but he is now helpless, so he blames his parents that he was cheated into an old woman. Age difference is one of the factors of breaking of marriages among couples.

Sometimes separation also takes place when there is a clash of personality in between the couple. The lack of adjustment thus, leads to separation. The song below belonging to *Jadur* category, is based on this theme, the lines of which are as follows:

1. *Jau do gatim chire, jạu dore sangaiṇg*
Dear friend and companion, we were forever
Kaji gelaṇg kaji leda
We had talked of one word
Jau do gatim chire, jau dore sangaiṇg
Dear friend and companion, we were forever
Miyad baṇkạr gelaṇg baṇkạr kena
We had talked of one word
Miyad kaji gelaṇg kaji leda
We had talked of one word
Miyad kaji dore baria jana
One word has now become two
Baria baṇkaṛ gelaṇg baṇkaṛ leda
We had talked of two words
Baria baṇkaṛ dore apia jana
The two words have split into three

2. *Miyad kaji gelaṇg kaji kena*
We had talked of one word
Bage seraṇ gehom seraṇ keda
You had thought of leaving me
Baria baṇkaṛ laṇg bankaṛ kena
We had talked of two words
Raṛa buidi gehom buidi ked
You did plan for divorcing me

The couple had very good time in their early days of their married life. They had very intimate relations and no one had ever dreamt that divorce is awaiting in their life also. They led a very happy life. But suddenly the mind of the bride changed and one day she left her husband forever. The husband could not perceive the plan of his wife. He came to know only when his wife was stepping out from his house. The husband reminds her with heavy heart of the promises they had made together which now have come out as false. The husband regrets over his own foolishness and thinks that his wife may have been making plans of leaving him silently since long time. There is now no way out but to bid good-bye to her with shattered heart.

In married life, there are occasions when many disharmonious situations arise and husband-wife relations become strained. But such situations do not continue for long in many a case and become normal in course of time. Particularly when either of the couple or both are mature enough to understand the life. The song below belonging to Lahsua category derives its theme from one such situation. The lines of the song are as follows:

Noko sate hiju lenam
From where did you come
Duar rem dube jana
You sat down on the door
Lokodor maina
O depressed dear
Kuli mere kame kakala
You don't respond when asked
Purbe tem hiju lena
You did come from the east
Duar rem dube jana
You sat on the door
Lokodor maina
O depressed dear
Kuli mere kame kakala
You don't respond when asked

The husband has returned from somewhere depressed. He sat down on the door of the house quietly. His wife asks him but she receives no response from him. When the husband-wife relations become strained, sometimes for days together they pass the time without exchange of a single word. In this song as stated the husband is expressing his unhappiness by keeping silence. The wife tries to break the silence of her husband.

There is the other side of husband-wife relations also. The song below belonging to Lahsua category describes the most cordial relations between husband and wife. The lines of the song are as follows:

Juṛi mor kahaṇ gel
Where did my beloved go
Juṛi binu khori suna bhel
The lawn is desolate without the beloved
Ho, hore, juri mor Muṛhu gel
O beloved mine has gone to Murhu
Juṛi binu khori suna bhel
The lawn is desolate without the beloved

The wife is feeling loneliness in the absence of her husband who has gone out somewhere for work. The wife is looking after everything alone and has become bored. This shows that there exists a deep love and respect among the husband and wife.

With the passing of days, the husband and wife relations become more intimate and enjoyable as they enjoy the life by living together. How they carry out their work merrily has been mentioned in the following song belonging to Jarga category, the lines of which are as follows:

Dhaṇkna dhapurna
O the loosely dressed one
Baba na rongo tana
The paddy is burning
Don tameya radoṛa
O the bearded one, please take down that
Babuyaiṇg koyoṇg kaja
The baby is on my lap
Ne na hene na
Look here it is
Simii na nelem sowan tana
The excrement of fowls is emitting bad smell
Her tameya gunda here
Drop some fine chaffs over it
Giṛi tare bolem jati senoga-haere
Will you loose your tribe if you throw it away

The relations between husband and wife are very cordial and harmonious. The song describes a very humorous and lyrical conversation between husband and wife which every couple share and enjoy in course of their daily activities. It is the general nature of every husband to ask his wife to do everything, however small and easy the job may be which the husband thinks beyond his duty. As mentioned in this song, the wife gives a fitting reply to her husband whenever he asks her to do something. The song indicates that the couple are so busy that they hardly get time to get dressed properly The wife has fastened her dress on her body very loosely and is attending every work in this very state. The appearance of the husband too is not so nice. His face is covered with full grown beard. He is sitting close to the oven where paddy on a pot has been settled. The wife is sitting at a distance with baby on her lap. The paddy started burning. At this the husband calls out to his wife to bring down the pot from the oven. But as the wife is taking care of the baby, she, in the same retorting words replies him to do the job by himself. A little later, the husband again asks his wife to throw away the excrement of the fowls which was emitting bad smell. The wife, instead of complying to the request jovially replies that he will not loose his tribe if he covers it with chaffs lying there. As for the practice, some works are considered exclusive for the females and males usually keep themselves away from such works, though there is no such strict division of labour. After the first issue, it is observed that husband-wife settle the matter of discord amicably by themselves. This song also reveals the universal feature of male chauvinism.

The marital life of the couple is thus full of tension, jealousy, hatred, joy and abundant happiness that is, the real life experience of agony and ecstasy mostly centred round the married life.

PART III

THE ENVIRONMENT AND TRIBAL PEOPLE

7

THE PHYSICAL ENVIRONMENT

It is a scientific fact that human beings and nature are symbiotically related to each other with virtual inclination of dependency of the former on the latter. With the systematization of social life, attitude of man towards nature changed from coexistence to purely an object of consumption, followed by accumulation and hoarding. This led to internal struggle among sections of human beings over the exclusive control of land and natural resources and its byproducts in the modern times. This followed unmindful exploitation and destruction of natural resources and eco-environment. In it, the most progressive and so-called advanced societies also developed unsatiable hunger and exploitative mechanisms *par-excellence.* The human society was, accordingly, identified in two civilizational sectors—one, the advanced and the other, primitive, tribal and backward. Human history is the story of the so-called civilized and advanced society which is full with the act of war, killing, subjugation, slavery and destruction which was unleashed on people and ethnic groups for the sake of control over the land and resources and pride. The process still continues today. In order to obtain maximum happiness, luxury and peace, besides robbing and killing the innocent people, they in modern times in the name of modernization, are engaged in the act of destruction and looting of natural resources through the establishment of industries. A reign of insecurity and terror has been unleashed on humanity due to the greed of advanced society. The woes have increased so much that today humanity is standing on the verge of annihilation, the destructions of most of the ancient civilization were the act of such greedy advanced people whose offsprings today are giving wrong analysis of the fact to hide the misdeeds of their ancestors.

The tribal communities, the world over, are eco-friendly and have preserved the sanctity and resources till today wherever they live. They are poor and backward in the eyes of the advanced communities because they are not like them who are engaged in all out loot of natural resources. It is an irony that modern living is possible at the cost of the poor and backwards who are sitting over the resources and wealth that can bring luxurious life to the affluents. Today, tribals are being uprooted from their habitation thereby destroying their whole social fabric, values and traditional knowledge. They have been robbed of their peace and happiness which the modernity cannot bring back. Against this environmental backdrop, the life and literature, sociocultural history and musical tradition of the Mundas may be seen through the creation of their music in the lines that follow.

Habitation

In Munda songs, we get ample description of the region of their habitation but with respect to their dwelling place, there are no such details. The songs under reference merely mention the names of the villages which are predominantly settled by the Mundas or which were once settled by their forefathers and thus, have historical significance.

The song below which mentions the names of the villages belong to the Bala category of songs, the lines of which are as follows :

> *Baṇdu bhai Koṇkeya*
> Baṇdu and Koṇkeya, O brother
> *Hasa, Bajigama, Mail, Meral*
> Duḍri Muṛhu, Khunti, Ḍoḍma,
> *Ranchi ho Ḍoranḍa*
> Ranchi and Ḍoranḍa
> *Hore kheil Khaṭaṇga, Ḍahu, Balaṇkel*
> Play around at Khaṭaṇga Dahu and Balaṇkel
> *Kheil Kodakel*
> Play at Kodakel

The villages mentioned in the song are all traditional villages settled by the Mundas. Someone tells the other that they play around in these villages. The names of the villages mentioned in the song are—Bandu, Konkeya, Hasa, Bajigama, Mail, Meral, Duri, Murhu, Khunti, Dodma, Ranchi, Doranda, Khatanga, Dahu Balankel and Kodakel. 'Hore kheil', and 'kheil' are the words to give the rhyme to the song and hillarity to the singers.

Below is another song composed with names of villages. It also belongs to the 'Bala' category of song.

Gidi, Lunguṭu, Kochaṇg, Siṇjuṛi, Salga, Sapaṛom;
Siti, Suti, Bisna, Tuyu;
Padogaon, Okoḍa, Ruṛi, Ghagra, Sardikel
Siri, Fatka, Tamba, Rania, Marcha, Karora;
Chidi, Chanduwal, Kudrig, Bala, Kudluṇg, Ruju, Koṭlo,
Jugu, Semla, Upar Guria;
Baṇḍu, Koṇkeya, Kuṭam, Jaṛia, Torpa, Diaṇkel,
Baṇḍu, Jana, Garib, Jate, Kotoa, Bamni, Sidum, Uli, Lowakel,
Goṛa, Baṛia, Buṛju, Tambakel,
Ḍidi, Ḍibḍhi, Gaṛi, Rengaṛi, Sowagi, Joria, Koronjotola,
Ḍoḍma, Haṭia, Ranchi

Below is another song which also is composed with the names of villages. The song belong to the category of 'Jadur' song.

Saṇdi pado, Budi Karakel, Kanaloya, re
Pimpi, Poje, Banabira, Turuṇḍu, Kuṭam, Kajol, re

Except the word, '*re*' which has been added at the end of each line, is for the sake of rhyme the rest are names of the villages.

The villages mentioned in the above songs, are inhabited by the Konkpat Mundas, and thus, we can locate their concentration in the map. The Mundas of this region share the same tradition of music and dance.

Climate and Weather Environment

In the month of June when the sun moves down to Northern Hemisphere in the line of Cancer, the summer heat becomes unbearable in Chhotanagpur but due to its topographical features and elevation, the severity of heat becomes lessened. The day and night temperature varies during the summer but it usually remains moderate. The southern and western wind blow day and night bringing the heat in balance, but sometimes in the evening, it becomes calm causing humidity. With the passing of night, however, coolness increases and by morning, it becomes very pleasant. In summer, till midnight, people spend the time in the open air, either on the courtyard or on the flat rocks outside the hamlets. And it is one of the best occasions when stories, legends, myths, etc, are narrated to the youngsters.

The trees become leafless at the beginning of the summer season. During this period, the whole botanical environment presents a dreary look everywhere. But it is hardly a matter of a week or two. The new saplings come out and life springs up again with vibration of joy and happiness. The trees got covered with green leaves and beautiful flowers. People, young and old both are usually seen under the cool shade of the trees during the midday. Humming bees and chirping birds, who do not care for the summer heat, add beauty to the environment.

In summer, the rivers and rivulets which are mostly rainfed, become dry causing great inconvenience to animals, birds, insects and water species. But summer brings with it variety of flowers and fruits. Despite heat in the open sky, the trees full of green leaves, provide great relief to the people and animals when they fan down cool breeze to them.

Rainy season has its own beauty. In brings great relief to the people from the summer heat. Monsoon, which begins with whirlwind and storms, is often accompanied by thunder and hailstorms. The trouble of poor man as well as birds and beasts can very well be imagined seeing the fury of the monsoon. The normal life becomes shattered when rain lashes out the region. However, the rainy season is a great boon to the agriculturist Mundas. The busy life during this season is vividly expressed in their songs.

During winter, the sun moves down to the southern hemisphere and the already wet weather receives little rays to warm itself up. The cold, thus, increases day by day. By October, the wind becomes dry and cold wind blows day and night During night dewdrops fall and the morning generally remains foggy. This type of weather condition continues from the month of October to February when occasional rain can also be experienced. Excess cold is felt during the months of December and January which sometimes extends to February when very often hailstorm lashes out in the region. It is during this period that people usually come out late in the morning and return early in the day time. People generally carry fire to the place of their work. Early in the morning and in the evening till late at night, people sit around the fire. Such occasions are always utilized for gossipping, planning the next day's programme as well as telling stories to children.

The intervening period between winter and summer is the occasion for sociocultural and ritual activities. The busy agricultural life is almost over after the winter. Autumn is the period for remembering and honouring of the ancestors and erection of memorial stones for the departed souls. People are now free from all emergency duties and undertake other sociocultural functions which are obligatory in nature, such as visit to relatives and friends, establishing of new social relations and participation in fairs and festivals. Most of these activities are future oriented. Construction and repairing of houses, agricultural lands and tools, ploughing the fields, digging the wells, collection of fire woods, wild fruits and flowers, etc, are carried out during this period.

The Munda perceive the season as a cyclical process in which no beginning and end can be demarcated. In each season, the impact of the earlier one lingers till the latter's intensity does not go up. The process is like an undulation which gradually moves up and down. It is due to this climatic feature that a Munda is unable to tell exactly the line of demarcation between the successive seasons. However, a Munda can very well perceive the beginning, lingering of and end of the season by observing the activities of animals, birds, insects and plant's life.

People generally perceive changes in weather and climate with the corresponding months, and accordingly arrange their socio-economic and ritual activities. The degree of change in weather and climate are, thus, perceived on the basis of months. But in fact, weather and climate have no specific association with month and variation is possible year after year. However, a general condition of weather and climate of the Munda region, can be perceived through Table 7.1.

There are, however, only two main seasons from the geographical point of view—general rain due to south-west monsoon (mid-June to mid-September) and that of continental winds or cold weather season (November to February). In between these, there are hot weather (March to mid-June) and retracting mosoon (mid-September to October).

TABLE 7.1 Weather Corresponding to Months

Months with Corresponding English Months	*Weather Condition*
1	2
1. Aghan-Paush (December-January)	Temperature goes down to zero, weather remains dry and cold, chilly winds blow throughout, often one shower falls.
2. Paush-Magh (January-February)	Intensity of cold continues, chilly and dry wind blows, occasional shower with stones, flowers starts budding.
3. Magh-Fagun (February-March)	Fine weather, dry temperature slowly increases, moderate wind speed, no rain, green leaves turn purple and fall down.
4. Fagun-Chait (March-April)	Fine weather, dry temperature increases little by litle, moderate wind speed, trees become laden with tender leaves, one or two showers likely.
5. Chait-Baisakh (April-May)	Dry temperature increases, no rain, moisture of the land become dry, all kinds of wild fruits ripen, trees become green all around.
6. Baisakh-Jeth (May-June)	Temperature further increases, hot wind blows during the day but under tree shade one may feel cool breeze, sometimes humidity increases when no wind blows during night, people spend night outside the houses or

1	2
	portico, all kinds of wild fruits become available, water level goes down.
7. Jeth-Asar (June-July)	In the first part of the month, day temperature reaches its height at about 2 p.m. temperature is felt till 12 p.m. at night, sometimes no winds blow in first part of the night, people spend the night in the open. In the second half of the month, during the day, whirlwinds blow and by the afternoon, black clouds arise in the horizon, rainfall with storm and thunder shower, temperature cools down.
8. Asar-Sawan (July-August)	Heavy rains continue intermittently, day temperature slows down, wind speed becomes normal, sky remains cloudy.
9. Sawan-Bhado (August-September)	Rainfall with intervals, sky remains clear after the rain but there remains patches, of clouds, heat is felt during the day, wind blows which carries away the cloud plays hide and seek with the sun.
10. Bhado-Kuar (September-October)	Fine weather, wind speed becomes normal and temperature too, there is one or two showers.
11. Kuar-Katik (October-November)	Very fine weather, clear sky, temperature goes down, cold is felt at night towards the morning, occasional drizzling.
12. Katik-Aghan (November-December)	Dry weather, clear sky, temperature further goes down, cold wind blows, no rain.

The songs below relate to the experience of the people and their way of looking at the whole phenomena. We can also see in these songs how climate exercises its influence on the people and in their way of life as well as the type of vegetation and animal lives it encourages or fosters. The songs also describe the activities and behaviour of the people and animals under various climatic conditions. A seasonwise portrayal on the mentioned aspects of life of the people as well as environmental features would be seen in the subsequent pages.

Winter Season

In the following two songs, cold has been taken note as an abstract phenomenon but conceptualized as a person and accordingly been treated and looked into. The song belonging to *Jarga* category runs as follows:

> *Ju rabaṇg, ju rabaṇg*
> Hasten away cold, hasten away cold
> *Ju rabaṇg senome, ju rabaṇg senome*
> Please go away cold, please go away cold
> *Mar̥ reyaṛ, mar̥ reyaṛ*
> O chill, O chill
> *Mar̥ reyaṛ birid me, mar̥ reyar birid, me*
> Please get up O chill, please get up O chill
> *Mar̥ rabaṇg senọme, bepari ko juṛi kamṛa-2*
> Please go away cold, tracers have pairs or blankets
> *Mar̥ reyaṛ birid me, ladna ko jota barki-2*
> Please get up O chill, pack bullocks have thick clothings
> *Seno doing senoga, jete singi kal-kal re-2*
> I will go away but during hot summer
> *Birid doing birida, jargi-da jurukuṇdu re-2*
> I will get up but during lashing down of rains

The song below too, which belongs to Jadur category has been composed with the same style and content as above with addition of few lines at the end. The lines are

1. *Ju rabaṇg, ju reyaṛ*
Hasten away cold, hasten away chill
Ju rabaṇg, ju senome
Please go away cold
Ju rabaṇg, mere reyaṛ
Go away cold and chill, please
Mere reyaṛ birid me
Please get up, O chill

2. *Ju rabaṇg senome*
Please go away, O cold
Bepari ko Juṛi kamṛa
Traders have pairs of blankets
Ju reyaṛ birid me
Please get up, O chill
Ladna ko kaṛe jota barki
Pack bullock have thick pairs of clothings

3. *Seno doiṇg senoga, ba maṇdi jom keyate*
I will go away eating food in *Ba* festival
Birid doiṇg birida, tenda illi nu keyate
I will get up drinking gruel and rice-beer
Ạm dore jati jumbṛi, Ba maṇdim kaji tana
You are too greedy, talking of *Ba* food
Ạm dore jati lalchi, tenda illim baṇkaṛ tana
You are too selfish talking of gruel and rice-beer

The winter cold has been conceptualized as guest who has come uninvitedly when the host has nothing to provide. He is being told or rather requested to move away to someone else house who have enough to provide. Urban traders regularly visit the weekly markets located in tribal areas in all seasons. After doing the day's business, they generally halt at the market place itself. Traders carry enough clothes to beat back the cold. The Mundas know about their own limitations, therefore, when one feels unbearable cold, he murmurs asking the cold to move away into the traders blankets. It is a way of psychological self-pacification during the tearing feeling of cold. The winter continues till the month of Fagun when Mundas celebrate Ba festival. Prior to this there is no question at all of the departure of the cold season. The song states that coldness in weather remains until summer or till rainy season sets in. The intensity of cold lessens down, as the Munda perceive, after *Ba* festival in the month of Fagun, that is, in March-April. A guest is given farewell after a feast which is arranged in honour of him. The cold, which is like an obstinate and greedy fellow who does not move an inch till he takes a sumptuous meal and drinks in *Ba* festival.

The song expresses the feeling and experience of a common Munda who leads a life of subsistence. For him, winter season is a very bad experience, but they are helpless and take it happily in the same way as a guest worthy of honour who visits them once a year. The song also reveals human nature of greediness and resultant sufferings of common man who are unable to cope with the situation. Despite tribulations and despairs, there is hope and expectation in life in the midst of one's relatives and friends.

The poor man's life and his experiences are more explicitly revealed in the following *Jadur* category of song. The lines of the song are as follows:

1. *Hae rabang, rabang, paṭi tale bano*
   Alas, cold we have no mat
   Hae, reṇge, renge, poṭom tale bano
   Alas, hunger, we have no grain in store

2. *Hae, rabang, rabang, jir adere leka-a*
   Alas, cold, it is like tearing out of heart
   Hae, reṇge, reṇge, tapa adere leka-a
   Alas hunger, it is like fanning in of air only

3. *Ayari go bapari, jir adere leka-a*
   Neither in the days of mother or father, it is like tearing out of heart
   Bapari go ayari, ṭapa adere leka-a
   Neither in the days of father or mother, it is like fanning in of air only

For the poor man, as described in the song, cold and hunger both are different situations to overcome. The feelings are unexpressible but people of similar condition, share the same experience. When a poor man has no clothes to cover his body during the winter, he feels it as if someone is squeezing or tearing out his heart. But how a man will feel when he has neither clothes to cover his body nor food to eat. The extreme of both the situations is fatal and unalleviable. There is no hope of improvement of the situation in future too. It is by sharing of feeling and experience only that the situation can be alleviated for a moment.

It is not that the poor only suffer and experience the cold. It can be felt by anybody when bitten by circumstances. The following Jadur song tells the pathetic condition of a traveller. He describes his own experience in these words :

1. *Deogi Dulmi re bareiṇg nida jan*
   Darkness covered me while in Deogi and Dulmi, nephew
   Koṭa, Kuṛumba re taiṇg siṇgi dubui jan
   The sun set while at Kota and Kurumba

2. *Degoing rabaṇg tana, degoiṇg reyaṛ tana*
   Please help, I am getting cold and chilly
   Dego niyaiṇg me, dego apaiṇg me
   Please open for me the door

3. *Dego niyaiṇg me dego oṛa: do*
   Please open for me the house
   Dego apaiṇg me dego, kapaṭa do
   Please open wide the door for me

The song mentions the experience of a married sister who was on her way to her brother's house. The sun set while she was at Kota and Kurumba villages and there was total darkness while she reached the village of Deogi and Dulmi. It was winter and the day time was short. Travelling was difficult due to darkness, but somehow she reached her brother's house late at night. She was shivering with cold. So, as soon as she reached the house, she called out for help as she wanted to get in quickly. She was feeling as if she was being frozen, therefore, asked her nephews to open ajar the door for her to get in.

The rain which lashes the region during the months of Magh, Asar and Sawan become ice-cold. It is during this period that old animals generally die. It is not only animals and birds that suffer from ice-cold rain but people also feel much inconvenience. In the song below, it is mentioned that a young damsel has been badly affected by rain water. The song belongs to *Jadur* category, the lines of which are as follows:

> *Magh mahina pala pani barisae*
> There rains ice-cold water in Magh
> *Banal chhokri ke pala mair le*
> A healthy damsel was hit by the frost
> *Asar-Sawan pala pani barisae*
> Ice-cold water rains in the month of Asar and Sawan
> *Banal chhokri ke pala mair le*
> A healthy damsel was hit by the frost

The above song seems to have been composed by a boy. The boys and girls do not postpone dance during the days of bad weather too. It may have happened that some girls did not turn up to *akhra* for dance in such condition. This became the subject matter of the song which the composer assumes that the girl has actually been hit by such frost.

Summer Season

As stated earlier, between winter and summer, that is, during spring, when people are free from busy agricultural life, they get some respite otherwise it is full of social, economic and ritual activities. It is during this period that visits to relatives are made, marriage ceremonies are arranged and Magh or *Ba* festival is celebrated. People remain busy in the construction and repairing of houses, wells, lands, etc, and firewoods are collected from the forest for the whole period of rainy and winter seasons. As the people work in the fields most of their time, summer heat and thirst for water are generally referred to in their songs. The song below which belongs to *Jatra* category decribes the condition of a thirsty person:

> *Pani dege nayo, pani dege*
> Let me have water mother, let me have water
> *Piyasi ahi ninda na awae*
> I am thirsty and am sleepless
> *Adho rati pani dege*
> At midnight, let me have water

Piyasi ahi pani dege
I am thirsty, let me have water

The person had no sleep during the night due to thirst, so he got up and asks water from mother. This song seems to have been composed by the thirsty person himself.

During summer, when most of the wells and streams dry up, travelling becomes very difficult. In such situation, when one arrives at in any village, he goes to anybody's house for water. In the following song of *Bala* category a woman asks a girl for water:

De Nuni pani, de Nuni pani
Let me have water Nuni, let me have water
Bara dur se ahi Nuni, piyasalain re
I have come from a distant land and am thirsty

What could happen to a person when he does not get a drop of water in wells and streams during burning heat in summer? This situation has been described in the following *Bala* category of song by someone who witnessed the pathetic situation of another person who did not get a drop of water in wells and streams in a widely spread forest region. The lines of the song are as follows:

Anko-banko bir ko tala re
In the midst of desolate forest
Ra:-ra: te da-ae asitan, jetae bankoa
Weeping, asking water, (but) there were none
Darie sen ken, dario anjed kana
Went to stream-well, but that too was dry
Kunwae sen ken, kunwayo dunda kan
Went to well but the water level was far below
Ra:-ra: te da-ae asitan, jetae bankoa
Weeping, asking water, but there were none

Such situation, as described in the song, is normally found in all parts of Chhotanagpur during summer. The water levels of the well and stream go down and also become dry. People usually store water in earthen pots. In some areas, water scarcity become so acute that people in group, during night time, go out for its collection even to distant villages.

During summer, people usually stay inside or take rest under the shade of the tree at noon time. Men, animals and birds all search for cool places. The composer of the following song, which belongs to Racha category of song, finds a bird sitting under the shade of *kansi* reeds. The lines of the song are:

> *Kansi rumbul re duba kora*
> Sitting under the shade of *kansi* reeds
> *Sirma situng te, note lolo te*
> Due to the heat of the sun and hot earth
> *Kansi rumbul re duba kora*
> Sitting under the shade of *kansi* reeds

During the last part of the summer season, the weather becomes vulnerable. Whirlwind blows during the mid-day and very often clouds of dust-storms engulf the region by the afternoon. In the song below which belongs to Lahsua category, a girl is advised to run back to the house as the storm was coming. The lines are as follows:

1. *Kansi piri hoyo dudugar*
   Dust-storm at Kansi field
   Nir mai re nir bolome
   Run into the house, O daughter
   Marang gara hoyo dudugar
   Dust-storm on the great river
   Sen mai re sen sekor sorome
   Walk quickly and hide yourself, O daughter

2. *Nir mai re nire bolome*
   Run into the house, O daughter
   Engam ora lo tana
   The house of your mother is burning
   Sen mai re sen sekor sorome
   Walk quickly and hide yourself, O daughter
   Apum ora bale tana
   The house of your father is in flame

People normally take extra-precaution during such duststorms to avoid any accident of fire as mentioned in the song. When dust-storm rises, elders warn the children and advise them to stay inside and avoid standing under the tree.

It is not only the men, birds and beast, that is, the land-dwellers that are affected in summer season, the water dwelling species too, feel uncomfortable. Many rainfed rivers and ponds dry up which kill various water species. The water species become easy prey to men, animals and birds when water level goes down. The following Jadur song mentions the pathetic condition of fish during summer:

1. *Chire gitil bumbuj, chirem obor kana*
   O sand-fish, why are you lying flat
   Chire chauli geṇger, chirem tabera kana
   Why chauli genger you are lying supported by

2. *Chire ote lolo te, chirem obora kana*
   Is it due to hot earth you are lying flat
   Chire sirma situṇg te, chirem tabera kana
   Is it due to sun's heat you are lying supported by

The composer of this song, in course of his moving around, noticed the fish in a helpless condition and it struck his feelings. It was not very difficult to know the reason of its helplessness. It was the summer heat that made all water living species uncomfortable.

Another close observation has been made by the composer of the song in the following Jadur category of song. He observes that date leaves which otherwise are strong, are also swinging when summer wind blows. The lines of the song are as follows:

1. *Khijuri hilelare, khijuri dolela*
   Khajur is swinging and swaying
   Khijuri balika lareka, khajuri luj parela
   Like little boy, the *khajur* is bending down

2. *Khijuri pate, pate me, khijuri hilela*
   Each leaf of *khajur* is swaying
   Khijuri ḍali ḍali me, khajuri luj parela
   Each branch of *khajur* is bending down

In Chhotanagpur, during summer, before mahua flowers start blooming, the grass and fallen leaves are burnt down to make the ground clean for easy collection of the *mahua* flowers. The fire sometimes spreads in quite a large area and pose a serious threat to wild animals, birds and other plant species. The plight of birds in such situation, has been conceptualized in the following *Jadur* song:

1. *Buru do lo tana chitri*
   The hill is burning, O partridge
   Buru geyona chitri
   The hill is in flame, O partridge
   Beṛa do bale tana askạl
   The valley is being reduced to ash, O *askạl*
   Beṛa jirpi jalaṇg
   The valley is burning in patches

2. *Buru do lo tana chitri*
   The hill is burning, O partridge
   Okorelaṇg atiṇga chitri
   Where shall we pick our food, O partridge
   Beṛa do bale tana askạl
   The valley is being reduced to ash, O *askạl*
   Chimae relaṇg gusạn
   Where shall we walk around

3. *Tara buru lo tana chitri*
   Parts of the valley is burning, O partridge
   Tara relaṇg atiṇga chitri
   We shall pick our food on the other parts, O partridge
   Tara bera bale tana askal
   Parts of the valley is being reduced to ash, O *askal*
   Tara relang gusạn
   We shall walk around on the other parts

Some parts of the forest are purposely burnt for better growth of plants and grass which sometimes spreads in a wider area. Burning of the forest is done after the celebration of Fagun festival.

The song below which belongs to Jadur category of song, is packed with emotions as it portrays the humane feelings. The song describes the plight of the *langur* whose dwelling place has been burnt down by men. The lines of the song are:

1. *Huring buru lo tana*

The small hill is burning
Gaṛi kin do dada, gaṛi kin ra-a: tana
A pair of *langur* are weeping, O brother
Sara-a kin do dada, sara-a kin eyạm tana
A pair of monkey are wailing, O brother
Kusude-kusude ho dada, gaṛi kin ra-a: tana
The *langur* are weeping unceasingly, O brother
Kusude-kusude ho dada, sara-a kin eyạm tana
The monkeys are wailing uninterruptedly, O brother

2. *Maraṇg buru lo tana*
The great mountain is in flame
Gaṛi kin do dada, gari kin ra-a: tana
A pair of *langur* are weeping, O brother
Sara-a kin do dada, sara-a kin eyạm tana
A pair of monkey are wailing, O brother
Kusude-kusude ho dada, gaṛi kin ra-a: tana
The *langur* are weeping unceasingly, O brother
Kusude-kusude ho dada, sara-a kin eyạm tana
The monkeys are wailing uninterruptedly, O brother

The composers of these songs have tried to draw the attention of the people towards the plight of the wild animals and birds when their dwelling place is burnt down. The sorrows and sufferings of these wild animals and birds during such situation keeps no bounds and touches the heart of everybody. They deserve compassion and sympathy from men. They have the same feelings and experience as the men have in such situation. The composers complain the burning of forest and have tried to spread message of love and compassion among the youngsters for wild creatures.

Rainy Season

The monsoon, generally, begins from the second half of the month of June, that is, last part of the summer season. The weather remains unstable during this period. Clouds move from one horizon to another. The atmosphere generally becomes calm before the storms. Black clouds arise in the western horizon by the evening and with gale of wind, rain lashes out the area accompanied by thunder and lightning.

The fury of monsoon creates fear among the children and adult alike. The following Bala category of song mentions this in these lines:

Bhanḍara kona me
In the north-western corner of the horizon
Badalije ghiṛikae, bijolije chamakae
The cloud thunder and lightning flashes
Dhuṇwaṇ je awae, ranarate awae
The smoke is coming running
Pani je awae, jhama kare awae
Rain is coming pouring down its water
Bhanḍara kona me
In the north-western corner of the horizon
Badalije ghiṛikae, bijolije chama kae
The cloud thunder and lightning flashes.

The observations and experience of the first monsoon have been expressed with feelings of thrills, excitement and fear in a most simple way. The experience of every person differs and so each form of expression reveals nature's unique features bit by bit by every individual. The following song mentions the experience of two friends who were caught by the fury of rain storms. The song belongs to Jadur category:

1. *Namin-namin hoyo gama re, okorem uku kena*
In so much stormy rain where did you hide yourself
Namin-namin rimil saṛi re, chimae rem danaṇg ken
During so much thundering clouds where did you shelter

2. *Aiṇg doiṇg uku kena, marangg buru kula lata re*
I hid myself in lion's den of great mountain
Aiṇg doiṇg danaṇg kena, huṛing naṛa bhalu lata re
I sheltered in bear's cave on the small hill range

3. *Kachi hoe hab ked me, maraṇg buru kula lata re*
Did he not bite you in lion's den of great mountain
Kachi hoe sodor ked me, huṛiṇg naṛa bhalu lata re
Did he not vex you in bear's cave on the small hill range

The two friends tell experience to each other after their fearful ordeal. The two were in different parts of the mountain ranges when stormy rains overpowered them. Each one of them was wondering about the miraculous escape of the other. While communicating their experiences to others, they immortalized this memorable events through the song. The thundering cloud and lightning create fear among all as stated earlier. The experience of personal nature are rendered into song on the very spot where the event takes place. Below is one such example of the song which belongs to Jadur category:

1. *Badarije ghiṛikate awae*
   The clouds coming thundering
   Kaese piyab chuṇwaṇ ka pani
   How shall we drink water from *chunwan*
   Haere, hae, kaese piyab chuṇwaṇ ka pani
   Alas! How shall we drink water from chunwan

2. *Haere, Badari je moke ḍaṛ lage*
   Alas! I fear the thundering cloud
   Kaese piyab chuṇwaṇ ka pani
   How shall we drink water from *chunwan*

This expression of fear is either of the boy or girl, most probably it is of the girl.

Similar fear has been expressed in yet another song, the lines of which need not be repeated here since the wordings are almost the same in this song too except with an additional sentence '*bijolije chamakate awae*', that is, lightning coming with a flash.

The youths often drink water from the nearby well or stream after or during the dance at night. During summer, it is but natural to feel thirsty. It were the girls who were talking about drinking of water from the *chunwan* but they were hesitating seeing the lightning and hearing of the thundering clouds. The boys, who heard the talk of the girls, composed the song on this very theme.

A friend expresses his curiosity to know as to how and where his friend got drenched in rain when clouds were nowhere to be seen. This often happens when flying cloud passes through all of a sudden. This event has been mentioned in the following Jadur song by way of reply:

1. *Sisi piṛi re gama ledingā*
The rain caught me in *sisi* field
Jam-jam marcha re rampi ledingā
It showered while I was on wide open field

2. *Loom jana ho lumaṇg liza do*
The silk dress of mine became wet
Reyare jana ho raṇga chari dhoti do
The coloured bordered dhoti became ice-cold

The composer of this song tells his friend as to how he was totally drenched in rain water when he was overtaken at an open field with no shelter closeby.

People are sometimes overtaken by rain when there is no sign of cloud in the sky. In such situation, the chance of avoiding the rain is zero. The following two Jadur songs mention the awkward situation of the persons who run for the shelters.

1. *Jibir-jibir go da-a: leda*
It rained thinly
De gatim chukuṛuiṇg me
Let us share your *chukuru* friend
Jalri-jalri go rampi leda
It rained lightly
De gatim chataring me
Let us share your umbrella friend

2. *De gatim chukuṛuiṇg me*
Let us share your *chukuru* friend
Raṇga saṛi go loome jana
The clourful sari all became wet
De gatim chataring me
Let us share your umbrella friend
Lumaṇg liza go reyaṛe jana
The silk cloth became ice-cold

The sudden rain was not at all perceived, this situation has also been mentioned in the following song:

1. *Noko-sa-a: re hende led*

The darkness arose somewhere
Noko sa-a: re gama led
It did rain elsewhere
Gatim re suru-suṭuing lume chaba jana
Friend dear, I was drenched totally
Gatim re de gatim chataring me
Friend dear, let us share your umbrella
Ho hore, gatim re, de gatim chataring me
O friend, let us share your umbrella

2. *Chetạn sa-a: re hende led*
It arose darkness in the yonder horizon
Latạr sa-a: re gama led
It rained beyond here
Gatim re de gatim chataring me
Friend dear, let us share your umbrella
Ho hore, gatim re de gatim chukuṛuiṇg me
O friend, let us share your *chukuru*

The composer of the song had never dreamt that there will be rain on that day as there were no dark clouds in the sky though only patches of them were there in the horizon, so he did not carry umbrella or *chukuru*. The rain surprised him. Anyway he ran to his friend and shared his umbrella and *chukuru*.

The tornado type of storm leaves behind innumerable problems for the people. In the song below, a girl is being requested by her mother to go out and see if some of the trees were uprooted. The song belongs to Jadur category:

1. *Chạl to maiya deikh abe*
Please go and see, O daughter
Ḍair ṭuiṭ gel re
The branches have broken down
Chạl to maiya chin abe
Please go and identify, O daughter
Pat jhair gel
The leaves have fallen down

2. *Dekhe keto deikh aloṇ*

I had been and seen it
Ḍair ṭuiṭ gel re
The branches have broken down
Chine keto chin aloṇ
I had been and identified it
Pat jhair gel re
The leaves have fallen down

Storms sometimes, uproot or break away trees and blow away roofs, etc. Sometimes lives are also lost. In the above song after a devastating storm, a girl is asked to see if some trees of their's have broken down.

Houses are generally repaired before the rainy season sets in, but many remain incomplete and there is every likelihood of collapsing of such houses during the rainy season. It was one such incident at Jarakel village that a church building collapsed like wall of sands. It was not a great event but as it became a subject matter of talk of the people everywhere, the Racha dancing youths composed a song on this theme. The lines of the song are as follows:

Jarakel bangela, haduṛ jana jo leyaṇg jana
The bungalow of Jarakel collapsed and melted away
Da-a: doe gama leda
It has heavy rains
Teser kena jo bojor kena
It fell flat into pieces like sands

Heavy rains also break embankments of fields, tanks and dams. The song below in *Jadur* describes one such situation in which a tank was overflooded and ultimately its embankments broke washing everything down below. The lines of the song are as follows:

1. *Chetaṇ redo hende leda*
It became dark in yonder beyond
Lataṛ redoe gama leda
It rained here below
Aṛi kunḍi pere: jana
It overflooded all embankments
Pokhari do charaṇg jan
The tank was overflooded

2. *Bual kedae, bual kedae*
   It carried away and away
   Kendaṛi buṭae bual kedae
   Kendari shrub was carried away
   Apaṇṛ kedae, apaṇṛ kedae
   It holed the embankments
   Seyari butae apanr kedae
   It made hole near *seyari* shrubs

Much inconvenience is felt by the birds who dwell on the trees and bushes. When hailstorms hit, many birds are killed and their nests are blown. In the song below of Jadur category, a Lipi bird mourns for the destruction of its nest. The lines of the song are as follows:

1. *Lipi tuka tada, gaṛa gena jhario re*
   Lipi made its nest by the side of a ravine of perennial stream
   Siṇgi rakab gama do, jhar-jhar-e gama leda
   The rain of the east fell incessantly

2. *Jhar-jhar-e gama leda, gaṛa doṛa pere: jana*
   It rained incessantly, all rivers and rivulets overflooded
   Tuka tạm atu tana, basa tạm bual tana
   Nest yours is on the current, home yours is carried away
   Lipi ra-a: eyạm tana, basa korem nameya
   Lipi is weeping and mourning, where shall it get the home

The composer was moved by the pathetic condition of the bird when its nest was washed away due to stormy rain. We saw the bird's helplessness. The bird was sitting on the twig watching its destroyed nest and was crying. This affected the composer deeply and he thought, 'where the bird will live now'. The home which the bird built laboriously and which took long time to complete, is now no more in existence. The song arouses human sympathy towards anyone and everyone in distress, may he be man, animal or bird.

Chhotanagpur is an undulating plateau of hills criss-crossed by rivers and rivulets. In rainy season, even small rivulets turn into a virtual sea making it difficult for crossing due to its sharp and swift currents. During rainy season, the area is turned into the land of million rivers. In the song below, which belongs to Bala category, this scenery has been portrayed vividly:

> *Chhoṭe moṭe nadia*
> A small rivulet
> *Bala je hilakate away*
> The sands are coming dancing
> *Sae samudaṛ milate away*
> Linking hundreds of seas
> *Poṭhi machhari malakate away*
> Pothi fish are walking up leisurely

It is during this period that fish are abundantly available in the region. Deforestation has led to soil erosion enormously in Chhotanagpur. It is but natural, therefore, that soil and sands roll down in large quantity filling up all deep of the rivers and bar-ring stones and rocks from the lands.

Crossing the rivers during this period is a great problem. A number of people, while crossing are washed away and die. The boatmen, in comparatively big rivers, are available to help the people crossing the rivers. The boat is made of single wood which is cut out at one side and is steered either by one or two men. They are locally known as *jhora*. They do not charge anything at the place of their duty for their services but visit each household twice in a year to collect the dues. It is not that everybody had to cross the river but even then, customarily they pay the boatman generously.

The song below which belongs to Lahsua category, mentions about the crossing of river. The lines are as follows:

1. *Chhoṭe moṭe kaṭhal ḍonga*
   A small wooden boat
   Kahe ḍhulu mulu re
   Why it is rolling
   Ḍhire-ḍhire jhora
   Slowly, O boatman
   Par karu dhire-dhire
   Get across it slowly

2. *Pani upar ḍonga*
Boat floating on the water
Ḍonga upar manoa
People on the boat
Kaṭh kera ḍonga, baṇs kera kheoṭa
With wooden boat and bamboo's steer
Ḍhire-ḍhire jhora, par karu ḍhire-ḍhire
Slowly, O boatman, take us across the river.

In yet another song below which belongs to Lahsua category of song, boatman's help is being sought to retrieve a piece of cloth being floated away by the currents. The lines are as follows:

1. *Ho hore jhora bhai kota tiya*
Alas, where did the boatman go
Donga chetan paṛhia liza atu tan
Upon the boat *parhia* cloth is being floated away
Ho hore, jhora bhai kota tiya
Alas, where did the boatman go

2. *Ho hore, jhora bhai Muṛhu tiya*
Alas, boatman is away to Murhu
Donga chetan paṛhia liza atu tan
Upon the boat, *parhia* cloth is being floated away
Ho hore, jhora bhai Muṛhu tiya
Alas, boatman is away to Murhu

Besides factual meaning, the cloth, in this song has symbolic meaning too. Here it also means a damsel—a young bride, who is running away from her husband's house by crossing the river on the boat. The boatman, that is, her husband, is not in the house and is away to Murhu. Somebody identified the bride and conveyed this news through song in a symbolic way. Only a few could understand the real meaning of the song who were aware of the whereabouts of the husband.

Danger lurks at every step where river and forest stand at every little distance. The following song which belongs to Lahsua category, mentions that rivers and forest infested with wild animals pose a great danger to the people. The theme of the song is derived from the Christian religious philosophy in which life is thought to be a journey which cannot be performed without the help of Jesus Christ. The background of the song is against the geographical features of the region. The lines of the song are as follows:

1. *Hora-hora sen hora*
   A journey through the path
   Hora redo ga gaṛa mena
   Ahead lies the river on the way
   Masih he ela masih mosate
   O Christ, come along with us
   Gaṛa chilkaing paroma
   How shall I cross the river

2. *Gaṛa parom sen hora*
   A journey beyond the river
   Hora redoga bir mena
   On the path lies the forest
   Bir redoga kula mindi menako
   The forest is infested with lions and bears
   Masih he ela masih mosate
   O Christ, come along with us
   Bir chilkaiṇg paroma
   How shall I pass through the forest

Crossing the flooded river as well as passing through the forest where tigers and bears roam about, both are dangerous undertakings. And Chhotanagpur was dreaded for these two reasons.

In Chhotanagpur, fairs are periodically held in traditionally selected places which are places of entertainment as well as selling and buying of goods and continue for a day or two. Below is one of the songs which belongs to Jadur category whose subject matter is the fair. The lines of the song are as follows:

1. *Nadi to nadi bhari gel*
   The river has inundated the banks
   Mela to mela lagi gel
   But the fair has been held
   Bapare gola bareda, lali ke lipi saparae
   How beautiful the bullock, decorating with red paste

2. *Nadia ka nara tire*
   By the banks of the river
   Gola bareda ke lipi saparae
   Young bullock is being decorated with red paste
   Bapare gola bareda, lali ke lipi saparae
   How beautiful the young bullock, decorated with red paste

There is flood in the river and fair has been held across the river. People have been held up due to the flood. They are, however, witnessing every activity of the people from the other side of the river.

Sometimes, as stated in the previous pages, clouds gather in the sky all of a sudden and start raining. Similarly, it also happens that shallow river becomes over-flooded without rain due to the rain in upper reaches which plays havoc and creates big problem for the people. A person tells his experience who was caught in such a flood. The song belongs to Lahsua category, the lines of which are as follows:

1. *Jae khana dekhaloṇ sukhala nadia*
   While crossing, I saw the dried up river
   Ho hore, phiraya se dekhaloṇ, duyo kuilo bar
   But alas, while returning found both the banks overflooded

2. *Je moke par kare*
   Whoever will help me in crossing
   Seke debo muṇga moti
   To him I will give pearl and ruby
   Ho hore, auro debo kire mua ke jabaṇ
   And I promise, I will give him more.

The person, who is held up due to unprecedented floods in the river, promises to offer precious stones to those who would help him in crossing it. In the song below too, mention of similar situation has been made in which a couple has been held up. There is none to help them to cross the river but they are in search of a means through which they can cross the river. The song belongs to Jadur category:

1. *Marang gara dore kau-bau tana*
The great river is swirling, O dear
Elare gatim lang kesed jana
O dear, we are held up

2. *Huring gara dore ebe-tobe tana*
The small river too is brimming its banks
Bapare sangaing lang taua jana
Alas dear, we have become stranded

3. *Mar ho gatim lang param geya*
Please dear, we must cross it
Hesel dutu dore gandia kana
A hesel log is lying crossed at the banks

4. *Mar ho sangaing lang tunda geya*
Please dear, let us fathom the depth
Tilae muli dore mulia kana
Tilae shrub has grown close by

5. *Mar ho sangaing lang tuna geya*
Please dear, let us measure the depth.

The couple are determined to cross the river by any means and measure the ebb and flow of the water at every moment. The song indicates that it is the wife who is more impatient.

When rain lashes the region during rainy season, a beautiful scenery is created. The following Jadur song describes the beauty in these lines:

Buru tati
The hill *tati* grass
Buru tati, leyon leka buru tati
The hill *tati* is swaying like waves
Bera baru
The valley Baru tree
Bera baru, lodob leka bera baru
The valley Baru tree is dancing rhythmically
Hoyo lere
When wind blows

Hoyo lere, leyon leka hoyo lere
When wind blows, it sways beautifully
Gama lere
When it rains
Gama lere
When it rains
Lodob leka gama lere
It dances rhythmically

In the months of *Sawan* and *Bhado*, the volume of water in the rivers remains considerably high and continues to remain so for a month or so. It is because, by this time, natural streams start giving perennial source of water even though the rain is not regular. But sometimes, in the month of *Bhado* too, there is good rain. The song below is on the rain of *Bhado* month. The song belongs to Jatra category and the lines are as follows:

Gaṛa jimtu dhire-dhire
Slowly the *jimtu* of the ravine
Kahe jimtu ekela bhele .... lekore
Why are you trembling, O Jimtu
Uṭhal bhado tire-tire
The sudden rain in Bhado is overflowing
Kahe jimtu ekela bhele
Why are you trembling, O Jimtu

Sometimes it also happens that even in rainy season there is no regular rain. Sometimes the rain starts a bit early, and during usual time, there is no rain at all for weeks. Sometimes, it starts in time, but it gives a very scanty rain. And, sometimes, there is no rain at all in the beginning of the season. Due to this irregularity of rains, people's economy suffer very badly. The song below which belongs to Jarga category, mentions that in Asar-Sawan months, when normally it rains heavily, it has no rain at all and Budu fish who live in shallow water are dying without water. The song runs as follows:

Icha haku chaṛab-chuṛub
The prawns are hopping about
Chaoṛa budu laṇgạb-laṇgạb
The up-land Budu fish are at the verge of death

Numana da-a: do gore kae gamaya, haena
Alas mother, there is no rain
Asar-Sawan seno jana
Asar and *Sawan* months have passed
Numana da-a: do gore kae gamaya, haena
Alas mother, there is no rain

The song mentions that there is no rain in the months of *Asar* and *Sawan* which are the usual periods of rain. The water from the up-land paddy fields have all drained out leaving behind small fish there. They are dying without water. Below is another song belonging to Jatra category which states the pathetic condition of the water species. The lines of the song are as follows:

Keyari ka pani sukhi gel
Water in small plots of land have all dried up
Budu re machhari ka gunani karae
What are you pondering, O Budu fish
Asar-Sawan chali gelain
Asar and *Sawan* have passed
Keyari ka pani sukhi gel
Water in small plots of land have all dried up
Budu re machhari ka gunani karae
What are you pondering, O Budu fish

Budu fish avoid pool and water current and so, like to stay in shallow water but with the passing of *Asar* and *Sawan* months, that is, when the period of heavy rains over, water from upland drain out leaving behind the small fish. These fishes have been stranded in shallow water at one place and no way to get out. The composer of the above song, looking at the gathering of the fish asks what they are thinking.

The song below too, which belongs to Lahsua category, describes the plight of the Budu fish who are moving downwards due to lack of water. The lines of the song are as follows:

Jhibir-jhibir pani
The shallow water
Pani nai barisae
There is no rain

Ho hore, budu hon dore gatim
Alas, the little Budu fish, dear,
Da-a: chetạn chetanate jalating tan
They are swimming around over the shallow water
Kuar katik rakab len
Kuar and Katik months have approached
Da-a: dore anjed jana
The water has dried up
Ho hore, budu hon dore gatim
Alas, the little Budu fish, dear
Da-a: chetạn chetanate ko arạgun tana
They are swimming down over the water

As soon as the rainy season is over, the upland becomes almost dried up due to lack of water. Budu fish, who do not live in deep pool as well as running water as stated above, are generally found in shallow water and so they become easy prey of frogs, crabs and birds, etc. In this song, as mentioned, Budu fishes are swimming down in search of some shallow pool of water. The movement of Budu fish, who are found thousands in number at one place, greatly impressed the composer.

8

THE FLORA WORLD IN SONGS

Environment of Plants

Chhotanagpur plateau has tropical climate. It receives moderately heavy rainfall, thus, there is lush growth of plants and creepers. In autumn, most of the trees, except date and palm, become leafless. Besides the natural growth of plants, some species are abundantly planted by the people like jackfruits, mango, *dau, edel, kasmar, koronjo*, tamarind, *hesa* (of all varieties), neem, bamboo, *kuda* (blackberry), *bari, kusum, dodari, putkal,* etc. These trees meet various needs of the people.

The trees that grow in the forest are of a variety of species. Some trees that are predominantly found in Chhotanagpur forest are Sarjom (*Shorea robusta*), Asan (*Terminalia tomentosa*), Kasmar or Gambhar (*Gamelina orboria*), Tiril (*Diospyros tomentosa* or ebony), Edel (*Bombax maluburicum*), Madukam (*Basia latifolia*), Tun (*Cedrela tuna*), Soso (*Dalber sia sisoo*), Hara (*Terminolia chebulan*), Karam (*Adina cardifolia*), Kusum (*Schlechera trijuna*), bamboo, Murud, etc. A variety of creepers also grow in which Gungu is the most important.

In rainy season, varieties of mushrooms (*ud* and *putkui*) grow which add to the delicacy of people's recipe. There also grow a variety of vegetable plants in rainy season. Some flowers and leaf vegetables are also found in the month of autumn. Grass vegetables are available all the year round around marshy lands and streams. Some wild roots from the forest are also the food items of the people. A scanty reference is found in Munda songs about the medicinal plants, though application of it is often referred.

Reference of botanical plants in Munda songs are made in variety of contexts, and sometimes carry a quite different meaning from its objective appearance.

Plants and Creepers

As stated above, the plants and creepers that are found in Munda country around their settlements, in fields, river banks, marshy lands and forest fulfil various needs of the people. It does not mean that they are unsuitable for the theme of songs. The fact is that any plant or creeper can be a theme for a song which strikes the composer's imagination or draws his attention in relation to a particular situation. Moreover, it is not the case that only useful and nice looking plants become the theme in song but even useless and charmless things also become the reference. Reference of plants or its different parts are made in different contexts and so carry different meaning and also make the situation meaningful which would otherwise be meaningless. The reference of plants in songs or its selection for it, is based not on the basis that it pleases the senses most but the choice depends upon the features that is thought to be common in plants and human beings. The selection of particular plant for elucidation of the theme of the song is, thus, culture specific and the reference always carry a meaning.

The song below which belongs to the Jarga category, illustrates the points made above. The lines of the song are as follows:

Tulsi daru, tulsi daru
The *tulsi* plant
Hale-hale re tulsi daru, tulsi daru, haere
The nice evergreen *tulsi* plant
Bindi daru bindi daru
The *bindi* plant
Sale-sale re bindi daru
The straight slim *bindi* plant
Dolarebu nele leyare
Let us see it
Hale-hale re tulsi daru
The nice evergreen *tulsi* plant
Mere rebu china leyare
Let us identify it
Sale-sale re bindi daru
The straight slim *bindi* plant

Tulsi is a herbal plant small in size and always remains evergreen. Bindi is planted in fence in the boundary of kitchen garden. From its seeds, oil is extracted which is used for lighting the lamps. It is also used as medicine. Its twig is used as toothbrush. So, both *tulsi* and *bindi* plants are useful for the Mundas. But the theme of the song is not its quality, it is the beauty and growth. The plants indicate the growth of children. The children grow so rapidly that if kept away from one's sight for a year or so, it may be difficult to recognize easily next time. Moreover, the children are always seen in cheerful mood like the *tulsi* plant which always remains evergreen.

Below is another song of this category which describes the beauty of the Karanj plant, but the meaning is quite different. The lines of the song runs as follows:

> *Hora gena ḍinḍa koronjo*
> The wayside maiden *koronjo* plant
> *Rinka-rore jo lena ḍinḍa koronjo, ḍinḍa koronjo, haere*
> The maiden *koronjo* became laden with fruits
> *Jo lena, rohoṛ lena*
> It bore fruits and dried up
> *Haṛṇsa latij meya ko ḍinḍa koronjo, dinda koronjo haena*
> You will be soundly thrashed, O maiden *koronjo*

Koronjo is another plant which grows or rather is planted abundantly in the Munda country. From its seeds, oil is extracted and is used in lamp for lighting the house. It is also used as hair oil and for massaging the body. Koronj seed, moreover, is used as herbs and its twigs as toothbrush. The Koronj tree under reference of this song, has bore fruits for the first time. When the fruits dry up on the tree, it is thrashed down with sticks. The composer of the song sees the tree laden with fruits, but in the meantime, thinks about the fate of the tree for it would be soundly thrashed because of the fruits. Motherhood of unmarried maiden is considered a social crime in the Munda society. And the composer of this song implicitly indicates towards crime and the punishment instituted by the elders.

It is not that plants always carry hidden meaning or reality of the society. It also describes the beauty of the nature as seen and perceived by the Mundas. The song below belonging to Racha category, a reference is made of the Koronj tree in its objective context in relation to rainy weather. The lines of the song are as follows:

> *Khunṭi shahar re koronjo ḍari, koronjo ḍari*
> The branches of Koronjo in Khunti town
> *Hoyo lere liyur kena*
> It stooped down when wind blew
> *Gama lere lodob kena*
> It rolled when it rained
> *Khunṭi shahar re koronjo ḍari, koronjo ḍari*
> The branches of *koronjo* in Khunti town

The composer of the song was very much impressed when wind and rain lashed the Koronjo tree. It appeared to the composer as if someone is dancing.

Neem is another tree which is abundantly planted in Munda region. A reference is made of the *neem* tree in the Racha song, the lines of which run as follows:

> *Neem ḍair, neem ḍair*
> The neem branches
> *Ke hilaela, ke hilaela*
> Who is shaking it
> *Malạk bain charalaiṇ*
> The playful sisters have got up
> *Sob ḍair, sob ḍair, hilela*
> All the branches are swaying

Neem is a very useful tree. Its tiny branches are used as toothbrush and oil is extracted from its seeds. Its leaf, bark and seeds are used as herbs by the tribals. Besides, it also provides firewood and timber for furniture. The juice of the ripened fruits are tasty and so the bats and the children often relish it. In this song, as stated, the girls have got up on the tree during the darkness, and so the branches are shaking. They are invisible due to the darkness and this has led to various sorts of imaginations.

Tamarind is yet another tree which is found in every village. Its wood is very hard and is used only for firewood but its fruits are very useful. It is due to the quality of fruits, sometimes girls are often compared with it. The song belongs to the Jarga category which runs as follows:

Hatu tala re ḍinḍa kuṛi, ho ḍinḍa kuṛi
A maiden girl in the middle of the village
Disum tala re binḍa jojo, ho binḍa jojo
Tamarind tree stands in the middle of the country
Dola rebu nele lia re, ḍinḍa kuṛi ho ḍinḍa kuṛi
Let us see the maiden girl
Mere rebu chakha leyare, binḍa jojo ho, binda jojo
Let us have a taste of the tamarind fruits

The Munda give great importance to unmarried girls at village as well as community level. Similarly, tamarind fruits also have significance in the daily recipe of the Munda food habit. In Naguri country, the whole village is generally settled by the segmentary lineages. In such cases, the whole village is a corporate family.

The unmarried girls, though they belong to a particular family, are considered to be the daughters of the whole village. Their services are obtained by each family at times of need, and during some social occasion, their services are immensely required. It is why the composer of this song locates her in the middle of the village who draws attention of everybody and is admired by everybody.

Tamarind tree, on the other hand, has its place among the trees. Its fruits add flavour to the food. Munda usually prepare fish with the juice of the tamarind which makes the dish exceedingly palatable. Fish as well as tamarind dish are the symbol of happiness and joy. It is why eating of these two items are prohibited whenever any death occurs in the family or village. The girl as well as tamarind both have, thus, got a significant place in the Munda society.

Reference of tamarind is also made in the following Khemta category of song, the lines of which are as follows:

Dubi rechi maḍi re kanṭari re
Whether in cowdung pit, *madi* or *kantari*
Bakaṛi reya kuṛi binḍa jojo
O girl, tamarind stands in the kitchen garden
Eesin saba-saba te kanṭari re
To remove sour boil it with *kantari*

Jojo morej-morej te binḍa jojo
To make it sour is tamarind

To remove the bitterness from any eatable, it is boiled with tamarind fruits. Flowers of jackfruit become tasty when tamarind juice is added in it as mentioned in the song.

In the song below, which belongs to Racha category, a reference of another plant, Churchu has been made. It is a wild plant which grows abundantly in Chhotanagpur forest. During summer, it is loaded with flowers white in colour which are full of sweet juice. The honey usually collect juice from it. The reference of Churchu plant has been made in some context. The Churchu plant in this song is located at the side of the Birinta hill which is known by the name of the village of Torpa police station in Khunti subdivision. The lines of the song are as follows:

Birinta buru suba
At the foot of Birinta hill
Churchu dinḍa lena kuṛi
Churchu plant had grown up, O girl
Churchu chhaḍa lena
The *churchu* was divorced
Chhaḍa koṛae roe leda
The divorced boy had planted
Churchu ḍinda lena kuṛi
Churchu plant had grown up, O girl
Churchu chhaḍa lena
The *Churchu* was divorced

In this song, *churchu* plant has got reference with respect to a social event, that is, divorce, otherwise it has neither the beauty nor utility for the Mundas except providing firewood. It is stated that a couple under the shade of *churchu* plant near the Birinta hill got separated after some period of unsuccessful married life. The *churchu* plant became the lone witness of the sad end of the married life of the couple. After the divorce, whenever anyone of them passes through the plant (as it was on the wayside), it reminds him or her of the painful event that had happened there. The *churchu* plant, even now, stands solitary and deserted.

Among the wild creepers which serve various needs of the Mundas, Bandu or Gungu is one of them from which leaf-cups, leaf-coat and leaf umbrella are prepared and from its fibres, rope is made. The creeper spreads on the trees and, thus, get support from it. In the song below, which belongs to Racha category, a girl asks a boy with whom she has got relationship, to cut down the Bandu creeper. The song runs as follows:

> *Chetan̂ redo bandu nar̤i*
> Bandu creeper on the top
> *Tola kana goiram tola kena*
> Has wrapped itself with, O *goiram̂*
> *Dej koete bandu nar̤i*
> On climbing up, the *bandu* creeper
> *Chopan̤ tame goiram, chopan̤ tame*
> Cut it down, O *goiram̂*

The song carries two meanings—one objective and the other subjective or symbolic. In the latter case, the boy is loved by two girls. One of the girl requests the boy to wrest all relations from the other girl so that they may live together without any interruption. In the Munda culture, like other Indian cultures, creeper usually symbolizes the fair sex who generally remain dependant on males.

Flowers

Flower is the most referred part of the plant in Munda songs. Its reference is made in different contexts to express the human mood and personality, and as a symbol of love and beauty.

In Chhotanagpur forest, various species of plants grow in which flowers bloom almost in all seasons, but it is during the spring that maximum plants are laden with flowers.

Flowers are used in personal decoration besides its ritual significance. The tribal youth usually establish friendship in the name of some flower which indicates their love for flowers. The reference of flowers, in Munda songs, are made in three different contexts: (a) to add to beauty, (b) as an object of ritual offering, and (c) in symbolism. The meaning or significance of flowers also differ in accordance with category of song. For instance, in Bala song, it mostly carries symbolic meaning, in Jadur as add to beautify and in

Racha, as a thing of beauty itself. The most beautiful flower which the Munda considers is the *kasom ba,* that is, cotton flower, not for its objective beauty but for its usefulness.

In Munda songs, as stated above, the appreciation of the beauty of the flower is less than its use in decoration. Reference of flower is made usually in some context and it is through that process that objective beauty of the flower is exposed. Below is one such song belonging to Jadur category, the lines of which are as follows:

> *Maraṇg buru re daru towa ba*
> In the great mountain stands the *towa* flower tree
> *Huriṇg naṛa re naṛi naṭa̯l ba*
> In the valley below creeper *atal* flower spreads up
> *Daru towa ba urae-baraeya*
> Towa flower tree has branches scattered
> *Naṛi naṭa̯l ba tare-taseya*
> Atal flower creeper has shady spreads
> *Gatu leka me urae-baraya*
> Stitch garlands if you can
> *Galaṇg leka me tare-taseya*
> Weave it if you can

Towa and Atal are two flowers that are widely referred in Munda songs. The composer of the song describes the appearance of the two flowers. Their appearance do not change even if they are stitched in garlands.

In the song below reference of *Dimbu baha* has been made in relation to stormy rain. The lines of the song which belongs to Racha category of song, are as follows:

> *Mid baka̤rio bare baka̤rio*
> A gardenful or two
> *Ḍimbu baha tara tegi leyona kana*
> Dimbu flower has leaned at one side
> *Hoyo lere*
> When the wind blows
> *Ḍimbu baha tara tegi leyona kana*
> Dimbu flower has leaned at one side

Gama lere
When it rains
Ḍimba baha tara tegi leyona kana
Dimbu flower has leaned at one side

Dimbu flower is a wild species of *Tulsi* plant. Boys and girls, when they visit *akhra* for dance, fair or market, insert Dimbu flower on the side of the ear or on head. It has medicinal value and also is believed to ward off the effect of evil eye. It is a bushy plant and grows thickly. The composer of the song observes that when the wind blows or when it rains, it cannot stand due to thickness and leans down to one side.

Change in nature or cycle in life is an indication of changing times which is very much visible in the falling of leaves from the trees, sprouting of tender leaves, budding of flowers and its decay. This very nature of life has been expressed in the following song which belongs to Racha category, the lines of which are as follows:

Buru ko chetan̂ re
Upon the hill tops
Kuṭi baha lena
Kuti flower bloomed
Beṛa ko laṭar̂ re
On the valley below
Sagai baha lena
Sagai had bloomed
Kuṭi baha yo notaṇg jan
Kuti flower too faded away
Sagai baha yo dopali jan
Sagai flower too fell down

The composer of this song once saw the hilltops and valley below covered with colourful flowers all around. A few weeks later, he found the area in a different look as no flower was left there at that time.

Flowers are usually seen by the Mundas as an object of personal decoration. The song below which belongs to Bala category of song mentions how the country is laden with flowers, but it looks beautiful if it is used in personal decoration. The lines of the song are as follows:

Gaṛa-gaṛa te gaṛa ludam ba
By the side of the ravines, *ludam* flower blooms
Tiṇjori buru ko chetan, Ramjaṛi beṛa ko laṭar
Upon the Tinjori hill and on the valley of *Ramjari* below
Baha lere raja baṇkoli baha
Nice is the *raja bankoli* flower on decoration
Tiṇjori buru ko chetan, ramjaṛi beṛa ko laṭar
Upon the Tinjori hill and on the valley of *ramjari* below

The flowers of *ludam* and *raja bankoli* are blooming all along the hills and valleys but the people seldom appreciate it. They are meaningless and insignificant if they are not used in personal decoration.

The reference of flowers are made in a number of ways in relation to the boys and girls in Munda songs. Some such situations are the look of the user of flower, place of availability, and its method of aquisition in the way of presentation to somebody and style and rhythm of garland making. The song below which belongs to Lahsua category, refers to one such situation. The lines of the song are as follows:

1. *Huṛiṇg-huṛiṇg guṭu re*
   On a small hillock
   Towa baha do baha len
   Towa flower had bloomed
   Ho, hore, mai re
   O daughter, dear
   Ne bahaete oko baha re pura-a: sugaram
   Leave aside this flower, on which flower you will be more beautiful
2. *Huṛiṇg-huṛiṇg guṭu re*
   On a small hillock
   Towa baha do baha len
   Towa flower had bloomed
   Ho, hore mai re
   O daughter, dear
   Towa bahaete Buṛju baha re pura-a: sugaram
   You are more beautiful in Burju flower than Towa flower

The youths, particularly the girls are fond of decorating themselves with flowers. During festivals, fairs and other social occasions, they are seen laden with flowers. The well decorated youth receives much appreciation from one's friends. The song as referred to is based on the expectation that if she would decorate herself with *Burju* flower instead of *Towa,* she would look more beautiful.

The song below which belongs to Racha category, is more explicit of this fact. The lines of the song are:

Hora re suku naṛi
The wayside pumpkin creeper
Buruduṛui ba lena re
Buruduṛui had bloomed
Ba lere, gutu lere
When decorated and on making garland
Bugi-bugi neloga re
It looks beautiful

As stated earlier, a flower's beauty is appreciated when it is used in decoration. The Mundas seldom plant flowers for the beautification of the spot. The ultimate purpose of planting flowers, is to use it in personal decoration or for the sake of its use in rituals.

The girls, whenever they go to the forest to collect forest produce, collect flowers too which are available there. One such flower collecting scene has been described by the composer of the following song which belongs to Lahsua category. The lines of the song are as follows:

1. *Ne jiliṇg sereṇg re*
   Upon this long rock
   Ne rengaṛ daru re
   Upon this seasoned tree
   Kodom baha do baha len
   Kodom flower had bloomed
   Ho chilkaing deja, ho chilkaing tebaga
   Oh, how shall I climb, how shall I reach out

2. *Baṇkayo tolere*
   Even with forked pole

Ti teyo tebae re
Even reaching out with hands
Ho, chilkaiṇg deja, ho chilkaiṇg tebaga
Oh, how shall I climb, how shall I reach out

A kodom tree stands at a place where there are rocks all around. Its flowers attract the girl. She tried to climb up the tree but failed. Then she got a long forked pole and tried to bring the flowers down but all in vain. The girl was disappointed. How the youths feel restless for flowers, has been described in the following song which belongs to Jadur category. The lines run as follows:

1. *Kon ṭoli ful fulela mai*
In which hamlet the flowers bloom
Kon ṭoli gamạk jaela
In which hamlet its scent spreads
Chhaela ka jiwa nahin manae
The youth is unable to control himself
Samaṭh lele dauṛela
Runs out carrying mortar

2. *Heṇṭh ṭoli ful fulela mai*
Flowers bloom in the hamlet below
Upar ṭoli gamạk jaela
Its scent spreads up to the hamlet above
Chhaela ka jiwa nahiṇ manae
The youth is unable to control himself
Samaṭh lele dauṛela
Runs out carrying mortar

Flowers and tender leaves when plucked remain fresh for some time and then wither away. This fact has been mentioned in the following song which belongs to Jadur category. The lines are as follows:

1. *Kuṭi ba riṛi suṛa gatim*
With *kuti* flower and tender leaves of *riri*, O friend
Gutu lem galaṇg leme
Stitch it and weave

2. *Towa ba baru suṛa sangam*
With *towa* flower and tender leaves of *baru, O* friend
Peṭe leme chagaṛ leme
Break and split it

3. *Gutu lem galang lem gatim*
Stitch and weave it, O friend
Chuṭi koṭo goso tan
Twig's tip is withering away

4. *Peṭe lem chagaṛ lem sangam*
Break and split it, O friend
Suba taṛa maila jan
Bottom end is shrinking

Garlands are made not only from flowers, but it is also made from dry fruits and seeds. In the song below which belongs to *Bala* category, a youth advises another friend as to what should be prepared from the flowers and what from the fruits. The lines of the song are as follows:

Chetan koto re lupung jo lena
Lupung fruits hang on the upper branch
Latar koto re lupung ba lena
On the lower branch, *lupung* flower bloomed
Jo te-jo te moti gutui me
Make beads garland from seeds
Ba te-ba te ba cha gutui me
Stitch flowers to make garland

Garlands can be made only by stitching flowers or fruits together and in course of such activity, minor accidents may occur. This very event is the theme of the following song which belongs to Jadur category. The lines are as follows:

1. *Ba kuṛi bapaṛi ba gutu leda re*
With flowers she stitched garland
Muṇga ba re chhaela ḍari galaṇg tan
With *munga* flowers the youth is weaving basket

2. *Ba gutu-gutu te tii gutu kedare*

While stitching flowers stitched his hand
Ḍari galaṇg-galaṇg te kaṭae galaṇg ked
While weaving basket, weaved his feet

A woman tells about the sore hand and feet of her husband to another woman. This conversation was overheard by a youth with interest and composed this song.

Flowers are collected from everywhere wherever they are available. In the following song, a girl requests her brother, who is going out to the forest, to bring flowers for her. The song belongs to Jadur category and runs as follows:

1. *Buru reya ho dada, buru lupuṇg baha do*
On the hill, O brother, *buru lupung* flowers bloom
Beṛa reya dada, beṛa baraṇgu baha do.
On the valley, O brother, valley *barangu* flowers bloom

2. *Auwa laṇg me dada, buru lupuṇg baha do*
Bring for me brother, the hill *lupung* flowers
Seṭeralaṇg me dada, beṛa baraṇgu baha do
Send for me brother, the valley *barangu* flowers

How impatient is the girl for flowers has been indicated in the following song. She makes a request to a parrot to bring flowers for her for he has seen almost all the forest and knows where the same is available. The song belongs to Lahsua category and the lines are as follows:

1. *Nam̂ dore salu suga*
O dear, green parrot
Soben brindam̂ nelana
Have seen all the forest
Sugare nagu leme sasaṇg ba, ho hore
Dear parrot, bring for me yellow coloured flowers

2. *Ḍari, ḍari torale*
You broke twig after twig
Ḍari mati bhulabe
Don't forget the twig

Sugare khosa bhari lele jhabarae
Dear parrot, full of hair-lock I will decorate it

This song seems to have been composed either by a girl who sees parrot flying over in the sky and thinks that they might have seen all the forest and desires that if they can bring flowers, she would decorate her hair-lock in full.

When flowers are exchanged between girls or boys, or are presented to someone else, it symbolizes their love and affection. One does not keep flowers for one's use only but are always presented to friends. This habit of the youths have been mentioned in the following Lahsua category of song which runs as follows:

1. *Huring-huring pokhera*
   A small lake
   Upal baha do baha len
   Lotus flowers had bloomed
   Upal baha do upal-dubai
   Lotus flowers float
   Okoe bahayae re haere, haere hae
   Who will decorate with it

2. *Huring-huring pokhera*
   A small lake
   Upal baha do baha len
   Lotus flowers had bloomed
   Upal baha do upal-duba
   Lotus flowers float
   Gatim bahayae re haere, haere hae
   The friend will decorate with it

The following Racha category of song describes how a youth who has been to the forest, is collecting flowers from unapproachable portion of the tree and always remembering his or her friends and decides to carry at least a twig or two for them. The lines of the song are as follows:

1. *Chuti muli re sarajom ba do, sarajom ba*
   At the tip of the stem, the *sarajom* flowers

Deje koete mide kotoyo
On climbing at least a twig
Sarajom ba do, sarajom ba
The *sarajom* flowers

2. *Mide kotoyo uyugai re*
If dropped at least a twig
Sarajom ba do, sarajom ba
The Sarajom flowers

3. *Gatim ke eediyai re*
If taken to a friend
Sarajom ba do, sarajom ba
The Sarajom flowers

4. *Gatim ke seṭerai re*
If carried for a friend
Sarajom ba do, sarajom ba
The Sarajom flowers

Tribal youths usually establish friendships in the name of flowers. After the establishment of flower-friendship, in reference or address, individual's name is not taken but it is the flower. This friendship is maintained throughout the life of the friend. At every auspicious occasion they remain present or invite each other and exchange the best thing. Such friends are treated by the parents like one's own son or daughter. Such friendship is usually established between the person of the same sex and of the same generation. The song below which is based on friendship, belongs to Lahsua category. The lines of the song are as follows:

1. *Kawan phula piriti joṛailo*
In which flower you established friendship
Kawana phula saṇge go delaigo madhu bone haere, haere, hae
In which flower you established friendship at Madhuban forest

2. *Champa phula piriti joṛailo*
You established friendship with *champa* flower

Kawana phula sange go de aigo Madhubone haere, haere, hae
With which flower the friendship was established at Madhuban

Flower friendship is established in a simple ritual by exchanging the particular flower before the firiends as witness. And it is generally established when they are out in the fields, hills and forests.

As stated in the previous pages, the beauty or attribute of the flower is seldom appreciated till someone uses it. And then only the flower is appreciated along with the user. The following Jadur song describes how bees as well as boys are being attracted towards the girl who has decorated herself with Towa and Atali flowers. The lines are as follows:

1. *Chikạn bahạm baha lena mai re*
   With which flower you decked yourself, O girl
   Hurum sukui biyuren ten
   The honey-bee is flying around you
   Chikạn bahạm ḍali lena mai re
   Which twig of flowers you did tuck, O girl
   Luti serom sekoren tan
   Lutiserom bee is hovering around you

2. *Towa bahạm baha lena mai re*
   You did deck yourself with Towa flower, O girl
   Hurumsukui biyuren ten
   The honey-bee is flying around you
   Aṭali bahạm ḍali lena mai re
   You did tuck bunch of Atali flowers, O girl
   Lutiserom sekoren tan
   Lutiserom bee is hovering around you

Attracted by the fragrance of Towa and Atali flowers, the bees are flying around the girl. But as described in the following *Jadur* song, the boys too, are making rounds of the girl who has decorated herself with colourful flowers. The lines of the song are as follows:

1. *Kahe phule jhaka-jhumair goi*
   With which flowers you decked yourself, O girl–

Kane phule malạk ḍair
Which bunch of flowers is hanging down
Hạm to alo tore love goi
Attracted by you we did come
Hạm kaese birasal jab
How shall we forget you

2. *Genda phule jhaka-jhumair goi*
You are decked with *genda* flower, O girl
Champa phule malạk ḍair
Bunch of *champa* flowers is hanging down
Hạm to alo tore love goi
Attracted by you we did come
Hạm kaese birasal jab
How shall we forget you

The sisters and brothers of married couples have *goi* and *eyar* relationships with each other. They maintain friendly relationship and exchange jokes freely. The *goi* has decorated herself with *genda* and *champa* flowers, but they have no attraction for it as they openly tell the girl. It is the colourfully decorated *goi* who brought them there and is unforgettable to them.

Flowers have ritual significance too. Flowers are rarely planted for ritual sake by the tribals. They are collected from the forest. If no flower is available in a season for ritual offerings, twig with leaves serve the purpose. And flowers do not form part of offering to Munda God at all occasions. It is during *Ba* festival that flowers are offered. The song below has been composed relating to *Ba* festival. The song belongs to *Japi* or *Jarapi* category and the lines are as follows:

Ba kuṛi bapari
The flowers, O girl
Ba aṛgu ledare goi sarạjom ba
Had brought down *sarajom* flower
Nikir boṇga ḍali nosor leda goi Tilae dali
Tilae branch was slipped down by Nikir bonga
Pahaṇṛ lagin ba aṛgu leda goi, sarạjom ba
Sarajom flowers were brought down for the *pahanr*

Pujar lagin ḍali nosor leḍa go Tilae dali
Bunch of Tilae was slipped down for the *pujar*

Every Munda village has usually a dozen or more dwelling places of the nature spirits which is known as Sarna. During flower festival, offering is made at *Ba Sama* for the supreme God Singbonga. Eekir bonga is the name of spirit of the deeps which also get offering during flower festival along with Singbonga. *Pahnr,* the village priest and *pujar,* his assistant, do the common ritual performance for the whole village community.

The trees that have religious significance for the Mundas besides sarajom are, bamboo, *madkam, sonso karam* and *tiril.* Among the grass, mention may be made of *dubla* grass, *Saga-a* and *ba-a-chom.* We may get reference of all these in subsequent pages in different context.

Symbolic and Contextual References of Flowers

As stated earlier, flowers in Bala or marriage songs carry deeper meaning than other categories of songs. Marriage is a happy occasion and reference of flowers in songs is, therefore, made to symbolize the moment of joy, happiness and emotions. This aspect of human life have amply been revealed in Bala category of songs. The reference of flowers on this very context has been made in the following song:

Chirchiti phuli gelaiṇ, chirchiti re
Chirchiti has bloomed in abundance
Chamaili phuli gelaiṇ gaḍa-gada re
Chamaili has bloomed bright
Ghoṛa je chale lagal, chale chhamaṛ-chhamaṛ
Horses are pacing with sound of tinkling bells
Hathi je chale lagal, suṇre nahiṇ sambharae
Elephants are moving with uncontrolled trunks
Chirchiti phuli gelaiṇ, chirchiti re
Chirchiti has bloomed in abundance
Chamaili phuli gelaiṇ gaḍa-gada re
Chamaili has bloomed bright

The song describes the status of flowers as well as the scene of marriage. *Chirchiti* and *chameli* are the two flowers mentioned in this song. *Chirchiti,* in particular, is a kind of grass whose flowers cannot be distinguished from its fruits. It is also not like any other flower whose colour is easily identified. On the other hand, *chameli* is a well-known flower. The composer of the song draws attention towards the phenomenon of two flowers, that is, blooming in abundance. It has two meanings in this context, in one case, it either indicates that the youths (the boy or the girl) has attained the marriageable age, and in the other, the marriage season has approached. The subsequent lines of the song clear up this ambiguity by referring horses and elephants who are marching together in unison with the sound of tinkling bells. Marriage among the Mundas is a most simple one and there is no association of horses and elephants in it at any stage. The reference of horses and elephants has been made to make the occasion a grand one. The *nagbansis as* well as big *zamindars* and *jagirdars* of the region during their days of reign, had to bring out such pompous scene of marriage procession which were often the reference in Munda songs.

In the following song, flower stands for the bride. Among the Mundas, it is the bridegroom who comes to the bride's house for marriage. The following Bala song has symbolized the bridegroom in these lines:

> *Buru-buru tega hiju lena*
> Came all along the hills
> *Umana buru baṇkoli ba*
> The hill *bankoli flower,* O mother
> *Gaṛa-gaṛa tega seṭer lena*
> Arrived all through the ravines
> *Umana gaṛa ludậm ba*
> The *ludam* flower of the ravines, O mother
> *Peṭe lere umana, buru baṇkoli ba*
> The hill *bankoli* flowers when plucked, O mother
> *Umana buru baṇkoli ba*
> The hills *bankoli* flowers, O mother
> *Gaṛa lere umana, gaṛa ludậm ba*
> Ravine *ludam* flowers mother when plucked

Umana gaṛa ludạm ba
The ravine ludam flower, O mother

In this song, Buru *Bankoli ba* and *Gara ludam ba* stand for the bridegroom. The girl tells her mother indirectly that the boy whom she met on the hills and ravines, is coming. The flower is the symbol of joy and happiness, and in this context, the bridegroom as flower, is happiness for the girl.

The song below describes the romantic scene of the would-be bride and bridegroom with the help of flower and a bird. The song belongs to Bala category and the lines are as follows:

Tetari phule rigi bigia
Tamarind blooms in multicolour
Kachnar phule kachera
Kachnar flowers in patches
Munga ko ḍari me baisae re rasabhaoṇra
On Munga twig is sitting *Rasabhaonra* bird

In this song, *tetar* and *kachnar* flowers symbolized the girl and *rasabhaonra* bird, a boy. *Rasabhaonra* is a small bird which lives on flower's juice. The bird is looking to the *tetar* and *kachnar* flowers from a distance sitting on a high twig of munga tree. It is ready to alight on the flowers. The composer of the song leaves the audience half way and forces them to imagine rest of the events. This is the very quality of Munda poetry. The sex does not get public expression in the Munda society unless it is ritually demanded. Nevertheless, the idea is communicated in a subtle way as in this song.

In the song below, the girl is symbolized in a different way and through it, a social custom of bride-price, has been brought into the light. The song mentions that the girl (symbolized by plant) grows up in a small household (symbolized as a small plot of land) and is sold away by the parent fetching them a huge amount. The song belongs to Bala category and the lines are as follows:

Chhoṭe-moṭe keyari nayo
A small plot of land, mother
Hirmicha sag nayo, hirmicha sag
Vegetable Hirmicha has grown, mother

Hirmicha sag nayo, sone phulan̯ phul
Vegetable Hirmicha has golden flowers, mother
Nayo rupe phulan̯ phul
Has silver flowers, mother
Sone phulan̯ phulae nayo
Has golden flowers, mother
Ḍaso ṭaka molae
Have been priced rupees ten, mother
Nayo biso ṭaka molae
Have been valued rupees twenty.

9

THE FAUNA WORLD IN SONGS

Chhotanagpur plateau is a good sanctuary for wild animals, birds and insects. Its undulating physiography and botanical environment provides suitable abode for both herbivorous and carnivorous species. The animals that are found in the region are of various categories in which mention may be made of elephant, tiger, bear, wild pig, deer, wild goat, nilgai, wild cat, hyena, jackal, fox, rabbit, mongoose, monkey, squirrel, etc. Various species of reptile, frog, crab, tortoise, spider, butterfly and insects, are also abundantly found in the region.

Like the animals, a wide variety of birds species are also found in the region. The prominent among these birds are peacock, wild fowl, wild duck, wild pigeon, dove, *titar* of various kinds, parrot, *maena,* crow, vulture, kite, crane, sparrow, owl, bat, etc.

Due to the denudation of forest and change in eco-environment, various species of animals, birds, reptiles and insects have gone extinct. The quantity of fish have also been reduced considerably due to irregularity of rain, drought and siltation.

Even in this changing eco-environment, songs with animals, birds, fish and reptiles are the favourite theme for the expression of human ideas and experiences.

We also get reference of domestic animals and birds such as bullock, cow, buffaloe, goat, ram, cat, fowl, etc, in Munda songs in different contexts.

Reference of fauna world is widely made in Munda songs in different context which reveal their beauty, their internal world, nature and character in relation to human beings. In songs, we also get the description of their habitation, movements and their behaviour.

In Munda country, regions are identified on the basis of its characteristic features like availability of hills, rivers and forests. They are accordingly identified as *Buru disum* (mountainous country),

Nai disum (country of the rivers), *Bir disum* (forest country), and *Piri disum* (country of the plain lands). Each region has its special features in the matter of flora, fauna and weather conditions.

People living in respective geographical or ecological zones are accustomed to its environment and identify a number of better facilities for themselves than the people of other areas. The better adjusted people are, however, those who live in *piri disum,* that is, region of treeless plain lands who fight all the time against the ecological imbalance. The people of each region, in their prolonged habitation in the area, cultivate in themselves many likes and dislikes for and against the respective areas. The song below which belongs to Jarga category mentions this difference of choice of the people. The lines of the song are as follows :

1. *Buru disum hoṛo ko*
   The people of mountainous country
   Buru gena ko hiatiṇga
   They desire the mountain sides
   Gaṛa disum hoṛo ko
   The people of riverine country
   Gaṛa disum ko chakatiṇga
   They aspire for the riverine country

2. *San sakạm nagen ge*
   For the sake of leaves and woods, dear
   Buru gena ko hiatiṇga
   They desire for the mountain side
   Hai kaṭkom nagen ge
   For fish and crabs, dear
   Gaṛa gena ko chakatiṇga
   They aspire for the riverine country

In *piri disum,* though the number of wild animals and insects are less, but their total absence is not assured. In this area, only small sized animals are found like fox, jackal, rabbit, squirrel, etc, who get easy hideout in barren rocks and ravines. There are some species of insects which are exclusively found in *piri disum.* The song below which belongs to Mage category of song portrays the distribution of some of them in *Bir, Buru* and *Piri disum*. The song runs as follows :

1. *Bir disum re, piṛi disum re*
In forested and in country of the plains
Barai rambṛa sonsorod-e, diriṇg-a: kana
The grasshopper of Barai-rambra has developed horns
Bir disum re, piṛi disum re
In forested and in country of the plains
Jugi hoṛe, jugie holad-a kana
On Hore plant, *jugi* (*kankato* insect) has barber's knife,

2. *Bir disum re, Buru disum re*
In forested and mountainous country
Buru gangai sara-e che-a loma kana
The hill *langur* has bunch of maize like tail
Piṛi disum re, beṛa oṭere
In the country of the plain lands and in valley lands
Beṛa irba-e hunie tolongana
The rat has tail like valley *irba*

In this song, mention of not only the habitation of animals and insects have been made, but the crops grown and the community who earns his bread by shaving the hair of others have also been indicated. *Barai rambra* (a kind of pulse) is grown mostly in forested area. On this crop, usually a long moustache grasshopper is also found. Hore—a wild grass grows in forest as well as in treeless region. Its leaves have sharp borders which can cut the skin like the barber's blade. *Kankata* a species of insect which have knife like hands, are also found in this region and mostly on Hore grass. Maize and *irba* (local name of crop) both have bunches of fruits which looks like animals tails with tuft of hair. Gari (a monkey) and rat both have tails with tuft of hair at its end which have been compared with that of fruits of maize and *irba.* It may be seen that these animals and insects as well as plants have at least one common similarity in their parts of the body. The singer composer of the song has made the close observation which otherwise the youths may have missed.

Chhotanagpur as seen, has many forest covered spots, marshy lands and water-pools which are the most suitable place for wild animals to live in. The following Jadur song mentions that these spots are meant for the animals like wild boars, elephants, etc. The lines of the song are as follows :

1. *Upal ba ikir do gule-gule*
   The lotus covered deep is silent blue
   Tarae ba jubila do bijir-balang
   The marshy land below the *tarae* flower spreads wide shining bright

2. *Okoe derang ko reyarente*
   For whom it is to be cooled down
   Chimae derang ko oyarente
   For whom it is to swim about

3. *Sukuri koge ko reyarente*
   It is for wild boars to be cooled down
   Kula koge ko oyarente
   It is for tigers to swim about

The source of spring and marshy lands away from human habitation, are the most peaceful spots. The places are for the exclusive use of wild animals and birds, and as the author of this song says, these spots are meant for them only.

In the midst of various species of animals, birds and insects, people feel homely even at desolate areas. Their peculiar sounds, movements, size, figure and colour all attract the attention of the people. While some avoid human contact, others roam about close to their habitation, some are harmful and dangerous. Their encounter with men generate automatic surprise and curiosity which are expressed through song by the Mundas. The wild life of three different species and their encounter with man have been described under three separate categories of animals, reptiles and insects and birds. In the category of animals and birds, wild as well as domestic, both are included.

Songs related to Animals

Among the animals that are found in Chhotanagpur forest, elephant is the biggest of them all. The song below which belongs to Racha category may have been composed more than hundred years ago for elephants are not so extensively found today in all parts of the Munda region. The lines of the song are as follows:

Madukam buta re, hantiya-mutia
Under the *madukam* tree, a couple of elephants
Hanti doe nir tana-2
The elephant is running away
Ramjari tonang te nir tana-2
Running away to *ramjari* forest

Elephants generally go on moving from one place to another, They do great harm to crops but people's experience tell that they are one of those well behaved animals who understand human signal. They never harm the person or his property when requested politely. As mentioned in this song, a pair of elephants were moving about under the *madukam* tree in search of its flowers but seeing the poor man, they moved away towards the forest of Ramjari village. As of today, no elephant is found in Ramjari forest.

In Chhotanagpur forest, once sambhar, nilgai, etc, were found in abundance. They are now located in few reserved forests only. The age of the song below too, may be very old for no wild buffaloes are now found in Munda region. The song belongs to Racha category which runs as follows:

Bono me rahle, bono bhainsa re
You lived in the forest, O wild buffalo
Bono kera mur mati kori-kori
Digging the soil of the forest from one's head
Hani-hani, dhani-dhani
Shoving and throwing away constantly
Sinja lakra re
No fear of either lion or tiger
Bono bhainsa re
The wild buffalo, dear

The composer of this song was moved seeing the fearlessness of the wild buffalo in the forest where lion and tiger roam about freely. It digs up soil with its horns showing the lion or tiger its prowess and ferocity.

In yet another song below which also refers to the buffalo in a different way. There is no difference in appearance between the wild and domestic one. The composer of the song, therefore, says that it is the domestic one that has gone to the forest for grazing. The song belongs to *Bala* category and the lines are as follows:

> *Bono re bono bhaiṇsa*
> O wild buffalo
> *Ḍih chhoṛi bono chare gela re*
> Leaving the village, went for grazing to the forest
> *Hare bono bhaiṇsa*
> O wild buffalo
> *Ḍih chhoṛi bono chare gela re*
> Leaving the village, went to the forest for grazing

Bears are generally found in hilly areas bordered by forest. They are feared for their ferocious paws. They rarely come out during day time. They depend on fruits, roots and insects. The following Lahsua song mentions about the bear:

1. *Bono me kawan raṭa-paṭa*
   Who is making rattling sound in the forest
   Ham̂ to sunalo
   We heard
   Bono me kawan raṭa-paṭa
   Who is making rattling sound in the forest
2. *Bono me dheṛi raṭa-paṭa*
   The bear is making rattling sound in the forest
   Ham̂ to sunalo
   We heard
   Hare, bono me bheṛi raṭa-paṭa
   Oh, it is the bear that is making rattling sound in the forest.

The youths usually visit one village after another for dance during night. It is one such detour, they heard the rattling sound in a bush and started speculation who it may be. Soon they came to the conclusion that it might be the bear. On arriving at the dancing ground, they rendered the experience into song. So long this kind of situation still exists during night travelling, the life of the song remains.

Hanuman or monkeys were once the most common animal in Chhotanagpur plateau, but their numbers have now considerably reduced. Their human like behaviour automatically attracts the attention of the children and adults alike. They like fruits very much and often come down to crops and after collecting, move away quickly. They are afraid of dogs. The nature of the monkeys have been reflected in the following Lahsua song. The lines of which are as follows:

1. *Kon baṭe kande ek Hanumaṇ bir, Hanumaṇ do*
   In which direction the brave Hanuman cries
   Hanumaṇ do heri johe jae re
   Hanuman is waiting
   Haere, haere hae
   Look how brave
   Hanuman do heri johe jae re
   Hanuman is waiting

2. *Purab baṭe kade ek Hanumaṇ bir*
   In the east the brave Hanuman cries
   Hae re haere hae
   Look how brave
   Pachhim baṭe heri johe jae re
   Goes to the west and waiting

Hanuman is one of the heroes in the epic *Ramayana.* The indication of this song is towards this brave Hanuman. The story tells that in search of epic heroin Sita, he was on her look out in all directions.

The song below also makes reference of the Hanuman but the meaning is obscure. The song belongs to Bala category, the lines of which are as follows:

Kono pahare, Hanumana kande, Hanumana roae
On which mountains, Hanuman wails
Detoge nayo, soṭaka tarowair, gaṛala barechha
Let me have mother, the hanging sword and pitched up spear
Hanumaṇ kande, Hanumaṇ roae
The Hanuman is wailing

In this song the boy asks his mother to give him sword and

spear to drive away the wailing Hanuman. It may be that monkeys were coming down to the standing crops on the field signalling other monkeys also.

Fox and jackals are the most familiar animals for they are found everywhere in Chhotanagpur. The song below refers to the fox indirectly. It is sung in Jadur as well as in Khemta category of songs equally. The wording of the song are the same but its tune differs in each category. The lines of Jadur song are as follows:

> *Lor-lor te metam*
> Through the ravines, I tell you
> *Lor-lor nokoe kakalae, metậm chimae rumbulae*
> Through the ravines who cries and growls, I tell you
> *Gaṛa-gaṛa te metậm*
> Through the rivers, I tell you
> *Gaṛa-gaṛa nokoe kakalae metậm nokoe rumbulae*
> Through the rivers, who cries and growls

Fox are the harmless creatures. They are found in pairs and sometimes in groups of three or four. The Munda term for them is Khai-Khai. They make peculiar sound in the evening and occasionally at night also. They are found in ravines and hillocks and eat fish and crabs. Their size is smaller than the dogs.

It is in the same category that *Tuyu*, that is, the jackals belong. They are found in good numbers everywhere and are of equal size to that of dogs. They are carnivorous and also take maize, *bajra* sugarcane, etc. They are so clever and steadfast in their objective that in every society their reference in the folklore of the people is found. They represent human character of cleverness, cheat, fraud, lie, etc. In the following Bala category of song the jackal personifies the bridegroom. The lines of the song are as follows:

> *Siru re pandey, siru re pandey*
> *O siru pandey* (jackal)
> *Kaese re murgi ke ḍharae*
> How you catch the hen
> *Siru re pandey*
> O *siru pandey*
> *Kaese re murgi ke ḍharae*

How you catch the hen
Gaon ker Muṇda Mahto
The Munda and *Mahto* of the village
Liha-liha karae
Cry for to catch him
Ṭola kera pahan
The *pahan* of the hamlet
Kaese re murgi ke dharae
How it catches the hen

The jackal always remains on the look out for the hen. At early morning when the hens come out it pounces upon them. At this hour of the day all persons remain busy and so the jackal gets enough time to get away with the catch. The subject matter of this very process of catching hen has been taken in the context of marriage ceremony. The groom represents the jackal and the bride, the hen. The marriage ceremony is performed in the presence of the village elders like Munda (village headman), *pahan* (village priest) and *mahto* (village watchman). The jackal (groom) carries away the hen (bride) even in the presence of great people of the village. This also indicates one of the forms of marriage called elopement marriage. In this form of marriage, the boy and girl both agree to run away and start life together. In such a situation, the village elders make great hue and cry against such union and also send some people behind them to get them back. The process is the same as with the jackal carrying away the hen after whom some dogs are let loose to catch it.

The song below mentions that at every nullaḥ and ḍitch hare and peacocks are dancing. As stated elsewhere, due to large-scale deforestation, the birds and animals may not be seen everywhere and this song is reminiscent of the past and may be over hundred years. The song is very simple in composition and so may appear to be a children's song. It is the song of Jarga category and the lines are as follows:

Lor bo, sokṛa bo
At the head of nullah and plot of fields
Kulae dumaṇg ru tana mai sigṛi-bigṛi
The rabbit is playing on Dumang pleasantly

Lor bo, sokṛa bo
At the head of *nullah* and plot of fields
Mara susun tana mai koncho-doṇṛo-kancho-doṇṛo
The peacock is dancing beautifully

But in the song below which belongs to Lahsua category, though the composition is simple, based on objectivity, it is poetically rich in imagination and impression. The composition has been made in a proverbial way but the temporal meaning is clear. The lines run as follows:

1. *Seta ko hatu re*
In the village of the dogs
Tiril jo lena, tiril ba lena
The *tiril* did bear flowers and fruits
Seta ko ruku tana, pusi ko halaṇg tana
The dogs are shaking the tree and the cats are collecting

2. *Tur ge ṭipchura kada*
The squirrel has raised its tail
Ho, ho, ho, neka samae re
How nice is the moment
Oko disum rem nela kada
Have you ever seen it in any land
Ho, ho, ho, saṇgiṇg disum reiṇg nela kada
I have seen it in distant land such nice thing

Tiril is delicious fruit and the trees grow abundantly in forest regions. There is no dogs village anywhere in the Munda country but the author, in the imagination, sees a village as such. The dogs and cats are busy in collecting the *tiril* fruit and the squirrel who likes this fruit very much, is simply looking on raising its tail due to fear of the cats.

Insects, Reptiles and Water Species

Various species of insects and reptiles are found in Chhotanagpur as mentioned earlier. They are harmful as well as useful to man. Not much reference of this class of species are found in the Munda songs. However, reference of only those have been made which are, otherwise, feared or which are supposed to have some economic value or simply for their curious activity and beauty. Its reference has come in different contexts and, therefore, only a few are described here.

Mosquitoes are menace everywhere in hilly and forest covered areas in Chhotanagpur. The wild variety are really dangerous for they inflict illness. Besides mosquitoes, there are varieties of other blood sucking insects, some are flyers and some non-flyers. Mosquitoes usually fly in groups and the following song is based on this very nature of theirs. The song belongs to Jarga category and the lines are as follows:

> *Gaṛa japa-japa te*
> Along the ditches
> *Sikriṇ kona era araṇdi tana*
> Sikriṇ are celebrating marriage, O lady
> *Nai ba rasi-rasi te*
> With the flowers juice of the river
> *Lowatiṇg kona era koraṇdi tana*
> Lowating are enjoying the feast, O lady
> *Upa̱l ba cheta̱n-cheta̱n*
> Upon the lotus flower
> *Chauḍal rena era sikriṇ aṛaṇdi tana*
> On the palanquin mosquitoes are celebrating the marriage
> *Kama̱l ba laṭa̱r-laṭa̱r te*
> Below the lotus flower
> *Lowatiṇg kona era koraṇdi tana*
> Lowating are enjoying the feast, O lady

In this song two species of insects have been referred—Sikrin and Lowating. Sikrin live in dark places while the Lowating are found either on the flowers or inside the fruits that are ripened. The imagination of the author is quite right and appropriate when he says that mosquitoes are celebrating marriage in ditches and under the lotus leaves for these places are hiding places for them. A peculiar sound is produced when they fly and to this the author says that they are singing, marriage songs. The Lowating, on the other hand, are also enjoying, marriage feast for they are always found on the flowers petals and inside the ripened fruits.

Insects who live on grass and leaves, are of a variety of species. The reference of two insects—Miru and Kare, who belong to the caterpillar species, have been made in the following Jadur song the lines of which are as follows:

Soso ren miru do
The *miru* of *soso* tree
Tilae ren kaṛe do
The *kaṛe* of *tilae* tree
Soso jom-jom te daṭae hende jan
Has blackened its teeth by eating *soso*
Tilae habe-habe te daṭae raṇgao jan
Has coloured its teeth while chewing *tilae*

Nature is not only beautiful in its topographical features and floral colours, but all creatures living over the earth, are the specimen of beauty itself. It is observed that most creatures carry the colours of their dwelling places. The colours of the insect living on *soso* and *tilae* trees, as mentioned in this song, are the same as the tree or the fruit.

Lac and cocoon are, of course, the most beautiful insects for the Mundas. These two insects are cultivated extensively in Chhotanagpur. They are the main cash crops of the people. Lac is cultivated on trees like *ber, baru, palas,* etc. On the first day when they are cultivated, the person who does the job takes bread of *kode* grain in bigger size than the normal one. The belief is that the lac cultivated through this process yields abundant crops.

People identify two kinds of cocoon—*Lareya* and *Barhaura.* Lareya variety of cocoon are small in size than the other one. The wild ones are found in almost all kinds of trees but particularly in *ber, sarjom, baru* and *tut.* The song below which belongs to Jarda category, mentions that whatever tree the *Lumangi*, that is, cocoon gets, it winds up itself on it. The lines of the song are as follows:

1. *Lumaṇgi do, lumaṇgi do*
   The cocoon
   Kita buṭa lumaṇgi do, *haena*
   The cocoon of the date tree, dear

Laṛeya do, laṛeya do
The *Lareya*
Sale buṭa lareya do
The *Lareya* of *Sale* tree

2. *Kita buṭa lumaṇgi do*
The cocoon of the date tree
Kita regi tolena haena
It winds itself up on the date tree, dear
Sale buṭa lareya do
The *laṛeya* of *Sale* tree
Sale regi neoṛan jan haena
It wrapped itself on *Sale* tree

3. *Bale opaḍ bano leka.*
As if there is no tender twig
Kita regi tolen jan haena
It winded itself on date tree
Linduṇg sarjom bano leka
As if there is no tender saplings of *sarjom* tree
Sale regi neoṛan jan haena
It wrapped itself on *Sale* tree

Cocoon in wild condition are rarely found as they are eaten away by birds. However, wherever they are found, they are collected by the people. The song below which belongs to Racha category, mentions about the cocoon collection. The lines of the song are as follows:

Siṇg ko choṭi re
At the top of the Sing tree
Korkoṭa naṛi ren lumang do-2
The cocoon of Korkota creeper
Halaṇgeme namsiṇg
Collect it, O namsing
Tumbaleme tumbalsiṇg-2
Pick it up, O Tumbalsing
Korkoṭa naṛi ren lumaṇg do-2
The cocoon of Korkota creeper

In this song, Namsing and Tumbalsing are not the personal names. It is simply an act of collection and picking up and have been used as personal names. The cocoon, as mentioned in this song is on the *korkota* creeper which is hanging on a very tall tree.

A wide variety of grasshoppers of different sizes, shapes .and colours are found in Chhotanagpur. They are found in all places—dry, wetlands, rocky, sandy lands and on grass and plants. Their colour matches to the place of their habitation. The song below which belongs to Bala category, finds the grasshopper in a happy mood. The lines of the song are as follows:

> *Chirchiti chuti faniga*
> The grasshopper on the twig's top of Chirchiti
> *Terem-resem tana re faniga, terem resem tana*
> The grasshopper is smiling and smiling

The grasshoppers which are found in *chirchiti* grass are slim and are of green colour. It can produce a rattling sound by rubbing its legs on the wings. The author of the song takes the process of producing sound as smiling and indirectly indicates the happy mood of the bridegroom.

How the insects living on *tilming* and *malan* crops appear, has been described in the following Jadur song. The lines of the song are as follows:

1. *Tilmiṇg tiju chiga, malạn uru*
   The caterpillar of tilming and fly of the bean
   Tilmiṇg tiju doe lemaṇg-lemaṇg
   The caterpillar of tilming is creeping
   Tilmiṇg tiju chiga malạn uru
   The caterpillar of tilming and fly of the bean
   Manal uru doe ruwaṇg-ruwaṇg
   The fly of the bean is hovering around

2. *Tilmiṇg tiju dogae lemaṇg-lemaṇg*
   The caterpillar of tilming is creeping
   Tilmiṇg goṛa regie lemaṇg-lemaṇg
   Creeping on the crop of the tilming
   Manal uru-regae ruwaṇg-ruwaṇg
   The fly of the bean is hovering around

Manal ba regae ruwaṇg-ruwaṇg
Hovering around on the bean's flower

These two species of insects are specific to particular plant and are not found in any other plant. The colour of these insects are also the same to that of the plants.

As stated earlier, there are variety of reptiles in Chhotanagpur and among it the snake is most dreaded one. While some are poisonous and others not. Some, as the people tell, are blood suckers and some milk takers, but almost all are carnivorous. Some carry poison on their teeth and some on tail, and some carry diamond on their head. The most often seen species are Pandu, that is, *nag, karait, dairdega, bandfora, burubing, naibing, sunumbing, lurbing, jamburbing* and *dundu*, etc. They are of different colours. Tigers and snakes are the two most feared creatures for the people. Their presence can be expected anywhere as the following Jarga category of song mentions. The lines of the song are as follows:

1. *Marchi bakṛi, bengṛa bakṛi*
   On chilli or brinjal garden either
   Biṇg na era biṇg, soṇ ken soṇ kena, haena
   The snake is hissing, O lady

2. *Marchi bakṛi, bengṛa bakṛi*
   On chilli or brinjal garden either
   Kula na era haṇ ken haṇ kena, haena
   The tiger is growling, O lady

3. *Dasi koṛa ke solka kija*
   It attacked the servant boy
   Biṇg na era soṇ ken soṇ kena haena
   The snake is hissing, O lady
   Kamṛi kuṛi ke hoạ kija, haena
   It bit the servant girl
   Kula na era haṇ ken haṇ kena, haena
   The tiger is growling, O lady

The hilly and forest clad area provides suitable hiding place for both tiger and snake and one can encounter regularly with these animals and reptiles. Sometimes, as mentioned in this song, they remain hiding in kitchen garden too, and the person unaware of the presence of any such creature, can become easy prey. Tigers, nowadays are rarely visible in most parts of the Munda region, but snakes are found everywhere. The snake, even creeps up into the dwelling place and thus they create the real danger to everybody. The song below, which has been taken from Jarga category of song mentions that a snake has got into the house. The song runs as follows:

> *Kuṇdam-kuṇdam te barachiti nae tunaṇg tana*
> Barachiti is creeping behind the house, mother
> *Salaṇdi-salaṇdi te, liṭa jaḍa nae kolaṇgia kana*
> On the wall, *lita jada* has spread itself, mother
> *Barachiti doe tunaṇg tana, jarma koṛae hua kia*
> Barachiti is creeping, it bit the young boy
> *Liṭa jaḍa doe kolaṇgia kana, ḍiṇḍa kuṛie sodor kia*
> Lita jada has spread itself, frightened the damsel
> *Jarma koṛae hua kia, ju dada baro guru ke namau kom*
> The young boy was bitten, call upon the twelve preceptors, brother
> *Ḍiṇḍa kuṛie sodor kia, ju dada hisibar chela ko naͅm payaͅr kom*
> The young damsel was attacked, bring the twenty-two disciples brother
> *Maͅr ho baro guru, jarma kora ho jo-aipe*
> O twelve preceptors, sweep down the poison from the young boy
> *Maͅr ho hisi bar chela ko, ḍiṇḍa kuṛi ho fukaipe*
> O twenty-two disciples, blow down poison from the damsel

Tribal people have their indigenous methods of curing the snake bite. In the method, it is cured by magic and prayer. The song refers to this very method of curing. In Chhotanagpur as well as in neighbouring states of Bengal, Orissa and Madhya Pradesh, Manasa and Nagmati cult is prevalent among various castes and tribes. The cult followers of Manasa worship the Manasa Devi, that is, snake deity but Nagmatias are the group of people who practise snake-bite curing through prayer and sacred performances. The teaching of the knowledge is imparted by a teacher to interested disciples. The preceptor teaches magic formulae to its disciples who undergo rigorous mental and physical discipline on the ritual process and learning of the formulae. When there is a case of snake bite, the Nagmatias are called upon to cure the victim. They never go alone but always with the teacher. They chant the magic formulae which, of course, is the story of the myth of Nagmati cult and follow the process in curing the victim as mentioned in the song. The followers of the cult members perform a ceremony called Deothan once in a year in the month of Asar and Sawan. During this ceremony, they observe penance for a fixed period of days and make offering of fruits and roots to their deity.

Snakes are of various sizes. The forest or mountain snakes are of big sizes and are locally called as Buru or Zada *bing*. Some of the snakes of this size are also found in water and particularly in rivers and are called Sunum or Nai *bing*. The river snakes become more active during rainy season when rivers are in spate. People who cross the river without boat, become easy prey of such snakes. The song below which belongs to Jadur category mentions the river snake who is coming up through the current of the river. The lines of the song are as follows:

1. *Nai-nai te rakâb lena re*
   Came all along the river
   Nai biṇg sunum biṇg, naisunum biṇg
   The river snake, the Sunum *bing*

2. *Gaṛa-gaṛa te upaṛ lena re*
   Arrived through the rivulets
   Gaṛa biṇg, dora biṇg, gaṛadora biṇg
   The rivulet snake, the Garadora *bing*

3. *Des nelae rakab lena re*
   Came to see the country
   Nai biṇg sunum biṇg, naisunum biṇg
   The river snake, the Naisunum *bing*

4. *Hatu nelae upa̤r lena re*
   Arrived to see the village
   Gaṛa biṇg, dora biṇg, gaṛadora biṇg
   The rivulet snake, the Garadora *bing*

Butterfly, scorpion, chamelion, lizard, etc, are the other insects and reptiles whose references are found in Munda songs in many contexts. The song below which belongs to Racha category, describes the beauty of the fish. The lines of the song are as follows:

Banai nai bichṛia haku dada
The Bichria fish of Banai river, O brother
Dumaṇg-a ru tana, dumaṇg-e saṛi tana
Are playing on dumang
Ru doe rue tana, jilibe-jilibe rue tana
Are playing on with a flair
Jolobe-jolobe saṛi tana
Are tuning with elegantly

The fish are playing in the river *banai.* The water is crystal clear and the fish are clearly visible. While swimming, their movement is swift and graceful, and when the sun rays reflect on their body, it glitters like lightning. The scene, as the author of this song says, it like dancing and playing on musical instruments.

Birds

Birds get wide reference in Munda songs. They are of different kinds, colours and sizes. The song makes reference of their colours, beauty, language, nature and also refers them symbolizing human nature. A few songs also are based on their daily activities and in relation to man. Maina, parrot, peacock and crane are the most referred birds in songs.

There are good variety of cranes, but their number is fast dwindling down. Birds generally get up early in the morning and go out in search of food. Most of the birds take rest during midday, either in group or in pairs. It is one such scene that the cranes have been referred to in the following Jatra category of song. The lines of the song are as follows:

Bakula re bhaiya
Brother crane
Raja leke kachairi baisae
Sitting together like holding royal court

Pokhera pindayo
At the platform of the pond
Raja leke kachairi baisae
Sitting together like holding royal court

Cranes during winter, in midday, are generally seen standing together, at the platform of a dam or pond. The scene is like holding a royal court by the king where people assemble and observe the court procedure silently. The cranes stand together hundreds in number, so also the people in king's court. This very song is also sung in Racha category of song, but in different tune.

Ash coloured crane is known by more than one term as *kansa baka, bilai baka* and *nai baka.* It is always by the side of water in the lookout of fish and frogs. Below is a song which belongs to Racha category of song in which the author of the song describes the accident that the *nai baka* met while meandering through the river's course but somehow it balanced itself and sat down on the reed. The lines of the song are as follows:

Nai-nai te
Through the river
Nai bakae napir tana-2
Nai baka is flying
Napir doe napir tana
It is flying on, but
Nai ko nachạl re thapa lora jan
Collided with the river's reeds
Kindu suṛa re dube jana
And alighted on the *kindu* foliage

It is the flying that attracted the attention of the author of this song. The river meanders and is full with big elongated rocks. The crane does not leave the serpentine course while flying, it collided with a standing reed ahead but somehow balanced itself and fell itself on green foliage.

The cranes, crows and sparrows always inhabit in the middle or closeby to human habitation. The cries of the birds, during day and night, make the whole environment lively. The song below which belongs to Dubung category, mentions of a lonely bird which came flying from nowhere and sat down on a tree in front of the house. The reference of two birds have been made in the song *kansa bakula* and *maina.* The lines of the song are as follows :

1. *Kahaṇ se nale re kaṇsa re bakula*
   From where did you come, O Kansa Bakula
   Baṇsa nupare baisae-2
   Sat down on the top of bamboo tree

2. *Purbe se nale re maina*
   Came from the east, O *maina*
   Baṇsa nupare baisae-2
   Sat down on the top of bamboo tree

In the song below too, which belongs to Jadur category, a hapless situation has been described by the author of the song in which a crane, because of the flooded river, returns back to its place of dwelling. The lines of the song are as follows:

1. *Kahaṇ se ale kaṇsa bakula*
   Where did you come, O Kansa *bakula*
   Joṛala daina tuṭi gel
   Pair of wings yours have broken
   Gaṇga-Jamuna nadi saki gel
   Ganga and Jamuna rivers have overflooded
   Hae briṇda bono poṛi gel
   Alas, the whole Birindaban forest is under the water

2. *Purbe se ale kaṇsa bakula*
   Came from the east, O Kansa Bakula
   Joṛala daina ṭuṭi gel
   Pair of wings yours have broken
   Gaṇga-Jamuna nadi saki gel
   Ganga and Jamuna rivers have overflooded
   Hae briṇda bono poṛi gel
   Alas, the whole Brindaban forest is under water

The Kansa Bakula—the crane of the river, has returned to its dwelling place early in the day time, for the whole area is under the flood water, and so it got no place to sit upon. In search of sitting place it lost feathers of both the wings. The crane looks in wearisome mood sitting alone on the tree.

This song might be of the very ancient times and most probably was composed when the Mundas were on Gangetic plains, for the flood scene of the wide scale as mentioned in the song is not to be seen in Chhotanagpur plateau.

Cranes, crow and kites are carnivorous. It is why, when they fly over the river, ponds, etc, the fish, frogs, etc, hide themselves from these birds. The song below belonging to Bala category describes how the fish are hiding seeing the crane. The lines of the song are as follows:

1. *Baka koga baka ko, puṇḍi baka ko*
   The cranes, the white cranes
   Gaṛa-gaṛa te jako apir tana
   Flying through the rivulets

2. *Kauwa koga kauwa ko, hende kauwa ko*
   The crows, the black crows
   Daru-daru te jako apir tana
   Flying through the trees

3. *Gaṛa-gaṛa te baka ko apir tana*
   Cranes are flying through the rivulets
   Hai ko doga ko ukun tana
   The fish are hiding themselves

4. *Daru-daru te kauwa ko apir tana*
   Crows are flying through the trees
   Ṭeṭeṇga ko doga ko nir ukun tana
   Chamelion lizards are running about for hiding

Fish and frogs are the food item of the cranes, similarly lizards for crows. It is why, when the fish and frogs see the cranes, lizards and crows, they run for their lives. The scene impressed the author of this song very much. The song below too, mentions how Budu fish are searching their hiding place seeing the crane flying close to them. The song belongs to Bala category and the lines are as follows:

1. *Kahaṇ se alere kaṇsa re bakula*
   Kaṇsa *bakula,* from where did you come
   Paiṇkhi hilaete, ṭhor dolaete
   Waving its wings and moving its beak
   Lukiyo gelain re budu re machhari
   The budu fish did hide themselves

2. *Purbe se alere kaṇsa re bakula*
   Kansa *bakula* did come from the east
   Paiṇkhi hilaete, ṭhor dolaete
   Waving wings and moving beak
   Lukiyo gelaiṇ re budu re machhari
   The *budu* fish did hide themselves

The *Kansa bakula* is of ash colour and easily mixes itself with the existing physical environment. The *budu* fish becomes an easy prey to this bird. When the bird flies over the water, the *budu* fish hide themselves but when it settles down, they again come up close to the crane unaware of its presence. The song also indicates a situation when the would-be bridegroom, for the first time comes to his would-be bride's house for preliminary discussions for marriage, all the girls of marriageable age hide themselves and peep through from somewhere. The bridegroom is a virtual *kansa bakula* for the girls as referred in this song.

While another singer-composer was attracted by the movements of two birds—Bakula and Toyan around a bush. The song belongs to Racha category and the lines are as follows:

1. *Baka kin chapa-churi*
   Pairs of cranes are running to and fro
   Toyaṇ kin goṛe lapa-luri
   A pair of *toyan* are wrestling
   Icha jaṭa jamri jaṭa
   In the dried up shrubs of Icha and Jamri
   Baka kin goṛe chapa-churi
   A pair of cranes are running to and fro
   Toyaṇ kin goṛe lapa-luṛi
   A pair of Toyan are wrestling

2. *Lasa lire, juṛa lire*
   When catching them with gum liquid
   Kalega laṇg galaṇgeya
   We shall weave feathers crown
   Jatra laṇg fada teya
   Decorate ourselves during Jatra dance
   Sendra laṇg fada biduṛ teya
   Attire ourselves till the end of Sendra dance

Colourful birds are generally snared, caught by gum-sticks and hunted down with bows and arrows for the sake of feathers. As mentioned in this song, the Baka and Toyan have actually been gummed by the side of the bush and so they are unable to fly away. The feathers crown are made for decoration during the *Jatra* dance.

The Hete Teyond and Tirung birds too as mentioned in the song below, which belongs to Racha category, are caught for the sake of feathers. The lines of the song are as follows:

1. *Nai gitil re*
   On the sand of the river
   Heṭe Teyoṇd jarom leda
   Hete Teyond had laid eggs
   Ṭiruṇg rage tana-2
   The Tirung is singing

2. *Lasa lekaime koṛa*
   Catch it with gum-sticks, O boy
   Pase lekaime koṛa
   Snare it, O boy
   Heṭe Teyoṇd jarom leda
   Hete Teyond had laid eggs
   Tiruṇg rage tana-2
   The Tirung is singing

The long legged bird known as Hete-Teyond is generally found in valleys, rugged uplands and river sands. Its cry is often heard during night also. It takes insects, fish and grasshoppers, etc, as food. They are always found in pairs or in group. Tirung is another bird with blue-brown feathers with a long tail. It is a small bird and always remains in group. It rarely comes down to the ground. It catches flies and insects while flying. It is one of the birds that welcomes rain.

Another beautiful bird-parrot, is also hunted down for its feathers. The song below, taken from Lahsua category, mentions the conversation of two persons with respect to the catching of this bird. The lines of the song are as follows:

1. *Bono me suga babu, bono me suga re*
   Parrots in the forest, O boy
   Chal̥ to babu dhanu tir dhair jabe
   Hasten, O boy with bow and arrow
   Bono me suga re
   Parrots in the forest

2. *Ṭhor yo lale lal*
   Beaks theirs all red
   Paiṇkh yo hariyar
   And feathers all green
   Chal̥ to babu dhanu tir dhair jabe
   Hasten, O boy with bow and arrow
   Bono me suga re
   Parrots in the forest

In the song below, beauty of the parrot is described. The song belongs to Jadur category and the lines are as follows:

1. *Kane suga hara-hara hariyaro re*
   Where is the parrot with green feathers
   Kane suga lal piyar
   Where are they red and yellow

2. *Ḍari me bais gelaiṇ*
   Sat down on the branches
   Ḍari ṭuiṭ gel re
   The branches have broken down
   Pat me bais gelaiṇ
   Sat down on the leaves
   Pat jhair gel
   The leaves have fallen down

3. *Chạl to bhaiya deikh abe*
Hasten to see it brother
Ḍair ṭuiṭ gel re
The branches have broken down
Chạl to bhaiya chin abe
Hasten to identify it
Pat jhair gel
The leaves have fallen down

4. *Dekhe keto deikh aloṇ*
I saw and returned
Ḍair ṭuiṭ gel re
The branches have broken down
Chine keto chin aloṇ
I examined and returned
Pat jhair gel
The leaves have fallen down

Parrots in good number alighted on a tree. Their feathers are green and beaks red. When the parrots sat down on a slim branch, it broke down. Some of them even sat down on leaves as all the branches were already occupied and that too fell down. The parrots were seen by elders, sisters or brothers. The scene was worth seeing and so they were insisting his younger brother to see it.

As stated earlier, some birds always inhabit in the midst of human settlement. Like the cock, they also knew the timetable by instinct, and though they sleep early, they get up at an interval of every two hours which they announce by chirping together all at once for a second and become silent again. Similarly, jackals also produce the hauling sound at fixed hours during the night, the first at 10 and at an interval of every two hours, and the last being at four in the morning. However, the only dependable clock is the cock who first makes sound at four in the morning. The people get up with the sound of the cock and begin their daily duties. The author of the following song which is taken from Jadur category, was much impressed with the chirping sound of the *maina* birds at night. He has expressed his impression in these lines:

1. *Kono ḍari sutạl re maina*
   On which branch are you sleeping, O Maina
   Kon ḍari jagạl re maina
   On which branch are you awake
   Chachirigi bigio maina
   In chirping sound, O Maina
   Sobere charaiya barabair
   All the birds are equal

2. *Purab ḍair sutạl re maina*
   You are sleeping on the eastern branch, O Maina
   Paschim ḍair jagạl re maina
   You are awake on the western branch, O Maina
   Chachi rigi bigio maina
   In chirping sound, O Maina
   Sobere charaiya barabair
   All the birds are equal

The author of the song says that some *maina* have slept on the eastern branch of the tree, while some on the western. When *maina* of the eastern branch make chirping sound, the *maina* of the western branch remains in deep slumber and *vice versa*. The division of duty among *maina* birds was closely observed by the author of this song.

Every Munda is generally well acquainted with the sound of every animal, bird and insects. He can tell the name of the animal or bird only on hearing his sound. In the song below, two friends are ascertaining the whereabouts of the bird whose sound they were hearing. The song belongs to the Lahsua category and the lines are as follows:

1. *Kone toṇgori bole*
   From which hillock the singing comes
   Tilaki paṇṛkiyo re saru
   O saru, the *tilaki* dove
   Kone toṇgori bolala miṇjur
   On which hillock the peacock cries
   Hore saru, konetoṇgori bolala miṇjur
   O saru, on which hillock the peacock cries

2. *Sone toṇgori Bole*
On the golden hillock the singing goes on
Tilaki paṇṛkiyo re saru
O saru, the *tilaki* dove
Rupe tongori bolala miṇjur
On the silver hillock the peacock cries

The Munda consider their area of habitation or the whole plateau of Chhotanagpur as silver, golden or land of diamond. The Chhotanagpur is often referred to as Hira Nagpur. In this golden land, animals and birds sing merrily everywhere. Even the rivers and springs are said to be singing songs during rainy season.

As stated above, the Munda identify every sound of the birds and often imitate it. In the following song which belongs to Lahsua category, the sound produced by the birds has been interpreted in the language of the people. The lines of the song are as follows:

1. *Kuhu bole kuhur-kuhur*
The cacoo sings 'kuhur-kuhur'
Miṇjuṛ bole keṇyor-keṇyor
The peacock cries 'kenyor-kenyor'
Hisir kaese bole re
How the Hisir dove sings

2. *Adho rati kuhur-kuhur re*
Sings 'kuhur-kuhur' at midnight
Pahaṛ rati keṇyor-keṇyor
Cries 'kenyor-kenyor' at half past midnight
Rani ghare raja piriti maṇgae
The king seeks friendship with the queen

The cacoo and peacock have no time for singing. They are heard singing even at midnight, The author of the song says that the singing of the cacoo, and Peacock are nothing but the voice of the king who is asking friendship with the queen.

Partridges are generally domesticated by the Mundas. They sing in the pitch of their voice. The singer-composer of the song below, on hearing the singing of the partridge in the mountain top, asks why not they come down the valley below where marriage is being celebrated with singing and participate in it. The song belongs to Jadur category and the lines are as follows:

1. *Buru chetan chitiri girio*
   Partridge is singing at its pitch at the mountain top
   Bera latar asekal do
   The *askal* in the valley below
   Chia chitiri kam arguna re
   Why don't you come down partridge
   Chia asekal kam nosoren
   Why don't you hasten down *askal*

2. *Engam ko arandin tana re*
   Mother ours are celebrating marriage
   Apum ko korandin tan
   Father ours are feasting
   Tere-nere ko arandin tana re
   Celebrating marriage with music
   Toro-roro ko korandin tan
   Feasting with sound of bugles

As stated earlier, *maina* and parrot are domesticated by the Mundas. It is told that they can learn the language of the people like any normal man. The song below is related to the domestication of *maina* and parrot. The song belongs to Jadur category and the lines are as follows:

1. *Kantar daru re maina*
   The *maina* on the jackfruit tree
   Maina, chere-bereya maina
   The *maina is* chirping
   Jojo ko choti re suga
   On the top of the tamarind tree
   Suga reyon-cheyon ya suga
   The parrots are talking

2. *Noko horo asul lija maina*
   Who had domesticated *maina*
   Maina, chere-bereya maina
   The *maina is* chirping

Chimae horo jatan lija suga
Who had nourished the parrot
Suga reyon-cheyon ya suga
The parrot is talking

3. *Munda horo asul lija maina*
The Munda had domesticated maina
Maina chere-bereya maina
The *maina* is chirping
Santa horoe jatan lija suga
The santa had nourished the parrot
Suga reyon-cheyon ya suga
The parrot is talking

Maina bird, as stated above, is domesticated and is put up in a cage which is prepared from bamboo splits or other wild reeds. In the song below, which belongs to Lahsua category, someone is being requested for making a cage for the bird. The lines of the song are as follows:

1. *Hore maina lagin*
For *maina* bird, dear
Maina lagin ho pinjra banae debe
Prepare a cage for *maina* bird
Ho maina lagin
For *maina* bird
Hore maina lagin
For maina bird, dear

2. *Sone ka pinjara, rupe ka tharia*
The cage of gold and door of silver
Ho maina lagin
For *maina* bird

As stated, cage is usually prepared from bamboo splits and reeds and sometimes from iron bars and rarely from gold and silver. The reference of golden or silver cage comes from stories and legends only. Such cage, if any, are found only in royal houses.

Maina birds generally make nests in caves or holes of trees. In Munda areas, earthen pots are placed on the branches of the trees for making nest in it. The song below, which belongs to Jatra category, mentions that *maina* bird was born in the bush in the forest. Though the song refers to some historical fact, it also tells where the *maina* birds make their nest. The lines of the song are as follows:

Maina re maina
O maina
Kera jharia me janạm lele
You were born in the banana bush in the forest pool
Rori ghate maina re maina
In the valley of Rori hill, O *maina*
Kera Jharia me janạm lele
You were born in the banana bush in the forest pool

The crow is carnivorous and notorious for the newborn birds. It carries them away from the nest. Below is a song belonging to Racha category in which the pathetic condition of *maina* birds whose children were carried away by the crow is told. The lines of the song are as follows:

Maina, maina
O maina
Ka lagin kandae maina
Maina, why are you crying
Maina ker chhauwa ke kauwa lei gelaiṇ
Children of *maina* were carried away by the crow
Se lagin kandae maina
The *maina is* crying for that

In the song below too, this very situation has been mentioned. The chicks are searching food in the garbage unmindful of the hawk who is preparing to attack them. The song belongs to Racha category and the lines are as follows:

Sim hon ko dili-diliya-2
Chicks are busy in searching
Dubi rechi sim hon ko dili-diliya
In the garbage, chicks are busy in searching
Na-e ege na-e arguna-2
At any moment it may come down

Sirmaeṭe buru kuṛid
The hill hawk from the sky
Na-e ege na-e aṛguna-2
At any moment it may come down
Na-e ege na-e idi kiya-2
At any moment it may carry away
Punḍi te punḍi sim hon
To an all white chick
Na-e ege nae idi kiya-2
At any moment it may carry away

The author of this song is observing that the all white chicks are busy in searching food in the garbage. A hawk is gliding high up in the sky which the chicks are unaware of. The author of the song sees the imminent danger to the chicks and thinks that in a second the hawk may come down at them.

The singer-composer of the following song was highly impressed with the bats who go on flying during the night and sleep in day time. The song belongs to Jarga category and the lines are as follows:

Dine to bhaduli gachha me taṅgal re
Bats remain hanging during the day
Hore bhaduli, rati to lapasate jae
The bats, glide on during the night
Jane-jane dumari pake
Wherever the *dumari* ripens
Tane-tane bhaduli
The bats are there
Hore bhaduli, rati to lapasate jae
The bats, glide on during the night

Bats are of different sizes. While the big sized bats live on fruit juice, the small ones on insects and mosquitoes. During the day time, they remain hanging upside down in some caves or trees, but as soon as darkness sets in, they come out in search of food and drink.

The reference of birds in songs are made either objectively or contextually. The following song which belongs to Bala category describes the beauty of the bird as well as symbolizes the bride and bridegroom. The lines of the song are as follows:

Panṛkire perowaṇ
Among the pigeon, the dove
Gunḍri re chitirewaṇ
Gundri among the partridge
Hare lawa-kawa re bakula
The crane, among the long legged ones
Bakula re haṇsa harila
And *hansa harila* among the cranes
Garuṛa re dani maina
Dani *maina,* among the *garura*
Sugawa re karaṇjua
Among parrot, the *karanjua*
Koepur re besra jora
And *besra* among the *koepur*
Hare lawa-kawa re bakula
The crane among the long legged ones
Bakula re haṇsa harila
And *hansa harila* among the cranes

The author of this song has given the comparative picture among the class of birds in respect of look and beauty and has indirectly indicated that would be bride and bridegroom are the most suitable pair among the host of girls and boys of marriageable age.

As above, in the following song too, the pigeon symbolizes the bridegroom. In this song the relative of the girl, requests the boy not to break the marriage. The song belongs to Bala category, the lines of which are as follows:

Kuyaṇ-kuyaṇ pani jhili-mili
The water of the well is dazzling
Hare pani hariyar
Oh the water is green
Nulaṭi nai jabe perowaṇ
Don't fly back pigeon
Palaṭi nai jabe re
Don't fly away hither
Tabe junu pabe perowaṇ
Then only you may get *perowan*

Kuyaṇ ka pani piyab re
Drink the water of the well

While the pigeon symbolizes the bridegroom, the water symbolizes the bride or her love. Similar symbolization is also found in the following Bala category of song too. The lines of the song are as follows:

Iṭa paṭa̭l kuwaṇ
The brick-walled well
Iṭa paṭa̭l kuwaṇ ge nayo
The brick-walled well, mother
Jhamaki-jhamaki pani pajharae
Water spring comes out slowly
Iṭa paṭa̭l kuwan
The brick-walled well
Dhiliki charaiya
The *dhiliki* bird
Niṇjhar pani piyab go sajani
Friend, we shall drink crystal clear water
Hare jhamaki-jhamaki pani pajharae
Water spring comes out slowly

The brick-walled well and crystal clear water, both indicate or rather symbolize the character of the girl. It indicates the chastity of the girl. There is no contamination in the girl's character who has grown up in a family environment like a brickwalled well.

In yet another song below, which also belongs to Bala category of song, water-crow symbolizes the bridegroom. The lines of the song are as follows:

Kahaṇ se nale re pain kauwa
Where did you come from, O water-crow
Tuku cheta̭n latarete
From above and below the rock
Niṇjhar pani piyab re pain-kauwa
Will drink the crystal clear water, O water-crow
Purab se ale re pain-kauwa
You came from the east, O water-crow

Tuku chetạn latarete
From above and below the rock
Niṇjhar pani piyab re pain-kauwa
Will drink the crystal clear water, O water-crow

Peacock is a lovely bird. It has very beautiful feathers. In the Bala category of song below, it symbolizes the bridegroom. The lines of the song are as follows:

Kone bone se nikasalaiṇ re jhail miṇjura
From which forest the long tailed peacock did come out
Paiṇkh tor bhuiṇ larakae, jhail miṇjura
Feathers yours are sweeping the ground, O long tailed peacock
Rone bone se nikasalaiṇ re jhail miṇjura
Did come from the Ronebone forest, O long tailed peacock
Paiṇkh tor bhuiṇ larakae, jhail miṇjura
Feathers yours are sweeping the ground, O long tailed peacock

Ghato is a migratory bird who crosses the Chhotanagpur plateau during winter from Siberia on way to Chilka lake in Orissa state. Sometimes it alights on ponds and dams. Ghato, in the song below, represents the bridegroom who comes down to the land from his flying sojourn fascinated by the frogs. The song belongs to Bala category and the lines are as follows:

Pagha jhora-jhora re ghaṭo
O ghato, drag on the pagha rope
Kuilo-kuilo kinara me utarae re ghaṭo-2
You alighted on the bank of the river Koel, O ghato
Machhari ka love, bengowa ka love
For the greed of fish and frogs
Pagha jhora-jhora re ghaṭo
O ghato, drag on the pagha rope
Kuilo-kuilo kinara me utarae re ghaṭo-2
You alighted on the bank of the river Koll, O ghato

Ghato birds are seen only during the winter season flying high up in the sky in a single file hundreds in number. They never fly in jumble like other birds. The children believe that *ghato* understands the language of the people. It is why, whenever they are seen in the sky, the children cry out in their pitch of voice—'*pagha jhora-jhora re ghato*', that is, make a single formation like a drawn up *pagha* rope. The *ghato* follow the leader who either remains in the middle or at its extreme right of the row. The *ghato,* thus, flying, sometimes suddenly fly back and start hovering in a circle in the same place for some time. The adults tell the children that the spirit of the place is not allowing to cross the area over which he has the jurisdiction. They are allowed only when one of them donates his quill. The birds, being migratory, they have to pay the tax whenever they come to the border of the other spirit. The spirits, as the Munda believe, inhabit everywhere, exercise control over the area of their jurisdiction. However, as the song is sung in the context of a marriage, *ghato* symbolizes the bridegroom and fish and frogs, the bride.

Crow is supposed to be a greedy bird. It never allows any one to take the thing alone. Whenever it gets difficulty, it remains waiting for some time for a chance. In the following Bala category of song, the author-singer perceives the intentions of the bride's relatives who do not like the bridegroom, but are helpless to oppose it openly. The crow, in the song, symbolizes the bridegroom. The lines of the song are as follows:

> *Kahaṇ se ale re kauwa*
> Where did you come, O crow
> *Semari gachh majhe ḍaṛ baisal re kauwa*
> Sitting on the middle branch of the *semar* tree, O crow
> *Purbe se ale re kauwa*
> You came from the east, O crow
> *Semari gachh majhe ḍaṛ baisal re kauwa*
> Sitting on the middle branch of the *semar* tree, O crow

In the following song a marriage ceremony has been described in which the host as well as guest are enjoying the occasion. The owl and peacock are engaged in singing the songs. The song belongs to Bala category and the lines are as follows:

> *Pecha raja, minjur raja*
> The king of owl and king of peacock

Chitiri charaiya surti bolaiṇ re
Partridges are singing sweetly

The song below describes the farewell of the daughter after the marriage. In this song the parrot symbolizes the bride. The song belongs to Bala category and the lines are as follows:

Lale-lale thor suga, hariyaro paiṇkh re
Parrot with red beak and green feathers
Aisan sundar̯ samae, sundar̯ samae kahaṇ pabe ho Ram
Such a nice time, where will you get
Late-lale thor suga, hariyaro paiṇkh re
Parrot with red beak and green feathers
Ḍari me baisa̯l suga, ḍario ṭuiṭ gel
Parrot sitting on the branch was broken off
Pate me baisa̯l suga, pateo jhari gel
Parrot sitting on the leaf also fell off
Aisa̯n sundar̯ samae, sundar̯ samae kahaṇ pabe ho Ram
Such a nice time, where will you get

In this song, the tree, branch and leaf symbolizes the parent and their protective hands. The parrot symbolizes the bride. Though the separation of the girl from her parent is a most pathetic one, it is one of the nicest time available once in the lifetime of any girl. The girl is given farewell and this very situation has been conceived as breaking off leaves and branches.

Separated from her parent, the girl in the song below has been indicated symbolizing a *tiri-tipi* bird. It is a small bird and is generally seen alone or in pair. The song belongs to Bala category of song and the lines are as follows:

Ṭiri-ṭipi charaiya, ṭiri-ṭipi charaiya ge nayo
The *tiri-tipi* bird, O mother
Ka hoire charaiya ḍera tora
What about your shelter, O bird
Ka hoire charaiya basa tora
What about your home, O bird
Leda ḍumaṛi tare
Under the spread up *dumari* tree

Hore, ka hoire charaiya dera tora
Alas, what about your shelter, O bird
Ka hoire charaiya basa tora
What about your home, O bird

The girl after marriage is being sent off to her new home with her husband. Initially, she feels all alone among the strangers like *tiri-tipi* bird in the forest. She is, however, told that she is not alone there. She will get a big house and loving people there, like a big spread up *dumari* tree. She will live among the new kin members under their care and love. The *dumari* tree is the symbol of extended family. The girl will feel happy and secure among them.

Tiri-tipi bird, as stated above, is seen alone in the forest crying on pitch of her voice all the time. In the song below the *tiri-tipi* bird coveys different messages. She symbolizes Sita, the heroine of the great epic *Ramayana,* who was forsaken by Rama in the forest. The song belongs to Lahsua category and the lines are as follows :

1. *Bono me kande ṭiri-ṭipi charaiya*
   The *tiri-tipi* bird cries in the forest
   Ho hore, kande kire Sita janame janam-2
   Alas, it is Sita weeping since generations

2. *Mae tora mori gel, bapa tora heri gel*
   Mother yours has died and father lost
   Ho hore, kande kire Sita janam-2
   Alas, it is Sita weeping since generations
   Mae tora mori gel bapa tora heri gel
   Mother yours has died and father lost
   Ho hore, Kande kire Sita janame ṭuar
   Alas, it is Sita weeping orphaned forever

This is an excellent example of poetic imagination. The theme of the song is loneliness forever.

The cry of the birds may be interpreted differently according to the context and situation. The cry of the bird, in the song below, is the cry due to trouble. The song belongs to Jadur category and the lines are as follows :

1. *Gaṛa kikir gole-gole ho, naija putam riyuṛ-riyuṛ*

The *kikir* of the ravines and the dove of the rivers are whistling
Gaṛa riya chi dova riya ho, nai riya chi ṭikura re
Is it is the ravine or pool, in the river or gorges

2. *Gole tegeiṇg ayum lia ho, riyuṛ tegeiṇg aten lia*
I heard and located in through its whistling
Bale bunum chetan ria ho, linduṇg sarjom chetan re
It is on the newly constructed dome of the white ant or on the tender twig of *sarjom* tree

3. *Chetanate hoyo leda ho, latarate rampi led*
The wind blew and rained lightly
Gaṛa kikire ra-a tana ho, naija putame iyam tan
The *kikir* of the ravine is weeping, the dove of the river is worried
Jati-matie ra-a tana ho, kili nalaṇg-e iyam tan
Weeping on the fate of her species, and worried of her clan

The above song may have been composed at the spot when hailstorm with rain disturbed the peace of the two birds. The author-singer was enjoying their music when all was gone in a moment. All were worried due to this abrupt event.

In the song below, which has been taken from Jarga category of song, husband-wife relations have nicely been portrayed through the cock and hen. The lines are as follows :

Jathriṇ chetan-chetan te
Along the side of the fence
Sandi sim gole duraṇge-2, haere
The cock is whistling-singing
Jathriṇ latar-latar te
Along the side of fence below
Budi sim landa jagare-2, haere
The hen is laughing-talking
Kuṛiteke nelante
Seeing his wife
Sanḍi sim gole duraṇge-2, haere
The cock is whistling-singing

Koṛa teke nelante
Seeing her husband
Buḍi sim landa jagare-2, haere
The hen is laughing-talking

It is a general scene that cock and hen go around together everywhere. Similarly, the young married couple live happily.

10

THE COSMIC UNIVERSE

Munda usually do not compose songs out of imagination or from preconceived ideas, but they are based on observations and experiences of the people. Most of the songs describe the objective reality of physical, social and cultural world as perceived and experienced by them. The myths and legends are not mere stories but it is the evolutionary history of the people. The universe is not an unperceptible world of the unknown. Anybody who has understood the structure, organization and functions of the society and culture of the community, can understand the universe too. The sun, the moon, the stars, the meteors, the rainbow, etc, are brought to the level of human understanding leaving aside the details of each element of the universe. In the event of any catastrophe, one is not driven into despair but the answer is available in the myth and legend as an open book. The concept is all poetic.

The songs concerning the cosmic world are in no way philosophical. They are composed in simple language. The song below which belong to Lahsuạ category, is related to the appearing and disappearing of the moon. The lines of the song are as follows:

1. *Kahaṇ se ugạl re chaṇdo*
   From where do you rise, O moon
   Kahaṇ se dubạl re chaṇdo
   Where do you set in, O moon
   Chaṇdo re chand bina dunia aṇdhar re
   Without you moon the world is in darkness

2. *Purbe se ugạl re chaṇdo*
   You arise from the east, O moon
   Pachhim me dubạl re chaṇdo
   You set in on the west, O moon

Chaṇdo re chand bina dunia aṇdhar re
Without you moon the world is in darkness

The moon has been eulogized in this song for without him the whole world may remain in darkness during the night.

In yet another song, the moon is requested to stay a day more as if he is a guest. The moonlit night is admired by all. The song belongs to Jadur category and the lines are as follows:

1. *Kahaṇ se ugạl re chaṇdo*
From where do you rise, O moon
Kahaṇ se dubạl re chando
Where do you set in, O moon
Aju ke dina re chaṇdo dina darile
Please stay for today, O moon

2. *Purab se ugạl re chaṇdo*
You arise in the east, O moon
Pachim me dubạl re chaṇdo
You set in on the west, O moon
Aju ke dina re chaṇdo dina darile
Please stay for today, O moon

In the song below which belongs to Jadur category, a person tells his experience while he was in journey through the hills and valleys of the rising of full moon and setting of some bright stars. The lines of the song are as follows:

1. *Buru-buru teiṇg rakab lena*
I travelled through the hills
Sagri chaṇdu dore tura kana
The wheel shaped moon has arisen
Beṛa-beṛa teiṇg aṛgu lena
I came down through the valleys.
Jono lpil dore hasur tana
The broomstick star is setting in

2. *Sagṛi chaṇdu dore tura kana*
The wheel shaped moon has arisen
Goṭa disum do maresạl kana

The whole world has turned bright
Jono lpil dore hasur tana
The broomstick star is setting in
Tara disum do akal jana
Part of the world suffered from famine

3. *Gota disum do maresal jana*
The whole world has turned bright
Soben horoko rasika tana
All the people are rejoicing

4. *Tara disum do akal jana*
Part of the world suffered from famine
Tara disum horoko iyam tana
People of part of the world are wailing

As stated in the above song, the appearance of full moon brings happiness and broomstick star and particularly the direction of its sticks, as the people believe, indicates and brings misery in that part of the world.

The song below which belongs to Jadur category, provides one of the instances how people make the correlation of events and thus predict other events. The lines of the song are as follows:

1. *Ne kalom lama pura-ā jana*
This year there is abundance of lama fruits
Ne kalom gaṛi ko arandia
This year monkeys may celebrate marriage

2. *Ne kalom burju isu ba jana*
This year there is abundance of *burju* flowers
Ne kalom sara ko koraṇdia
This year *langurs* may celebrate marriage

3. *Ne kalom lamā jang taka te*
This year seeds of lama fruits are priced rupee one
Ne kalom gaṛi ko koraṇdia
This year monkeys may celebrate marriage

4. *Ne kalom burju jang sikate*

This year the seeds of *burju* fruits are priced annas four
Ne kalom sara ko koṛaṇḍic
This year *langurs* may celebrate marriage

Such forecast of events are made in every aspect of life of the people and they regulate their activities accordingly.

As described in the previous pages, the relationship of the Mundas with the nature, is symbolic as well as objective. The life is revealed on the nature, the cognition of which differs from culture to culture. The different aspects of nature are perceived or symbolized either as human beings or behaving like human or as material objects having features of aesthetic beauty or quality which satisfy various needs of the people. The different qualities of nature, moreover, reveal different characters and personalities of the individuals. The unknown cosmic world is made known either through personification or categorization of it into one of the known object or species. Thus, the unknown is easily made known through the already known. This is how the people adjust and accommodate themselves even with the hostile environments. The training and communication to this ethnic knowledge is specific to every culture.

PART IV

THE SOCIAL WORLD AND THE PHILOSOPHY OF LIFE

11

SOCIALIZATION AND PEOPLE OF OTHER CULTURES

Social life emerges in living together and mutual help and Co-operation among the people, which helps in the formation of the society. A society, being a complex organization of human relations and activities involving different kinds of persons, social life does not always go on smoothly and often there erupts conflict and tension among the members. While living together, the people also feel the experience that some habits and practices are essential for happy and carefree living. This helps growth of culture and traditions of the society. For the smooth sailing of society morals and values enshrined in the culture and traditions need continuity and preservation. The process of socialization or orientation of the members in these values and behaviour is an essential function of the society. But in traditional or tribal societies, the process of socialization or enculturation is diffused and not uniform as no institution has developed for the purpose. However, some devices to maintain social order in conformity to accepted values and norms exist to maintain peace, stability and continuity. For this purpose almost every community has evolved ways and means for maintaining social order among the members which are basically of two kinds—firstly, as a structured organization or administrative organ, and secondly, through diffused process by customary ways in the form of manners, etiquette, norms and values, etc. The Munda society has both these devices of social control. The administrative mechanism is of two types but it has no structural linkages between them. The first, known as *Parha* or *Patti* engulfs the whole or part of the community while the functional jurisdiction of the second is limited to geographical boundary of the village. Offences arising out of socio-cultural nature and behaviour are dealt by the *Parha* or clan organization, while social crimes and maintaining of peace within the jurisdiction of the villages, is looked after by the village organization comprising the office of Munda, Pahan and Mahto.

We have references of these systems in songs in some other context. In the ensuing paragraphs, we shall restrict ourselves to references in songs dealing with self-regulative ways related to behavioural restrictions of the members of the community. It is observed that enculturation or orientation values to members begin at a very early age which continues throughout the life. To understand and to interpret the behaviours of other members, one has to know the traditional and customary laws of the community thoroughly. The encroachment of these values do not always invite corporal or pecuniary punishment but sometimes social sanctions are enforced or simply warnings are issued or advice are offered. The best ways to discourage socially unaccepted behaviour is to ridicule the person or pass some unpalatable comments against the person of such character. Among the Munda community, boys and girls are always kept under the watchful eyes of the elders, but it is the girls, who mostly face comments. It is beacuse the Mundas consider the women as preceptors and preservers of social values and are the symbols of dignity and honour of the society. The ill-conditioning in values may lead to social pathology and devaluation of ideals.

The songs that we get in pages that follow, relate to comments against men or women whose activities, it is thought are contrary to social norms and values.

The following song which belongs to Racha category, pass a comment sarcastically on a woman who has let loose her long hair. The lines of the song are as follows:

1. *Bhauji ka keṇsa*
   The hair of the sister-in-law
   Lahur-lapur keṇsa re
   She has floating long hair
   Khori majhe lahsate jaela
   Goes about floating in the open field

2. *Lajo nai lage, bijo nai lage*
   She has but no shame and regard
   Khori majhe lahsate jaela
   Goes about floating in the open field

At adolescent age, the girls are regularly guided and advised on proper conduct and behaviour. ignorance or negligence of these are considered improper and become the subject of gossip and invite criticism as mentioned in the above song. Keeping hair loose by the married woman is considered immoral and obscene and is strictly prohibited.

Reference of songs related to a newly married woman who is in her parents-in-laws' house, have already been made under dress, decoration and dance in different context. She is criticized and abused for her negligence and ignorance in customary ways and in the household affairs. The girl who does not attend work is also criticized. The following song belonging to Baroya category is based on this theme. The lines of the song are as follows:

> *Kone bone se nikasalaiṇ*
> From which forest did she come out
> *Kadam̂ tare ṭhaṛ re*
> Stood under the *kadam* tree
> *Hare, rahṛi tare bahin sobhae*
> She would look beautiful on the *rahri* field

The girl is loitering about in the forest aimlessly without any work. She is a beautiful girl but the elders say that she will look more beautiful in crop's field. The *rahri,* the pulse crop is ready for harvesting, while the family members are busy in one kind of work or the other, the girl is loitering about somewhere else. This has erked the elders and criticized the girl.

In another case, a boy has been criticized by the elders for his indulgence in dance during the period when his parent expired. This is a serious offence or behaviour. The Munda customarily prohibits dance, music and merrymaking in the village when there is death in a family. The song based on this theme has already been referred to under dance.

The teaching and orientation in behavioural practices on customary ways are diffused in character and not formalized by the Mundas. The responsibility of leadership on this area rests on the shoulders of the elders of the society.

Inter-Community Interaction

Socio-cultural change and development is noticeable in every society today which has helped in the diffusion of knowledge and skills in wider scale. In the past, it was not so when there was a lack of modern system of communication. This also has facilitated people's migration from one region to the other, resulting in wider interaction of the people. Though Mundas have always lived in isolated condition relatively, there is ample evidence which suggests their contact and cooperation with various other communities during the ancient past. The story of their interaction with other communities is found in *Kurshinama* or oral tradition of the community as well as in other epics and legends. The ethnic interaction in wider scale with the Mundas, however, began only during historical period and particularly when hordes of non-tribal communities made inroads to the Munda region of Jharkhand. The reaction of interaction with non-tribal communities is a mixed one and mostly on unequal terms which have been well recorded in their ethno-history. Here we shall confine ourselves to events and reactions which are of the nature of first hand impression generated out of the first contact of the people and which have been incorporated in the folk song of the Mundas. In human history, we have ample of such impressionistic records on other people and culture. Such records do not present the true picture of the people and often give distorted ones. Thus, tribal people of India suffer from poor vision due to insufficient records of other people available in epics, legends and history. The Mundas have composed a number of songs based on impression regarding the people and their culture with whom they first came into interaction.

Language and Dressing

We have reference of two songs as given below which belongs to Bala category and describe the language and style of dressing of the two non-Munda communities, that is, Muslim and Bengali. The lines of the first song are as follows:

> *Chaibasa musalman*
> The Muslim of Chaibasa
> *Hindi Hindiyari hinti-minti sinti-minti bat bolae re*
> Speak Hindi in *hinti-minti, sinti-minti* tone
> *Muṛe me topi ahe*
> They have cap on the head

Ghencha me chandoa ahe
They have locket on the neck
Chhati me jhula ahe
They have shirt on the body
Ḍanḍa me dhoti ahe
They have worn dhoti on the waist
Gore me juta ahe
They have shoes on their feet
Chaibasa musalman
The Muslim of Chaibasa
Hindi hindiyari hinti-minti, sinti-minti bat bolae re
Speak Hindi in *hinti-minti, sinti-minti* tone

The lines of the second song is as follows:

Dekhali Bangalia
I was a Bengali
Ḍanḍa dhoti chhati daiya
Wearing waist-dhoti on the chest
Chhati luga pahirae
Covering his body with cloth
Dekhali Bangalia
I saw a Bengali
Okhaṛi samaṭhe chhati daiya
His chest is like mortar and pestle
Chhati luga pahirae
Covering his body with cloth

The above two songs are the impression of a Munda about language and dress of Muslim and Bengali communities when he first saw them in the bordering areas of Munda country. Hindi language was quite foreign to the Mundas and when they heard people speaking in Hindi, they could only reproduce the sound and no words. The language problem is still there in India and today it is a one way process that is, the language of the dominant people is always thrust upon the weakest group. Due to this forcible attitude of the people of the dominant language, many languages, however rich they may be, are in rapid process of decay and death.

The way or style of dressing of Muslim and Bengali communities described in the song, portray the correct picture of these communities and no other description of their ways of dressing, in a nutshell, can be given.

Today most Munda understand Hindi language and the dressing pattern of the Muslim and Bengali do not attract their attention, for these communities are now found in almost all areas of the Munda region.

People in early days of contact with the Mundas were usually recognized even from distance by their style of dressing. The dressing pattern of the Mundas itself have now changed a lot. About a century ago, they used to wear very scanty dress on their body. The male used to wear only loin cloth on the waist and the female sari, the rest of the body was almost naked. And if a person's dress was different from one's own, he would surely be a stranger belonging to other communities.

In the song below which belongs to Racha category, it is stated as to how a stranger was identified. The lines of the song are as follows:

1. *Kahaṇ kera pa̭rdesia*
   The strangers of which country
   Lale-lale pagari bandhae
   Have red turbans on their heads

2. *Muṛhu kera pa̭rdesia*
   The stranger from Murhu
   Lale-lale pagari bandhae
   Have red turbans on their heads

The stranger described in this song belongs to the Munda community itself but from different parts of the region and the people of that part of the country have their distinct pattern of dressing which differs from the rest. The stranger is wearing red turban, and the Mundas where the above song was composed, do not wear red turban, so the person was identified as a stranger and from Murhu region of the Munda country.

Ploughing with the Horse

Ploughing of the fields for the sake of cultivation of crops is mostly done with the help of cattle and particularly from bullocks and water-buffaloes by most of the tribal people of India. Ploughing with the help of horse is not found in India, however, they are employed for drawing of cart. Ploughing the field with the help of horses was there in European countries. Where did the Munda see ploughing with the help of horses, is a matter of investigation, the reference of which is found in the following Jadur song. It is a matter of curiosity for the Mundas for they never think of ploughing with the help of horses. The lines of the song are as follows:

1. *Sadom teko si tana re*
   Ploughing with the help of horse
   Chuṭa bhair nekela tan
   The hair of the middle head only are shaking

2. *Dolarebu nele lia re*
   Let us go to see it
   Mare rebu china lia re
   Let us identify it

3. *Nale dole nele lia re*
   We had but seen it
   Sadom teko si tan
   Ploughing with the help of horse

4. *China dole china lia re*
   We had but identified it
   Chuṭa bhair ekela tan
   The middle hair of the head only is shaking

For the Mundas, ploughing from horse is a curiosity and perhaps nobody will believe that horse can also be harnessed as plough cattle. The song also does not indicate as to who are the people who do ploughing with horses. There is the problem of identification of people by name but it is thought that some Mundas had seen people ploughing from horses. During First and Second World Wars, a number of Mundas were in military service and had visited Middle East and Eurpoean countries during the wars and may have the chances to see ploughing from horses. The narration of events heard from these servicemen may have been rendered into song by the youths.

Transport and Communication

A great stride has taken place in the field of transport and communication after the industrial revolution. Formerly, there was no means of transport in the Munda region and the Mundas rarely used animals for such purpose and travelling to distant land was next to impossible. They would generally visit their relatives by walking down the distance.

The song below belonging to Jadur category describes the difficulty of travelling during the days when there were no means of transport. The lines of the song are as follows:

1. *Do mai sondari, do mai seneme*
   Let us proceed, O sondari daughter dear
   Mare mai lalakari, mar mai hojorem
   O little daughter, please go on jogging

2. *Horayo jilinga, mandiyo rengeja*
   The path is long and we may be hungry
   Pariyo chakara, da: yo tetanga
   The path is zig-zag and we may feel thirsty

A little girl is accompanying her father in his journey. The girl does not know the difficulty of the journey and is too happy when she accompanies her father. The destination is too far and the path passes through the hills and valleys. Due to this difficulty, the father wants to complete the journey early. They may also be carrying food and drinks for consumption during taking rest on the journey.

Below is another song belonging to Jadur category which describes that the journey was long but was completed by running the path and arrived the destination at sunset when the women were preparing the evening meal. The lines of the song are as follows:

1. *Nire kedam chire sene kedam*
   Did you run or walk, dear
   Hora ra: dhuri soben otang jan
   The wayside dust are flying

2. *Ka reng nire keda, ka reng sene keda*
   Neither did I run, nor walk

Hora ra: sengel sukul dudugar jan
It is the kitchen oven that brought out the smoke on the way

Now the situation has completely changed as the automobiles and trains have been introduced in the region, but a few persons only avail all the facilities. The rest, and particularly the illiterates never have the opportunity to travel on any such modern conveyance. The song below belonging to Jadur category mentions the impression of the people about the transport systems. The lines of the song are as follows:

1. *Rele gadi hudu-hudu*
The train is running with *hundu-hudu* sound
Hoyo leka sesen tan
It is running like wind

2. *Hoyo leka sesen tan*
It is running like wind
Horo ko deja kan
People are riding on it

How the modern transport aviation system has brought changes in the whole system of transport, is to be found in the following Lahsua song, the lines of which are as follows:

1. *Gara dora motre chale*
Motor car runs over ditches and ravines
Sarke bicycle ho
Bicycle on the road
Pahia-pahia rail gidikate awae
The train comes whizzing on the rails

2. *Motar ka chario chaka*
The four wheels of the motor car
Rele ka baro chaka
The twelve wheels of the train
Uranbaj ka tino chaka
The three wheels of the aeroplane

Uṛala akas ho
Flies over the sky
Haere, haere hae
What a wonder
Uṛaṇbaj ka tino chaka
The three wheels of the aeroplane
Uṛala akas re
Flies over the sky

How the days of the tiresome journey have passed away and how it has brought the distance close and saved the time, has been mentioned in the following Lahsua song, the lines of which are as follows:

1. *Haṭia hora re*
   On the way to Haṭia
   Jojo sakạm gạsạr len
   The leaves of tamarind tree had fallen down
   Maire, okorelaṇg hijo senoga
   How shall we cover our journey, O dear daughter

2. *Ranchi ya Duruṇḍa*
   May it be Ranchi or Durunda
   Relegaḍi gidi-gidi
   The train runs with gidi-gidi sound
   Ho hore
   How nice
   Mai re rele telaṇg hiju senoga
   We shall travel by train, dear daughter

Formerly, when there was no transport, it took much time to reach Ranchi or Durunda. The journey was difficult in summer when the trees shed their leaves. Now, there is no problem as these towns have been joined by roads and rails and as stated in the song, the father and daughter can now travel by train.

Whenever any new means of transport passes through the village, people, irrespective of age and sex run towards it. The following Lahsua song describes the curiosity of the people as well as the speed of the train. The lines of the song are as follows:

1. *Rele gaḍi kaisana sundar*
   How beautiful is the train
   Chalure dekhe jab
   O dear, let us go to see it
   Rele gaḍi kaisana sundar
   How beautiful is the train

2. *Rele gaḍi hawa ke saman*
   The train runs like wind
   Chalure dekhe jab
   O dear, let us go to see it

Travelling by modern means of transport is prone to serious accidents and loss of life. This has been described in the following Jadur song:

1. *Asansol hare muni re*
   At Asansol, my dear
   Rele teko sesen tan
   People travel by train
   Haṭia hare muni re
   At Hatia, my dear
   Lauka teko tunaṇg gen tan
   People travel by boat

2. *Rele teko sesen tana re*
   People travel by train
   Rele ḍanḍi doraṇg jan
   The beam of the train was broken
   Lauka teko tunaṇg gen tana re
   People are travelling by boat
   Lauka ḍanḍi rochod jan
   The steering rod of the boat was broken

3. *Rele ḍanḍi doraṇg jana re*
   The beam of the train was broken
   Rele koṛae iyam tana
   The train man is lamenting
   Lauka ḍanḍi rochod jana re
   The steering rod of the boat was broken

Lauka koṛae rage tana
The boat man is weeping

Accidents may take place in any means of transport, may it be aeroplane, motor car, train or boat and may leave behind remorse among the authorities and irrepairable loss and grief to the relatives of the victims of accident.

Changes in Nature

The time is fast changing and all are aware of this change. There are revolutions and wars. In this fast changing world, people often feel insecure. The Munda perceive this change when he observes the contrast—the contrast in nature and culture. The cultural change is perceived observing the change taking place in nature. How this change in nature is to be perceived has been described in the following Jadur song, the lines of which are as follows:

1. *Disum dada neka giya*
   The nature of the world is such, brother
   Hoṛo kaji disum ulamali
   People say the world is in turmoil
   Disum dada neka giya
   The nature of the world is such, brother

2. *Ranchi dada neka giya*
   Ranchi is such, brother
   Hende sakam pundi jana
   The green leaves have turned purple
   Ranchi dada neka giya
   Ranchi is such, brother

Passing away or change in time is clearly visible in the change of colour in leaves. A green leaf, in course of time, turns purple or grey and falls down giving way to new ones. The world or the country changes either through revolutions or wars.

But the society or culture changes silently like the colour of leaves unnoticed.

Usually every revolution brings some sort of change in the society—in thinking or attitude. Sometimes change in the established socio-cultural life takes place through the abrupt human actions of dislocation of population as at present in mining and industrial areas and catchment areas of big dams. Sometimes natural calamities like earthquake and famine also brings about changes in the socio-cultural life of the people abruptly. The following Lahsua song gives an instance of such change. The lines of the song are as follows:

1. *Kalau re chibu chikaya*
   What shall we do in famine
   Hoṛo nelte kuṛi chuṅgi nu tan
   Seeing the men smoking, the women are imitating them
   Kalau re chibu chikaya
   What shall we do in famine

2. *Bangla re kuṛi jati bagi jan*
   The women were left behind in the house
   Kalau re chibu chikaya
   What shall we do in famine

During slack season or famine usually a number of persons of a family move out in search of work in distant lands. And it is during such period that males as well as females imitate or acquire the habits and practices of other people contrary to their cultural norms. The females, who do not smoke *bidi,* etc, when they stay in distant land, develop the habit of smoking seeing others. All the more, when the male persons go out in search of work leaving behind the females in the household with little or no work at their hands, they develop the easy going life. Nowadays, ladies also stay back in their houses due to change in the general work ethics of the people of neighbouring communities.

The Beliefs and Traditions

The traditional religious beliefs and practices of Mundas rest basically on the living together and inter-communion among the men on this earth and with that of supreme God Singbonga and with the spirits of one's departed ancestors. This belief system engulfs the whole life activities and organizational pattern of the community. The relationship between the living and the departed are continuous in nature and durable whose objective manifestation is always recorded in nature. Structurally the Munda belief system consists of: (1) belief in life after death, (2) belief in one Supreme being, and (3) belief in uninterrupted relationship between the living and the dead as well as with the Supreme God Singbonga. There is also the belief on peripheral spirits whose role in life is always felt by the Mundas. This latter belief is responsible for the development of various cult institutions among the community. But in Munda songs we do not get the detailed portrayal of the belief system, what we get is the passing reference of a few ritual categories. Besides, we also get few songs of impressive nature in the ritual activities of other neighbouring non-tribal communities.

Singbonga and Baranda

The Supreme God of the Mundas, Singbonga is supposed to be a male figure. He is the creator, supporter and destroyer. There is an elaborate myth about the creation of the universe and all animate and inanimate objects. Singbonga's associate or attendant is known by the name of Baranda. Baranda downgraded his own status by evil activities and was driven out from the heavenly abode by the Singbonga. Since then all actions of Baranda are against the will of the Supreme. He misguides human beings who are the best creation of the Singbonga and whom he loves most. A constant struggle is going on between Singbonga and Baranda, that is, between the good and the evil.

The song below which belongs to Jadur category, refers to Singbonga's action against Baranda when He went out to punish the wicked and mischievous. The lines of the song are as follows:

Oko rege cha̩m uku kena
Where did you hide yourself
Ba̩randa raja bonde turku do
King Baranda in the guise of a Muslim
Chimae rege cha̩m darang kena
Where did you keep yourself out of sight
Ba̩randa raja bonde̩ turku do
King Baranda in the guise of a Muslim
Bisun si̩ng lala barangu
Dear Bisum sing lala barangu

Ing do hoing uku kena
I did hide myself
Marang buru bana lata re
In the deep cave of the great mountain

It is told in the myth that Baranda went on hiding the wrath of Singbonga. A detailed description of chase is found in the prayer song of the Mundas. When driven out from the heavenly abode, Baranda befriended human beings. He usually participates in every ceremonial dance and music unnoticed from the people. The song below belonging to Jadur category describes how he, along with his wife, is participating in dance. The lines of the song are as follows:

1. *Sirma re Singbonga*
   Singbonga in heaven
   Dasi re kora do
   His servant boy
   Bondol tege hale bore-bore
   Has long sweeping loincloth

2. *Marang neota re*
   At a great feast
   Kamri kuri
   His maidservant
   Paela tegi hale jirpa-jalang
   Has elongated floating saree

3. *Bondol tegi hale bore-bore*
   Has long sweeping loincloth
   Goto tala regi argu lena
   Had descended in the midst of the gathering

4. *Paela tegi hale jirpa-jalang*
   Has enlongated floating saree
   Gohonda tala regi nosor lena
   Had slipped down in the midst of the assembly

The Liquidation of Asurs

Asur legend is one of the most important part of Munda religious system. The *asur,* it is stated, did not obey the order of the Singbonga in spite of repeated appeal and persuasion. They were defiling the God's creation. At last, the Singbonga vanquished their arrogance and subdued them. The following Gena song describes the event in these lines:

> *Sirma redo Singbonga*
> Singbonga in His heavenly abode
> *Singbongae elang tana*
> Singbonga is getting heat
> *Ote redo marang deota*
> The great god on earth
> *Marang deotae elang tana*
> The great god is getting heat
> *Baro bhai* asur *honko*
> The twelve asur brothers
> *Baro bhai* asur *honko sipud tana*
> The twelve asur brothers are engaged in mixing up the clay
> *Tero bhai deota honko*
> The thirteen brothers of deities
> *Tero bhai deota honko lebed tana*
> The thirteen brothers of deities are in piling work
> *Ema singi do, ema singi ko sipud tana*
> For seven days, they are engaged in mixing up of clay
> *Ema nida do, ema nida ko lebed tana*
> For seven nights, they are engaged in piling up of work
> *Ena tegi do Singbonga, ena tegi do marang deota*
> For that reason, the Singbonga and the great god
> *Ena tegi do deota ar bonga, ena tegi doe tayur jana*
> For that very reason, they were liquidated to spirits

The above song describes how the asur worked day and night, that is, 24 hours for seven days of the week continuously without rest. The Singbonga ordered them to work at any one time—either at day or night but not continuously for day and night as they do. The *asur* did not obey the orders of the Singbonga and, therefore, they were liquidated.

In the details of the *asur* legend—the traditional unwritten document on which the present system of religious feast and rites are based, have been recorded for the first time in the history of human beings, about protection of environment from human destruction. The legend as well as human consciousness about environment and concern for its protection relates to the period when metal and particularly the iron ore was detected by man as extremely useful for the development of human beings. The furnaces and smithy fires of the *asur*, blazing day and night, caused a disastrous drought on earth and even inconvenienced Singbonga up in heaven and so on (*Encyclopaedia Mundarica:* 210, Vol. 16). Because of heat generated by furnaces, the water resources and plant life dried up, air and water became polluted, life on earth became insecure for all living beings, even the God was disturbed. This was the birth of industrialization and reaction of human beings as was first perceived by the Mundas. Environment is the prime concern of humanity today which for the Mundas is not new. When man was after the materialistic world for satisfaction of the insatiable hunger, the Mundas had by then already attained maturity in wisdom and thinking and saw the foolishness of man in such activity and cautioned the humanity about environment degradation.

The song also indicates the situation of the changing time and people's reluctance to such changes. A great transformation was taking place in the history of man's thinking, society and economy. The leader proclaimed the work ethics, as in *asur* legend, by declaring a rest after either working at daytime or night. People were increasingly becoming consumerists and nature was considered to be an abundant supplier of wealth, therefore, a reckless exploitation of it began with competitive mentality under the garb of development. The change was there not only in the field of economy but the change was also visible in social organization, philosophy and values.

And the legend goes—when the *asur*—a technologically advanced group of people, did not obey the Singbonga's order. He himself came down to earth in the guise of an orphaned boy suffering from incurable disease to punish the haughty *asur*. A detailed story in the form of prayer song is found among the Mundas which gives a picture of struggle between traditionality and modernity, the result is the birth of a new social order, philosophy and values.

The *asur* legend provides a very deep insight in the then existing situation on the one hand, and a foresight into the future on the other. The legend depicts strong belief of the Mundas that there is an existence of power in the universe identified by them by the name of Singbonga beyond which no human being can go, whose existence was from the very beginning of the universe and who will remain for ever in future also. All human beings must accept this fact. He is there for ever whatever change and development may come in human history.

Asur legend as story has been told in a very simplistic way but it is full of deep meaning. The story describes His coming, stay, activities and final work and ascension to heaven. In all traditional culture there was no difference and discrepancy among people and between individuals but modernization has it all. It is against this trend of development which is thought to be catastrophe to human beings, an adjustment between the old and modern for the betterment of human being is brought about through the actions. The modernization and development has brought greediness and it has no limit but entails self destruction. The legend tells this fact very clearly.

The legend also tells how a host of changes were introduced in the Munda society and religious thinking. It is in the course of ascension, as the legend tells, the *asur* women clung all over His body so as to force Him to stay along with them on earth and support them. But He shook them off throwing them down to earth. He, however, made them dependent on the Mundas, that is, human beings for their sustenance. It is these women whom the Mundas consider as spirits and identify them by various names such as, *Ikir bonga, Buru bonga,* etc. These names are derived by the place names of their dwellings. The communication between the spirits and the men have been made possible as per arrangement of Singbonga through the middle men known as *Deonra*. Since then, the belief of spirits other than. The High God Singbonga and Baranda and institution of the cult of Deonraship has come into existence among the Mundas. The appointment of a Munda for performance of ceremonial worshippings to Singbonga was done by the Singbonga Himself who is known as *Pahan*. He is the village priest who is to be found in every Munda village. Appointment of *Pahan* as village priest is found in yet another myth of the Mundas. So in Munda society, *Pahan* and Deonra have their respective place and jurisdiction of activities. The belief on spirits and evil actions of the witches has become a part of the total belief system of the Mundas. The concept of spirits and witches are the result of change taking place in the overall situation in the Munda society. There was great impact of change on the profane as well as on sacred aspect of life of the Mundas. The result of interaction with outside community was the introduction of the concept of evil eyes and witch due to competition and jealousy. Besides, many non-sacred concepts related to psychological and philosophical aspects of life were incorporated in the religious thinking of the Mundas, like *roa*—the innate personality of the individual and belief in omen. The latter is supposed to be the objective manifestation of the will of the Supreme God Singbonga revealed in nature for the guidance of human beings in their day to day life.

The spirits who were made dependant by the High God Singbonga to men here on earth for their existence, create problems if they do not receive offerings and so it is an obligation of the people to make the offerings to them. This philosophical thinking of the Mundas is quite contrary to otherwise widely held thinking of the social scientists that the concept of spirit and witchcraft is the outcome of the fear psychosis of the tribals. The Mundas never bow down to the spirits but they order and command them. They are feared because of their evil actions. God Singbonga is the most benevolent one for the people. He is the member of every Munda family like a *haram* that is, an old person. The Munda share the food and drinks in their daily communion with the Supreme God Singbonga and with ones ancestral spirits. During every social and religious festivities the Munda dine together with unforeseen forces to the satisfaction and happiness of everyone.

So, there are a number of spirits who are identified by the place names of their dwellings, by their nature of behaviour or by specific names. In Munda villages there are number of places called *sarnas* like *Keda sarna, Baha Sarna*, etc, which are supposed to be the permanent dwelling places of these village spirits where the village community annually make offerings during ceremonies and festivals.

The song below which belongs to Jarga and Japi category indicate about their dwelling places and also mentions of their engagements. The lines of Jarga song are as follows:

Kuda umbul gule-gule ho
The shade of blackberry tree is pitch black
Ikir bongae duba kana
Ikir bonga (spirit of the deep) dwells here
Bari toyor bijir-bijir ho
The plot beyond banyan tree is glittering
Nage erae jarua kana
Nage era (spirit of the marsh) is overshadowing it
Ikir bongae dube kana
Ikir bonga dwells
Ikir bongae lo tana
Ikir bonga is burning bright
Nage erae jarua kana
Nage era is overshadowing
Nage erae bale tana
Nage era is lighting bright

Ikir bonga and *Nage era* are both water spirits whose dwelling places are normally located in deeps of the river, natural springs and marshy lands where there is perennial source of water.

People have a firm conviction that without making offerings to the dwelling spirit of the area concerned, the success in economic activities and particularly in hunting and gathering is doubtful. These spirits are considered to be the guardian of the nature—both animate and inanimate aspects of it and without making any offerings to them or obtaining prior permission from them, either the success will be little or the offender may face the wrath of the spirit. Such beliefs hindered the people in their wanton destruction or clearing of the forest areas as well as the fallow land and also prevented them from hunting, fishing, and gathering of flora and fauna at will. This religious philosophy as well as the customary laws of the people protected and preserved the nature and natural resources. Reference of such protection offered by the spirit has been made in the following *Japi* song, the lines of which are as follows:

Madukam jayar do
The Jayar of the Madukam tree
Senderae seno jana bhai, senderae seno jana
Has proceeded to hunting
Papra chandi do
The Chandi of the Papra tree
Karengae birid jana bhai, karengae birid jana
Has departed for gathering
Madukam jayar do
The Jayar of the Madukam tree
Tuing jilu-e seno tana bhai, tuing jilu-e seno tana
Is proceeding to hunting
Papra Chandi do
The Chandi of the Papra tree
Daran-baran-e birid tana bhai, daran-baran-e birid tana
Is departing for gathering
Madukam jayar do
The Jayar of the Madukam tree
Kutungan kulhai bhai, kutungan kulhai
Has shouldered a rabbit, brother
Papara Chandi do
The Chandi of the Papara tree
Hataran mara-a: bhai, hataran mara-a:
Has carried a peacock on her back, brother

People usually do some ritual performance while proceeding to hunting or collection in the forest. The activity may bear no fruit if no offering is made to the guardian spirit of the area.

The following Karam song states that all labour is lost if no proper offering is made to the concerned spirit. The lines of the song are as follows:

San agure kam bonga ledare
You did not offer while proceeding to firewood collection
Sakam he-re kam checha sakam led
You did not break leaf while proceeding to leaf collection
Hende simte kam bonga ledare
You did not perform ritual offering of black fowl

Ceremonial hunting by women in men's attire celebrated once in twelve years

Ara merom te ka̭m checha saka̭m led
You didn't do ritual breaking of leaf in the name of brown goat
Hasa uli re ka̭m boṇga kedare
You did not make offering at Hasa mango tree
Mara: buru re ka̭m checha saka̭m led
You did not break leaf at Mara buru

In the above song, the person is reminded of the reason of trouble or failure in his activity, and that is lack of proper offering to spirit concerned before undertaking such activities.

Prior to the introduction or adoption of *asur* legend, the Mundas had to invoke the offering to supreme God Singbonga, Baranda and ancestor spirits only. A complex of ritual details have since been introduced in the religious belief system by the Mundas. The spirits demand offering as their right as stated elsewhere. Domesticated cattle, and birds, particularly fowls, fruits and grains are the basic offering objects to these spirits.

The following two songs belonging to Jadur and Bala category describe how ritual offerings are being made by the villagers in which they are sacrificing goat and hen. The lines of the Jadur song are as follows:

Gaṇga thala chire samuda̭r thala
In the centre of either Ganga or ocean
Gaṇga thala reko boṇga tana
Ritual offering is being performed in the middle of the Ganga
Karia pathia ko boṇga tana
A black shegoat is being offered
Samuda̭r thala reko puja̭i tana
Offering in the middle of the ocean
Kaseya pathia ko puja̭i tana
Ash coloured shegoat is being offered

The lines of the *Bala* song are as follows:

Ne hatu ren Munḍa Pahaṇ ko
The Munda and Pahan of this village

Hare do siman parom re
At the confluence of the border of the villages
Tene-nene tan, kara-bara tan
Murmuring musically
Puṇḍi sim kalṭi ko boṇga tan
Offering white hen

Festivals

Mundas do observe a number of festivals. The most important of them is the *Magh* or *Ba* festival which is celebrated in the month of *Maghe* corresponding to the English month of February-March. The season being the spring when plants become laden with colourful flowers, *Ba* is the festival of flowers. The Munda observe it as a thanks giving festival to the God Singbonga. During spring, the plants bear new leaves, flowers and fruits. The Munda abstain from using these till *Maghe* or *Ba* festival is celebrated. After the harvest, people become free from heavy works. When the day of celebration of the festival is announced by the village *Pahan*, the preparation gets into full swing and particularly by the womenfolk. The floors and walls of the houses are plastered and cowdung cleaned, new earthen pots are purchased, rice is husked, rice-beer is fermented and clothes are cleaned. For children, festival is an occasion of joy and merriment and they await it eagerly.

In one of the following Jadur songs, a child reminds his mother the size of the bread and portion of meat that he would like to have during the ensuing Maghe festival. The lines of the song are as follows:

1. *Ne kaiom Maghe redo engaiṇg-2*
   In the ensuing Maghe festival, my mother dear
   Tai barabari soṇgaṛ lad ladaiṇg me-2
   Bake for me a plain bread of the size of a pan

2. *Ladaiṇg-ladaiṇg do eṇgaiṇg*
   If at all you bake for me, mother
   Bạr rokom ladaiṇg me
   Bake for me of two varieties

3. *Enga sim bu goii redo*
If we kill a hen
Salom japa jilu salaing me
Select for me a piece of meat of the chest

How the women are busy in their household work in the preparation of the festival, has been described in the following Jadur song, the lines of which are as follows:

1. *Ba chandu mulu lena mai*
Ba month has arrived, my dear daughter
Ba hasam ader tana
You are collecting clay for the *Ba* festival
Singi doe tikin tana mai
It is becoming noon, my dear
Narka hasam lowade tan
You are watering the soap-clay

2. *Ba hasam adere tana mai*
You are collecting clay for the *Ba* festival, dear
Okoe lom jalome
With whom will you do plastering
Narka hasam lowade tana mai
You are watering the soap-clay dear
Chimae lom narkan
With whom will you clean your hair

3. *Ba hasam adere tana mai*
You are collecting clay for the *Ba* festival, dear
Gatim lom jalome
You will plaster with your friend
Narka hasam lowade tana mai
You are watering the soap-clay dear
Sangam lom narkan te
You will clean your hair with your friend

The work is thus, carried out with the help of friends and others. As stated above, items of sacred offerings are collected by the males and cleaning, preparation of food and drinks, by the females. The following Jadur song mentions that flowers and tender leaves have all been collected and a chicken for offering is also ready. The lines of the song are as follows:

1. *Titi-titi ela bolome*
Come in fowl
Kuṇḍa̯m rem chiab-chiab a
You are crying in the back of the house
Titi-titi ela soṛo me
Hurry up fowl
Salaṇdi rem kere boreya
You are cackling on the wall

2. *Titi-titi ela bolome*
Come in fowl
Sa̯rjom ba tendera kana
Sarjom flower have been kept ready
Titi-titi ela soṛome
Hurry up fowl
Suṛa sagen siduba kana
Branch of green tender leaves have been kept ready

Similarly, as above, on the day of the festival, when ritual offering is being performed at one of the Sarna's people and particularly the *pujar,* that is, the helper of the *pahan,* collects flowers from Sarjom trees for offering. The following Jarandi song describes for whom the flowers are being collected. The lines of the song are as follows:

Ba kuṛi bapaṛi
What a beautiful flower, O girl
Ba a̯rgu ledare gui Sa̯rjom ba
Had brought down 'Sarjom' flower, O friend
Nikir boṇga ḍali nosor eda goi tila̯e ḍali
For Nikir *bonga,* Tilae flower have been brought down
Pahaṇ lagin ba guṭu leda goi sa̯rjom ba
For Pahan garland from Sarjom flower have been prepared
Pujar lagin ḍali nosor eda goi, tilae ḍali
For Pujar, twig of *tilae* plant have been brought down

Penance is part of the ritual in every religion and the Mundas are in no exception which they observe at every religious performance. However, the bachelors, spinsters and children are excluded from such observance. They also are restricted from sharing in the offerings. As the ladies remain engaged and abstain from eating and drinking on the day of offering, food also is not cooked by them. Because of this the children suffer as they do not get food. However, the young are assigned all sorts of duties on this day as the elders remain busy in sacred performance.

The following Jadur song mentions how a small girl because of ritual performance by the elders feels neglected and unattended and weeps at a corner. The lines of the song are as follows:

1. *Eṇgạm ko ba katạb tana mai*
   Mother yours is observing penance, O dear
   Kuṇdạm rem tiṇgua kana
   You are standing in the back of the house
   Apum ko giṛi toroe tana mai
   Father yours is performing the ritual of throwing away ash
   Salaṇdi rem japa kana mai
   You are standing by the fence wall, dear

2. *Kundạm rem tiṇgua kana mai*
   You are standing by the back wall, dear
   Kunḍạm hasa haṇdiṛi tana
   The back wall is falling down
   Salaṇdi rem japa kana mai
   You are standing by the fence wall, dear
   Chandae da: do joro tan
   Water from the roof is falling down

3. *Kuṇdạm hasa haṇdiṛi tana mai*
   The back wall is falling down, dear
   Med da: do joro tana
   Tears yours is rolling down
   Chandae da: do joro tana mai
   Water from the roof is falling down, dear

Uli da: do oṛoe-toṛoe
The saliva is rolling down

The girl is hungry and, therefore, is weeping. She is not being allowed to get in the room of the house as the ritual performance is going on. There is drizzling and the girl who is standing by the wall is getting wet. In the mean time, the parents are sharing the ritual offering, while the girl, who is hungry merely looks on. The water from her mouth is rolling out to see the eatables.

Though there are religious leaders like *pahan* and *pujar* for performance of ritual details of community festivals, the family head or the head of the lineage or seniormost of the male member in the family does ritual performances and offerings in the household. It is why, everyone in the household, and particularly the eldest male person has to learn from the very childhood the ritual details of worshipping.

The two Jadur songs given below relate to the learning of such ritual offerings and mentions its paraphernalia in the following lines:

1. *Ba doga eṇgaiṇg Ba teba tana*
   Ba festival is arriving, mother dear
   Dali doga apuiṇg, dali seter tan
   The festival of the twig is arriving, father dear

2. *Boṇga buru eṇgaiṇg kaiṇg ituana*
   How to worship I don't know, mother dear
   Sewa susar apuiṇg kaiṇg saria
   I have no knowledge of the ritual details, father dear

3. *Isu heṛem jagaṛ te, itu aiṇg me eṇgaiṇg re*
   Teach me in sweet words, my mother dear
   Isu heṛem kaji te udubaiṇg me apuiṇg re
   Tell me in sweet words, my father dear

The boy as above is eager to learn the ways of performing ritual offering from his parents. The following song mentions the ways of ritual process. The lines of the song are as follows:

1. *Ba dope Ba tana haga go*
   You are celebrating *Ba* festival brother dear, but

China hope chikaya
What will you do
Ḍali dope ḍali tana misi ko
You are celebrating the festival of the twig, sister dear, but
Mere hope rikaya
How will you do

2. *Ba dope Ba tana hago ko*
You are celebrating *Ba* festival brother dear, but
Sukar̤ sim boṇgai pe
Sacrifice a young chick
Ḍali dope ḍali tana misi ko
You are celebrating the festival of the twig sister dear, but
Tapa̤n ko chipae pe
Prepare rice-beer for offering

The festival is the occasion of joy and merriment for the young and the old alike. The day of *Ba* festival differs from village to village as the day for its celebration is determined by the villagers themselves, however the month, that is, *Magh* remains the same. During this period, the environment becomes scented from green foliages and flowers. And as almost all the villages celebrate the festival as per their convenience, the whole month is enjoyed by the people as song and dance resounds in the region day and night. Any traveller, during the period can guess as to where the festival is being celebrated. The lines of the following Jadur song mentions this in these lines:

1. *Oko reko Ba tana, Ba soan tana*
Where the *Ba* festival is being celebrated, there is the scent of the flowers
Chimae reko ḍali tana, Dumaṇg saṛi tana
Where the festival of the twig is being celebrated, the sound of *dumang is* being heard

2. *Bunḍu reko Ba tana, Ba soan tana*
Ba festival is being celebrated in Bundu, the scent of flowers is coming from there

Tamaṛ reko ḍali tana, Dumang saṛi tana
Festival of the twig is being celebrated in Tamar, the sound of *dumang* is coming from there

A few Dubung and Lahsua category of songs also describe about the *Karam* festival. This festival is not celebrated by the Mundas of the Naguri country. However, the song with the theme of Karam festival is also found in this part. The following Lahsua category of song describes the day of celebtration of the festival in these lines:

1. *Bhado ka ekadasi karame gaṛae re*
   Karam plant is pitched on the eleventh day of *Bhado* month
   Hare, Lil mai, kone dine karame gaṛae re
   O Lil dear, on which day *karam* plant is pitched

2. *Etwar ko balu uthe*
   Sands are collected on Sunday
   Somar ke jawa jage re
   Maize seeds are sown on Monday
   Hare, Lil mai, Maṇgar ke karame gaṛae re
   On Tuesday *karam* plant is pitched, dear Lil

The lines of the other song is as follows which gives the picture of celebration of the festival accompanied by music and dance.

1. *Gaṛailo bono kera ḍair go*
   Twig of the forest was pitched, O dear
   Sajani goi, gaṛailo bono kera ḍair
   Friend dear, twig of the forest was pitched
   Hilo khosa, lagṳr lasa-lagṳr lasa
   Hair of the head swing up and down
   Gaṛailo bono kera ḍair
   Twig of the forest was pitched

2. *Kacha ho baṇsa ke ḍalia ṭangae goi*
   Basket from tender bamboo plant is fastened on it
   Gaṛailo bono kera ḍair
   Twig of the forest was pitched
   Hilo khosa lagṳr lasa-lagṳr lasa

Hair of the head swing up and down
Garailo bono kera dair
Twig of the forest was pitched

The following two songs which belong to Dubung category, mentions the place where the *karam* tree is pitched as well as the persons who do the ritual details. The lines of the first song are as follows:

Ohre koronjo buda
How beautiful is the *koronj* plant
Bahre do siman
What a nice place the conjoint of the two village boundary
Laere do siman majhe karame garae
Karam tree is pitched at the boundary of the village
Khelare haere, Ohre do siman
Play and dance at the boundary of the village
Do siman majhe karame garae
Karam tree is pitched at the boundary of the village

Karam tree is worshipped by seven damsels who do penance all through the days of the celebration of the *karam* festival. The following song describes this as under:

Karam karale, sato karam garale
You celebrated *karam* by pitching seven branches of *karam* plant
Hae ho sato karam bahin sewa karae
All the seven *karam* plants are being worshipped by the sisters
Ujhal-pajhal dhoti, ujhal-pajhal dhoti nayoge
The white clean dhoti mother
Ujhal-pajhal dhoti ayo sewa karae
Wearing white clean dhoti, mother is worshipping
Hae ho ujhal-pajhal dhoti
How nice, the white clean dhoti
Ujhal-pajhal dhoti, Sato sae bahin sewa karae
Wearing white clean dhoti, seven hundred sisters are worshipping

As stated in previous pages besides the festivals, some cultural fairs are also held. This cultural fair is called *jatra.* Such cultural fairs are held twice in a year and are identified by different names. The fair which is held in winter is called *Ind jatra* and that in summer *jethua* or *Jeth jatra.* During *Ind jatra* a flag, representing clans or tribe is pitched at the centre place of the fair after performing ceremonial ritual. The song below which belongs to Lahsua category mentions about the *Ind* variety of the fair. The lines of the song are as follows:

1. *Niṇdi choṭi kaisana sundaṛ, chalure dekhe jāb*
   How nice is the top of Ind post, let us go to see it
   Hore, chalure dekhe jāb
   Let us go to see it
   Niṇdi choṭi kaisana sundaṛ
   How nice is the top of Ind flag

2. *Heṇthe to puja dhaja*
   Ritual worship is performed at the base
   Nupare to niṇdi choti
   The Ind flag is on the top
   Hore, chalure dekhe jāb
   Let us proceed to see it
   Niṇdi choṭi kaisana sundaṛ
   How nice is the Ind flag

Spirits

Spirits are generally feared by the tribals. And it is this psychology of fear that has helped in the development of various superstitious beliefs. In reality, the spirits never engage themselves in frightful activities which the song as recorded here indicates. The song belongs to Karam category and the lines are as follows:

Da aguiṇg sen kena, chi chubuṛ-chubuṛ re
I had been to fetch water, what is splashing in the water
Choke koga chubuṛ-chubuṛ, caiṇg boro tana re
It is the frogs that are splashing, I fear not from them
Sakam he-iṇg sen kena, chi paṭa-paṭa re
I had been to pluck leaves, who is making rattling sound

Kula koge raṭa-paṭa, kaing boro tana re
They may be tigers, I am not afraid of them
San aguing sen kena, chi rosod-rosod re
Had been to collect wood, what is making rattling sound
Ṭeṭeṇga ko rosod-rosod, kaiṇg boro tana re
It may be lizard, I am not afraid of them

The above song describes the various situations that may create fear in an individual. But in most cases such fears are found baseless when reality comes to light as mentioned in the song.

During night, such fear situations increase manifold due to distortion of figures. One such situation has been mentioned in the following Karam category of song:

Da aguing sen kena
Had been to fetch water
Chikạn jatie duba kana
What species are sitting on the way
Ocho mur kara, Chika teiṇg sena dur kara
It desists me, how shall I dare to pass through

Spirits, though invisible, are said to assume any biological figure at will, and it is because of this ability to sudden change in figure that they are feared. It is believed that some spirits inflict injuries to people when encountered and so they are feared. Spirits are visible to a very few people. The Munda believe that only those people can see the spirit or the spirits become visible to those who have *rambal roa* that is, light shade. The *roa* is an intrinsic quality or personality character or *gun* of an individual and carries some magic power with him. The persons of *rambal roa* or heavy shade, on the other hand, cannot see the spirits and so no encounter with spirits is recorded by such people. It is the persons of *rambal roa* who are supposed to lack deterrance of diseases.

The end of life is painfully felt by the survivors in any family or by the community among the Mundas. And this painful memory has been recorded in some Jadur songs. One such instance has been recorded in the following Jadur song on a person who is unaware of the death that has occurred of his dear friend. The lines of the song are as follows:

1. *Gaṇga tala chire samudar tela*
   In the middle of the Ganga or the ocean
   Gelbar gossaiṇ ko duba kana
   Gossain, twelve in number are sitting together
   Gaṇga tala chire sumudar tala
   In the middle of the Ganga or the ocean
   Hisibar Bamre ko jarua kana
   Brahman, twenty two in number have assembled

2. *Kachi reko udubad meya*
   Did they not tell you
   Sidaren gatim ko hoyon tana
   They are shaving in the name of your previous friend
   Kachi reko chundulad meya
   Did they not signal you
   Tayom ren saṇgame ko hor nam tana
   Performing last rite in the name of your friend

3. *Hiyatiṇg mone-iṇg re chakatiṇg sanaiṇg*
   I deeply feel and remember with heavy heart
   Sidaren gatim ko hoyon tana
   They are shaving in the name of your previous friend
   Hiyatiṇg mone-iṇg re chakatiṇg sanaiṇg
   I deeply feel and remember with heavy heart
   Tayom ren saṇgame ko hori nam tana
   Performing last rite in the name of your friend

Service of the Gossain and Brahmin are taken by the Mundas of the Hasada country during life ritual ceremonies, no such service is taken by the Mundas of Naguri country from Hindu priests.

On Major Religions

In Munda country, people and communities belonging to or professing other religions such as Hinduism, Islam and Christianity are also found in good number. The Munda region was once the field of religious activities of sects like Brahmo Samaj, Kabir Panthi, Hari Baba, Vaisnavism and Krishna Bhakti cult besides Christian missionaries. While the Hasada country was swept over by various sects and cults of Hindu religion, the Naguri country by Christian Missionaries of various denominations. We have a good number of songs which are derived from the themes of these religions in the traditional songs of the Mundas. While the Karaṃ and Lahsua category have good number of songs on the themes of Krishna Bhakti, the Bala category records from the *Bible* and *Ramayana.* Some of these songs are as follows:

> *Kroos daru suba re*
> Under the cross
> *Nalo Mariam rageya*
> Don't weep Mariam
> *Ama lagin Prabhu gi menaiya*
> The Lord is there for you
> *Tee kaṭa reko kila kija*
> He was nailed on hands and feet
> *Kuṛam reko kila kija*
> He was pierced on the chest
> *Da: leka mayom liṇgi jan*
> Blood flowed out like water
> *Nalo Mariam rageya*
> Don't weep Mariam
> *Ama lagin Prabhu gi menaiya*
> Lord is there for you

The above song belongs to Bala category and is based on the theme of crucification of Lord Jesus Christ.

The song below has a philosophical content of Christianity, the line of which are as follows:

> *Chetan̥ latarete da: lingi tan hada-hada*
> Water is failing from above down below with ferocious sound
> *Ne jiu bicharem, gaṛa chilkaiṇg paroma-2*
> Think over my soul, how shall I cross over it
> *Tee kataiṇg peṭe jana, med lutur bano jana re*
> Mẏ hands and feet are broken and am deaf and blind
> *Ne jiu bicharem, gaṛa chilkaiṇg paroma-2*
> Think over my soul how shall I cross over it

According to Christian philosophy, sinful life is like broken hands and feet as well as a deaf and mute soul. This is a great hindrance in the journey towards God, the ultimate aim of every human soul. Sin is, moreover, like an ocean and infirmities as stated, it is next to impossible to cross the ocean. And it is here that Lord Jesus Christ stands to help everybody.

The song below which belongs to Bala category, relates to an episode of war between Lord Rama and Ravana. In the song under reference, Lord Rama is being advised to organize the warriors in a better way, the lines of the song are as follows:

Siri Prabhu Bhagwan, dạl ke saṇwara re
O Lord, organize the battalion
Hare, age pichhe chale sena dạl re
The warrior battalion should walk in front and behind
Gawali moe Hari bol
I shouted *Hari bol*
Hare sirinagare bahute moe rahaloṇ
I had stayed in the state capital for long
Hare, age pichhe chale sena dạl re
The warrior battalion should walk in front and behind

The following Lahsua category of song describes the life of Lord Krishna, the lines are as follows:

Heṇde-heṇde a dhoti tada
Clad in blue coloured dhoti
Uri gai koe gupi tana
He is tending the cows
Bir bhitạr diri re duba kana
Sitting on the rock inside the forest
Ogo dhoni, rutu tedo aiṇge nutum tana
O dear, taking my name through the sound of flute
Jire rutu gutu jana
The sound of flute got into my heart
Nida siṇgi-iṇg lo tana
I am burning day and night
Bir bhitạr diri re duba kena
Sitting on the rock inside the forest

Ogo dhoni, rutu tedo aiṇge nutum tana
O dear, taking my name through the sound of flute

There are a number of songs which are based on the *Ras Lila* of Lord Krishna with *gopinies* and the memory of the latter for Him when He deserted them. These songs are found in Karam and Lahsua category.

Though the Mundas do not believe in fate, but the following Lahsua category of song has recorded this. These songs may have been composed by the sect leaders of Bhakti cult like Budu Babu etc. The lines of the song are as follows:

Ne disum tala re, janạm kana bu re
We have taken birth in this world, dear
Duku-suku soben mena
Pleasure and pain coexist here
Bidhi ol tada re, elare taiṇg subodhini
The Almighty have written this, dear Subodhini
Elare taiṇg iṇg chika leka
Alas dear, what shall I do
Navdhana jire do diri tena kana re
Stone is laying over the heart of Navdhan
Ayar tayom uṛu keyate duraṇg bai tana re
Song is composed thinking pros and cons of the life

12

THE PHILOSOPHY OF LIFE AND WORLD VIEWS

"The philosophy is the formulation and logical exploration of concepts." It is based on the fact of life of the community or society generated through life experience and controlled observation and perception, So it gives direction for social action and behaviour to the people. There are few songs which reflect the philosophy of life of the Mundas.

The following Bala category of song, though its reference has already been made in other context, relates to the well known proverb which states—'where there is will, there is a way' or 'where there is life, there is a way'. The song conveys the message that one should not attach oneself emotionally too much to a particular place or group of people. There is life everywhere. The song is sung in pacification to the daughter who is married away to a distant place and strange family. The lines of the song are as follows:

> *Eke kose pani*
> A *kos* wide water belt
> *Biso kose jungal bhitarege nayo*
> Inside the forest spread over in twenty *kos,* mother
> *Duyo bhaiya-bahina kaṇḍae ge nayo-2*
> Brother and sister both are weeping
> *Aisana jana to aisana baja toge nayo*
> Such an unknown place, mother
> *Jahaṇ jina tahan morna ge nayo*
> Where there is life, death is there too, mother

The last line of the song carries the lesson for the people. Tribulation and joy is the life of man and one should not lose hope even during the trouble. This message is found in the following Jadur song too, the lines of which are as follows:

1. *Kita daru sile-sile*
The slime and straight date tree
Gidi toe tuka tana
The vulture is making nest
Sale daru sale-bole
The straight and slime sale tree
Kari doe aṭed tan
Kari is laying foundation of the nest

2. *Gidi doe tuka tan*
The vulture is making nest
Kita daru gure jana
The date tree fell down
Kari doe aṭed tan
Kari is laying foundation of the nest
Sali daru rauṛe jana
Sali tree fell down

3. *Kita daru gure jana*
The date tree fell down
Gidi doe ra-a: tana
The vulture is weeping
Sali daru raure jana
Sali tree fell down
Kari doe niyạm tan
The kari is moaning

4. *Alo gidim rageya*
Don't weep vulture
Lika gire gidi sagenoa
It will sprout today itself, O vulture
Alo karim niyame
Don't moan *kari*
Gapagi kari suṛaoa
Tender leaves may come out tomorrow itself, *kari*

The mixture of joy and sorrow is the nature of life and one should be hopeful of happiness in life even during trouble. This message has been conveyed in the following Lahsua category of song, the lines of which are as follows:

Ne hatu tala re china ko chaka tan
What is being done in the centre of this village
Reṇge-rabaṇg duku-suku, bidhi ol kedae re
Famine and poverty, joy and tribulation is the God providence
Bidhi dore ol ked, bhabhi dore nel ked
God made providence was seen by the sister-in-law
Reṇge-rabaṇg duku-suku, bidhi ol kedaere
Famine and poverty, joy and tribulation is the God providence

The song mentions that though God made the providence of joy and tribulations in life of every man, happiness blossoms in the family only when there is mutual respect among all the family members, otherwise the life is hell. And it is in the hands of sister-in-law who comes in the family by marriage, that happiness of the family depends. This is what has been mentioned that *bhabhi* saw the lines of the sentence written by the God.

When one falls in trouble or sees trouble in the neighbourhood or in the world, like famine, diseases, revolutions or wars, he should not be affraid of it for it is natural for such things to happen. The change is natural and imminent, just as the green leaves turn into purple which ultimately fall down and in its place new ones comes out. The same is the case with life. The following Jadur song has the content of the changing nature of human life. Though the song has been referred to in previous pages also in the context of change, it has the philosophical content and is worth noting in this context too. The lines of the song are as follows:

1. *Disum dada neka giya*
   The nature of the world is this, brother
   Hoṛo kaji disum ula-mali re
   It is in the revolution, the people say
   Disum dada neka giya
   The nature of the world is this, brother

2. *Heṇde sakaṃ puṇḍi tan*
   In the turning of green leaves into purple
   Puṇḍi sakaṃ heṇde tan
   In the turning of purple leaves into green

Hoṛo kajo disum ula-mali re
It is in the revolution, the people say
Disum dada neka giya
The nature of the world is like this, brother

All are subjected to natural law or law of the providence and no one can escape from it, that is, growth, maturity and decay is the law of nature. The following Jarga category of song has the content of this vital aspect of life. The lines of the song are as follows:

1. *Lo tana lo tana*
   It is burning
   Sengel te lo tana re soben daru-2
   All the trees are burning by the fire

2. *Atu tana atu tana re*
   It is floating down by the current
   Gaṛa da: te atu tan soben jubila
   The soils are floating down with the current of the river

3. *Lo tana lo tana nai*
   It is burning, mother
   Tiril sahạn lo tana raṭa-paṭa
   Tiril log is burning with cracking

Similar to the above, the song below too has the message that, irrespective of difference in race and in colour, all are subjected to the same natural law of decay and death, and therefore, all should live in harmony and peace. The lines of the Jarga song are as follows:

1. *Jau jubila, jeta jubila*
   The marshy lands of all kinds
   Gaṛa da: te atu tan soben jubila
   All marshy lands are over flooded by the river water

2. *Ja jati jetan jạti*
   Whatever may be the caste
   Hora te seno tan soben jati
   All are travelling on the same path

3. *Lilair gore, bapair gore*
Since generations
Hora te seno tan soben jati
All are travelling on the same path

4. *Lilair gore, bapair gore*
Since generations
Gaṛa da: te atu tan soben ubila
All marshy lands are over flooded by the river water

Life is but transitory in this world. Birth, growth and death of a person is like a plant that sprouts, grows, and bears buds, blooms and ultimately fades away. This message has been given in many a Munda songs. The song below belonging to Dubung category states that human life is like flowers. The lines of the song are as follows:

1. *Ka janạm dele ge nayo*
Mother, in which species did you give me birth
Jharia-jharia phula janạm dele ge nayo
I am like flowers of the spring side

2. *Manus janạm dele ge nayo*
You gave me birth as human being mother
Jharia-jharia phula janạm dele ge nayo
I am like flowers of the spring side

Education on works and good living are informally given to children. Real life activities are but a practical lesson to children which they learn by involvement. Theoretical instruction is meaningless unless it is associated with practicals. The following Jarga song has this content. The knowledge comes only through the participation in works. The lines of the song are as follows:

1. *Eṇgaiṇg kin, apuiṇg kin*
My dear, parent
Sel kuti re tiṇgu taiṇg ben
Please help me to stand by the pestle
Eṇgaiṇg kin, apuiṇg kin
My dear, parent
Kaṛba ḍanḍi re japa taiṇg ben
Please help me to stand by the handle of the plough

2. *Engaing kin, apuing kin*
   My dear, parent
   Sona kaji do kajiyaing ben
   Tell me the words that have value of gold
   Engaing kin, apuing kin
   My dear, parent
   Rupa bankar do bankaraing ben
   Please speak to me in words that have value of silver

3. *Mar babu, mar bachha re*
   Dear son
   Sona kaji do sel kuti reya
   The words of the value of gold lies with the pestle
   Mar babu, mar bachha re
   Dear son
   Rupa bankar do karba dandi reya
   The words worth silver in value is with the handle of plough

In Munda community, the household responsibility is usually shouldered by a person only after his marriage, though exceptions may be there. A man can understand the reality of life when he gets himself involved in life activities as responsible person. Usually the children enjoy life so long as the parents are alive. The following Jadur song has this very content the lines of which are as follows:

1. *Manri-manri te uru bolo tana*
   Anxiety is getting in slowly
   Dhire susuaete med da: joro tana
   Tears rolling down while sobbing

2. *Apuing goe jana, uru bolo tana*
   Father expired, anxiety is getting in
   Engaing chaba jana, med da: joro tana
   Mother is no more, tears are rolling down

Time flies away very fast. This is perceivable in the sequence of birth, maturity and death. Every Munda is aware of it. The youths are usually advised not to while away time in useless activities. The following Lahsua song mentions that time once wasted is gone for ever and cannot be available again. The lines of the song are as follows:

1. *Samae misa geya*
   Time available is but once
   Kocha kuni danṛae re kage namoa
   In searching out every corner of the world, it cannot be availed again

2. *Mid samae seno jan, bar samae seno jan*
   Chance once or twice lost
   Samae misa geya
   Chance is but once
   Kocha kuni danṛae reyo kage namoa
   In searching out every corner of the world, it cannot be available again

3. *Bale samae seno jan, ḍinḍa samae seno jan*
   Childhood days passed and youthful age gone
   Samae misa geya
   Chance is but once
   Ḍinḍa samae seno re kage namo
   Once youthful age gone, it cannot be available again
   Samae misa geya
   Time is but once

In this scientific age, change is taking place very rapidly in every sphere of life. Change is visible somewhere and others not. This changing scene has been mentioned in the following Jadur song. The lines are as follows:

1. *Sida do disum taikena*
   The state of the world in bygone days was
   Bursi sengel leka, bursi sengel leka
   Burning slowly like amber
   Na: do disum lo tana
   The world is now burning
   Diya leka lo tana, diya leka
   Burning like lamp, like lamp

2. *Sida do disum taikena*

   The state of the world in bygone days was
   Pasaṇgi seṇgel leka, pasaṇgi seṇgel leka
   Like burning log, like burning log
   Na: do disum lo tana
   The world is now burning
   Jara leka disum lo tana, jara leka
   Like burning forest, like burning forest

The changing world has brought with it many evils. A considerable change in human behaviour is rampaging the world of the peace loving people. The following Jadur song vividly mentions the trend of change now taking place in human behaviour. The lines of the song are as follows:

1. *Sida samae taikena, sotoyug taikena*
   The state of the world in bygone days was, where *Satyug* prevailed
   Na: samae rakạb lena, kaliyug rakạb lena
   The days of this age has dawned with *Kaliyug*

2. *Satyug taikena, samạrom gele lena*
   When there was *Satyug,* the truth blossomed
   Kaliyug rakạb lena, chenṭa te pere-akna
   When *Kaliyug* dawned, jealousy prevailed in fullness

3. *Samạrom gele lena, disum ho marsạl lena*
   When truth blossomed, the world glowed bright
   Chenṭa te pere-akna, disum ho nuba jana
   When jealousy prevailed in fullness, the light of the world gone forever

The song describes the present day situation of the world with a tone of lamentation. The achievement made in materialistic comfort in this scientific age is usually not welcomed by the tribal people. Earlier, people lived in peace with love and compassion. There was no greed, no hatred, no jealousy among the people. Now the peace has been writ large from the face of the earth instead it has been engulfed with greed, anger, hatred and jealousy where anguish, despair and death prevail.

PART V

ECONOMIC PURSUIT FOR A LIVING

13

THE ROLE OF NATURE, MAN AND SPIRIT IN TRIBAL ECONOMY

Music emanates from the heart of an individual and is an expression of his total perception and experience of the whole life situation and the environment which he encounters while carrying out various activities in life. His social and physical geography, his beliefs and economics for living influences his emotions and feelings most. A major part of an individual's life during the day is usually devoted to some sort of economic pursuit. The tribal communities are traditionally directly depended on nature for a living and so most of their economic pursuit are linked with nature. People always have some view or opinion about the physical milieu in which they live. Thorough knowledge of the geography is an asset for the people in their economic activities. The deeper the knowledge of the environment and the efficiency with which it is used, greater is the likelihood of improving the life situation. The material condition provided by geography, on the one hand, affects food supply situation and regulates economic activities of the people through variations in seasons, and on the other, is supposed to be responsive to social organization, ritual process and world-view of the people.

The whole economic process of the people belonging, particularly to simple societies can conveniently be viewed through three broad angles: (a) its materialistic apsects, (2) its sociological basis, and (3) its customary beliefs, values and rituals. These aspects of economy are not exclusive in themselves but are related to each other. The first would include the material condition of the people, their resources, means and technology of exploitation, process of production, distribution, preservation and its method of consumption as well as the skill and knowledge required in the whole process of economic activity. The second would deal with the organization and manipulation of productive system, social relationship of the people engaged in economic activity and their norms and etiquette with respect to economy, viewed as a human resource investment for a happy and peaceful living. It is a fact that the economy of the traditional and simple societies like hunters, food gatherers, fishermen, pastoralists and agriculturists, etc. are full of contingencies which often pose a serious danger to their existence. In such societies, in normal condition, there is a tendency to continuity and preservation of existing system. People generally rely on past experience for it provides a pattern for living and a ready model for action. The socio-economic relationship in such cultures is structured and organized on the basis of established values, skills and capabilities, truth and experience. The cultural contents and experience are handed down to next generation through oral transmission and direct demonstration. The process is both diachronic and synchronic.

Thirdly, the customary beliefs, values and rituals are needed for economic security. The simple and traditional community of self-supporting economy, which usually depend on nature for existence, faces numerous natural hazards in their economic pursuit. A drought, a hailstorm or a blight might mean famine for the simple agriculturist communities. All their several crops, their herds and their game might easily be affected by the same catastrophe. The reserves in store are never large. Such communities are fully conscious of their immediate dependence on the powers that bring rain and sunshine, thunder and hurricane. But these acts are capriciously and terribly uncertain. At all costs they must be compelled, cajoled or conciliated with. So, they seek the help of benevolent forces to control and ward off noxious powers by rituals, incantations and charms. It is at such situation that belief in supernatural forces and system of magic to achieve that compulsion or a ritual to ensure that conciliation receive confirmation from the people, as such belief becomes a solace in the terror of life that one dare not surrender (V. Gordon Childe, 1956 : 100).

Besides the sacred and ritual approach as stated for economic security or success in economic operation, there are other factors which play major role in the operation and management of economy. One must be fully aware of one's natural environment and its effects on economy. The knowledge of astrology, climatology, topography, geology, bio-chemistry, zoology and botany are essential to achieve better results in economic operation and above all, lore of agriculture, mechanics, metallurgy and architecture.

In order to survive, the society keeps an adjustment to its environment and supports itself by exploiting the natural resources of its territory. The individual must be aware of the prevalent natural philosophy of the society. In economic exploration, he is being helped by the tradition and culture of his community which he learns through lore and practical experience. The success depends on everyone doing what has proved to be the right thing at the right time and in right way, it imposes a complete pattern of behaviour on all the community members. This pattern finds expression in social institutions and in traditional rules and prohibitions. It is often sanctified by magico-religious beliefs and fears. Just as the practical acts of life are accompanied by appropriate rites and ceremonies, so also the mystical forces and particularly the souls of the departed among the Mundas are supposed to watch over the traditional rules and avenge any transgression of them. The established economy is reinforced by an appropriate ideology. The forces of such beliefs consolidate and maintain the established social institutions and economic arrangement enormously. The adjustment achieved, after all, is precarious as stated above. An insufficient or excessive rain or floods, an untimely hailstorm, a plague of locusts might imperil the whole community, for its resources are limited and reserves small. The disasters threatening life are mysterious and even today incalculable. It may easily be regarded as the anger of supernatural forces for the transgression of customary rules of behaviour. Any deviation from established practice, any departure from behaviour that has been found safe and effective, might theoretically provoke such punishment. Any innovation or change in the established practice would naturally call to public criticism. Such reaction seems to be inversely proportional to the community's economic security. The change is inevitable in the culture and society, but as stated above, people are reluctant to adopt any innovation in the initial stage and it is justifiable in the absence of other alternate means of livelihood considering the existing economic condition and resources of the people so affected. The change may occur either by the internal forces or external or both, which may bring in new elements in the existing culture or economy created appropriate to the environment and may either exert adverse effect to it or may prove a boon for progress. In the changing situation, there would be a great impact on the existing prescriptions, prohibitions, the rites and ceremonies regarded as essential to life in their environment. In Jharkhand region which was a few centuries ago inhabited exclusively by tribal communities and in virtual isolation from outside world, the immigration of numerous nomadic and trading communities brought them into contact with people of strange customs, cultures and practices and there developed economic interdependency among them. A host of material products new to the people were introduced by the community of traders. In the self-sufficient economic tradition, a market economy was introduced which replaced the traditional barter system of exchange.

When the alien forces such as the Mughals and British trading companies illegally took control of the region, it opened the road for immigrants who were in search of virgin areas for livelihood. The mobility of non-tribal communities put an adverse effect on the whole life systems of the tribals, and particularly, on their economy which is based on land and forest. The tribals were hard-pressed for survival and were forced for large-scale migration to outside region. Those who stayed back had to eke out their living on a piece or two of land and on forest products. The nature which was never treated as commodity by the tribals, became a spoil of the cherish of the immigrants. This, on the one hand, led to the denudation of forest and spoiling of natural resources and environment and on the other, there ensued jealousy and hatred among the communities. No history of the Jharkhand region is complete without mentioning of the struggle of the innocent tribal people which still continues in various forms as justice is in no sight. How long a community can keep its dignity, social values and culture in situation of insecurity, plunder and poverty? The fear of unknown, however, helped the tribals to struggle for survival, continuity and maintenance of their culture and unity in the community which is amply reflected in their songs. Below is one such song in which the young generations are advised not to leave the native place of one's ancestors. The song belongs to Jadur category and the lines are as follows:

1. *Sambharae paṇḍe hale guchu paṇḍu jana*
   Beard ours have turned white, tells Sambharae Pande

Hatu kabu bagia marbu Jadura
We shall not leave the village, let us dance Jadur

2. *Disum talang sambarao-yalang*
We shall keep the country going
Dasi nabu, goti nabu
Even if we have to earn our bread by selling labour
Hatu kabu bagia, marbu Jadura
We shall not leave the village, let us dance Jadur

The above song refers to an episode when the landlord of the village, Sambharae Pande by name, was once requested by the Maharaja Loknath Sae of Chhotanagpur to leave the village and join the service of Harinath Sahdeo of Jariagarh estate who was the then king there. It is told that Sambharae Pande refused to join the service, on the ground that he has become old and preferred to stay in the village. This became a reference to the Munda youths who would advise others not to leave the village in any circumstance like Sambharae Pande even if they had to live a life of starvation for it would be better to die in one's village than in a foreign land where there will be nobody to offer a lump of earth when one dies. The fear of the unknown and emotional attachment with one's relatives and one's land is too deep for the tribals and provided solace when uncertainty prevailed at every step of life and fastened them to their land and country in the situation of economic uncertainty and restrained them from mass exodus to Assam and Bengal in search of job. The song below belonging to Jadur category states the situation in the following lines:

1. *Gara ho dora ko or keda*
All through the rivers and ditches, chains were drawn
Gatim re oko telang seno mulina
Where shall we take shelter, dear
Assam telang seno mulina
We shall proceed to Assam

2. *Assam telang seno re, haga hon jetae banko jan*
There will be no kin if we go to Assam
Gidi Kurid Tuyu-e Jom langa
Vultures, kites and jackals may devour us

It is but natural to human beings to be worried when any unprecedented things happen against otherwise a peaceful settled life. The song relates to a historical event among the Mundas when Jharkhand region came under the control of the British Company. In order to streamline the land rent, the company undertook survey settlement of landholdings which were supposed to be at the disposal of each individual household. The tribals could not understand the real purpose of the company. They thought that land is being surveyed for acquisition by the company and never for permanent settlement of holding in an individual's control as such the concept was inconceivable to the tribals. A situation of total confusion and fear of dispossession from one's ancestral land was imminent in the minds of the tribals. The above song describes the operation of the survey and the resultant situation of panic among a couple. The couple are panicked by mere thinking of the situation when they will be dislodged from their land which is a permanent source for support of the family. This fear was genuine as they see no alternate source of livelihood in the environment familiar to them, The only alternative is to earn their livelihood by selling their labour in a far off land among the strangers just introduced in tea gardens in Assam. This was equally dangerous, as leading a life among the strangers means to cut off one's relationships from the kinsmen who, in traditional system, would always remain at their side in the hours of joy and trouble. They will not be able to avail this facility in far off land and the condition when they would die, would be most disdainful. Nobody will be there to bury their deadbody. The mere thinking of such end of life restrains the couple from taking any positive step towards earning a livelihood in unknown foreign land. They, therefore, prefer to stay back in the ancestral homeland determined to face any situation that may come to them. Even today when an air of change is sweeping over the country, tribal way of thinking still persists.

The economic life of the Mundas is an intricate structure and organization of socio-economic and ritual process set against the ecological environment which is the result of their ingenuity in human resource organization and management, distribution and utilization of wealth, developing thereby complex socio-economic and political institutions, beliefs and values. It is in economic pursuit of the Mundas that we get the total picture of the economic man which exposes his achievement in arts and crafts, science and technology, philosophy and world-views and socio-political institutions in relation to the environment. The economic image of Munda man is, however, relative and cannot be perceived only through his works and product alone. His sense of perception of the total situation in which he is placed and the ways of communication of the contents and the resultant behaviour pattern of the individuals, all make to form the social, political and ritual reality which are recorded through songs.

Organization of Production Relations

Mundas are the settled agriculturists practising monsoon cultivation by harnessing the cattle energy through simple technology of plough. They are totally dependent on rain water for cropping. Besides the main crops of rice and millets, a variety of grains, pulses, tubers and vegetables besides some commercial crops like lac and cocoon, etc, are also produced. As the Mundas are dependent on rains for cultivation of crops which generally begins in the middle of June every year and intermittently continues till April, a thorough knowledge of weather and climate is essential to get the desired yield from the land. The monsoon is often late or early and this affects the planning of work of the individuals. Heavy and scanty rainfall also very much affects the production of crops. Sometimes unprecedented hailstorm, blight as well as drought washes out all hopes of the individual of getting a good yield from the crops. Thus, all his toil and labour may go waste.He should be physically as well as mentally ready to face such a situation. A cultivator must know the weather and climatic conditions, the nature and quality of each crop, the quality of land and also the quantity of water it requires for growth. The movement of insects and birds is also to be carefully watched.

A cultivator must be fully aware of the land management system under his possession, for the land of the Munda country is relatively infertile, particularly the uplands. There is marked difference in the elevation of land, its slopes, soil texture and moisture and content of humus from area to area. Rice is a crop of the heavy soil of the clayey lowland able to retain moisture for a longer duration. The rice lands are invariably terraced and the upper terraced lands are given to autumn paddy, the lower ones being reserved for winter paddy. Due to sloping, the upper layer of the soil is washed away during every monsoon and so, manuring is essential to maintain the fertility of the lands. The main suppliers of manures to the Mundas are the cattle heads. Green manuring is not the regular practice of the Mundas but wherever possible, they adopt this method of manuring also. Per acre yield, therefore, varies from land to land and crop to crop.

In agricultural operations, besides considering nature of each crop and physical features of the land, the Mundas also take into account the climatic environment. The crop yield, is thus, a contingent affair. Besides the adoption of various practical methods to protect the crops, the Mundas also ensure the yield through the practice of magic and ritual performances.

The Mundas closely study the symbol of nature and its events. Prediction of many events as well as weather condition can be had from the activities of animals, birds and insects. For instance, the start of monsoon can be detected much earlier by seeing the insects carrying their eggs from one place to another. This insect is known as *Bhalu-mui* by the Mundas. Also the crying of the water bird during night time, its closeness or distances from the earth, as well as number of cries as well as the croaks of toads etc, are sure signals of the nearness of the monsoon. Similarly, the circle formed around the moon during night from the clouds is a clear indication of early or late rainfall. Early falling of dewdrops and slant and parallel form of spider's net on the grass tops are also an indication of withdrawal or continuity of the monsoon. Water level below the earth can be easily detected by analysing the soil brought out by ants.

In fishing expedition, the presence and absence of fish in the pool or on rolling water can be detected by observing the soil and stone submerged under water or by simply studying the water colour. The depth of the pool can be fathomed by dropping a small pebble in the water and the sound so produced is analysed.

In hunting expedition, identity as well as presence and absence of animals and birds in a particular area or locality is analysed through their footprints, excrement, hair, feathers and sound of cry.

Similarly, when one is out in the collection activities and gathering of medicines and mushrooms, etc, he or she is guided by some signs particular to that species.

All such techniques and knowledge are learnt and acquired

through practice and guidance by others who have already acquired such skills. And the scientific tempers of the like are developed in consonance of the cultural tradition of the people. These are but few instances of how people maximize their resources, energy and time in course of their economic activities in agricultural pursuits, hunting, fishing and gathering, etc.

The Munda economy have considerably been influenced by the immigrants since the last hundred years or so who made inroads in the tribal region from time to time. There are three phases of immigration in the tribal region. The first phase is marked by the moving in of a number of occupational and servicing communities, other than the tribals, who settled down in the tribal villages. There developed a functional relationship of mutual interest of coexistence with these communities which was very harmonious and cordial. They brought with them their own cultural traditions and values and continue to maintain it in the area of their new habitat. As these communities were occupationally skilled the Mundas were economically much benefited. They also brought with them the calendar of months and days which the tribals adopted regularizing their sequence of time and its conception.

In the second phase, there came hordes of business and trading communities who were educationally and economically far advanced than the first immigrants. They brought with them new materials into the Munda region and were closely associated with the feudal system. With them a new economic institution and values were introduced in the region. The most important features of this phase was in the area of human social relations. The immigrants, though belonged to different communities among themselves, they shared the same values and attitudes which put them together in a quite opposite position in relation to the Mundas. These people were highly conscious of their socio-religious status and asserted their superiority as such. In behaviour pattern too, they were opposite to that of the tribals. They were shrewd, cunning and clever. Their only aim was how early one could amass wealth and exhort others and usurp their property. Human kindness and mercy was totally absent in them. There begain a sharp deterioration in the socio-economic condition of the tribal people. The ethno-history of the tribal records this inhuman situation as well as the revolution they undertook to redeem themselves against such treacherous people in their songs.

The third phase which began just after the independence, brought a complete different set of people. To manage and run the new administrative set-up, development projects and programmes, factories, industries, mines and other institutions, thousands of government servants and workers were deputed from the north Bihar or were appointed starting from the peon and chowkidars to the most senior government officers, they were followed by countless job seekers. And as the statistics now indicate the native tribals were outnumbered relegating them to a minority. Further, the tribals have been constantly deprived of their lands and forests and other natural resources despite the enactment of laws to its protection which has left them in perpetual poverty.

The government is more interested in implementing the policy of integration of tribal people in the national mainstream, and is very unsympathetic towards the tribals as the existing situation of the tribal people has amply proved. The laws meant for the protection of the tribal people, the schemes and programmes meant for their upliftment and development, have been proved today as instruments of exploitation and plunder. Tribals have been reduced to, stream of labour class of people or beggars. These situations have been recorded by the Mundas in their songs.

Economic Organization and Management

The household is the basic unit of economic organization which operates at the family level. It has been shaped to the best fulfilment of the family needs. Its productive functions are organically linked with the totality of its economics, society and cultural functions. The management pattern affects the family cohesion and the patriarchal model of relations between members which hampers individualization of attitudes. Ownership of resources rests on the family, though for political reasons it may be recorded either in the name of one person or more. Economic production is the result of cooperative efforts of the members of the family and on the basis of age and sex, everyone has its role and duty in the overall economic operation and management. The household or the family is the primary institution for the education and training of the younger generation in all aspects of economic operations, techniques and technology, physical and environmental sciences and ideological concepts. In other words, the household not only certifies the continuity of traditional knowledge, skills and values, but also retains technologies and other material objects useful to the existing condition as well as examines and adopts new technologies and products for improvement in the existing economy. These include above all, the compact and highly expressive linguistic formulae often put into songs, riddles and proverbs which contain meteorological information, facts about climate, information relating to agricultural farming and animal husbandry and diseases and medicines associated with it, magic formulae, moral and practical instructions as well as the whole realms of experience forming what is popularly known as 'wise sayings'.

The economic role of the lineage members among the Mundas has a great significance. The land normally belongs to the lineage as a whole. Every family or the member has the right to cultivate one's portion of land and enjoy its crops but he has no right to transfer it permanently to any person outside his lineage. Preservation of ancestral property for the descendants is one of the main obligation of the lineage. What the family cannot do in normal course, is done by the members of the lineage as their duty and not as their voluntary work. The lineage people assist each other in all types of social and economic activities in agricultural operation from preparation of fields for cultivation of crops in sowing, weeding, harvesting, threshing and storing, in construction of houses, wells, etc. The other feature of the lineage system is the sharing of material products, technologies and other resources such as foodstuff, portion of land, cattle wealth and money. Every family of the lineage comes forward to help each other in the hours of emergency like famine, shortage of food, etc. Old and handicapped persons are given special care by the lineage irrespective of their belongingness to the family. Children get training and guidance from the lineage members in all aspects of life activities, ideologies and values.

An individual's economic, social and political interests are, thus, secured in the lineage, lineage as a corporate body preserves, distributes, settles disputes, takes decisions in the matters of mutual interests and interacts with other lineages in the village.

The village as a conglomeration of lineages along with

neighbouring villages, play a vital role in the socio-economic and political matters in preservation of peace and harmony among its members. The various lineages within the territorial jurisdiction of the village, function for the preservation and continuity of socio-cultural traditions. The social relationship of the lineages is based on mutual help, cooperation and coexistence. Certain portions of the natural resources are set aside in the village for common use such as forest, rivers, lakes, groves, pastures, etc. Some economic activities such as hunting and fishing are jointly carried out by the lineages of the village and sometimes in cooperation with neighbouring villages also. The village sacred centres such as common graveyard and sacred groves such as *sarnas* and lakes and fairs and festivals emotionally hold up the lineages of the village.

Besides the above, the village is a big platform for social interactions where informal as well as formal gathering take place regularly, where gossipping to serious matters are discussed. The holding of such gatherings normally takes place either in the house, community hall or at public places like *akhra*, at the place of work or at places of ceremonies or while in journey, market places and fairs, etc. Such contacts and gatherings provide opportunities for the renewal of relationships and exchange of views and sharing of experiences of matters of mutual concerns. The subject matter of gossips or conversation often range from local events and household and community affairs as well as news from the wide world. Numerous tales, riddles, proverbs with legendary, mystical and magico-religious character are also talked at such occasions. Their subjects centre around various figures belonging to the world of popular demonology spirits of the dead ghosts and devils, tales of good as well as malicious kings, queens, persons and animals, etc. It contains many practical hints on how to protect oneself from evil forces or how to implicate them. They also have ethical and moral lessons, stressing the point on reward for good deeds and punishment for the wrongs. There are also indications of events and experiences under different situations which the Mundas in general encounter in real life situations which reflect deep emotions, desires, attitudes and values. They also provide information on economic processes, geographical and cosmological environments and nature and character of various floras and biological species.

Life in Nature

Munda being basically agriculturists, live in the lap of nature. For them, nature is animate as well as inanimate. As inanimate, it is a source of life and as animate it is a friend and companion whose actions and reactions are shared throughout the life.

Besides cultivation of crops, Munda supplement their economy by gathering, fishing and hunting and of late through services and lending out their labour. It is during these economic pursuits that they come into close interaction with nature. The observation made and experience gained and communicated through the form of songs, is the total perception and conception of the people about the nature. The ideas and conception about the nature have been made at the level of their culture which reflects the degree of culture conditioning and its internalization by individual members. As the culture conditioning differs from individual to individual and the experience too, its expression on the subject are of varied forms.

Collection and Gathering

Collecting as an activity is not a pastime or leisure but is a part of the total economic activity of the people. We get few songs on this aspect of activity which gives a total picture of its environment under which the collection activity is in process.

Just after the spring, during summer, a variety of fruits ripen. These fruits are usually collected by young boys and girls. The collection of fruits are made while they are out in the fields and forest in pursuits of their normal work. In the song below which belongs to Jadur category, it is stated that much time was devoted in the collection of mango and pear, the trees which stand beyond the river away from the settlement. The lines of the song are as follows:

1. *Nai ko parom re, sinduri uli do*
Vermilion coloured mango fruits beyond the river
Gaṛa ko parom re, kajor baṛi do
Banyan fruits in black beyond the ravines

2. *Huduma-huduma te, siṇgi doe ḍubui jana*

The sun set down while throwing pebbles on it
Lebeda-lebeda te, Chaṇḍu ape muli jana
The moon arose while throwing sticks on it

The mango fruits beyond the river have ripened. Its colour is red like vermilion and hence the name of the fruit *sinduri uli*. In another case, banyan fruits beyond the ravines have also ripened, giving the fruits deep blue or black colour. The beauty of the fruits has attracted everyone's attention. The trees are tall and the fruits cannot be easily approachable. The composer of the song describes the location of the fruit trees, beauty of the ripened fruits and the time devoted to collect the same. The composer states that after crossing the river and ravines, he came to the tree. As the tree was tall and located on sloping hill and on the ravine, he could not climb the tree and went on pelting stones and tree branches on the fruits. As he could not stand properly due to sloping and ravine, he could not hit the fruits directly many a time. Nevertheless, he was not disheartened and continued his attempt. He was so busy in throwing the stones or sticks on the fruits that he totally forgot to see the sun which has already set down beyond the mountains and the moon has appeared on the sky. Though the collection was meagre, the experience was memorable which is conveyed through the song.

The following song too, which also belongs to Jadur category, relates to the scene of fruit collection. The lines of the song are as follows:

1. *Ber pake, pipa̤r pake*
   When bair and pipar fruits ripen
   Dhaṇgoṛi ririyaela
   Damsels run about merrily
   Girae debe salue suga
   Drop down, O parrots
   Achera me jhokaela
   Collect the same on dressing cloth

2. *Daṇg lele, tuṇki lele*
   Carrying pole and baskets
   Dhaṇgoṛi ririyaela
   Damsels run about merrily

Girae debe salu suga
Drop down, O parrots
Achera me jhokaela
Collect the same on dressing cloth

The composer of this song observes that when *Ber* and *Pipar* fruits ripen, girls carrying poles and baskets go out in groups for its collection merrily. Through poles they strike down the fruits and collect in the baskets or on the cloth's borders of their dress. They also collect the fruits which are dropped by parrots. So the season when the fruits ripen, is the occasion of merriment and joy for children and birds alike.

The song below also relates to collection of fruits which mentions how friends help each other in the collection activity. The song belongs to Jadur category and the lines are as follows:

1. *Ḍal Baṛi, dal Baṛi*
   Banyan fruits hang on every branch
   Baṛi re gatim uyugaiṇg me
   Drop it for me, O friend dear

2. *Sereṇg regim uyugaiṇg redo*
   If you drop it on the rock
   Sereṇg, sereṇg sowana
   It may smell like rock

3. *Gitil rem nosoraiṇg redo*
   If you drop it on the sand
   Gitil, gitil re siṛinja
   Its odour will be like sand

One of the friends, as mentioned, is on the tree and other stays on the ground below as he is unable to climb it. The friend, who is down below, requests his other friend on the tree indirectly that he should not drop the fruits on the ground for it may either fall on the rock or on the sand as in either case the fruit may give out its odour on the object it has fallen on. The taste of the fruit may, thus, be spoiled. This is a lesson for others.

In the song below it is mentioned that a person is desperately in need of fruits but there is nobody except the birds. The song belongs to Jadur category and the lines are as follows:

1. *Dato kauwa, hora ra jojo hesa*
   Let, me have the sour Hesa fruits, O crow
   Dato kauwa metạm uyugaing me
   Drop it for me, I request you, O crow
   Dato kauwa hora ra rol bari
   Let me have banyan fruits of the way side, O crow
   Dato kauwa metạm nosoraing me
   Bring it down for me I request you, O crow

2. *Dato kauwa metạm reṇgej teiṇg nobor baṛan tan*
   I am rolling due to hunger, O crow
   Dato kauwa metạm uyugaiṇg me
   Drop it for me I request you
   Dato kauwa tetaṇg teiṇg taver baṛan tan
   I am crawling due to thirst, O crow
   Dato kauwa metạm nosoraiṇg me
   Bring it down for me, O crow

It is summer time and the composer of this song is out on a journey. He is exhausted completely due to hunger and thirst. He could not even reach the nearby village and took rest under a *jojo Hesa* or banyan tree which stood on the wayside. The tree was laden with fruits and were ripening. A variety of birds were on the tree enjoying the fruits. The composer was so tired that he lay under the shade of the tree and could not move though he was feeling hungry and thirsty. He satisfied himself by eating few fruits which were dropped by birds. There was no wayout for him but to request the birds to drop more fruits.

This was the personal experience of the composer and anybody can have such experience. The feeling of hunger and thirst is so intense that it makes the body weak and feeble. It is due to such experience that Mundas have developed and internalized the values of kiṇdness, fellow feelings and generosity towards everybody and extend warm hospitality to the needy and helpless.

Below is another song belonging to Jadur category which relates to gathering of fruits. The lines are as follows:

1. *Dadaya buru Tiril*
   The hill Tiril, brother

Dadaya rukuwalaṇg me
Shake off for us, brother
Dadaya Beṛa Tarob
The valley Tarob, brother
Dadaya daṇgsiyalaṇg me
Trample it down for us, brother

2. *Reṇge tan tetaṇg tan re*
During hunger and thirst
Dadaya rukuwalaṇg me
Shake off for us, brother
Jeṭe lolo, hoyo gama re
During summer heat and stormy rains
Dadaya daṇsiyalaṇg me
Trample it down for us, brother

In this song, young boy or girl request the elder brother to help him or her in getting some fruits of *Tiril* and *Tarob*—the two well-known wild fruit trees of the forest in Chhotanagpur plateau. It is late summer and the children are out in the forest in search of the fruits. It is at this period of the summer month that these fruits ripen. The children are hungry and rēquest the elder brother to get *Tiril* and *Tarob* fruits for them.

The songs here provide us valuable ethnographic information which is generally missed even by experienced enthnographers. They tell about the season when various kinds of fruits are available in Chhotanagpur forest, geography and environmental condition of the region, location and availability of fruit trees, its methods and means of collection, methods of identification of ripe and unripe fruits, care to be taken during collection, how people cooperate in collection activity, intensity of hunger and thirst when out in the forest, sharing the joy with animals and birds while eating fruits, etc. And last of all, sharing of the knowledge and experience and imparting training to youngsters to help continuity of the culture.

One of the most important tree that is abundantly available in the forest, is the *madukam*. Its flowers and fruits as well as seeds are of immense use to the tribal people of Chhotanagpur. The song below which belongs to Bala category of songs relates to the collection of this flower. The lines of the song run as follows:

Chhoṭe-mote toṇgori
Upon the small hillock
Jhali-jabâr mahua
Stands a gigantic *mahua* tree
Hare mahua bichhauya ke ketai maya lage-2
Alas, the collectors of *mahua* feel piety
Mahua sirai gel
Mahua flower is not more available
Hare dori aisạn jori kahaṇ pabe-2
Alas, better companion than *mahua* fruit will be available nowhere

The interpretation of this song can be offered by two ways: (a) objectively, and (b) implicitly. Seen from its objective angle, the gigantic *mahua* tree is standing on a small hillock. The tree is laden with *mahua* flowers. The composer of the song feels piety for the hillock upon which the gigantic tree stands almost covering the whole hillock and that too laden with flowers. The hillock, though small supports the gigantic tree on its bosom and so deserves compassion.

In the song, the meaning is implicit. It is to be noted that the song is sung during the marriage ceremony. The *mahua* tree, among the Mundas, symbolizes fertility, prosperity and wealth. It is why the Mundas during marriage, pitch a branch of *mahua* tree at the middle of the canopy erected for the shelter of the marriage party where marriage ceremony is performed. The flowers symbolize the bride, the collectors of the flowers to that of bridegroom's relatives who have come in the marriage party to take away the bride with them, the hillock symbolizes the bride's parents who look very small in the august gathering of the marriage party who will soon be left with fruits only, that is, the bridegroom when the flower, that is, the daughter will be taken away. At the falling down of flower the relationship is broken with the tree and when it is collected the relationship is broken from the house or hillock as in the song. The relationship of flower and fruit is eternal and so the married couple.

How the *mahua* flowers drop and how these are collected, has been described in the following Bala category of song. The lines of the song are as follows:

Mahua je girae
The *mahua* flowers fall
Ṭipake-ṭipa̱ke mahua girae
Fall one by one
Hare rate bichhae jane-kane
It is collected by all during the night
Dine bichhae mahua mauwar
The owner of the tree collects it during the day
Hare ṭipake-ṭipake mahua girae
Fall one by one

There are two kinds of *mahua* trees—the flowers of one kind fall during the day time (either in the morning, noon or evening time) and the other, during the night. The flowers fall one by one constantly for two to three hours. Generally, *mahua* trees are owned privately except the trees that are found in public forests. Families where the number of members is small and who have good number of trees, all the flowers cannot be collected during the night, it is during the day time that they are able to collect. So flowers that fall during the night time are generally collected by the public. It is common scene during the flowering season of the *mahua* that people with baskets are seen guarding flowers under the trees from animals and birds. The composer of this song has made two important points worth noting, firstly, that *mahua* flowers fall for a fixed period and for an appointed time only and the other, thạt the flowers that fall during the night, are collected by the public.

Firewood and green leaves for making leaf cups are regularly collected by the villagers. Below is a song belonging to the Jadur category which describes as to how the ladies are returning from the forest after collecting the above-mentioned materials. The lines of the song are as follows:

1. *Saha̱n china̱m dupila̱n*
Are you carrying firewood, mother
Seta̱m satuga̱n
Being followed by a dog
Saka̱m china̱m hatara̱n
Are you carrying green leaves on your back, mother

Pusim hataṛan
Carrying a cat on your back

1. *Iṇyaṛi goṛe, bapaṛi goṛe*
Neither during the time of mother or father
Sahaṇ chinaṃ dupilaṇ
Are you carrying firewood mother
Setaṃ sutugaṇ
Being followed by a dog
Iṇyaṛi goṛe, bapaṛi goṛe
Neither during the time of mother or father
Sakaṃ chinaṃ hataraṇ
Are you carrying green leaves on your back, mother
Pusim hataraṇ
Carrying a cat on your back

A woman depending on her age, is generally addressed as mother by the children belonging to the younger generation. She is returning from the forest loaded with a bundle of firewood and leaves and is carrying a cat along with the leaves on her back, followed by a dog. These two pets are her good companions, on the way and in the forest. This scene is extraordinary for the composer of this song. In this song we do not get the description of difficulties in firewood collection, such as covering ups and down of the hills, loneliness in the forest, hunger and thirst and load carrying difficulties etc. But the composer was simply fascinated by the scene that presents her auntie, the so-called mother on her way back home. The pets have followed her to the forest. The cat could not travel the long path like the dog, so she carried her on her back along with the leaves. This scene has been made memorable by composing the song as cited above.

Another song which relates to firewood collection but with different themes is given as follows. The song belongs to Bala category and the lines are as follows:

Gaṛa gena pasaṇgi
Log of firewood by the ravine
Gaṛa gena pasaṇgi ge nayo
Log of firewood by the ravine, mother

Dhuṇgiya-dhuṇgiya nuṛi gela re
Emitting heavy smoke
Dhuṇgiya-dhuṇgiya naṇgor bhela re
While emitting smoke, it caught the flame
Baba khojal pasaṇgi
The log collected by the father
Nayo khojal pasaṇgi ge nayo
The log collected by the mother, O mother
Dhuṇgiya-dhuṇgiya nuṛi gela re
Emitting heavy smoke
Dhuṇgia-dhuṇgia naṇgor bhela re
While emitting smoke, it caught fire

The song indirectly indicates the season when the marriage is mostly celebrated by the Mundas. It is winter and fire is burning to warm up the guests. They are singing and it is during this occasion that they composed the song about the fire that is burning. There arose heavy smoke in the beginning but slowly it caught fire and emitting of smoke stopped. The singers presume that the log of wood must have been collected by the mother or father of the bride from the ravine.

Below is another song which also belongs to Bala category and relates to collection of firewood of shrubs variety and also describes the scene as to how the guest of the marriage party are sleeping by the side of the fire peacefully. The lines of the song are as follows:

Khojalaiṇ jaṭa-jori re
Collected twigs and shrubs
Joralaiṇ pasaṇgi samạn-2
Burned it like log
Khojalaiṇ jaṭa-jori
Collected twigs and shrubs
Joralaiṇ pasaṇgi samạn-2
Burned it like log
Sutalaiṇ kukura samạn-2
Slept the dog's way

It is stated that the marriage party collected dried up twigs and shrubs themselves to warm up. There is no arrangement of fire to warm up the guests from the side of the host party. It is winter but the members of the marriage party have not brought sufficient clothes to cover them. Anyhow the guests themselves collected some twigs and shrubs and set fire to it. It burned like a log of wood. The guests warmed themselves up and most of them lay down by the side of the bonfire and slept. The composer of the song states that they slept like dogs as they huddled themselves up together, The trouble and joy experienced during marriage and community gatherings cannot be easily communicated through language. But such experiences for future undertakings are recorded in songs as a precaution and young boys and girls are advised to carry enough clothes.

The collection of toothbrush twigs is also as essential as that of firewoods and green leaves. The Mundas do collection of toothbrush twigs from trees of *sarjom, neem, koronjo, bindi,* and sometimes from *putus* shrubs and mango trees but most important is *sarjom.* Below is a song belonging to Dubung category which mentions the toothbrush collection. The lines of the song are as follows:

> *Kone bone datuna toralaiṇ re, datuna toralaiṇ*
> In which forest they collected toothbrush
> *Bija bone*
> In Bija forest
> *Datuna toralaiṇ re, datuna toralaiṇ*
> Collected toothbrush

When toothbrush is collected from forest, it is done from *sarjom* tree. The toothbrush, as stated in this song are being collected from *Bijabon* forest. The song also indicates that collection is going on *en masse.* This is how in every activity, the Munda do cooperate.

Leaf Vegetable Collection

In the Munda region, various kinds of roots, creepers, flowers, fruits and leafy vegetables are abundantly available. While some are cultivated by the Mundas themselves, others grow wildly. These are all seasonal. It is why some are preserved for odd periods when they are not available. In the latter case, the vegetable is first half boiled and then it is spread for drying. As for cooking of vegetables, we have a number of songs. The song below which belongs to Bala category mentions the collection of vegetables. The lines of the song are as follows:

Nadi kinare silimari sag
By the banks of the river, grow *silimari* vegetable
Jato beṭi re torio lanbe
Daughter dear, go and bring it collecting
Nadi kinare koenara sag
By the banks of the river, grow *koenara* vegetable
Jato beṭi re torio lanbe
Daughter dear, go and bring it collecting

Silmari is a grass vegetable and grows at the place where moisture remains on the soil throughout the year. *Koenara*, on the other hand, is a tree plant whose tender leaf is taken as vegetable. *Koenara* is planted by the people for the sake of vegetable. Collection of vegetable is usually done by the females. In this song a daughter, may be the newly wed bride, is asked by the mother to collect *silmari* and *koenara* vegetables from the banks of the river.

Below are few songs of Jadur category which relate to the collection of various kinds of vegetables. The song describes the identity, place of availability and methods of collection of each vegetable. The lines of one of the songs are as follows:

1. *Chikan̺ ara: gom side kena*
What vegetable did you pluck, O girl
Tereṇg kaṭa go losodan̺ gi
Leg yours have spotted with soil
Chikan̺ ḍaṛi gom da: au kena
From which brook did you collect water, O girl
Suba sunupid ba chuṭi reyaṛan gi
The roots of the hair-knot and tip of flower yours are wet

2. *Muchri ara: gom side kena*
You plucked muchri vegetable, O girl
Tereṇg kata go losodan̺ gi
Leg yours have spotted with soil
Buchi ḍaṛi gom da: au kena

You collected water from broken brook, dear
Suba sunupid ba chuṭi reyaṛan gi
The roots of the hair-knot and tip of flower yours are wet

Muchri vegetable grows on marshy land and on shallow pool of water. It is why the legs of the collector of this vegetable become soiled and wet. Similarly, when someone collects water from broken brook, the sign of dampness is visible on the hair-knot as well as on the flower pitched on it. This song is in the form of conversation between two girls who meet during the day. It is in this way the information are disseminated among the people.

The song below which belongs to the Jadur category, also mentions the availability of a particular species of vegetable and its method of collection. The lines of the song are as follows:

1. *Buru re buru re mani do*
   Hills after hills, *mani* plant has grown
   Beṛa re beṛa re rai
   And valley after valley, the *rai* plant
   Chuṭi reko sideya mani do
   Mani plant is plucked by the top
   Suba reko chagaṛe rai
   Rai is splitted plucked by the bottom

2. *Chuṭi soben goso jạn mani do*
   Top of the *mani* plant have withered away
   Suba soben lamạ jạn rai
   The *rai* plant have been splitted down to the bottom

In the song below, reference of another variety of vegetable plant has been made mentioning the method of its collection. 'Leper ara' and 'Sirgiti' are leafy vegetable plants which grow on the pit of the garbage. The lines of the song belonging to Dubung category are as follows:

1. *Dubi rechi madi re najina*
   It is on the cowdung or garbage pit, sister
   Dubi sirgiṭi do najina

The *sirgiti* of the cowdung pit, sister
Maiṇd leper aṛa: do
The *leper ara* of the garbage

2. *Dubi sirgiṭi do najina*
The *sirgiti* of the cowdung pit, sister
Leyona-leyona, najina
Has grown straight, sister
Maiṇd leper aṛa: do
The *leper ara* of the garbage pit

3. *Dubi sirgiṭi do najina*
The *sirgiti* of the cowdung pit sister
Jokona-jokona, najina
Has grown with thick dense leaves, sister
Maiṇd leper aṛa: do
The *leper ara* of the garbage pit

4. *Chuṭi reko sideya najina*
It is plucked by the top, sister
Dubi sirgiti do najina
The *sirgiti* of the cowdung pit, sister
Suba reko chagareya najina
It is splitted broken by the bottom, sister
Maiṇd leper aṛa: do
The *leper ara* of the garbage

5. *Chuṭi soben goso jạn najina*
Top of the plant withered away, sister
Dubi sirgiṭi do najina
The *sirgiti* of the cowdung pit sister
Suba soben lamạ jạn najina
The plant was splitted down to the bottom, sister
Maiṇd leper aṛa: do
The *leper ara* of the garbage pit

While the mustard seeds are sown upland, on hills and valleys, the *sirgiti* and *leper* ara vegetable leaves grow widely on open fields and kitchen gardens. The *sirgiti* and *leper* ara are also available on dried up cowdung pits and on garbage pits. The plucking of these vegetables are done with the help of fingers and only the upper or tender portion of the plant is plucked. The instruction as outlined in this song is for the novice who do not know how to pluck and collect the vegetable. While collecting grass vegetables, the Munda never uproot the plant but only they collect its tender portion. It is observed that non-tribal communities, generally uproot the plant while collecting, thereby destroying the very species of the plant. It is why many species from the tribal region have vanished because of such wrong methods of collection. The Munda strongly oppose such methods of collection.

Fetching of Drinking Water

The daily activity of the Munda womenfolk usually start with the cleaning of the sleeping and sitting rooms, kitchen, cowdung shed, courtyards and surroundings. The next step is the cleaning of the household utensils by taking them either to the well or the brook. Fetching of drinking water is most essential before taking up the job of cooking of food for the day or going out to the field. All these works take up much of the time but the womenfolk usually get up early in the morning and complete the job before the sunrise. While attending these works, many problems crop up and interesting events take place. As a precaution, the following Lahsua song advises the girls not to go to the brook in a hurry otherwise the earthen pitchers may break down:

1. *Dhire jabe pani lane*
   Go slowly to fetch water
   Thes lagal fuṭe tor gagari mai
   Or else, pot yours may break with the stumbling of feet, girl
   Dhire jabe pani lane
   Go slowly to fetch water

2. *Muṛe upre binḍa*
   Pitcher's pad rests on the head
   Binḍa upre gagari
   The pitcher rests on the pad

Thes lagal fuṭe tor gagari mai
Or else, pot yours may break with the stumbling of feet, girl
Dhire jabe pani lane
Go slowly to fetch water

In this song, the girl is advised not to go hurriedly to fetch water otherwise the pot may break with one tumble. The other thing to remember is to place the pad on the head properly so that pot may be placed on it upright and safe. A pad is placed on the head to keep the pot intact on its place and also to protect the head from getting hurt. The pads are prepared by the womenfolk themselves from straws, grass and with fine bamboo splits. They pass this knowledge to their children as a part of cultural continuity.

The following song, belonging to Lahsua category mentions the conversation of two sisters who are planning to go to the brook to fetch water:

1. *Nai gitil ruguṛi sud*
The pebbles made brook on the river sand
Da: nau going sen kena
I had been to fetch water
Hore, bucha chaṭu dupil kete dolaṅg
Let us proceed to fetch water carrying broken neck pot
Dolaṅg daigo da: nau te dolaṅg
Let us go to fetch water, sister dear

2. *Bo: redo binḍa mena*
There is pad on the head
Binḍa redo bucha chaṭu
The broken neck pot rests on the pad
Hore, bucha chaṭu dupil kete dolaṅg
Let us proceed to fetch water carrying broken neck pot
Dolaṅg daigo da: nau te dolaṅg
Let us go to fetch water, sister dear

In this song four notable points have been made, (a) the location of the brook, (b) the broken neck pot, (c) companionship while fetching water, and (d) technique of keeping pot on the head.

As stated in the song, the location of the brook is on the river bed and is far away from the main settlement of the village. It thus takes much time of the ladies and they have to take into this time factor for they have to attend other jobs also. The reference of broken neck pot has importance in this context for it may create inconvenience in the speed of work to be completed.

The Munda carry load on their heads. While carrying load, a pad is always placed in-between the load and head. The young girls are taught as to how a pad is placed on the head and the load on it.

In this song, the elder sister asks her younger sister to accompany her in fetching of water from the brook located on the river bed. The neck of the pot is broken. The young girls usually do not like to carry water in broken neck pot. The elder sister however, requests her to take the broken neck pot and details her as to how to place it on the head to avoid dripping down of water.

In the song below which belongs to Jadur category, other kinds of problems have been mentioned, the lines of the song are as follows:

1. *E'maina Gangi Jauni*
O girl, Gangi and Jauni
Hasa chaṭu guli tana
Earthen pot is rolling away
E'maina Gangi Jauni
O girl, Gangi and Jauni
Sutạm binḍa guli tana
The thread pad is rolling away

2. *E'maina gatim mena re*
O girl, you have companions
Gatim ko sabe ruaṛe
Companion may hold it back
E'maina sangame mena re
O girl, you have friends
Sangame ko chapu ruaṛe
Friends may pull back

The girl has gone to fetch water where accident occurred when pot and pad went on rolling away because of undulating nature of topography. She is asking help from the girls by the name of Gangi and Jauni. The girls express their inability and tell her that if she would have friends, the accident would not have happened. In fine, during odd hours, friends always stand for each other.

Similar to the above other variety of inconveniences may occur while fetching water. In the song below which belongs to Racha category mention of an accident have been made. The lines of the song are as follows:

Eṭa paṭal kuṇwaṇ re
The brick walled well
Jhamaki-jhamaki pani pajharae
Water in stream shooting out
Daṇg-yo tuṭi gel
The pole too broke
Basanayo fuṭi gel
The earthen pot too broke
Pani bharal rani beṭi kandate awae re
The water fetching princess is returning weeping

The song describes how a water fetching girl met her accident in which she lost her earthen pot when the pole which broke hit it, while falling down. The song mentions the brick walled well which is found in urban areas only. In rural areas, the Mundas make stone walled well only.

Accident of serious nature may also occur while collecting water from wells or brooks, etc. The song below which belongs to Bala category, has reference of such accident. The lines of the song are as follows:

Chhoṭi moṭi chhokṛi pani lane jae re
A small sturdy girl went to collect water
Giri gela re beṭi ḍubiyo gela re-2
She slipped and drowned
Gurguṛia chuṇwaṇ niramala pani
In the narrow brook with crystal clear water
Hare sona aisaṇ beṭi ḍubiyo gela re-2
Alas, the only daughter like a gold was drowned

Drinking water, as stated above is collected from brook, spring and well. *Chunwan* or *sud* is a narrow mouthed well which is constructed on a perennial spring. Its depth varies from four to five feet only. The water generally flows out from such well. As the water is easily reached, small children, who usually accompany the elders, are allowed to collect it. But sometimes they go alone unnoticed by the elders. The girl, as stated in the song may have gone out alone to the well and so the accident took place. This song is a sort of warning to the small children.

So, it is in the collection of drinking water that much time of the ladies is lost. Below is a song belonging to Racha category in which a girl requests her elder brother to dig up a well close to the house to save time:

Aṇgena me dada kuṇwaṇ koṛi le
Dig up a well at the courtyard brother
Dada pani baṛa dur
Water we bring from a distant location, brother
Dada re kuṇwaṇ koṛailo
The brother dug up a well
Bhauji re pani bharailo
And sister-in-law is using it

As it is the girls who generally attend all household duties, they are straightforward in pointing out any inconvenience that they face while carrying out their jobs. In the present song the girl points out the difficulties of the distant location of the brook or spring and requests to dig up a well in the courtyard. At her request, a well was dug up in the courtyard but before its completion, she got married to a distant village. The brother also got married in due course, and it is the sister-in-law now who is the beneficiary of the facility. The well was dug up at the request of the sister but she could not use it. Now her sister-in-law does not have to go out for collecting water. The girl is envious of this. In her view it is not justified to enjoy the fruit at the cost of other's labour.

Hunting

Besides cultivation of crops, hunting and fishing activities are part of the food quest of the Mundas which has got its continuity since generations and has formed part of their total culture. The preliminary requisite for hunting expedition is the presence of forest for it is the home of wild animals and birds. Today dense forest are no more available in the Munda region except in a few patches and wherever it exists, it is under the control of the government where hunting is prohibited. With the depletion of forest community hunting is no more practised. This has changed the hunting culture of the Mundas. Some hundred years back the position was quite different when this was a regular practice among the community as well as individual. At the height of its importance, hunting had developed an interesting feature in its culture which is visible in (a) totemic clans, and (b) hunting by women called *Jani Sikar*. Almost all clans of the Mundas are totemic, that is, they derive their surnames from plants, animals and other natural objects. Killing and eating of totemic animals by clan members was socially prohibited. This custom of the people protected the species of plants, animals, birds and fish from wanton destruction and killings.

At one stage of the developmental history of Munda culture, hunting expedition became a prestigious activity. The females were normally debarred from taking part in the expedition because of physical hazards that it entails. Since hunting was a prestigious expedition and women were the constant companion of the males in all spheres of economic activity, they could not be excluded from this prestigious activity. The women, as the ethnohistory of the Munda tells, have shown their courage and valour in times of emergency when the males were totally helpless. It is to recognize their heroic deeds and with an objective to reward them suitably, the custom of hunting by women came into practice. Till this day, the tradition is followed with all pomp and gaiety by the womenfolk of the Jharkhand region which is celebrated once in 12 years.

Hunting is not an easy task as it appears superficially. A Munda learns hunting from the very childhood. The first lesson is the handling of hunting implements in which the main item is a bow and arrow and shooting practice. It is at this very age, they occasionally engage themselves in hunting of small birds and animals and learn many tricks and techniques. They also closely study the living environment of the birds and animals and their habits and receive knowledge and guidance from the elders in the technique of hunting as well as in making hunting implements.

During community hunting expeditions, Mundas take various precautionary measures and often take the help of supernatural forces. The songs that follow illustrate some of the hunting techniques, means and methods and experience gained during such expeditions.

The song below which belongs to Racha category mentions hunting of birds by a boy:

> *Ee gaon me eke goṭo bair gachh*
> Single strawberry tree stands in this village
> *Suraṇgi suga baisae*
> Beautiful parrot is sitting there
> *Deto ge nayo mor dhanu tira re*
> Mother, let me have my bow and arrow
> *Suraṇgi suga baisae*
> Beautiful parrot is sitting there

Parrots are hunted down by the tribals not for the sake of their meat but it is for their feathers which is used in making feather flowers for decoration on head during annual dance. The boy is asking for a bow and arrow to shoot down the beautiful parrot who is sitting on the only one strawberry tree of the village. Parrots usually come on such trees which have nuts in their fruits.

The song below too, which also belongs to Racha category of songs mentions the hunting of Tonyan and Baka birds. Tonyan is a multicoloured feathered bird having white, green and blue, while crane have all white colour. These birds are also hunted not for the sake of meat but it is for their feathers. The lines of the song are as follows:

1. *Icha jaṭa jamri jaṭa*
   Inside the bush of Icha and Jamri
   Toyaṇ kin goṛe lapa-luṛi
   A pair of Toyan birds are struggling
   Baka kin goṛe chapa-chuṛi
   A pair of cranes are running to and fro

2. *Lasa lire jura: lire*
   If caught through gum sticks

Kalega laṅg galaṅg teya
We shall weave feather ornament
Jatera laṅg fada teya
And decorate ourselves during *Jatra* dance
Seṅdera lang fada biduṛ teya
Use it during *Sendra* dance

The feathers of above mentioned birds are used for making decorative ornaments known as *kalga*. The feather ornaments, that is, *kalga* made from three different birds having three different colours—green, blue and crystal white when decorated during dance, receive much admiration from the masses for their beauty.

Hunting of birds are also done for the sake of meat. The following song belonging to Jadur category has theme on this, the lines of which are as follows:

1. *Jharia-jharia, bone-bone*
Beside the pools and in the forest
Noṛe giyae ṭuṭi ya
Does hunting of birds

2. *Noṛe ṭuṭi-ṭuṭi te*
While shooting birds
Ṭuṭi mail a̭m ade kedare
Lost his arrows
Hathowal doraṅg jan
The bow string too broke

The elders of the family generally dislike hunting all the time by their sons. The young boys often get reprimanded for being too much engrossed in hunting. In this song the young boy is taken to task for his whole day engagement in hunting. But sometimes they are encouraged too. Below is a song on this theme which belongs to Racha category of song:

1. *Ḍoḍri re Ḍoḍri re*
The Dodri bird
Ḍoḍria puta̭m doe rage tana-2
Ḍoḍria dove is singing

2. *Lasa lekai me koṛa*
Catch it through gum stick, O boy
Pase lekai me koṛa
Catch it by snaring, O boy
Ḍoḍria putạm doe rage tana-2
Dodria dove is singing

In the above song, the boy is asked to catch the bird either by snaring or through gum stick.

Besides using of bow and arrows in hunting, gum sticks, nets or snares or traps are also used as stated in the above song. In the song below too which belongs to Jadur category, birds catching through nets have been mentioned. The lines of the song are as follows:

1. *Patera re uṛala guṇḍaria*
Quails flew away from the heap of leaves
Hare guṇḍri, piṛi guṇḍri
The field quails

2. *Nane suta ker jal moe ganthaloṇ*
I weaved a net from fine threads
Bajhi gelaiṇ piṛi guṇḍri
The field quail was snared

The field quail is a partridge specy of bird and is generally found in bushes and in heaps of leaves. Its colour is grey or brown and cannot be easily visible for it mixes up with the colour of the surroundings. However, it is trapped with the help of a net specially prepared for the purpose. Traps are of different shapes and sizes and are made from different materials. As mentioned in the present song, the net has been made from fine thread to trap the *gundri* bird.

Similar to the song above, there is yet another song having double meaning which also belongs to Jadur category of song, the lines of which are as follows:

1. *Chetạn tola ḍaṛida: re putami,*
On the spring located in upper hamlet, O dove
Alom aṛgunaya putami
Don't come down there, O dove

Latar tola sud da: re paraelu,
On the spring located in lower hamlet, O pigeon
Alom nosoren
Don't alight

2. *Chetan tola Munda hon-e putami*
The son of the Munda in upper hamlet, O dove
Atae lasa tanaya, putami
Putting gum sticks, O dove
Latar tola Santa hon-e paraelu
The son of Santa of lower hamlet, O pigeon
Bale atam tan
Spreading eatables

3. *Munda hon-e Putami*
The son of Munda, O dove
Ata tam geya putami
May catch you through gum
Santa hon-e paraelu
The son of Santa, O pigeon
Bale kem ge
May ensnare you

The above song carries double meaning (a) objective, and (b) symbolic. The birds usually come down at the spring to drink water where the Munda and Santa boys are spreading up traps to catch them. In the latter case, the dove and *paraelu* symbolize the girls with whom the Munda and Santa boys are in love and both of them are waiting on spring, for the arrival of the lady love. The girl is cautioned about the plan of the boys.

As stated above, the young boys usually go out to catch birds. In the song below, which belongs to Baroya category, a boy is stated to be busy in placing his traps in the grove where birds regularly come. The lines of the song are as follows :

1. *Kahan se ale ti rio-rio re*
From where did you come, O flutist
Bagicha re lasa ropae
Putting gum sticks in the grove

2. *Purbe se ale ti rio-rio re*
   You came from the east O, flutist
   Bagicha re lasa ropae
   Putting gum sticks in the grove

Now deadly weapons such as firearms are used in hunting. Use of firearms in hunting began to be used during the days of the Mughals and it came to be used extensively during British rule. The song below which belongs to the Bala category describes hunting of birds with the help of gun which kills each and every bird. The lines of the song are as follows:

Gaṇga ko tira raja
By the side of the river Ganga, O king
Sara-hara, sara-hara bolae
The cries of sound is being heard
Nadi nara kuilo charai kinara me bolae
On the river and rivulets all around the birds cry
Sisa ka goli babu
The bullet of lead, O dear
Bindi-bichi, bindi-bichi sobe charai marae
Kills all the birds one by one
Nadi nara kuilo charai kinara suna bhela
There is no sound of chirping of birds on the banks of the river

The meaning of the song is quite clear. Once the river banks were resounding with chirping and cry of birds. But it is now desolate and deserted. There is an eerie silence in the atmosphere as no noise of the birds are being heard on the river banks. The composer-singer of the song laments over the situation created by men which has rendered the river banks in such a state from full of life to no life. And it is all due to inhuman attitude and reckless use of firearms by civilized men.

How a wild boar was killed with the help of gun, has been mentioned in the following song belonging to Lahsua category. The lines of the song are as follows :

1. *Kado saiṇ laṭapat, suari re baroyaṇ*
   The wild boar besmeared in clay

Ho, hore naho, suari chhoralaiṇ bijabon re
The boar may have come out from the Bijabon forest

2. *Ḳado saiṇ laṭapaṭ suari re baroyaṇ*
The wild boar besmeared in clay
Ho, hore naho, panjora me goli bambakae re
The bullet may have pierced the ribs

The wild boar was hit on the ribs when it was lying in the swamp but somehow escaped from the hunter's hand and came out towards the settlement. The composer has narrated the people's reaction on the plight of the wounded boar.

The song below describes how the big and dangerous animals were hunted down by the king and his men with the help of firearms. The lines of the song belonging to Jadur category are as follows:

1. *Machia baithalaiṇ maharaj*
A platform was erected by the emperor
Egoi bono me
In the forest, dear
Machia baithalain maharaj
A platform was erected by the emperor

2. *Kacheraiyo kait-kait, ata re baithae re*
With fresh chopped wooden poles sitting platform was set up
Banduka ke delaiṇ othoṇgae
And kept the gun leaning against it
Egoi bono me
In the forest, dear
Banduka ke delaiṇ othoṇgae
And kept the gun leaning against it

As stated in the song, a sitting arrangement is being prepared by erecting a raised platform with the help of freshly chopped down wooden poles. The platform is on the high up from where the hunter can see all around with ease and also is out of reach of the animal when attacked. Sometimes fenced cabins are prepared on elevated ground which are covered with bushes so as to make it invisible.

The hunter sits on the platform safely and awaits the coming of the animal. With the introduction of firearms, it is observed, wild animals and birds have vanished at alarming rate from the forest.

The Munda always share the game animal specially when the size of the game is big. But when the size of the game is small it is given only to one's friends or near relatives. The youths, when they catch some prey, they usually keep off some piece of meat for their friends or for one's brothers and sisters. Sometimes these pieces are kept for weeks till they meet. The song below belonging to Lahsua category derives its subject matter based on this theme. The lines of the song are as follows:

1. *Daru chetaṇ daru re, mide koto Lupung*
   On the tree upon tree, one Lupung twig branches off
   Chuṭi re kodo muli Suriem chi bagi chepeda-2 haere
   On the top of the twig upon the flower, Suriem drinks juice

2. *Mahra koṛae lasai re, mani laṇg sunumia*
   When the shepherd boy catches it, we will cook it with mustard oil
   Chiṛia koṛae juṛai re, rai laṇg rasuṇia
   When the crop guarding boy catches it, we will fry it with *rai* and garlic

3. *Mani laṇg rasunia, gati laṇg seṭeraiya*
   When cooked with mustard oil we will send it to the friend
   Rai laṇg rasuṇia, misi kelaṇg seteraiya-2 haere
   When fried in *rai*, we will send it to the sister

Fishing

Like hunting, fishing is also a subsidiary economic activity of the Mundas. The Munda region is far away from the sea and there is no big lake or river and so the area of fishing is very small. But there are numerous small rivers and rivulets which accommodate a good quantity of fish of various types in it. These rivers and rivulets are seasonal and so the fish are not available in lean season. Nevertheless, these rivers and rivulets have numerous pools and deeps where the water level does not come down even during summer. Fishing by the Mundas is normally done during rainy season and in winter through various means and methods. In deeps and big pools of the rivers community fishing is carried out, In almost all fishing activity, some precautions, such as warding off of the evil eyes or help from the supernatural forces are sought to ensure a good catch. The ensuing paragraphs refer about the songs that mention various methods of fishing, fishing implements, people's involvement and the experience of hardships and joy during fishing activity.

One of the method of catching fish is through the fishing rod with an iron hook. The song below which belongs to Jadur category of song mentions detailed process of this method:

1. *Okote-kotem seno tana dada*
   Where are you proceeding brother
   Ela dada ruaṛ me
   Please come back, brother
   Na:-chi mai reiṇg ruaṛa re
   How can I come back now, sister
   Hai baṇsiṇg seno tan re
   When I am proceeding to fishing

2. *Dahaṇg rado duir mena*
   There is thread on the rod
   Duir redo baṇsi mena
   A hook is there with the thread
   Na:-chi mai reiṇg ruaṛa re
   How can I come back now sister
   Hai baṇsing seno tan re
   When I am proceeding to fishing

The elder brother is out for fishing. He meets his sister on the way. In the conversation that follows with his sister describes the fishing implement that the Mundas generally use.

The following song which belongs to Bala category gives more details of the fishing rod and other accessories of the implement. The lines of the song are as follows:

Deto ge neyo mor banal baṇsi
Mother, let me have my fishing rod
Moe to jabo Ganga-Jamuna machhari marek-2
I shall proceed to Ganga-Jamuna (river) for fishing
Baṇs kera daṇgowa
The rod made of bamboo
Koa kera ḍuir
The thread made of cocoon
Miṇjur kera paiṇkh
The quill made of peacock feather
Gobar kera jonkṭi
The earthworm from cowdung pit
Guthi lalaiaṇ, thuki lelaiṇ
Inserting the earthworm, they spit on it
Ganga-Jamuna machhri marek-2
Fishing on the river Ganga and Jamuna

As mentioned in this song, the boy himself has prepared the iron hook known as *bansi*. The rod is from bamboo plant and thread from cocoon. To ascertain whether the fish has eaten up the hook, quil from peacock feather is attached with the thread. When the fish eats up the hook, the quill sinks in the water. Feathers of birds are needed when fishing is done on still waters like pool or pond or river where one can easily see the quill. Fishing is also done on shallow waters like lowland paddy fields during winter where no quill is needed. To attract fish towards the hook, earthworms are generally inserted in the hook, it also keeps the hook invisible. Insects are the favourite food of the fish, so they are attracted easily towards the bait. The Munda boy when he does fishing with the fishing rod, he spits on the bait before letting it down in the water which is more of a practice than for serving any purpose. The song is like a prescription for the youngsters who always would like to learn.

Fish are also caught through various other fishing implements. Mention of some have been made in the following Jarapi category of song, the lines of which are as follows:

1. *Kumuni kumuni re*
The Kumuni

Kumuniṇg tupu leda, kumuniṇg tupu leda
I put up the Kumuni

2. *Jhimb̂ri, jhimb̂ri re*
The Jhimbri
Jhimb̂riṇg aṭed leda, jimb̂riṇg aṭed leda
I had set up Jhimbri

3. *Bolo bolo do*
It entered but
Budum boloken, budum boloken
Budu fish had entered

4. *Soṛo soṛo do*
It had slipped into but
Ichâm soṛo ken, Ichâm soṛo ken
Lobster had slipped into

Of the most handy, time and energy saving fishing implements are *kumuni* and *jhimbri* which are made from split thin sticks of bamboo. Both the traps are used for small fish. While the *kumuni* is put up on rolling water, the *jhimbri* is put on still water. And as mentioned in the song, Budu fish who live in still water, are trapped. They always like to move on from one pool to another. The Icha fish or the lobster, on the other hand, prefer to live on the still water where pebbles of stone and other hiding objects like grass are available. It is in search of their hiding place that they get trapped.

Below is another song. belonging to the Bala category which describes how the fish are getting into the trap. The lines of the song are as follows:

Gaṛa gena Jamuna
By the banks of river Jamuna
Tiro-rio baṇsuri bajatạn-2
The sound of flute is being heard
Made sakạm chonga re-2
In the pipe made of bamboo
Hare, biyur tana re, sekor tana re
Alas, they are revolving
Soben hai ko jaman tan
All kinds of fish are getting assembled

Duar re haṛam kaṭkom laṇda tan
An old crab is laughing at the gate

Water of the river is rapidly flowing down producing a great musical sound which has been compared as sound of the flute. A bamboo pipe (fish trap) has been put up at one side of the water current. All the fish swimming downwards through that side are being trapped in the pipe. They are unable to get out from the pipe. A crab is sitting at the door of the trap and is looking at the pitiable condition of the fish, and as stated in the song, it is laughing. The composition of the song is very poetical. In the river where the flow of water is heavy but manageable, a specially made trap called *janjid* is put up to catch fish. *Mad sakam chonga* mentioned in the song indicates to this very trap.

Fishing is also done through the net. The following two songs which belong to Bala category, describe fishing from net. The lines of one of the songs are as follows :

Pokhri pinde pendo chhauwa
At the banks of pond's platform, the child fish
Hare chali gelaiṇ pokhri pinde
Went up to the banks of the pond's platform
Pokhri pinde pendo chhauwa
At the banks of the pond's platform, the child fish
Pendo chhauwa kheiṛ khelae
The child fish are playing
Jal feko
Cast the net
Bajhi gelaiṇ bhaiya baini
Brother and sister both were trapped

Snails of various kinds also move along the flow of water and they also get trapped along with the fish in the trap. The lines of another song which mention the trapping of snails, are as follows:

Kon kona baṇdh baṇdhale
In which direction you constructed the dam
Kon kona pain chalale
In which direction you constructed the drainage

Majhe to guṇgi resawaṇ
Snails lay at the middle
Bhaṇwar jal fekaṭ jamuna goi raṇgar-raṇgar
Rattling sound is heard at the casting of net
Purab kone baṇdh baṇdhale
You constructed dam in the east
Pachhim kona pain chalale
Constructed drainage in the west
Majhe to guṇgi-resawaṇ
Snails lay at the middle
Bhanwar jat fekaṭ jamuna goi raṇgar-raṇgar
Rattling sound is heard at the casting net

The dam was constructed and a drainage was taken out in the western corner of it. Somebody cast his net, but, alas, there were no fish but snails only which made rattling sound when pulled out from the water.

Another method of catching fish is by draining out the water from the pool. The song below which belongs to Bala category describes the operation of fishing as well as taste of the fish when cooked with tamarind juice. The lines of the song are as follows:

Numana, kuda ikir baru toyor do
Mother, the deeps under the blackberry tree and streams beyond Baru tree
Numana, hile ken, hile ken
Mother, rises waves high
Numana, gule ken, gule ken
Mother, it is bluish deep
Numana, arej lere, ehepa lere do
Mother, when embanked and drained
Numana, sisiṇgari menaja
Mother, Sisingari fish is there
Numana, ḍiri kaṭkom menaja
Mother, there is stone crab
Numana, jojo lire, kaṇjigi lire do
Mother, when cooked in tamarind juice or sour water
Numana, isugi hereṃa

Mother, it may taste too sweet
Numana, jale-chotabe sibila
Mother, it may taste like licking fingers

As mentioned in this song, after draining out the water, the Munda not only catch the fish but they catch crabs and snails etc too. The fish are usually cooked with tamarind juice.

As stated in previous pages, people of other castes and communities have also settled down among the Mundas. They either do specialized job or do business of essential commodities like cloths, spices and salt, etc. Munda usually receive goods and services from these communities. Some of the implements used in fishing activity are supplied by these commuities. The following song which belongs to Racha category relates to the economic relationship of these communities with that of the tribals:

1. *Arejeme nai*
   Drain out the water of the river
   Turi banal tuṇki tegi arejeme-2
   With *turi* made basket, drain out the water

2. *Chhekademe babu re*
   Make embankment, O dear
   Badae banai kuḍi tegi chhekademe-2
   From spade made by blacksmith make embankment

3. *Sabe kome babu re*
   Catch them, O dear
   Turi banai tuṇki regi sabe kome-2
   In the basket made by turi catch them

In catching fish by draining out water from the pool, help from implements like spade and basket are taken which are made available by blacksmith and Turi communities.

The Munda also depend on other communities such as potters, *malars, sonars* and traders for the supply of pottery, earthenwares, brasswares, utensils, ornaments, salt, oil and spices, etc. The song below, which belongs to Bala category, mentions this as under:

Piṛi re jojo
Tamarind tree on the field

Gaṛa redo hai ko
And fish in the river
Hare Malạr bidya
And the knowledge of Malar
Kunkạl chaṭu reko, choṇge, choṇgeya-2
And the frying is done on the potter's made pot
Turku re buluṇg
Salt from the traders
Baṇiyarẹ sasaṇg re masala
From *baniya*, the spices
Malạr bidiya
The knowledge of Malar
Kunkạl chaṭu reko, choṇge choṇgeya-2
Frying is done on the potter's pot

The above song describes how the life has become easier with the cooperation of the communities. The Mundas are the primary producers of food items while other subsidiary things are supplied by other non-tribal communities. We may take the example from simple economic activity like fishing. The fish are available in the ponds and rivers which the Munda catch. In this operation, they get necessary objects like spade from blacksmith, basket from Turi community, pot and other utensils from potters and brasswares from brassware making communities and salt and spices from traders.

The Munda also catch fish by poisoning the water. The method is particularly adopted when neither of the methods like, draining out of water, fishing by net or other methods are feasible. The song below which belongs to Dubung category mentions this method in the following lines:

1. *Kane daha re hilo karae*
   On which deep is being poisoned
   Bhaiya re, kane daha re machhri marae
   And on which deep fishing is going on, brother

2. *Upạr daha re hilo karae*
   The upper deep have been poisoned
   Bhaiya re heṇthe daha re machhri marae
   Fishing is going on in the lower deep, brother

Fishing by poisoning is a week long affair and it involves people of one or more villages who usually claim share in the common pool. The poisonous plants are first collected by the villagers and on an appointed day, usually determined by the village priest and after some ritual performance, the deep is poisoned. Such ritual performance is essential in order to ensure a good catch and to avoid any untoward incident during the operation. The water linking the deep is first diverted by erecting a strong block. On the appointed day and time, the catching of fish is taken up which also ends within the time schedule as predetermined. The catch so collected is gathered and distributed to each family irrespective of the number of participants of fish catchers from the family. Such fishing is done once in every year after the harvest and normally after the *Ba* festival.

In gathering, hunting and fishing activities, a person is not always rewarded, sometimes, he may have to return empty handed. The following song belonging to Jadur category mentions this in the following lines:

1. *Soso kuṭi baru jola re, saṇga ho dile doṇgoba*
   Under the *soso* tree in the valley of Baru, sweet tubers grow abundantly
   Icha lor Bandu sokora re, hai ko ho sigil-bigila
   In the Icha drainage on Bandu plot, fish overcrowded it

2. *Saṇga ho dile doṇgoba, saṇga ho ura laṇg me*
   Sweet tubers grow abundant, dig up for us
   Hai ko ho sigil-bigila, hai ko ho are: laṇg me
   Look the overcrowding fish, drain out to us

3. *Sanga hoiṇg ur kena, sanga ko red chaba jan*
   I dug up the tubers, it all turned out to be fibres
   Hai ko hoiṇg are kena, hai koho choke chaba jan
   I drained out the water for fish, but there were frogs only

In the activity as mentioned above, the labour and energy of the person all were simply wasted as he got nothing out of his labour. These are but simple experiences out of life worth remembering.

14

THE AGRO-ECONOMIC ACTIVITY

The physical features of Chhotanagpur region are characterized by hills dissected by numerous small rivers and valleys. Once the region was covered with dense forests but now, except for reserve forest, they are found in patches only. The land under cultivation has considerably been reduced due to various reasons and the land-use pattern has also changed. Traditionally, the cultivable lands are classified into uplands and lowlands. The lowlands are fertile due to its alluvium, while the uplands vary considerably from place to place on the basis of soil texture and fertility. Some plots of these lands are left for growing grass and every year some plots are left fallow to enable it to regain its natural vitality and fertility. Due to denudation of forest, the water level too has gone down and swampy lands are rare which once were in abundance. The fertility of lands has considerably been reduced as upper layer of the soil are washed away every year during rainy season. All this, has affected the production of crops, besides other environmental and natural calamities.

The Agricultural Operation

The Munda has to toil all the year round in the preparation and management of the land. The agriculture and related activities take considerable time of the Munda. The life is full of hardship but there is joy in it which the Munda share as would be seen in the pages that follow.

Clearing and Preparation of Land

It is rather difficult to state as to which of the activity in agricultural operation is the initial one which may generate other activities. The songs which have detailed records of the process of economic activity also do not indicate to this point. However, to present a systematic picture of economic activity, preparation of the field for cultivation has been chosen as the initial activity in the whole process of agricultural operation. The song below belonging to Jarga category describes the subject as follows:

1. *Bakula loyong rata-pata*
   The plot full of Bakula shrubs is being cleared
   Dhangori ko chalu tana
   The girls are digging

2. *Jubila loyong lata-pata*
   The marshy land is being operated upon
   Dhangora ko sii tana
   The boys are ploughing

The song presents the scene of work in which the girls and boys are engaged. The girls are clearing the land from thorny shrubs, while the boys are ploughing the swampy land which is equally difficult and tiresome.

Below is yet another song which mentions that while ploughing the field, stones are also being removed from there. The song belongs to Lahsua category and the lines are as follows:

1. *Jhibir-jhibir pani*
   It is showering thinly
   Pani nai barisae
   There is no rain
   Ho hore, nam dore gatim dirim tusang tana re
   O friend dear, you are picking up stones

2. *Dasi korae sii tan*
   The servant boy is ploughing
   Kamri kuri tusang tan
   The servant girl is picking up
   Ho hore, nam dore gatim dirim tusang tana re
   O friend dear, you are picking up stones

The uplands usually contain stones and pebbles which need to be removed before sowing the seeds. As stated in the song, the servant boy and girl are engaged in this job.

Clearing and ploughing the upland, particularly when it is dry, is a tough job. The song below belonging to Maghe category describes this in the following lines:

1. *Chalu tanae piṛi badi*
   Digging up the upland plot
   Kudlạm te chalu tanae piṛi badi
   With spade digging up the upland plot

2. *Kara tanae gaṛa loyoṇg*
   Levelling the lowland
   Haḍa-keḍate kara tanae gaṛa loyoṇg
   With the help of bullock and buffalo, levelling the lowland

3. *Laga janae chalu tani*
   The person digging up has become exhausted
   Chalu-chalu te laga janae chalu tani
   While digging he became exhausted

4. *Kuba janae kara tani*
   The person levelling has become crooked
   Kara-kara te kuba janae kara tani
   While levelling, he became crooked

5. *Idiyaipe chalu tani*
   Send something for the person digging
   Basi da: ko idiyaipe chalu tani
   Send some leftover water to the person digging

6. *Seṭeraipe kara tani*
   Carry something for the person levelling
   Chuna-tamku seṭeraipe kara tani
   Carry lime and tobacco for the person levelling

When there is whole day work and when the place of work is far away from the settlement, the ladies usually carry breakfast, etc, to the person working in the field. As mentioned in this song, the ladies are being told to carry light food and tobacco, etc, for the persons working in the field.

Working in the field is not an easy job. There may be variety of work situation some may be working in bush and forest, some on hilly, rocky, some on plain land and some on low and marshy lands. The experience of working on different types of fields may differ from person to person. Sometimes serious accidents also occur while working in the field. The following song of Jadur category illustrates few of such experiences. The lines of the song are as follows:

1. *Siyu-siyu chi chalu-chalu*
   Ploughing or digging
   Keṭe ote reiṇg paṇdil yana
   I Was thrown upon the hard soil

2. *Siyu-siyu chi chalu-chalu*
   Ploughing or digging
   Karatạd losod reiṇg tali jana
   I slipped on liquid soil of the levelled field

The song below belonging to Jadur category add up some other kind of experience, the lines of the song are as follows:

1. *Sii tạd duṛa chi kara tạd losod*
   Ploughed up dust or levelled up clay
   Sitạd dura teing otaṇg lena
   I was sprayed up with ploughed up dust

2. *Sitạd duṛa chi kara tạd losod*
   Ploughed up dust or levelled up clay
   Karatạd losod teiṇg pasir lena
   I was sprinkled up with levelled up clay

3. *Sitạd duṛa teiṇg otaṇg lena*
   I was sprayed ploughed up dust
   Chitiri lekaiṇge chitri jana
   I was coloured like partridge

4. *Karatạd losod teiṇg pasir lena*
   I was sprinkled with levelled up clay
   Tur leka geiṇg onol jana
   I was stripped coloured like squirrel

The ploughman working on hard soil could not handle the plough properly and is often thrown away. On the other hand, ploughman working on wet soil, slipped and fell down. When the hard soil is thoroughly ploughed up making it like flour, the ploughman is sprinkled turning his look like a squirrel. While the ploughman working on the wet soil when sprayed up with liquid, soil, his appearance changed like the colour of the partridge. The experience that a person gets while working on the field as stated, leaves a life long mark in his memory. The song as above was composed by one such person.

Paddy Cultivation

Before the sowing of seed or transplantation of paddy saplings in the field, the land is thoroughly ploughed and all kinds of shrubs and pebbles are removed from the field. The song below belonging to the Jadur category describes how the land is being prepared. The lines of the song are as follows:

1. *Kahaṇ se ale re guḍu re muṣa*
   From where did you come, O Gudu mouse
   Hare, bhusu̯r-bhusu̯r maṭi bigae-2
   Throwing soil out at ease

2. *Ropa khete dibḁl dobol*
   Floating all over on the field of transplantation
   Chhao data kaṛa re
   The full grown up water buffalo

3. *Ulaṭi palaṭi paṭa marae*
   Levelling the soil to and fro
   Chhao data kaṛa re
   The full grown up water buffalo
   Hare ulaṭi palaṭi paṭa marae
   Levelling the soil to and fro

The burrows of the Gudu mouse are found everywhere on the embankments of the plots of the crop field. They make their burrows easily and throw out the soil from inside. This leisurely operation of the mouse is called *bhusur-bhusur*. Similarly, a grown up water buffalo levels up the liquid soil to and fro smoothly and easily.

Transplantation of paddy is a tedious job. First, the seed saplings are uprooted and then transplanted in another field. This process along with the condition of work has been mentioned in the following Bala category of song. The lines of the song are as follows:

Eko goṭo dhana kera biṛa mae bunaloṇ
I sowed paddy seed for sapling in a plot of land
Hare, dhuchuṛ-dhuchuṛ, dhuchuṛ biṛa jiwa ke janjal
The job of uprooting the sapling is too tedious and boring
Jotauya je thaki gel
The ploughmen were all tired
Ropauya je thaki gel
The transplanters were all exhausted
Hare, dhuchuṛ-dhuchuṛ, dhuchuṛ biṛa jiwa ke janjal
The jobs of uprooting the sapling is too tedious and boring

The transplantation of the paddy is to be taken up at right time and also to be completed within a stipulated time frame. This tight schedule makes the people very busy during the transplantation period. If one has enough land for transplantation, the uprooting of paddy sapling as well as preparation of the land for transplantation and actual work of transplantation become a very tiresome job. As stated in this song, the uprooters of the saplings, ploughmen and the transplanters all were exhausted. The work in any case be completed within the right time and this allows no body for rest. But completion of work may also depend on many contingencies. One such situation has been mentioned in the following Bala category of song. The lines of the song are as follows:

Eko ana kera jamin
One anna worth land
Tin khanḍi kera biṛa
Three *khandi* worth seed sapling
Ropi debe banihar
Labourers please do transplant
Sirae debe banihar
Please complete the job, O labourers

Hara dukhe nayo biṛa sario gel-2
Paddy sapling remained unused because of the lack of plough

The song states that the quantity of paddy sapling and the size of the plot of land on which transplantation is to be made both are on high side. A good quantity of paddy sapling could not be transplanted due to want of plough as the land on which transplantation is to be done could not be ploughed. There are either one or two ploughs in the house which could not take up the whole job. And as all families are engaged in their respective work of transplantation, no spare plough could be availed. Even the labourers on payment are not available. Majority of the Mundas possess one or two ploughs only. And those having one plough find it very difficult to complete the work in time. The work in the village is, however, carried out through cooperation and this makes the task easy. One may expect desired production of crops if the work is finished in time.

As far as the ploughing of field for transplantation is concerned, it is done through cooperation and no payment is made to the ploughmen, however, feast is hosted for them. But for transplantation work, it is always done on payment—either cash or kind as per the existing practice. It is also done on reciprocal basis without making any payment. Below are few songs which relate to work through payment. The song belongs to Lahsua category and the lines are as follows:

Asaṛ chanḍu teba lena
Asaṛ month has arrived
Dola maire roa nala te
Let us do labour work in transplantation, dear
Hatu ren hoṛọ kodo uṛuṇg lena
The village people have all come out
Soben ko seno tana ko
All are going
Mid ta: rebu kamia panti-panti ge
We will work at a place in rows
Siṇgi doe dubui lena
The sun has set

Dola maire nala tela te
Let us proceed to collect payment, dear daughter
Nala bu tela keda
We collected our payment
Rurung geya bu, mandiyabu
We will pound, clean and cook it
Hon-hopon tenda kobu nuya
Let us all family members drink the gruel

A beautiful scene has been presented in the above song on how people are proceeding to work in the early hours of the morning. It may be noted that in transplantation work as labourers, it is the females only that participate in it. No male person does labour work in the job of transplantation as they remain engaged in the preparation of the fields for transplantation. This is why as stated in the song, it is the females only who are proceeding for transplantation work. The economic condition of almost all families in the village is average, so, many families get their daily meal when they get payment after day's work. In such a situation, even the gruel is shared by all members of the family.

Even living under the condition of poverty, the tribals continue to sing and dance during the night after the day's work. The following Lahsua category of song describes this feature of the tribal life in the following lines :

1. *Disum horo ko seno tan*
The people of the country are going
Kami nala ko seno tana
All are going for labour work
O mai jojohatu, seno medo roa nala te
Go to labour work in transplantation, O dear Jojohatu

2. *Seta: getem roa kena*
You did transplantation work from morning
Tikin sa:-gem hoka jan
You stopped work at noon
Nire sene jolam rakab keda
Running and walking you did cross the hills and valleys
Jojohatu nalam tela kena
You did collect payment, O Jojohatu

3. *Tela dorem tela ked*
You collected your payment, but
Rurung dunduam tayom jan
In cleaning and cooking, you became late
Akhra re dumang sari lena
The sound of *dumang* did hum at *akhra*
Dhangri ko tingu tangi tana
Girls are waiting for you

Music and dance are the regular features of the Munda village. The young boys and girls, after day's labour, assemble at *akhra* at night. As most of the families are poor, they have to earn their daily meal through labour as mentioned in the song. Music and work are inseparable part in the life of the Mundas. As stated in the song, a married girl goes for labour work in the neighbouring village by crossing the hills and valleys. After day's work, she returned through the same route, pounded the paddy, cleaned and cooked it. All this took much of her time. It was a long process to complete the job of cooking and she was already late when dance started in the *akhra* where all her friends were waiting for her.

The following song provides a very fine example of the whole economic process relating to sowing and transplantation of paddy to cleaning and storing, celebrating at the completion of which, through music and dance. The song belongs to Bala category and the lines are as follows:

Gola bareda har jotae re
Gola bullock is ploughing
Gola bareda har jotae, har jotae re
Gola bullock is ploughing continuously
Hara chhora kire babu moroli bajae-2
Plough boy is playing on flute when the ploughing was over
Hara binu, kara binu, juathi binu
Without the plough, platter and yoke
Nadha binu, paina binu har jotae re
Without yoke, rope and stick, is ploughing
Jotala khete sario gela re
The ploughed up field remained unsowed

Dhana moe bunaloṇ
I sowed the paddy
Seo dhan fuṭi gel
This paddy bore ears
Seo dhan paki gel
It then ripened
Heṇsua me katalaiṇ
They harvested with sickle
Dora me bandhalaiṇ
They fastened it with rope
Cheguri me ghusalaiṇ
They inserted cheguri on it
Dahar̤-dahar̤ bohalaiṇ
Carried it through the path
Kharian me charalaiṇ
Brought it to the barn
Dhan moe chhitaloṇ
I spread up the paddy stalks
Gola bareda, chaoṇra bareda
Gola and Chaonra bullocks
Khundalaiṇ misalaiṇ
They trod and squeezed with their feet
Dhanyo jhari gela
The paddy got separated
Pora ke fekalaiṇ
They threw away the paddy straw
Dhan ke osalaiṇ
They spread up the paddy for drying
Daura me sajalaiṇ
They collected it in the basket
Mora bandhalaiṇ
And stored it in *mora*
Ḍorayo ṭuṭi gel Chuṭiya kisan ker
The rope of the Chutiya farmer too broke
Gola bareda har jotae re
Gola bullock is ploughing

Gola bareda har jotae, har jotae re
Gola bullock is ploughing continuously
Hara chhora kire babu moroli bajae
Plough boy is playing on the flute after the ploughing is over
Hara chhora kire babu baṇsuri bajae
Plough boy is playing on flute after the ploughing is over

The boy is ploughing the field with a pair of well grown up bullocks. The name of the bullocks are Gola and Chaonra. The field was first ploughed up thoroughly and then seed was sown. It grew, bore fruits, ripened and was harvested. The paddy was carried to the barn for separation, cleaning and storing. One gets relief and great satisfaction at the successful completion of the work which at community level is always celebrated with joy and merriment with accompaniment of music and dance.

One may feel happy to see the growth of paddy after its transplantation. In the song below which belongs to Jadur category, the beauty of the growth of paddy has been mentioned. The lines of the song are as follows:

1. *Sud hora nan baba re*
   Fine paddy on the path to stream
   Hare nan baba do
   What a nice fine paddy

2. *Oko honae roe leda re*
   Who had planted it
   Hare nan baba do
   What a nice fine paddy

3. *Santa honae roe leda re*
   Santa boy had planted it
   Hare naṇ baba do
   What a nice fine paddy
   Hare nan baba dore
   What a nice fine paddy, dear
   Tului-lusui, dhimir dhila tilasari
   Swaying to and fro beautifully laden with luscious growth

Sometimes there is a good yield. The following song belonging to Lahsua category describes how *maga* and *tilming* crops are full of seeds that produce nice musical sound. The lines of the song are as follows:

1. *Gaṛa ko parom re maga*
   Across the ravine *maga* crops grow
   Seke ken seke ken
   Producing tinkling sound

2. *Nai parom kore tilming*
   Beyond the river Sesame crops
   Rolo ken rolo ken
   Producing nice rattling sound

A good growth do not always provide desired yield. There are many contingencies upon which the production of the crops depend. The following song belonging to Lahsua category indicates to this fact. The lines of the song are as follows:

1. *Gaṛa parom siyu kami*
   Ploughing beyond the ravine
   Jiṇga baba iṇg her leda
   I had sowed Jinga paddy
   Ada kara, isu daru jana dai
   What an abundant growth, dear sister
   Ji do ji ge suku jan
   My heart is full of joy

2. *Okoe mene mod bandi*
   Some would predict the yield would be one bandi
   Okoe mene bar bandi
   Some would say, it would yield two bandi
   Ada kara, isu daru jana dai
   What an abundant growth, dear sister
   Ji do ji suku jana
   My heart is full of joy

3. *Latarete hoyo leda*
   The wind blew from beyond

Sururi ko rakab lena
The pest had infested
Chainya chiprud ko jom chaba keda
The insects destroyed everything
Hare, ainga jido jige lo tana
My heart is burning with anguish

As stated, the growth of the plant, was very good to the joy of everybody. But when the ears of the crop appeared on the stem, a strong north wind blew bringing with it a swarm of pests who ate up the milk of the grain reducing it a mere chalf. All labour of the person was lost which he had to bear throughout the year.

Life of a Cultivator

Below is another song which states that the life of the cultivator is not an easy life. The poor cultivator is the worst sufferer. The song which belongs to Lahsua category points out some basic problems in the following lines:

1. *Da: tare hita bano, hita nạm tare da: bano*
   When it rains, there is no seeds, when seeds available, there is no rain
   Her tare chainya-chiprud jorn chabayako
   When seed is sown, it is eaten away by pests

2. *Apsul mundi bano, apsul mundi bano*
   There is no way out in life how to live
   Her jeṭe rurub jome, roe baba banki jome
   Seeds sown during summer are eaten away by insects and transplanted saplings are affected by diseases

3. *Gele tan re chainya-chiprud jom chabayako*
   While bearing ears, it is attacked by pests
   Apsul mundi bano, apsul mundi bano
   There is no way out in life how to live

At every stage of crop cultivation—from sowing to harvesting, there are innumerable problems which the cultivator faces. The above song describes the major problems which the cultivator is helpless to ward off. People are fully depended on rain water for crops cultivation and as monsoon is very irregular, they are placed in a very awkward situation, particularly the poor who hardly meet the needs of the day. For such families, rain is of no use for they have no seeds for sowing. Such families when they manage seeds, it becomes too cumbersome to wait for the rain and are forced by the situation as they have no alternative left for them but to consume the same. If somehow the seeds are sown the delay of rain may allow insects and birds to eat away all. The transplanted saplings, on the other hand, are attacked by insects and various kinds of diseases such as '*banki*' which hampers the growth or destroys completely. The insects or pests called '*chainya-chirud*' again attack the crops when ears of grain come out. Looking at all these problems, the cultivator says, as mentioned in the song that there is no way out in life. The situation of the cultivators continue as mentioned in the above song as there is no canal irrigation system in Chhotanagpur plateau and the use of chemicals for the protection of the crops has yet to gain its popularity.

Farming of Pulses

Crops are not only destroyed by birds, animals, insects, pests and diseases, natural calamities also do havoc to the crops. Against natural calamities, people have not invented any protective device that can be effectively used when such situation arises. In the following song, the hailstorm with hailstones destroyed the standing *arhar* crop at the time when the plant was covered with flowers. The song belongs to Bala category and the lines are as follows:

> *Jeṭe rari moe bunaloṇ*
> I sowed the summer variety of *arhar*
> *Hare nane-nanedari me jhabarae*
> It was laden to the tip of the slim stem
> *Seo rari forae runu-jhunu*
> The fruits were full of seeds
> *Hare pakhna pani*
> Alas, the hailstorm with hailstones rained
> *Pani nai barisae*
> There was no rain

Hare, ḍari chhori, pate chhori
Alas, it spared stems and leaves
Phori me marae
Lashed down the fruits alone
Jato beti mae tor ke pūchh anbe
Go and ask the mother, my dear
Hare, supli dani, mauni dani
In the winnowing fans and baskets
Rari ke bichhi lanbe
Collect the *rahri* fruits

The meaning of the song is quite clear. *Rahri* crop—a kind of pulse, have been sown. The pulse is of summer variety and ripens during spring when the region is vulnerable to hailstorms. The stems were all laden with fruits and were raw when the hailstorms with hailstones lashed out in the region. The plants were all denuded. As the fruits were unripe, it could not be kept for seeds. The family members, however, collected the fruits for use in the breakfast. All the labour of the family was thus lost in vain.

Besides natural calamities, the *rahri* pulse is also subjected to various kinds of plant diseases making the cultivators' labour worthless forcing him to live under the poverty situation for rest of the year. The following song which belongs to Jarga category, describes how the standing crop of *rahri* was attacked with disease:

1. *Buru re rahṛi ko her leda*
   Rahri was sown on the hill
   Buṭaete chuṭi jaked na moe te goso jana, haena
   Alas, all the flowers withered away from bottom to top

2. *Dola tobu nel leya re*
   Let us go to see it
   Mare tobu china leya re
   Let us inspect it
   Butaete chuti jaked na moe te goso jana, haena
   Alas, all the flowers withered away from bottom to top

In this song as stated, the bud of *rahri* fruits before its blooming was infected with disease and all the buds fell down. There was no way out to save the buds and the cultivator remained helpless except expressing his anguish on seeing the condition of the buds.

Separation of Grain from Husk

After the harvest, people remain busy in the operation of separation of grain from the straws and its cleaning and storing. Separation of grain from straws is done, if the grain is paddy, either by treading over with animals or by squeezing it by feet from individual persons. The song below belonging to Jadur category, describes the process of separation of grain by individual persons by squeezing it with their feet:

1. *Chire tika mesa baba mena*
   Is there the paddy lying for treading
   Chire tika mesaya
   That you will mix up by treading
   Chire charpa mesa chauli mena
   Are there the rice laying for squeezing
   Chire charpa mesaya
   That you will mix up by squeezing

2. *Kare tika mesa baba mena*
   There is no paddy for treading upon
   Kareing tikamesaya
   I will not mix up by treading
   Kare charpa mesa chauli mena
   There is no rice left for mixing up by squeezing
   Kareing charpa mesaya
   That I will mix up by squeezing by feet

The process of separation of grain from the straw is a tiresome and monotonous job. When the grain is separated by treading with cattle, one has to walk around along with the cattle for hours in the barn. Some cattle may express their resentment by kicking back or by running out from the barn. In the song below as mentioned, a boy has been assigned the job of driving the cattle on the paddy straw heap for its separation but he refuses as one of the cattle kicks back. The song belongs to *Racha* category and the lines are as follows:

1. *Kairka lo*
Dear Kairka
Jabere babu dauṇri khede
Go to attend the treading job, dear
Jabere babu pora nikae
Go to bring out the straws, dear

2. *Nahiṇ jamu dada*
I will not go brother dear
Gola bareda dhusi morela
For Gola bullock attacks with its horn
Chaoṇra bareda laṭi morela
For Chaonra bullock kicks back

Separation of grain from straw is a time consuming job and is taken up from very early morning. All members of the family have to remain busy in this job, The song below describes a typical scene of the barn generally observed during the harvesting season in every family and village. The song belongs to Jarga category and the lines are as follows:

1. *Kimin koja, kimin ko*
Look, the daughters-in-law
Gudlu busu reko duba kana
All are sitting over the heap of Gudlu straw
Hoṇjar koja, hoṇjar ko
Look, the fathers-in-law
Bende busu reko jarua kana
Are sitting around over the heap of Bende straw

2. *Papṛa gandu ḅano leka*
As if there are no stool made of Papra tree
Gudlu busu reko duba kana
Are sitting over the heap of Gudlu straw
Jimtu paṭi bano leka
As if there is no mat made of Jimtu grass
Bende busu reko jarua kana
Are sitting around over the heap of Bende straw

It is winter and the time is morning hours. All the members of the family are on the barn attending the grain separation job. They are taking rest after the tedious job of separation of grain from the straw. The composer of the song closely observes them. The daughters-in-law, at one side, are taking rest on the soft straw of Gudlu. At a separate side, the fathers-in-law, too are sitting around over the Bende straw and are engaged in gossip. The sun is slowly rising up in the sky and all are enjoying the warmth of the morning sun resting over the straw.

Value in Greater Numbers of Members and Cattle

Agricultural work cannot be carried out single handedly. It requires the helping hands and cooperation of all members of the family in day-to-day activities. Even the children and the disabled are assigned duties according to their abilities. Children are always given necessary guidance and training in all kinds of work. The following song belonging to Jadur category mentions of a person who has got no helping hand. The plight of the person is narrated from the mouth of the person himself in the following lines:

1. *Miyad geyae taiṇg leda-leda sedom*
   I have got but one dwarfed horse
   Bora koiṇg laḍiya chi aiṇg deja
   Shall I load burden or I myself shall ride upon

2. *Miyad geyae taiṇg aṛandi kuṛi*
   I have but only one married wife
   Haṛkae dupila chi tailae sabe
   Will she carry box or will she hold bag

3. *Miyad geyae taiṇg banḍi-banḍi guḍi*
   I have but a single tail-less cow
   Deḍe reiṇg joraiya chi nao reiṇg jorai
   Shall I yoke it in the right or in the left

The work of cultivation can be smoothly carried out when there are sufficient number of persons as well as cattle. Lack of individuals, gents or ladies, in the house badly affects the family economy and so does the lack of cattle. So a good number of persons in the family is always desired. Some will take care of the household works while others the outside, though such division of work is never conclusive and final.

The Young Girls at Work

Each type of work has its own importance and is equally difficult and it is the person who can perform the task efficiently, is preferably deputed on that particular work. But the novice are always encouraged to take up all kinds of work. And as stated in the previous pages, they receive proper guidance from the elders. The following Lahsua category of song describes the desires of the minor girls for learning the job:

1. *A̭m leka suta̭m takui ber-ber*
   Swinging and spinning like you, dear sister
   Kana dai kaiṇg ituana
   I don't know, sister dear
   A̭m leka chari chaṭa: sa̭r-sa̭r
   Splitting the sewing sticks swiftly
   Kana dai kaing sariyana
   I have no knowledge of it dear sister

2. *Alo dainam eraṇgiya re*
   Don't abuse me, dear sister
   Kana dai kaiṇg sariyana
   I have no knowledge of it, dear sister
   Kana dai kaiṇg juṛi tiṇga re
   I am not of your age, dear sister
   A̭lo dai a̭m eraṇging
   Don't abuse me, dear sister
   Kana dai a̭m jota tiṇga re
   I am not of your equal, dear sister

In this song as stated, a young girl is inquisitive of knowing the secret of speedy work like swinging the spin and splitting the sewing sticks. The girl is a novice and she has no knowledge of these works. She constantly asks her sister about the methods of spinning and splitting. She is abused by her sister for which she begs an apology for she is ignorant of doing such works. However, as she is not of the sister's age and equal to her, but she is confident that with attainment of age, she will be able to learn all these works.

The following few songs of the Lahsua category mention how the young children are guided by the elders:

1. *Sahạn agum seno redo*
   If you go to collect firewood
   Sakạm hejem birid redo
   If you go to pluck leaves
   O hore maina, Hora rem naki supi dena
   My dear, you comb your hair on the way

2. *Seta rem birida, roka tokạm senoa*
   You got up early and proceeded hurriedly
   O hore maina, hora rem naki supi dena
   My dear, you comb your hair on the way

3. *Naki taben me gatim, supid taben me*
   Comb your hair and dress yourself quickly
   Songe kodo ko nir bage langa
   We will be left behind by our colleagues

The girls are proceeding to the forest to collect firewood and leaves. Two friends are making hurried preparations for the outing. In one case, one of the girls does not get time even to comb her hair and does it on the way. While in the second, one of the friend advises the other to make haste in combing her hair otherwise their friends may leave them behind. The girls are proceeding together to the forest in the early hours of the morning.

One should know one's requirement and needs and take up work accordingly. Even the young girls understand this necessity. In the following Jadur category of song, the young girl requests her elder sister to proceed to the forest to collect firewood and leaves. The lines of the song are as follows:

1. *Dolabu dai bir teho*
   Let us proceed to the forest, sister dear
   Sahạn sakạm agute
   To bring firewood and leaves

Saha̭n saka̭m okoe agua bua
Otherwise, who will bring firewood and leaves for us
Apa̭n jiu re bichareyabu bole
Let us think over it by ourselves for a moment

2. *Sekerabu senoa.*
We shall proceed hurriedly
Tikin siṇgi jeṭe-a
By noon it will become hot
Jeṭe lolo okoe sahatiṇga
Who will bear the scorching sun
Apạn jiu re bichareyabu bole
Let us think over it by ourselves for a moment

The work is generally taken up early in the morning but there are some persons in the family who do not like to leave the bed so early. The elders always keep a watch over such persons and remind them their work. The song belonging to Jarga category has this theme which runs as follows:

1. *Aṇg jana tur jana*
It is morning and the sun has arisen
Chia mai guri kạm giṛiya
Why don't you clean the cowshed, daughter

2. *Aṇg jana tur jana*
It is morning and the sun has arisen
Chia mai racha kam jo-o-ya
Why don't you clean the courtyard, daughter

3. *Aurige eṇgaing kore, tee sakom taiṇg sakom koa*
Wait for a minute, mother, let me wear bangle on my hand

4. *Aurige apuiṇg kore, kaṭa andu taiṇg andu koa*
Wait for a minute, father, let me wear my leg ornament
Aurige eṇgaiṇg, paṛia kichiri taing kichiri koa
Wait for a minute, mother, let me dress with *paria* cloth
Aurige apuiṇg, pachon paṛia taiṇg paela koa
Wait for a minute, father, let me dangle *pachon paria* on my body

The elder sister, as stated in the song appears to be lazy that is why she is getting up from her bed late. She is asked by her parents to clean up the cowshed and courtyard. The girl takes it lightly and tells her parents to let her wear her ornaments and dress properly first. The parents like to see that at the rising of sun all household work must be completed.

The work, as stated elsewhere, are all of equally important as well as difficult. But some are of specialized nature which the novice cannot be singly assigned. How difficult is each work, this subject has been taken up in the following song which belongs to Jadur category:

1. *Uri gupi bugina chi hoṛe tud bugina*
   Is it easy to tend the cattle or to uproot the *hore* plant
   Goṭa buru hoko daura keda
   They did run on all the hills
   Uri gupi bugina chi hoṛe tud bugina
   It is easy to tend the cattle or to uproot *hore* plant
   Goṭa goṛa ho taiṇg buta teya
   It is spread over the whole field

2. *Goṭa buru ho ko daura keda*
   They did run over on all the hills
   Ayur sāiṇg hara chi tayom sāiṇg hara
   Shall I control the forward or backward
   Goṭa goṛa ho taiṇg buṭa teya
   It is spread over the whole field
   Haṇ sāiṇg tuda chi ne sāiṇg tuda
   Shall I uproot there or here

3. *Miyad geya ho taiṇg tiril ḍanḍa*
   I have but only one *tiril* stick
   Ayur sāiṇg hara chi tayom sāiṇg hara
   Shall I control the forward or backward
   Baṛiya geya ho taiṇg tu-tud tee
   I have but a pair of working hands
   Haṇ sāiṇg tuda chi ne sāiṇg tuda
   Shall I uproot there or here

Tending cattle is not as easy as one may think, for they run about all the time and one may have to run after them. It is not either easy to uproot *hore* plant from the paddy field for its roots go deep in the soil and grow all over the field. It is hard to uproot the plant and the hands too may get swollen and bruised. The work becomes more difficult when a person is alone. He cannot control huge number of cattle alone in the field for when he is after the two or three cattle at a time, the others may go away in other direction. Similarly, he cannot uproot *hore* grass all alone which are spread over the whole field. So work is generally carried out through cooperation. Such cooperation not only comes from the family members and kin groups but from other non-community members also who specialize in many aspects of agricultural technologies or services. The services of these communities for the Mundas cannot be underestimated. The reference of their cooperation with specialized occupational communities have been made in the song by the Mundas.

The Blacksmith Community

The following Racha category of song refers to the blacksmith—a non-Munda community, who supply or repair iron implements which are used by the Mundas. The lines of the song are as follows:

Uthu guru, uthu guru
O master, please get up
Bihạn bhela
It is morning
Chạm chipuwa guru susuwaela
The skin fan is breathing, master
Babu lagi sanṣi koṭasi
Pincers and hammer for the boy
Maiya lagin metạm chạm chipuwa
The skin fan for the girl

The above song describes division of work among the family members of blacksmith community. The operation of *chipuwa,* that is, skin fan is handled by the females and iron implements like pincers and hammers are at the disposal of the male persons who repair all kinds of agricultural implements of the Mundas.

The services of the blacksmith have got an important place in the Munda economic system. All sorts of iron implements used by them in agricultural operation are made and repaired by these communities. They also participate in many socio-cultural ceremonies of the Mundas. In lieu of their services they get fixed amount of grain from each household after each harvest annually. As stated in the above song, they have division of work among themselves too. The males handle the main job of mending and making new implements and females work on the skin made air blowing machine called '*chipuwa*'. The blow can be operated either by hand or feet. In one of the songs below, which belongs to Jadur category, the blacksmith is requested to prepare knife and basket maker to supply basket to the person. The lines of the song are as follows:

1. *Sa̭rjom suṛa sagen re*
   When the sarjom flowers bloom
   Kapi re badae teyariṇg me
   Prepare a knife for me, O blacksmith
   Maduka̭m chuti ruchu re
   When the madukam flowers are in the bud
   Turi re tunki teyariṇg me
   Make a basket, O Turi

2. *Kapi re badae teyariṇg me*
   Prepare a knife for me, O blacksmith
   Sa̭rjom hese jom te
   To cut down the sarjom twig
   Turi re tunki teyariṇg me
   Supply me a basket, O basket maker
   Maduka̭m halaṇg jom te
   To collect madukam flowers

The song below also relates to the same subject which belongs to the Bala category. The lines of the song run as follows:

Lohra bhaiya
Brother blacksmith
Hiṇsua mor ke banaiyo debe lohra
Make a sickle for me, O lohra

Hiṇsua mor ke baniyo debe
Make a sickle for me
Seo hiṇsua ghas kaṭaloṇ
I cut the grass from that sickle
Seo ghas ke gaiya khiyalo
I fed the cow with that grass
Seo gae dudh delak
The cow gave me the milk
Seo dudh kauwa pilak
The crow drank up the milk
Seo kauwa painkh delak
The crow gave me the feather
Seo painkh tir patalo
I used the feather in the arrow
Seo tir me harin maralo
I hunted a deer from that arrow
Seo harin siṇg delak
I got horn from that deer
Seo siṇg me maṭi koṛalo
I dug up soil with that horn
Seo maṭi kumhar̭ leglak
That soil was taken away by the potter
Seo kumhar̭ chuka delak
The potter gave me a pot
Seo chuka Telin leglak
That pot was taken away by the oilwoman
Seo Telin tel delak
The oilwoman gave me the oil
Lohra re bhaiya
Brother lohra
Hiṇsuwa mor ke banaiyo debe lohra
Make a sickle for me, O lohra
Hiṇsuwa mor ke banaiyo debe
Make a sickle for me

This song describes how various occupational communities and the Mundas are related through economic services which they render to each other. It also indicates how a particular work leads to another work thereby interlinking all occupational communities and the Mundas. The song is a fine example of how a piece of work generates another work or occupation.

The Potters

Below is yet another song which appreciates the work of the potter in making beautiful tiles which the Munda get for roofing the house. The song belongs to Racha category, and the lines are as follows:

Kahaṇ kera kumhạr bhaiya
Brother potter from which village
Khapra kera bangela bhale re sobhae
The bungalow tiled with *khapra* looks beautiful
Nao jagale kumhạr bhaiya
Brother potter you earned your name and fame
Khapra kera bangela bhale re sobhae
The bungalow tiled with *khapra* looks beautiful
Re kumhar dahaiya
O brother potter
Khapra kera bangela bhale re sobhae
The bungalow tiled with *khapra* looks beautiful

The potters not only supply various sizes and shapes of earthen pots and utensils but they are the main suppliers of tiles to the Mundas. The Mundas either purchase readymade tiles from the potters or they are invited to make tiles in the house. In either case, the dealing is made in cash.

The Bania

Similarly, the Mundas get various articles of merchandise such as salt and spices, etc, from the Bania or trading communities. Bania communities do not believe in credit and so they do not give the articles through lending. The following song belonging to Bala category describes the sale and purchase of articles among the Bania communities and the Mundas:

Bania re Bania, ho hore Bania
O dear Bania
Marchi bechab re Bania
I shall sell chilli to you, O Bania
Bania re bania, ho hore bania
O dear Bania
Rokae lebo, rokae debo re bania
I shall take and make the payment at the spot, O Bania

The Associated Economic Activities

Besides the main agricultural activities, Mundas also remain busy throughout the year in other economic activities. Some such activities are making and repairing of agricultural implements, guarding the crops, tending and looking after the cattle, kitchen gardening, house construction and its repairing and weaving of various articles of use and also cooking and preparation of various food items. With the pressure on land, a good number of Mundas also do labour work either within the community or outside. All these activities have got references, somehow or the other, in their songs. Except construction work and repairing of houses, all other works are being done side by side along with other agricultural activities during the hours of recess.

Guarding of Crops

Guarding of crops from birds and wild animals is essential to get a good harvest. In the song below belonging to Bala category, the watchman is being praised for the endurance he undergoes while carrying out his duties. The lines of the song are as follows:

Bono re bono baroya
The guard in the forest
Kheti majhe re kumba derale
You have erected rest house in the middle of the crop
Jug jitale bono baroya
You did create the tradition
Manoa ke hari manale
You defeated the human endurance

The watchman of crops spends all his time in the field guarding the crops day and night cut-off from the family and community members leaving behind all joys and happiness there in the village. It is for this sacrifice and endurance that he receives praise from the community people.

Guarding of crops starts from the day the seeds are sown in the fields. The following Racha category of song states that the grain was all taken away by birds as there was nobody to guard it. The lines of the song are as follows:

> *Buru ko chetạn re nir gele lena re*
> On the hills Nir grain had sprouted its ears
> *Beṛa ko latạr re nirwa ḍimbu lena-2*
> On the valley below, *nirwa* had born its buds
> *Chuṭi-chuṭi do suga nidi kedare*
> All the top of the grain was taken away by parrots
> *Suba-suba do kaṭeya nobor ked*
> All the roots were harvested by the mouse

Similar to the above, in the song below too it is stated that crops were all grazed over by the deer during the night. The song belongs to Racha category and the lines are as follows:

> *Jad buru re masuri moe bunclo*
> On the Jad hill, I sowed *masuri* pulse
> *Harina chari gela-2*
> The deer grazed over it
> *Dekhbe re raja ghare sipahia*
> Look O policemen of the king's palace
> *Harina chari gela-2*
> The deer grazed over it

Making of the Plough

While guarding the crop, other work like plough making, spinning, weaving and repairing works are also attended. The song below which belongs to Racha category mentions about the making of plough. The lines of the song are as follows:

> *Jojo buṭa re*
> Under the tamarind tree

Nayalae bai tana, nayalae bai tana
Is making the plough
Nidiyai meja hili
O sister-in-law you would have carried for him
Loṭa re da-a, tunki re kalewa
Water in a brass-pot and breakfast in a basket

Plough making also takes a lot of time. As stated in the song, a person is engaged in plough making under the tamarind tree away from the house. He is so busy that he cannot come to the house even to take water or breakfast. When his younger brother came to know that his elder brother has taken nothing since morning, he asks his sister-in-law to carry water and breakfast for his brother. So in tribal community, everybody is anxious for the welfare of the other as happiness and joy is shared together. When there is a lack of cooperation, one can demand it. The work is normally carried out through cooperation and help.

Household Work

The song, below gives a very fine example of how the husband and wife, who have no other family member to help them in the work, attend their work in a relaxed atmosphere sharing each other's jokes. The song belongs to Jarga category and the lines are as follows:

Dhaṇkna-dhapurna
O, the dishevelled dressed one (wife is addressed)
Baba na roṇgo tana-2
The paddy is burning
Don temeya radoṛa
O the bearded one (husband is addressed)
Babuyaiṇg koyoṇg kaja-2 haere
The baby is on my lap
Ne na hene na
Look here it is (wife is addressed)
Simii na nelem sowan tana-2 haere
The excreta of the fowl is emitting bad smell
Her tameya gunḍa heṛe (husband is addressed)
Cover it with the chaff

Giṛi tare bolem jati senoa-2 haere
Will your gender spoil if you throw it away

In the above song, the conversation between husband and wife is very enjoyable for the audience as both of them are using selective words of abuse for the other while doing nothing but pretending to be most busy. Each one is asking the other to do the same job. As everybody remains busy in his own way, request for doing a particular job on emergency basis is also, not always granted. In this song as stated, paddy put up on the oven, in one case, is burning, and on the other, the excreta of the fowl is emitting bad smell. But in both cases, the person requested is also busy and is natural to be attended by the person from whom the request was initially made.

Oven is prepared by the womenfolk only. Its method of preparation has been described in the following Dubung category of song, the lines of which are as follows

Lal miṭi koir-koir chulha re banae
Digging out red soil oven is prepared
Chulha upar gagari chaṛae-2
Pot is placed on the oven
Kathi jori bich-bich
Firewood is burnt at intervals
Aig kathi karae re
Firewood is pushed in at intervals
Aigi ko bhelaiṇ bhinsar re
It became morning in the process

Oven is usually prepared from red clay in which paddy chaff is mixed. Three horned oven is usually made by the Munda women. The above song indicates how the women burn firewood in the oven while cooking food. In this song it took much time to burn the wood as the oven just prepared was wet and so it took hours to catch fire in the wood.

The song below which belongs to Jadur category, describes how a woman while watching the crop, is also attending her other works. The lines of the song are as follows

1. *Masuri piṛi re kita hom galaṇg tana*
   You are weaving mat while guarding the *masuri* crop

Kewaṛi badi re chari hom chaṭa tana
On the Kewari plot you are splitting sticks

2. *De masuri metạm re ote gem tiruba*
When asked for *masuri, you* look down to earth
De chari metạm re, sirma gem saṇgila
When asked for sticks you look up to the sky

3. *Ote rechim topa keda ote gem tirruba*
Have you buried it in the earth that you look down to earth
Sirma rechim haka tada sirma gem saṇgila
Did you hang up in the sky that you look up to the sky

The woman as mentioned in the above song is so busy that she is steadfastly looking down on the earth or looking up to the sky. The procedure of work is different in both types of jobs.

Spinning

In yet another song which belongs to Racha category the composer of the song describes the spinning scene. The hands which do the spinning job is not handling an ordinary thing but it is as valuable as gold. The lines of the song are as follows:

1. *Duṛum tanạm mami*
You are sleeping auntie
Takui tanạm mami lodob-lodob
You are spinning gracefully

2. *Eke hathe sone je taulae*
Gold is weighed by one hand
Duyo hathe rupa je taulae
The silver is weighed by both hands
Duṛum tanạm mami
You are sleeping auntie
Takui tanạm mami lodob-lodob
You are spinning gracefully

Auntie is spinning cotton thread, it is night. Cotton fibres are white like silver which she is holding in one hand but when it is made thread and clothes from it, its value become worth of gold. The auntie is feeling exhausted and sleepy but she looks graceful in this mood also.

Food Recipes and its Preparation

The daily duties of the womenfolk, as stated in the previous pages describe their busy life since the dawn of the day. Paddy husking, cleaning and cooking food are the routine duties of the young ladies and girls. The staple diet of the people of Chhotanagpur is rice. Rice is separated from the paddy through long process. The paddy is first half boiled, then it is dehydrated and dried up in the sun. It is then pounded in the instrument called *dhenki* in Mundari. *Dhenki* is one heavy log of wood and is operated by feet. The following song describes the process of separation of rice from the paddy which is done by feet operated instrument called *dhenki*. The song belongs to Bala category and the lines are as follows:

Tetari tare nayo
Near the tamarind tree mother
Dhana moe ghataloṇ
I spread up paddy
Garowaṇ charai hiri-jori utarae-2
The sparrows are alighting on it on after the other
Dhanayo sukhi gel
The paddy too dried up
Supe me uthaloṇ
I collected it on a winnowing fan
Dheki me sajaloṇ
I put it in the *dheki*
Dheki me kuṭe chhamar-chhamar-2
Pounded it on the *dheki* rhythmically
Kuṭe keṭo kutaloṇ
I pounded it but
Supali me pechhorae
And cleaned it through the winnowing fan

Dheki me kuṭe chhamar̥-chhamar̥-2
Pounded it on the *dheki* rhythmically

Separation of rice from the paddy is a time consuming process. The process involved as stated earlier is first of making rice half boiled and then dehydrating it by putting it into the pan over the fire. It is then allowed to cool down. The next step is to spread it on a mat allowing it to dry in the sun. It is during this time that sparrow birds come down on the paddy. While drying it is regularly checked so that it may not overdry otherwise when it is pounded, it will be reduced into small grain. To keep the rice in its usual shape, the paddy is moderately dried up. It is then pounded in the *dhenki* and the chaff is separated through a winnowing fan. In the above song, the girl describes how she separated rice from the paddy.

There is yet another instrument for separation of rice from the paddy. This instrument is called *tuku* in Mundari. It is hand operated. In this process single person can do the job but to save the time more than one person can participate in the operation. The song below which also belongs to Bala category, describes this process of rice separation in the following lines:

Ḍiṇḍa ge chhoṇṛi
O young damsel
Ḍih ṭangera me kute chhamar̥-chhamar̥
You are pounding rhythmically on the village rock
Ḍiṇḍa rahle maiya
While remaining spinster
Chhoṇṛi rahle maiya
And remaining young
Hare, ḍih ṭangera me kuṭe chhamar̥-chhamar̥
You are pounding rhythmically on the village rock
Supli me jhunṭi
You have decorated the winnowing fan with toe rings
Baṛhni me phudena
And colourful thread flowers in the broomstick
Samatha me ghughura
And tinkling bell metal in the mortar

In this song as mentioned *samath*, that is, mortar which is called *tuku* in Mundari is the instrument used for pounding the paddy. The song also mentions how the work environment has become musical through rhythmic sound of tinkling bells which are tucked with the instruments. The place of pounding the paddy have also virtually been turned into a dancing ground and the operation producing a rhythm of dance with colourfully decorated instruments—a feast to the eyes and ears for the audience. The girl's whole body is rhythmically moving while pounding the paddy. The elders observe that such musical work atmosphere can be created by the girl so long as she remains unmarried and young. It is during this age that nobody can raise any question about the activity and behaviour, that is, decorating the pounding instruments of the girl.

The Munda also cultivate *kode* or millet for bread. The grain is floured in the grinding stone, called *janta* by the women. The following song not only describes the grinding of millet but also mentions other human behaviour with respect to sharing of the bread. The song belongs to Bala category and the lines are as follows:

Eke paila maruwa
One *paila* worth millet
Pise lagal chhokri
The girl is grinding
Hore, janta baje ghunure ghunur
The grinding stone is producing the sound of *ghunur-ghunur*
Pise keto pisale
You have grinded, but
Paka keto pakale
And baked also, but
Hare, kahe bhauji gal tor ke phulale-2
But alas, sister-in-law, why are you annoyed

The social atmosphere is congenial if the members of the family agree on certain points without any differences. The work can be easily completed when they develop understanding of mutual respect with each other. In this song as mentioned the sister-in-law is not happy over the sharing of bread. As the quantity of millet was small, the size of the bread that the girl baked was also small. It was, therefore, natural that the amount that was distributed among the family members when each one got the share was too small. This was the fact that made the sister-in-law unhappy.

Cooking the Food

Cooking of food also takes much time of the ladies. The Mundas prepare only one or two recipes or vegetables besides the main item of food. Cooking of vegetables is also too simple. In cooking of vegetable, generally no spices are added but it is always fried in oil after the cooking. Below are few songs which relate to the preparation of food. *Rai* and garlic besides onion are used while frying the vegetable or pulse. The reference of *rai* and garlic have been made in the following Jadur category of song. The lines of the song are as follows:

Rai buru re rai Rasuṇṛi
On the hill *rai* and *rasunri* grow
Tilasari buṭa teya
It has spread up roots
Gena-gena daha teya
It has tubers on the sides
Rai bura re rai Rasuṇṛi
On the hill *rai* and *rasunri* grow

The above song only mentions where the *rai* and garlic are produced and how they appear. The following Jadur song describes how the Munda ladies cook the vegetables. The lines of the song are as follows:

1. *Chikaṇ aṛa: tarakari tana pere*
What vegetable are you cooking, dear
Rasuṇṛi ka soṇd foraṇ momolagi
The fragrance of fried garlic is spreading

2. *Losod aṛa: tarakari tana pere*
You are cooking *losod ara,* dear
Rasuṇṛi ka tel foraṇ momolagi
The fragrance of fried garlic in oil is spreading

3. *Muchuri aṛa: tarakari tana pere*
You are cooking *muchuri ara,* dear

Rasunri ka sond foran momokagi
The fragrance of fried garlic is spreading

When green vegetables—leafy or fruits—are cooked, they are first semi-boiled and then are fried in oil with garlic or mustard seeds. Usually no spices are added in the vegetables when cooking.

The song below which belongs to Khemta category describes where the fish are available and the materials which are added in it during cooking. The lines of the song are as follows:

Gara redo hai ko
Fish are available in the river
Piri redo jojo
The tamarind in the field
Jojo utu re hai ko sibila
Gravy with tamarind juice make the fish tasty
Sasang surumi farka regi re masela
Leave aside turmeric, spices and oil
Jolo utu re hai ko sibila
Gravy with tamarind juice make the fish tasty

Cleaning and Cleanliness

There are few songs also with the theme of cleanliness with respect to the body and clothes. Food is generally taken after taking bath and no soap is used while taking bath but hair are cleaned with clay-soap which is locally available on the field. The song below is related to the cleaning of hair. The song belongs to Jadur category and the lines are as follows:

1. *Deto ge nayo mure misna mati*
   Mother, let me have the clay-soap
   Hare, bendo jharia me nare kensa ke jharae
   I will wash my fine hair in the stream of Bendo

2. *Detoge nayo dubuni me karanji ka tel*
   Mother, let me have *karanji* oil in a cup
   Hare, bendo jharia me nare kensa ke jharae
   I will wash my fine hair in the stream of Bendo

3. *Detoge nayo katha kera kakai*
Mother, let me have the wooden comb
Hare, nane kensa ke jharae-2
I shall comb my fine hair

After taking bath and washing the hair oil is used in the body and hair with *karanj oil* which is available from *koronj* tree. The hair is combed with comb made of wood or bamboo. The above song is also sung during marriage and the song can be categorized under Bala category.

The clothes are generally clean—washed by the ladies of the family. No soap is used in washing the clothes. The clothes are first boiled in ash and then taken to some stream for washing. Some clothes and particularly the personal dress are, however, washed by the gents also. The song below belonging to Jadur category has mentioned this in the following lines:

1. *Binga-bange sereng re*
On the stripped spreadup rock
Kichri sobod kora
The cloth washing boy

2. *Kachi koram nelana*
Don't you see the cloth
Kichri atu tana
The cloth is being carried away by the current
Gamcha bual tana
The cloth is floating downwards

Animal Husbandry

Tending or looking after the cattle is one of the important works of the agricultural communities. The animals which include water buffaloes, bullocks and cows, goats and sheep, pig and horses are the assets of the Mundas. Tending or looking after the cattle, requires one or two persons engaged in the job all the time. There are a good number of songs relating to different aspects of the job describing the situation, environment, mood and temperament of the person associated in the job and the cattle which indicates problems as well as the joys and happiness that one gets while remaining engaged in the job. The tending of cattle is always done together and the job is done by all age groups and gender of people. It is during the tending of cattle that youngsters receive training on various activities and gain knowledge and experience of the practical life. Each day the cattle are taken out to different areas of the village for grazing. The song below belonging to Jadur category mentions the plan of the cattle tending boys and girls which they are making for next day's outings. The lines of the song are as follows:

1. *Uri kobu ha̭r koa, maraṇg charia jana̭r te*
   We shall take out the cattle to the wide and spacious valley
   Merom kobu ha̭r koa, huring charia lata̭r te
   We shall take out the goats to the little greenery valley

2. *Maraṇg charia jana̭r do chakoṇḍa pereya kana*
   The big and spacious valley is full of *chakonda* plants
   Huriṇg charia lata̭r do bakula dalob kana
   The little greenery valley is covered with thorny shrubs

3. *Uri kobu ha̭r koa, chakonda chako joma*
   Will the cattle eat *chakonda* plants if we take them there
   Merom kobu ha̭r koa, bakula chiko haba
   Will the goat eat *bakula* if we take them there

Before taking out the cattle for grazing, the availability of grass and water in the area is taken into consideration. The people while tending, also collect grass, leaves, hay, etc, for the cattle. The cattle are usually fed before they are taken out or after they are brought back to the house from the field. Paddy hay is usually piled in stacks for them and used during the lean season when there is unavailability of green grass. The cattle are also fed with green leaves and oil cakes.

When the cattle are taken out to distant and hilly areas, the calves are usually left behind in the house as they cannot walk along with the herds. In that case they have to remain without mother's milk till the evening. In case of accident of the mother, say by killing of tiger, the calf may face great trouble. The following two *Bala* categories of songs are based on this theme:

Bono re bono bhaiṇsa
The wild water buffalo in the forest
Ḍih chhoṛi bono chare gela re-re
Went for grazing to the forest leaving behind the village
Na dharu re baghoa
Don't catch, O tiger
Na dharu re sapoa
Don't catch, O python
Najuko janamalaiṇ bachharu
The newborn calf
Dudhase dukhe morae
May die without milk

The owner of the water buffalo is anxious for it has gone to the forest for grazing leaving behind its newborn calf There is danger of being killed by the tiger or eaten away by python snake in the forest and in such cases the calf may die without milk. The owner hopes that the water buffalo would return safely without any harm from the tiger and python. The composer of the song has not mentioned the result and has left to guess for the audience. The result will either be a great joy and happiness for the owner in case the buffalo returns and if not there will be grief and crying.

Similar to the above, the song below too have the same theme. The song belongs to Racha category and the lines are as follows:

Buru ko chetạn re gaya mor tharki
My rattle ornamented cow went for grazing to the hill
Beṛa ko latạr re gai ko dipir-dilo-2
On the valley below the cows are grazing gracefully
Hare mor bachharu dudha binu morae
Alas, my newborn calf is dying without milk
Hare mor bachharu piyase morae-2
Alas, my newborn calf is dying thirsty

The cattle have been taken out to the hills and valleys for grazing, leaving behind their calves. As the cows would return late in the evening, the calves have to remain without milk. The owner is very much worried for the calves are thirsty and hungry.

Construction and Repairing of House

Shelter is one of the basic needs of the people. So one of the activity of the Mundas after the harvesting is construction and repairing of houses. The activity takes much time and labour of the people. This work is generally done through mutual help and cooperation by the lineage members. Normally, houses are made of mud walls with roofing by earthen tiles. Roofing is also done with special variety of grass which are grown for the very purpose. There are few songs which relate to construction of houses and the condition of house during rainy season. All the songs referred here belong to Bala category. The materials, methods and design of house construction by the Mundas have been systematically described in the song. One of the song belonging to Bala category gives the following description of house construction.

> *Bata moe chholaloṇ*
> I cleaned the (bamboo) planks
> *Baṇgela moe banaloṇ*
> And constructed a bungalow
> *Hare, ke moke kai samujhae mono dil ka bata re-2*
> Alas, who will tell me the words of heart and mind
> *Dharti nupare khuṇṭa moe garaloṇ*
> I pitched the poles on the ground
> *Malwa upare dharna moe charaloṇ*
> I placed the centre log on the Malwa
> *Dharna upre maniktham moe charaloṇ*
> Put up *maniktham* on the *dharna*
> *Manikthaṁ upre kaṇḍ moe charaloṇ*
> I placed *kand* upon the *maniktham*
> *Kaṇḍ upre bata moe charaloṇ*
> I placed bamboo planks on the *kand*
> *Bata upre khapra moe charaloṇ*
> I placed the tiles upon the bamboo planks
> *Hare, moke kai samujhae mono dil ka bata re-2*
> Alas, who will tell me the words of heart and mind

The song describes one of the methods and process of house construction. In this method, the poles are first pitched on the ground and thus a structure is prepared by placing other wooden poles and planks of wood one upon the other and lastly earthen tiles are placed upon it. The person desires that somebody should advise him other methods of house construction. In this method, the roof supported by poles have been made. This is a shed type of house which has no walls. In case of need, braided walls from planks of bamboo or wood can be erected or be replaced by mud walls.

The Bala category of song below too describes the same methods of house construction in the following lines:

Ghar kera ghar nayo
The house to live in mother
Ghar kera ghar re
The house to live in
Ghar kera ghar nayo lambe-lambe-lambe
The long houses to live in mother
Ghar nupare khunṭa gaṛae
Poles are pitched in the house
Khunṭa nupare malwa chaṛae
Malwa is placed on the poles
Malwa upre bhanḍia chaṛae
Bhandia is placed on the *malwa*
Bhanḍia upre kanḍ chaṛae
Kand is placed on the *bhandia*
Kanḍ upre bata thokae
Bata is nailed on *kand*
Bata upre khapra chaṛae
Tiles are placed on *bata*
Khapra upre pani nai barisae
There is no rain on the tiles
Ghar kera ghar nay ghar kera ghar re
The house to live in mother
Ghar kera ghar nayo lambe-lambe-lambe
The long house, mother

Besides the systematic description of house construction, items which have been used in it have also been given. The wooden poles when given to different shapes and sizes to serve the different purposes in house construction, are given different names. The names cited in this song are *khunta, malwa, dhanra, bhandia, maniktham, kand* and *bata.*

Doors are usually made of solid plank of wood, but doors with bamboo splits which are woven to the size of the door are also made. The following song of Bala category describes how the door is being prepared. The lines of the song are as follows:

> *Raṭa-raṭa keoṛa*
> The door with cracking sound
> *Hare ke re bhai bhagina deota kholala keoṛa re-2*
> Who the god like brother and nephew are opening the door
> *Lenga hathe rukna*
> Holding chisel in left hand
> *Dayeṇ hathe mugera*
> And hammer in right hand
> *Hare, ke re bhai bhagina deota kholala keoṛa re-2*
> Who the god like brother and nephew are opening the door

The door makes sound whenever it is opened so it was repaired. The lady of the house was fed up with the cracking sound of the door and requested to repair it early.

The song below belonging to Bala category describes the palatial size of the door in the following lines:

> *Chhoṭe moṭe kuṛia purbe duar re*
> A small house with door facing the east
> *Hare tala lagal bajara kewaṛ re*
> It has strong solid lock on the planks
> *Sone kera kuṇjiwa*
> It has gold key
> *Rupa kera talawa*
> The lock is made of silver
> *Hare, tala lagal bajara kewaṛ re*
> It has strong solid lock on the plank

Houses are generally made single storied but sometimes double-storeys are also made. The beauty of such houses have been described in the following Bala category of song:

> *Chote chhani chharae, diya baro cahani chharae-2*
> Small and big houses were constructed
> *Chharailo-chharailo chandana chaupari*
> A four storied house was constructed
> *Sona hole badalae*
> If I had gold I would have purchased it
> *Rupa hole badalae*
> If I had silver, I would have purchased it
> *Jiwa kaese badalae*
> How shall I exchange my soul
> *Chhote chhani chharae diya baro cahani chharae-2*
> Small and big houses were constructed

The house constructed is so beautiful that the owner does not want to sell it even with gold and silver. The house as stated is of four storeys which is an indication itself of the richness of the owner and his living standard.

The house is the indication of the living standard of the owner. The houses of wealthy persons are generally built in number of storeys and well designed which reflect the beauty of the house. On the other hand, the poor people built the house with great difficulty and that too with poor materials and badly designed. The life becomes difficult during rainy season when rain water percolates down into the badly constructed and roofed houses. The following song belonging to Bala category mentions this situation in the following lines:

> *Jati kera ghorena*
> Walled with mat
> *Mati kera chhabena*
> Plastered with clay
> *Dino-dino ratio sagar chuwela-2*
> All through the day and night it percolates
> *Upre to kera patai dabena*
> With banana thatched roof

Niche to meral patai chhabena
And floored with *meral* leaves on the ground
Dino-dino ratio sagar chuwela-2
All through the day and night it percolates

Generally Mundas construct the house with mud walls but the song mentions the house whose walls are of mat and roof that of banana leaves, the flooring has been done with *meral* leaves. Thus the house has been very poorly built. It is as such but natural that the house gets overflooded with rain water during rainy season. It is a nightmare to stay in such house during the monsoon.

Below is yet another song which also mentions the condition of the poorly built houses during rainy season. The song belongs to Bala category and the lines are as follows:

Jhimir-jhimir pani nai barisae-2
It is scantly raining
Ja tore chocha re charaiyo
Proceed, O *chocha* bird
Khijur patai chirio lanbe, bhangio lanbe
Split and break the date leaves and bring it here
Ghar mor chuwela-2
House mine is percolating

The *chocha* bird makes its house with date leaves, these are thought to be waterproof that is why it lives comfortably during the rainy season. Man has not been able to construct such a waterproof house. The knowledge and skill of man stands nowhere in the construction of waterproof house. So the poor men with dilapidated house desires to engage the *chocha* bird and avail its services in the construction of the house.

15

BARTER AND MONETARY ECONOMY

To cope with the variety of works and to complete it within the time schedule, besides family members, help is sought from community and other people. But such help and cooperation is not available everyday. The Mundas have, therefore, developed the practice of keeping the helpers of either sex on fixed amount of grain on annual basis. The male helpers in Mundari are called *dasi* and female *kamri*. They are not looked upon or treated as servants, as in the modern sense but as one of the family members. It is mostly the young persons who offer their services in lieu of grain as per agreement for a year which can be renewed every year. The song below belonging to Jadur category describes the experience of a person who had begun his life by working as *dasi* in other's house in his early age. The lines of the song are as follows:

1. *Bale:-bale: regeiṇa dasi kena*
   I did my duty as *dasi* in my childhood days
   Tire mayom ka aṇjed jana
   When baby blood in my hands were still there
   Liṇduṇg-liṇduṇg regeiṇg guti kena
   I did start my service at the age of infancy
   Kaṭa jambar oga dage jaṇa
   The sole of my feet became moistured

2. *Tire mayom-O aṇjed jana*
   The blood in my hand too dried up
   Okore taiṇg saṇgaiṇg oṛa:
   Where is the house of my friend
   Liṇduṇg-liṇduṇg reiṇg guti kena
   I did start my service at the age of infancy
   Okore taiṇg a hagaiṇg oṛa:
   Where is my brother's house

The boy under reference in this song seems to be an orphan. He may have been picked up and looked after by a family other than his kin. He does not know who are his friends and brothers nor he remembers his village of birth. He started working as *dasi* in someone's house from his very childhood days.

As stated above, *dasi* or *kamri* are initially employed on contract basis for a year. On completion of the period, he may leave for his house or may renew for another year that may depend upon the need and satisfaction of the family who employs or the desire of the concerned person for continuity. In the former case a situation of uncertainty prevails till the decision is arrived at by the employer, This theme has been taken in the following Jadur category of song :

1. *Mage munḍi dore teba lena*
The month of Magh has arrived
Ne Munḍa do reko bage-iṇg deraṇg
These Mundas may not continue my service
Bachor neda dore nachur lena
The period of service is nearing completion
Ne Munḍa do reko bage-iṇg deraṇg
These Mundas may not continue my service

2. *San gatiṇg reiṇg farga koa*
I shall cut wood for them, friend
Ne santa do reko raṛaiṇg deraṇg
These *santas* may not enter into further agreement
Sauṛi saṇgaiṇg reiṇg ira koa
I shall cut *sauri* grass for them, friend

3. *San gatim reiṇg farga koa*
I shall cut wood for them, friend
San gatim re nonolad geya
The wood when burnt leaves behind black stain
Sauṛi saṇgaiṇg reiṇg ira koa
I shall cut *sauri* grass, friend
Sauṛi gatim re sasaga
Sauri grass too pinches

The two friends are talking about the continuity of service in their respective households as they are not sure of it. Both the families where they work have made remarks against their respective *dasi* regarding their way of working and so they are doubtful of their continuity.

These songs indicate how the Munda economy as well as its process of management is changing day by day. The land being limited and as division of land takes place at each generation, it reduces the per capita holding making it uneconomic and ultimately reduces the production which hardly supports the family. The only alternative is living by labour either in the local area or outside.

Fresh clearing of land is now no more possible as unoccupied fallow land are not available in the village and forest areas are reserved by the government, so establishment of new settlement is now a matter of history. The people from neighbouring states and districts too are now pouring in who are all interested in having some portion of land in this region thereby restricting the locals into their own land. All these factors have reduced the size of holding among the Mundas and as the society and culture of the Mundas are fast breaking down which would, otherwise have held together the members of the community, a tendency of individualism is developing among them which breaks a family into multi-families and each claiming a portion from the limited ancestral inherited land. With the dwindling of forest region, the fertility of land has gone down enormously, it is unable to support the family members. The other natural resources which were once found abundantly in the region, are no more in existence due to environment degradation. In this situation, labour is the only alternative source of livelihood left to the Mundas. Trade, business and white-collar jobs are quite a new field for the Mundas, they lack courage for its undertaking. Almost all Mundas live in villages among the community people and migrating out for the sake of labour work is against the likings. It is not that the high income and other facilities and benefits do not attract them but leaving one's kith and kin is deeply felt by most of them. In Munda songs we get a blend of themes on this aspect of joy, mirth and danger of unknown which may await a Munda labourer in a distant land cut-off from one's relatives and community people.

When the Mundas were passing days of uncertainty, a number

of tea gardens sprang up in the far eastern corner of the country in Assam during the last part of the 18th and first part of the 19th century which needed labourers to work over there. This was the only area known to the then Mundas where they could earn something for their family. The news of requirement of labourers in tea gardens of Assam, etc, was welcomed by the tribals. A good number of Mundas migrated to the tea gardens to earn their living. As the land of their habitation was too dear to them, they seldom remained their for a long time. A couple, as in the song below which belongs to Jadur category, decides to migrate to Assam to earn something. The lines of the song are as follows:

1. *Dolaṇg gatim re Assam disum te*
   Let us proceed to the country of Assam, dear
   Dolaṇg sangaing re kachhar gamae te
   Let us proceed to the village of Kachhar, dear
   Assam disum re paisa do dibua kana
   The money has become very cheap in Assam

2. *Dolaṇg gatim re suku telaṇg, raina*
   We will live there happily, let us proceed, dear
   Kachhar disum gatim sirma leka
   The land of Kacchar is like paradise, dear
   Dolaṇg gatim relaṇg kami joma
   Let us work and live there

In the above song, the wife insists to her husband to proceed for Assam and Kachhar to work and live there as she has heard that money is easily earned there which may purchase the paradise like happiness for them.

On hearing the news that money can be earned easily in the tea gardens of Assam and Kachhar, enough for leading a good and happy life, a good number of people proceeded there. Many people, who otherwise had no intention to visit Assam, also joined the goers as it was a new country and experience for them. The unknown land and its people, the journey and the idea of meeting the strangers *en route* to Assam and back enthralled the Mundas and the more they heard and thought about it, the more restless they got to go there. The song below belonging to Lahsua category describes the state of mind of the Munda under the situation as above :

1. *Ranchi redo dipu mena*
There is a depot at Ranchi
Daigo iṇku lo: seno gi sanaiṇga
Sister dear, I would like to go with them,

2. *Maraṇg Ganga teba lena, lauka reko dub jana*
When they arrived to Ganga all of them got into the ship
Daigo iṇku lo: doing landa jagạr geya
Sister dear, I would like to talk and have jokes with them

3. *Maraṇg Ganga teba lena, lauka reko dub jana*
When they arrived to Ganga all of them got into the ship
Daigo iṇku lo: do jati mạti jetạn jati banoga
Sister dear, among them there is no discrimination of caste and creed

To control the movement of labour and to check the spurious agent, the government opened a depot at Ranchi to flush out unscrupulous elements. When one successfully crosses these checkposts, there lies ahead awaiting a land of wonder and joy for him.

When some persons heard about the land and condition of life there from persons who had already returned, they told others about it. In the song below which belongs to Lahsua category, a person tells his own experience in the following lines:

1. *Assạm disum sene kenaiṇg*
I had visited Assam
Assạm disum isugi suku giya
Happiness abounds there in Assam

2. *Dola to gabu seno gabu*
Let us proceed there
Assạm disum isugi suku giya
Happiness abounds there in Assam

While some, who had visited the tea garden, had mixed experience. The following song belonging to Bala category describes this in the following lines:

Pardese ko sen kenako, kami kenako
They visited foreign land and worked there

Isu sukuwa ko meneya
There is happiness over there, they say
Sen kenale, kami kenale
We visited and worked there
Banoa suku do, duku do kasaka giya
There is no happiness but sufferings abound
Khunṭi sahar̥, Ranchi sahar̥, mered bayar̥ tola kana
Metal wire links Khunti and Ranchi towns
En bhitar̥ re sen kenale kami kenale
There we had been and worked
Banoa suku do, duku do kasela giya
There is no happiness but sufferings abound

While tea gardens were being opened in Assam for the first time, the towns of administrative and business centres were also being connected with telegraphic wires which the song above has indicated. All these were new developments, that were taking place during the early years of British rule. These were great wonders for the simple Mundas.

There is no easy going life in working in foreign lands as nothing can be predicted what would happen there, the elders would not allow the young to leave them behind. The following Lahsua category of song mentions the uncertainty of life in foreign land :

1. *Mage chanḍu seṭer len*
The month of *Magh* has arrived
Saredar ko hiju seno tana ko
The agents are coming and going
Numana aiṇga jido seno mone inga
My heart yearns to accompany them, mother

2. *Nalom sena babu re*
Don't go my dear
Nalom sena bachhare
Don't go my child
Babure duku-suku, pahạm-fikir mena:
There is happiness, sufferings and anxiety, dear
Gidi, kuṛid, tuyue jojoma
Vultures, kites and jackals may devour

When tea gardens in north-eastern part of the country were opened in Darjeeling, Jalpaiguri, Bhutan, Sikkim, Manipur, Assam and Kachhar, the tribal labourers were exported out to these gardens. Sardars, that is, agents of the company were sent out to tribal areas of Chhotanagpur to assemble the labourers at the depot at Ranchi during the month of *Magh* and *Fagun* when the people were free from routine jobs of agriculture. Working on tea gardens was on contract basis from a period of six months to three years. The agents would explain to the people about the rate of payment, facilities and other benefits which easily lured the young boys and girls. But the elders who have seen the days and are aware of the pros and cons of the situation, as mentioned in the song, are not consulted and brought into confidence.

Visit to tea gardens, even for few months, is not welcomed by the other family members of the couple. In cases when wife does not accompany the husband, the former does not allow the latter to leave them behind as they always think of each other's welfare and no one knows what would happen to the other after separation. In the following song which belongs to Lahsua category, a wife fervently makes appeal to her husband to postpone the decision to visit the foreign land. The lines of the song are as follows:

Jori re rasika
O beloved husband
Mati jabe paradesh
Don't go to foreign land
Ho hore rasika, more jabe bukhe re piyas
O my beloved one, you may die of hunger and thirst there
Na mile marua, na mile gondli
No corn of bread will be available there
Ho hore rasika, mori jabe bukhe re piyas
O beloved one, you may die of hunger and thirst

But separation is sometimes inevitable when circumstances are beyond the control, though it is painful, particularly to the young couple. Sometimes the husband leaves the wife without her knowledge. The following Jadur category of song describes the situation that existed a day prior to the departure of the husband. The lines of the song are as follows:

1. *Auj lele saparạle rani*
   You have decorated today like a queen
   Kaul lele bipatạl jae
   Trouble may befall on you from tomorrow
2. *Joṛi tora chali gela rani*
   Beloved yours have gone away, O queen
   Kalikata Koṛae raji
   For digging work at Calcutta

The husband has left for Calcutta and his wife has no knowledge of it. Unmindful of the situation that is befalling her, she is decorating herself. The departure of her husband is conveyed to her by other persons.

In the following Jadur song description of a wife has been given which has been created at the sudden departure of her husband. The wife has been left in a precarious situation and she is unable to bear the pangs of separation. The lines of the song are as follows:

1. *Jori re rasika*
   My beloved husband
   Chali gela re Assạm raij
   Have left for Assam
   Dhaṇgoṛi ka lora pani dhimir dila re giral jae
   The girl is shedding tears incessantly

2. *Adho rati, pahạr rati*
   At day in and day out
   Chali gela re Assạm raij
   Have left for Assam
   Dhaṇgoṛi ka lora pani dhimir dila re giral jae
   The girl is shedding tears incessantly

3. *Ranchi ka rail gaṛi*
   The train of Ranchi
   Chali gela re Assạm raij
   Took him away to Assam
   Dhaṇgoṛi ka lora pani dhimir dila re giral jae
   The girl is shedding tears incessantly

The wife was, thus left behind in perpetual agony to bear it alone. The service in distant land, on the one hand, widens the knowledge and experience of the people about the world beyond and on the other, a bit of extra cash in their hands disturbed the peace of family life. The experience of the outside world was taken as an adventure, the agony born silently by the close relatives, are equally eventful and memorable. These are all remembered and shared by the members of the community through the song of their creation.

Thus, among the Mundas, money economy was slowly introduced and it became the medium of exchange between the traders and also replaced the barter economy among them. It is stated that prior to the introduction of currency in the tribal regions, the material of one's need passed through from one hand to another by way of barter or exchange. This system still exists in villages in which occupational castes usually receive grain in lieu of their services or materials produced by them. The system has come to be known as *Bhownri* among the Mundas. In this system, a person carries his products or articles and makes a visit to every village announcing the names of the articles he is carrying. This system of exchange was introduced among the Mundas by the non-tribal traders. The traders in their early years of immigration to Munda region did carry various items of merchandise to villages on mules, horses back and bullocks. And as there were no weekly markets, they would travel to every village with their articles like nomads often camping in some village to pass the night. They introduced various articles among the Mundas which were mostly urban products. The use of articles which were new were demonstrated to the Mundas. The sound of metal bells hanging from the body of the animals of burden, would indicate the arrival of the traders and the women would come out to do the purchasing from them. The sound of bell metal was a matter of curiosity for the young and the old alike. The song below belonging to Jadur category indicates the curiosity of the people. The lines of the song are as follows:

1. *Kuṛumba ṭikura do salu*
   The streets of Kurumba village, O friend
   Chi riṛiṇg-riṛiṇg
   What sorts of riring-riring sound

Salga bera do salu
In the valley of Salga, O friend
Mere rarang-rarang
What is ringing, rarang-rarang

2. *Beyopari ko hora re*
The traders on the way
Chi riring-riring ho
What sorts of riring-riring sound
Landna ko dare re
The pack animals on the way
Mere rarang-rarang
That is making *rarang-rarang* sound

And as stated above, they would usually encamp under some shady tree during the night and move to other villages at day time. For the villagers the sight was interesting. The curiosity of the villagers has been expressed in the following Jadur song :

1. *Uli suba, jojo suba*
Under the mango and tamarind trees
Beyopari ko dera tada
The traders did encamp
Uli suba, jojo suba
Under the mango and tamarind trees
Ladna ko basa tada
The pack animals had taken rest

2. *Chi ho ko chika tana*
What they are doing
Beyopari ko dera tada
The traders did encamp
Mere ho ko rika tana
What they are performing
Ladna ko basa tada
The pack animals had taken rest

3. *Bulung geko tula tana*
They are selling salt

Beyopari ko ḍera tada
The traders did encamp
Rasuṇṛi ko gaṇḍa tada
They are displaying garlic for sale
Ladna ko basa tada
The pack animals had taken rest

Thus, the Mundas in the early years of their contact with strangers and visit to foreign lands, were aquainted of the life that exist there as well as the foreign goods and their sale and barter. The traders who visited the villages would prefer exchange of goods in kind as it was most profitable for them and as the Mundas had no money in the form of coins, the barter exchange was most easy and suitable. The traders slowly developed market economy in a regular way and later on number of market centres came up in the form of quarterly or weekly markets where the sellers and buyers would gather. The tribals were able to earn cash with the coming of labour in the market and slowly the barter system of exchanging things were replaced with currency.

The Economy of Abundance and Scarcity

Munda shares his joys and sorrows with the fellow Mundas in his day to day life. The saving of a family, if any, gets distributed by various ways either through work, ceremonial functions, or simply by exchange. The well-to-do Munda seldom feels proud of his wealth, nor the poor one ever complains of the plight he is living by. The economic condition of a family is a matter of contingency and fortune and misfortune lurks everybody's door alternately in a man's life. The poor economic condition or its abundance in an average family, depends upon how the resources at one's disposal, are managed. The Munda does not show keenness in the gathering of wealth in abundance and so, not a single song is available on this theme. The song below which belongs to Jadur category records the conversation of two friends who belong to two different areas of the Munda region. The two friends are talking about the economic condition of the people living in respective areas, and the one who belongs to the area of better economic condition, invites the other to come to his area. The lines of the song are as follows:

1. *Ale sate laṇga chi ape sate laṇga*
Shall we proceed to our area or your area
Tala-mala bir relaṇg napa̭m jana
We have met in the middle of the forest
Ale sate laṇga chi ape sate laṇga
Shall we proceed to our area or your area
Biyur-sekor ḍare relaṇg napa̭m jana
We have met in the circular path

2. *Ale disum icha chiṇgṛi ba*
Our area is laden with flowers red
Ale disum heṇde hariya̭r
Our area is evergreen
Ale disum towa aṭa̭l ba
There bloom *towa* and *atal* flowers all over in our area
Ale disum sae danuwa̭r
There are hundreds of *danuwar* in our area .

3. *Ale disum towa tabena*
We have abundance of milk and beaten rice
Ale disum ili maṇḍia
Ours have an abundance of food and drinks
Ape disum ḍuku kasala
Agony and distress abounds in your land
Oko disum telaṇg senoa
To which country shall we proceed

4. *Ale disum ḍuku ukṛa*
Ours is trouble infested country
Ape disum suku sugṛa
Happiness blooms in your country
Disum taiṇg laṇg doya bagiya
Let us leave behind my country
Ape disum telaṇg senoa
Let us proceed to your country

Thus, it is not only the blood relatives that are welcomed during the hours of crises but others also receive the same treatment.

As stated above, it is the managerial skill of the members of the family, that even with scarce resources they manage their affairs. One such instance has been given in the following *Jadur* (*gena*) category of song:

1. *Kolom latar loyong dore dada*
   The plot below the barn, brother
   Alom dada bandareya
   Don't mortgage out, brother
   Miyad giyae bandi gundi dada
   We have but a single tailless cow, brother
   Alom dada kundariya
   Don't let out in mortgage, brother

2. *Dasi nalang guti nalang dada*
   We shall sell our labour, brother
   Alom dada bandareya
   Don't mortgage it, brother
   Udareya lang painchayalang dada
   We shall take loan, brother

3. *Mid bita la-e natin dada*
   For two finger tips lengths stomach, brother
   Alom dada bandareya
   Don't mortgage it, brother
   Chapu sunum mocha lagin dada
   For the sake of a finger's tip oil, brother
   Alom dada kundareya
   Don't let out in mortgage, brother

This is how the brother and sister, who have no other member in the family, eke out their living under the situational pressure of abject poverty.

The people who cannot support themselves from the annual production of crops are many. For many, the production hardly goes for six months. For the poor Munda family, summer and rainy seasons are the lean months. In the song below which belongs to Jatra category, a depiction of a poor family has been made who is hardly able to manage his family. The precarious condition of the family has been narrated as follows:

Jeṭe siṅgi seṭer lena
The summer month has arrived
Hoṇko doko rage baṛa tana
Children are crying all around
Pati babae au leda
She brought paddy worth a seer
Hoṇko doko laṇda baṛa tana
The children are laughing all around

Life becomes hell for such families when prices of the food articles rise or when there exists a general famine situation in the region. As the economy of the people is wholly depended on monsoon, the untimely and scanty rain both affects the economy badly. During such situation, prices of every commodity shoot up. The song below belonging to Jadur category describes the state of affairs in these lines:

Khunṭi re taka baba gel pati jana
At Khunti ten seers of paddy did cost a rupee
Siṇri gutu re jambira chauli soṛo dibua jana
At sinri gutu *jambira* rice did cost sixteen *dibua*
Akriṇg kodo ko rasika tana
The sellers are rejoicing
Kiriṇg kodo ko iyạm tana
But the purchasers are lamenting

The age of this song might be more than 100 years since its composition when it is stated that people could not carry paddy which was purchased in one 48th part of a rupee, that is, in the rupee value of pre-independent period. The song portrays the life of a very poor family. Every year the people still face the situation of scarcity when traders gain the maximum benefits. As stated in the above song, the traders are rejoicing as the price of the paddy had gone up, on the other hand the common people whose purchasing power was almost zero, had to lament for the soaring prices.

The song below which belongs to Jadur category, states the apprehensible mood of the two friends at the onset of famine. The lines of the song are as follows:

1. *Riṇga do golaiṇchi hiju tana*
The starvation has set in, O golainchi
Supid golaiṇchi joṛur tạm
Apply oil on your hair-lock, O golainchi
Akạl do mocho kuli seṭer tana
The famine is arriving slowly asking its way
Paela mocho kuli buṛui tạm
Let your saree fall down behind

2. *Riṇga do golaiṇchi hiju tana*
The starvation has set in, O golainchi
Supid golaiṇchi risa jana
Hair-lock of yours have become dishevelled
Akạl do mocho kuli seṭer lena
The famine has arrived asking its way
Paela do mocho kuli checha jana
The saree yours have become taterred

When the economic condition of the people remains normal, they carry out all sorts of activities in normal and regular way and wear or decorate themselves according to their liking. In this song two friends are talking about the famine and starvation which is about to set in. One of them asks the other to utilize his available time and resources in decorating herself before the setting in of the famine when it becomes too late. During famine life comes to a standstill which affects the people both physically and mentally. To avoid poverty or starvation, people all the time remain busy in one kind of economic activity or the other and work out ways to ameliorate the situation. All social, political and religious institutions are directed towards the maintenance of normal life of the people.

PART VI

THE POLITICAL HISTORY OF THE PEOPLE

16

THE DIFFERENT PERIODS IN HISTORY

The Traditional Government

The oral history of the Munda tribe is rich and varied in content. It gives us an account of their early migratory history in India and records the events that happened during the course of their sojourn. It also provides an account of the development of socio-religious and political institutions such as clan, Munda-Pahan, Parha-Patti and mankiship which later on helped in the development of chieftainship or kingship among them. Through these systems, the pattern of social relationship among the Munda themselves as well as with others was established and maintained and emerged as an influential and powerful force in the region which helped in resolving conflicts and establishment of peace and good government. This also helped in the integration and adaptation as well as in the continuity of tradition and culture among the ethnic groups of the region. The system itself also saw of its own growth and transformation.

The songs which have been taken up in this chapter with content of politico-historical facts provide more on politico-historical condition of different phases of socio-cultural development of the Munda tribe than recording facts of historical interest. These phases may roughly be categorized into two: (1) Pre-independence period, and (2) Post-independence period. The first phase includes the British period and prior to it. Besides, there are events which have neither a political hue nor historically very important, but indicates out of the way cultural factors that may have the force of socio-cultural transformation among the Mundas. The politico-historical situation as described through the song shows the interrelationship and interaction of the people with the authorities in power, thereby giving a course in cultural transformation of the people.

There are very few songs with the content of traditional administrative system. And whatever there are, it provides us only a piece of information of the system. It is stated that a two tier administrative system existed among the Mundas at (a) community level, and (b) village level. The former dealt with the issues of social nature and was responsible for maintaining peace and order in the society. The latter, on the other hand, dealt with issues of civil and criminal nature within the limited jurisdiction of a village.

Socially, Mundas are divided into clans as stated in the previous chapter. Each clan was organized which was known as *Parha* headed by a chief called *manki* who had his courtiers from people of kin clan. The *Parha* would resolve all social problems within the existing norms and traditions. Thus, there are as many *Parhas* as the number of clans. These *Parhas* would further, make confederation of such organizations of eight to twenty, as the case may be, which is headed by a chief called *maharaja*. The whole community is, thus, brought under clan or *Parha* organization.

The village organization, on the other hand is independent of the clan organization and there is no interference in either of the affairs. The village chief is known as *Munda* who is assisted by a dignitary called *Mahato* whose duty is like a watchman and makes reports to the Munda of offences of civil and criminal nature. The religious affairs are looked after by another dignitary called *Pahan*. Generally, all the three functionaries should belong to three separate lineages. But there are exceptions also when there is either two or uni-lineage in the village. The village organization which consisted of *Munda, Pahan* and *Mahato* administers the village affairs through an assembly of representatives from every family member in the village. The responsibility of maintaining the community's religious tradition is at the hands of *Pahan* who is assisted by a person called *Pujar*. The village organization is responsible for maintaining the law and order situation in the village and settles all criminal issues.

As stated above, the social issues in general and inter-clan and inter-community nature are taken up by the clan organization of *Parha*. The *Parha* functions as guardian of the community tradition and customs and keeps records of the ethnic history. The Mundas pay deep respects to the elders, at least this was so before the present social situation among them. The custom of ancestor worship and erection of memorial stones for the departed souls, are the indicators of these sentiments. They also remember their ancestors, besides daily offerings and prayers as well as ritual festivals in memory of them, through stories and songs as tradition. For the existence and continuity of the generation, they express their gratitude as described in the following Jatra category of song, the lines of which are as follows:

Naṇg ren hoṛo ko, naṇg ren hoṛo ko
The people of bygone days
Hatu ko dub keda-2 lekore
Sing hail, for they established villages
Piṛi loyoṇg ko bai keda-2 lekore
Sing hail, for they cleared fields and also constructed plots

It is the people of the bygone days who cleared the forest, made the fields and plots for cultivation and established villages on which their present generations are settled. For this act of their forefathers, the Mundas sing songs of praise and express gratitudes.

Some villages, in the process of their settlement history, were settled by the order of their chiefs. Some of the villages which were settled by the chief themselves are mentioned in the following song belonging to Jatra category, the lines of which are as follows:

Haṭia, chuṭia sirjala
Hatia and Chutia villages were established
Haṭia, Chuṭia, Korambe ke raje
O the king of Hatia, Chutia and Korambe

In the course of developmental history of the society, a number of groups and clans branched off from the original one and the expansion continued uninterruptedly. The identity and its maintenance has been an important area for social solidarity among the Mundas and it was one of the prime functions of the *Parha* organization. Besides personal name, a person can be identified by the lineage he belongs to in the village, that is, *Munda, Pahan* and *Mahato*; his clan or *Parha* name, that is, Topno, Surin, Bage, Guria, etc. by the name of the village, that is, Marcha, Banabira, etc. and by the name of the pargana he belongs to, that is, Sonpur, Belsinya, etc. Till pre-independence days, this was the most common practice of giving identity to a person in the society. We get the reference of *marki ko* and *surin ko* (the clan name as common name) in conversational language which indicates a close interclan relationship that exists among the members of the community.

All the clans have equal status in the society and have been interlinked through the *parha* organizations. No clan feud is ever reported in the ethnohistory of the Mundas. Though in the following song which belongs to Jadur category, a communal colour has been given to the feud of two persons belonging to two separate clans. The two persons have been identified distinctly through their respective clan names. The song runs as under:

Alore marki kora
Desist, O Marki boy
Alorem mapa ga
Don't kill each other
Alore surin kora
Desist, O Surin boy
Alorem tupuing ga
Don't shoot arrows to each other

The song does not refer to the clan feud, but it refers to the fighting of two persons belonging to two separate clans each. These two clans are neighbours to each other.

We have good number of songs which relate to the local chiefs or rajas and British administrative system, but no song is found based on the theme of traditional Munda administrative system, though indirectly its reference are found in a number of songs. While some songs distinctly relate to the events arising out of the situation under the administrative system of local kings, others depict the situation to that of the British. Some songs are based on both the systems as the age of the song is the same and involvement of these administrative organizations in a single event, is not an extraordinary one. However, for the sake of clarity and better understanding of the situation under each system, the songs have been classified accordingly in two different chapters. As the local rajas or chiefs are an extension of the traditional tribal administrative system in its changed form, it will be given a preference dealing. It may, however, be noted that except the lines of songs, no details are available about the events they relate to. Moreover, the songs too are not sequential and systematic. Nevertheless, it provides us an important clue or instrument to peep into the then prevailing situation of politico-historical nature of the people and region in the absence of recorded and authentic documents.

Arrangement of song text in sequence on the basis of historical events is dispensed with, for the composer is not the same individual who may have composed the songs on the basis of personal interest or gravity of the situation as perceived by the composer himself or the people. The songs are, therefore, an indicator of matter of concern of the people or the individual composer.

The Local Chiefs and Rajas

With the crowning of first chief or *manki* as raja from out of the traditional mankiship in the *parha* organization, the foundation of kingship as well as a line of Nagbansi dynasty was laid in Chhotanagpur. The song below which belongs to Bala category, is sung in the context of marriage where the marriage crown, in Hindu tradition occupy an important place and refers to crowning of Nagbansi king. The comparison has been made because of similarity of the situation. The lines of the song are as follows:

> *Siri bharno utaralaiṇ Nagbaṇsi raja*
> Nagbansi king came down to Siri Bharno village
> *Hare daiya, niṇda nahiṇ awae*
> Alas! Sister, there is no sleep
> *Lala topri pahiralaiṇ Nagbaṇsi raja*
> Nagbansi king was crowned with red cap
> *Haere daiya, niṇda kaise awae*
> Alas! Sister, how the sleep will come

It appears that the bridegroom has been impersonated as Nagbansi king who is being crowned with red turban. The song makes a psychological impact on the bridegroom on hearing its content, he will think of himself as king on being crowned.

Besides the kings of Nagbansi dynasty, there were numerous rajas, *jagirdars* and *zamindars* who also virtually ruled like a king in their own jurisdictions. The song records their activities which were related to the construction of palaces, temples, roads, ponds, implanting of trees in the groves, etc, as well as celebration of marriage, war, feuds and rivalries among themselves and often exposing the sinister motives and characters of some kings or chiefs and related socio-economic condition of the people and their reactions under different situations. For instance as in the following song which mentions how one of the local king held court. The song belongs to Lahsua category and the lines are as follows:

Kone raja umaṛalaiṇ
Which of the king was dethroned
Kone raja sambhaṛalaiṇ
Which of the king was crowned
Kone raja ho kacheri baisae ki leṇga sahare, haere
Which of the king held court in the left side of the town
Muṛhu raja umaṛalaiṇ
The king of Murhu was dethroned
Tamaṛ raja sambhaṛalaiṇ
The king of Tamar was crowned
Bamaṇ raja ho kachaeri baisae ki leṇga sahare, haere
The brahman king held court in the left side of the town

During or just prior to British rule, almost every *pargana* was ruled by a chief or raja either independently or as a tributary to Nagbansi king. Murhu and Tamar, then *pargana* but now police *thanas*, were ruled by a raja each and rivalry between them existed. Holding court by the raja, though not a new thing for the Mundas, but it is the grandeur that aroused their curiosity most.

The song below as in the above, mentions the holding of court by a king. The song belongs to Bala category and the lines are as follows:

Kon kone me Gobindsae raja
Where is the king Gobindsae
Kon kona me kachaeri baisae-2
Where he is holding the court
Purab, pachhim, uttar, dakhin

East, west, north and south
Seo kona me kachaeri baisae
He is holding the court in that direction
Hare, pancho Kona me kachaeri baisae-2
O, he is holding court in all five directions

Gobindsae was the king of Nagbansi dynasty during the early part of 19th century. During his period, the British government introduced, for the first time, the police *thanas* which he was entrusted to implement. He was quite reluctant to introduce it. So prior to its introduction, he held number of courts with his *jagirdars* and *zamindars* and with Mundas *parha* leaders separately for consultations. After attending one such meeting, the Mundas bade farewell to the king. The reference of this event is found in the *Jatra* category of song below:

Sonpuria Bhuiṇyara ke
To the original inhabitants of the *pargana* of Sonpur
Bida debe Gobindsae raja
Bid farewell, O king Gobindsae
Pan-kasaili se bhuiṇyara ke
With beatle leaf and arecanuts to the original inhabitants
Bida debe Gobindsae raja
Bid farewell, O king Gobindsae

The above song has now been adopted as custom and is normally sung after the public gathering is over and people get separated bidding farewell to each other and particularly after the meeting like *Parha* organization.

The above event as stated was the talk of the day among the people which the composer of the song selected for the theme. The two songs clearly indicate the ups and downs of the political situation as prevalent during the period when one king of *murhu* was dethroned and the king of Tamar took his place and in another case, the king was holding courts in panic with his people.

War and Feuds

As stated above, ever since the local chiefs and kings were made tributaries to the Mughal king, a new economic order, that is, payment of *malgujari* or tax were introduced among the people. The chiefs were helpless and for the people, the system was quite impracticable. The system, however, enhanced the social status and economic power of the chiefs and rajas at the cost of the common people. The system proved to be a weapon in the hands of the chiefs and rajas to control the tribal people who were, till then, not under any outside administrative suzerainty. This system was adopted by those chiefs too, who were not made tributaries by the Mughal due to the reason as stated. This led to constant feuds and even wars among the families themselves and with neighbours. When the British came into the picture, they simply certified the system and war and feud among the chiefs continued unabated. The British seldom interfered in the internal matters of the local chiefs as they were concerned with the dues imposed on them only and the former were left in complete freedom to exhort it from the people. The people who were otherwise leading a peaceful life, it shattered their way of life and thinking. The *parha* organization of the tribals had no provision to withstand the outside threat in whatsoever forms. The people were left unguarded as no immediate defence mechanism could be incorporated in it. As the chiefs and rajas did not belong to the cultural ethos of the people, the war and feud were looked upon as strange events. But each war or enmity between the chiefs or among the family members of the chief, engulfed the people in one way or the other, also it was but natural to be affected by such events. The following song belonging to Racha category describes such involvement of the people. The lines of the song are as follows:

> *Bareṇg do na bareṇg do*
> Brother mine, O mother
> *Okotiya goṛe okotiya*
> Where did he go
> *Kamḍa reko mapa tana*
> There is a war at Kamda
> *Okotiya gore okotiya*
> Where did he go

The sister is worried about the welfare of her brother. She asks her mother of his whereabouts. But she is apprehensive that he may have gone to Kamda where fighting between the chiefs is going on.

During British days when the capital of the Nagbansi king was at Palkot, similar event happened when several hundred people were either injured or killed. This has been described in a Bala category of song which runs as follows:

> *Palikoṭo sahar re, relegaṛi chalae*
> At Palkot town, train was introduced
> *Relegaṛi chalate banduka dheralaiṇ re*
> While running train, guns were heaped up
> *Banduka je chhuṭe lagal*
> Firing guns were booming
> *Goli je gire lagal pani ka buṇd re*
> The bullet is falling like raindrops
> *Manukha je rowe lagal*
> People were weeping
> *Raja ka banduk baba, goṛe biṛi ḍanḍa paga*
> The result of king's gun, led to chaining on leg and roping on waist
> *Hathekaṛi chalan karu re raja beta*
> The prince was sent away in handcuffs
> *Raja ka banduk baba, goṛe biṛi ḍanḍa paga*
> The result of king's gun led to chaining on leg and roping on waist
> *Hathekari chalan karu re raja beta*
> The prince was sent away in handcuffs

The song is related to an event in which the king of Surguja estate while on his way to king's court at Palkot was killed by the prince of the Palkot and his people.

At Palkot, there is no train line but it indicates the presence of the British force there who made captive of the prince after the incident.

It is told that Raja Deonath Sahdeo of Nagbansi dynasty was a treacherous and deceitful king. The people believe that the act of injustice and immorality of the king caused famine during his time. The following song belonging to Jatra category mentions one such act. The lines of the song are as follows:

Kuṇwara Thakur ke marale Deonath raja
You killed the Kunwar and Thakur, O king Deonath
Raji to akala bhela Deonath raja
Famine has befallen in the country, O Deonath raja

Sometimes there were bitter enmity among the sons of the chief or king or near relatives for inheritance or division of the estate or for *jagir* in which ministers and advisers of the court were also involved. Below is one such song which relates to the event which occurred during the period of the kingship of Raja Deonath Sahdeo. The song belongs to Jatra category and the lines are as follows:

Ka hoire Khudi Raja Pandey
What will happen, O Khudi Raja Pandey
Ka hoire dub raj Lal Kuṇwar
What will happen O prince, Lal and Kunwar
Hari gelaiṇ Khudi Raja Pandey
Khudi Raja Pandey was defeated
Jit gelaiṇ dub Raj Lale Kuṇwar
The prince Lal and Kunwar won the war

Enmity and fighting for the sake of power and property were routine affairs among the chiefs and *jagirdars* during British rule. One such incident which shook the pargana of Murhu is described in the following Jatra category of song as under:

Kahaṇ kera baitḁl telenga
The mad enemies of which land
Kari majhe naga gossaiṇ ke marae
In the mid-field killed the Naga gossain
Muṛhu kera baitḁl telenga
The mad enemy of Murhu
Kari majhe naga gossaiṇ ke marae
In the mid-field killed the Naga gossain

One Raja Chander Sae, a local chief instigated a particular community, called Malar, to fight the Mundas for non-compliance of his order by the latter (see *Kurshinama*, p. 100). The song belongs to Jatra category and the lines are as follows:

Malar ka larai dekhu ho Chander Sae raja
Look at the fight of Malar, O king Chandar Sae
Malar ka larai dhela-pakhena
The fight of Malar are with pebbles and stones
Malar ka larai dekhu ho Chander Sae raja
Look at the fight of Malar, O king Chander Sae

Dukhan Sae and Mani Sae were once the chiefs of Sonpur and Basia respectively. The two chiefs were relatives of each other. A number of songs have been composed on the two chiefs which have been recorded in the book *Kurshinama*. The following song, the reference of which has been cited relates to Dukhan Sae, the Chief of Sonpur pargana.

The flag was the symbol of status, power and authority which the Chief Dukhan Sae once did possess. Many had an eye on the flag and everybody was planning to have it somehow or the other. Some battles were also fought for control over the flag and often it was stolen. The following song relates to one such event which belongs to Jatra category, the lines of which are as follows:

Dukhan Sae raure lili jhanḍa luṭala jaela
Robbery is being committed to your blue flag O Dukhan Sae
Shikaro danḍe
On the hunting field
Raure lili jhanḍa luṭala jaela
Your blue flag is being taken away forcibly
(See *Kurshinama*, p. 94).

Once a British, Simon saheb, by name, also tried to get the flag of the Munda tribe by force. Mention of this event has been made in the following Jatra category of song as follows:

Munḍa ka jhanḍa
The flag of the Mundas
Utaru re Simon raja
Bring it down, O king Simon
Munḍa ka jhanḍa lili jhanḍa
The blue flag of the Mundas

Munḍa ka jhanḍa
The flag of the Mundas
Utaru re Simon raja
Bring it down, O king Simon

Developmental Activities of the Kings and Chiefs

The kings and local chiefs introduced the money economy and a new economic order and also did some welfare work but mainly for their own benefits. Construction of roads, ponds, temples, *dharamsalas,* that is, rest houses and residential palaces for self were some notable activities. During this period when the kings, *jagirdars* and *zamindars* came into prominence, traders and various occupational communities made inroads into the tribal region and established liaison with them for supply of items of merchandise and articles of daily use as well as services. As stated in previous pages, they roamed about in the region as nomads initially and slowly spread network of contact with the king and his men. Gradually market centres were developed in a number of places. Below is a song belonging to Lahsua category which mentions that market centres were started by the king. The lines of the song are as follows:

Noko rajae raja lena
Which of the king was crowned as king
Noko Munḍae Munḍa lena
Which of the Munda was made the Munda
Hore, elare dolare
O dear, let us proceed
Ne hatu piṭi re saṇgina re
This village market is very far away
Hatu Munḍae Munḍa lena
The village Munda was made the Munda
Bir rajae raja lena
The king of the foreign country was crowned as king
Hore, elare dolare
O dear, let us proceed
Ne haṭu piṭi re saṇgina re
This village market is very far away

Initially there was no medium of exchange even when the traders came into the region. Currency as medium was totally absent in those days. The sale and purchase was done through the exchange of articles which were rarely in equal terms. It is stated that Gobind Sae, the Nagbansi king, introduced cowrie as currency for medium of exchange for the first time. This is remembered in one of Jatra songs which is as follows:

Gobind Sae Raja, paisa nai chale
Gobind Sae Raja when currency was not in use
Cowrie ke chaliyo dele
You introduced cowrie then
Chatera sahạr re
At Chatra town
Paisa nai chale
When currency was not in use
Cowrie ke chalaiyo dele
You introduced cowrie there

In the song below which belongs to Lahsua category, request is made to King Gopinath of Nagbansi dynasty for repairing of the road, which he did. The lines of the song are as follows:

Saṇdika ke karu dachina Gopinath Sae
Call a tender for the road, O Gopinath Sae
Saṇdika ke karu dachina-2 haere, hae
Call a tender for the road
Saṇdika ke karu jabitae-2 haere, hae
Take control of the road, O Gopinath Sae
Neecha ke uṇcha karu
Raise up the lower level
Uṇcha ke neecha karu
Level the elevation
Saṇdika ke karu jabitae, Gopinath Sae
Take control of the road, O Gopinath Sae
Saṇdika ke karu jabitae
Take control of the road

Planting of mango trees on the groves and on the roadside and construction of ponds were extensively taken by the kings, *zamindars* and *jagirdars*. Below is one such song which mentions construction of ponds and planting of mango trees on the platforms. The song belongs to Bala category and the lines are as follows :

Pokhra koṛale ho raja beta
You dug up ponds, O prince
Pinde-pinde maṭi bigalaiṇ re-2
Threw away soil on the platforms
Dhaire-dhaire namba ropalain re-2
Planted mango trees in rows on it
Nane-nane ḍair jhabaralaiṇ re-2
There grew thick tiny branches in it
Jhopa-jhopa amba foralaiṇ re-2
It bore mango fruits in bunches
Lale-lale amba pakalaiṇ re-2
The mango fruits all ripened red

Among the Nagbansi kings, Durjan Sai is remembered as palace builder. At Doisa, he constructed a beautiful stone palace which stands even today. The following song which belongs to *Jatra* category describes the beauty of the palace in the following lines:

Kone nagare
In which city
Baṇgela tora diyale ho raja lekore
You constructed the palace, O king
Ḍoisa nagare
In the city of Doisa
Baṇgela tora diyale ho raja
You constructed palace, O king

Below is another song of this category which also is related to the construction of this very palace. The lines of the song are as follows:

Kae paṭain diyale ho raja
How many storeys did you construct, O king
Kaṇsa perowaṇ uṛala jaela
That ash coloured pigeons are flying in and out

Nao paṭain diyale ho raja
You did construct nine storeys, O king
Kaṇsa perowaṇ uṛala jaela
That ash coloured pigeons are flying in and out

The people appreciate the beauty of the stone palace constructed at Doisa by Durjan Sal. The palace stands in nine storeys and is called 'Naoratangarh'.

Construction of temples and holding of fairs and festivals were the other major activities of the kings, zamindars and jagirdars. Dussehra festival was celebrated with great pomp and show where hundreds of animals were sacrificed on this occasion. The song below which belongs to Jatra category describes how the king, during this festival killed hundreds of water-buffaloes to appease the god. The lines of the song are as follows:

Ka deota manale raja deota
Which of the god did you worship, O king
Palikoṭo sahare sae kaṛa marae
You killed hundreds of water-buffaloes at Palkot town
Satkhaṇḍi manale raja deota
You did worship the god Satkhandi, O king
Palkot sahare sae kaṛa marae
You killed hundreds of water buffaloes at Palkot town
Sae kaṛa raji ke marae
You killed the country by killing hundreds of water-buffaloes

In the last line of the song, the composer has conveyed the sentiments of the people stating that by killing hundreds of ploughable water-buffaloes, the king killed the country. This shows that the king had no love for the country from where he was getting his life support.

During the Dussehra festival not only the animals but even human beings were also sacrificed by the king. The song below which belongs to Jatra category gives an indication of this fact, though the incident was taken as accident. The lines of the song are as follows:

Khedana kaṛa marae
Killing the buffalo by driving

Kahe manoa ke marae
Why the man was killed
Tamasa dekha maharaja
Look at the show, O king
Kahe manoa ke marae
Why the man was killed

As would be inferred from the song below, the objective of construction of ponds were to build temples on its platforms as well as in the centre of the pond. Worshipping is normally performed after taking bath in the pond. The song below which belongs to Bala category describes that the king installed the statue of the god in the temple built in the middle of the pond and during his worship, goats were sacrificed by the Brahmin priest. The lines of the song are as follows:

Pokhera kera le ho Baman̂ beṭa
You dug up the pond, O the son of Brahmin
Pokhera ko bhitare machhiamara deota
In the middle of the pond, there is god *machhiamara*, that is Kali
Pooja karu re Baman̂ beta
Worship him, O son of Brahmin
Kaseya bakaṛa ke dakhina karu re
Sacrifice an ash coloured goat
Karia pathia ke pooja karu re baman̂ beta
Sacrifice a black she-goat, O son of Brahmin

In some places, particular kinds of plants that were considered sacred, were also planted by the king. For instance, the following song belonging to Jatra category states that at Turiyara by the side of the brook, keora plants were extensively planted to worship god Ma-Maru. The lines of the song are as follows:

Ṭuṛiyara ḍaṛi ghate
In the valley of Turiyara at the brook
Keora bagicha lagae
Garden was made of *keora* plants

Ma-Maru pooja karae
To worship the god Ma-Maru
Keora bagicha lagae
Garden was made of *keora* plants

It was not the Dussehra festival only that was celebrated on a grand scale, but Holi and Sohral festivals too were equally celebrated by the chiefs and kings. The composer of the following Jatra song describes his impression of the manner the Holi was then celebrated. The lines of the song are as follows:

Ke bhaiya hori khelae
Who are playing Holi, brother
Nagpure dhuri uṛala jaela
Dust are flying up in the sky over Nagpur
Babu bhaiya hori khelae
The nobles are playing the Holi
Nagpure dhuri uṛala jaela
Dust are flying up in the sky over Nagpur

Games and Pastime

The leisure time was usually spent by the king and his nobles in gambling of various sorts locally known as *jua*. Besides these competitive games they also used to spend their leisure in the game of hunting. The song below belonging to Jatra category mentions how one Kinaram Rautia by name, lost his daughter in bet in gambling. The lines of the song are as follows:

Karanpure juha je khelae kinaram babu
Kinaram, the noble is playing gamble at Karanpur
Juha je khelae, beṭi je harae
Lost his daughter in gambling

This game not a thing of the past but even today the princely descendants and other non-tribal people of the plateau region play games where they put everything in stake and sometimes even lose their wives and property.

The king and his nobles had to go out on hunting expedition very often. The song below describes hunting in groups and jointly with people of neighbouring villages. The song belongs to *Jatra* category and the lines are as follows:

Sonpuria ke hanka parae
Sonpuria was called upon
Gena (i.e. Kena) pahare sikaro khelae
Hunting will be carried out in Gena hill
Gena pahare lila harina
There are blue deers in Gena hill
Gena pahare sikaro khelae
Hunting will be carried out in Gena hill

Sonpuria is the name of the pargana which has been used here as personal name as per the practice among the Mundas and represents the inhabitants of the Sonpur pargana as a whole. The deer of either blue and black as stated in the song are found nowhere now in the region except in the reserved forest in Orissa. This song mentions how the whole pargana at the call of the king, was involved in the hunting expedition. Hunting was so popular that the courtiers often requested the king to undertake the expedition. As in the song below which belongs to Jete Jatra category, the king is being requested for such an expedition as it has not been undertaken since many years. The lines of the song are as follows:

Kai bachharo chhuṭala
Many years have passed
Chalu raja sikaro khelae
Let us proceed to hunting, O king
Lawa chiṭiri mareke
To hunt partridges
Chalu raja sikaro khelae
Let us proceed to hunting, O king

Hunting were usually done with firearms. Following song belonging Jatra category describes how the prince used to hunt birds and animals. The lines of the songs are as follows:

Sisa ka goli chalae yuvaraj
You fired the bullet of lead, O prince
Janṭa baithle kauwa ke marae
You sat on the platform but killed a crow

Sisa ka goli hajaro rupaiya
The bullet costs thousand rupees
Sisa ka goli chalae yuvaraj
You fired the bullet of lead, O prince

The hunting by the prince was not successful and the bullet of high cost was spoilt as it killed the crow. But the following Jatra song gives a success story of hunting of the prince who killed a wild buffalo. The lines of the song are as follows:

Sisa ka goli chalae yuvaraj
You fired the bullet of lead, O prince
Bono bhitare bono bhaiṇsa ke marae
In the forest you killed a wild buffalo

The following Jatra song describes how the king hunted down a deer who was grazing on the open field:

Marecha me harina charae
Deer is grazing on the open field
Bhikhuwa raja harina ke marae
King Bhikhuwa killed the deer
Chari kona najari chalae
Looks at in all directions
Dekhu ho raja harina ke marae
Look how the king is killing the deer

Social Life of the Chiefs and Kings

The chiefs and kings had a network of social relationships in and outside the region with people of the same or similar status and influence. Such relations followed the movement of people and facilitated them for settling down in each other's areas. As the chiefs and kings were non-tribals or non-Mundas, the people who settled down in each other's region were the non-tribals. The marriage procession, the scene of reception and camping of marriage party, all evoked curiosity among the tribals as they were strange customs for them. The local tribal people were also involved as attendants to carry palanquin, articles of dowry, food and other paraphernalia of the marriage party. All these jobs were taken from the tribals with no payments which was usually known as '*bet beggar*'

Mundas have recorded some events in their songs which were the talk of those days. One such song is related to the birth of Harinath and Jaganath, though both of them belonged to two separate generations. Harinath Sahdeo was the brother of Nagbansi king Dripnath Sahdeo who was the great-great grandfather of Jaganath Sahdeo.

In Munda songs, usually the birth of male child is symbolized as the sun and that of female child as the moon. But in the song below, the birth of Harinath and Jaganath have been symbolized to moon which is contrary to the above mentioned thinking but may have some implicit reasons for the two are remembered not for their good work by the Mundas. The song belongs to Lahsua category and the lines are as follows:

Kare janamalain chaṇdo re
Where did the moon appear
Suja Harinath ho
Prince Harinath
Kare janam Jaganath re, ho hore-2
Why did Jaganath take birth
Dharti janamare chaṇdo re
On earth the Moon did appear
Suja Harinath ho
Prince Harinath
Dharti Jaganath re, ho hore-2
On earth Jaganath too

The song below gives an account of the orphanhood of one of the most remembered chiefs. The song belongs to Jatra category and the lines are as follows:

Chhoṭe me mae tora mori gela
While in childhood mother your's died
Chhoṭe me tuwaro bhela Manisae raja
You became orphaned in childhood, O king Manisae

There are a number of songs which relate to marriage ceremony. The following Bala category of songs describe different stages and features of the marriage such as searching of the bride, about the match maker, marriage procession, farewell to the daughter, dowry, etc. These songs give only the glimpse of the social life of the chiefs and kings. The lines of one of the songs are as follows:

> *Kadam Taregana raja*
> The king of Kadam Taregana
> *Kadam Taregana raja ge nayo*
> The king of Kadam Taregana, O mother
> *Kadam tare ḍera diyae re*
> Is camping under the *kadam* tree
> *Kadam tare raja basa mangae re*
> Asking shelter under *kadam* tree
> *Saparu hai ko, saparu baṛai ko*
> Get ready all courtiers
> *Chithi likhi-likhi kaneya mangae*
> Searching bride through writing letters
> *Puthi paṛhi-paṛhi kaneya khojae*
> Searching bride through consulting horoscope
> *Suno baba sona chandan*
> Listen dear, O golden sandalwood
> *Suno baba, rupa chandan*
> Listen dear, O silver sandalwood
> *Boto pani nutarai*
> The flood of first rain is flowing down
> *Kadam Taregana raja*
> The king of Kadam Taregana
> *Kadam taregana raja ge nayo*
> The king of *Kadam Taregana*, O mother
> *Kadam tare ḍera diyae re*
> Is camping under the *kadam* tree
> *Kadam tare raja basa mangae re*
> Asking shelter under *kadam* tree

The song is about the king of Kadam Taregana who is out in search of a bride. Once he wrote letters after letters to the guardians of the prospective brides asking their horoscopes and other times, he personally visited a number of them. This took much time and the monsoon has already set in forcing him to postpone his further search. The chiefs and kings were almost all Hindus and so they followed Hindu customs which were strange customs for the tribals.

The song below belonging to the Jatra category mentions about go-between or middleman of the marriage ceremony The function of the go-between in marriage is very important. He takes the responsibility of searching of bride, helps the bridegroom in making suitable selection, helps for settlement of acceptable dowry, fixation of marriage and other paraphernalia as desired by the parties. The song is based on actual events and mentions the accepting of the job of go-between by the barber. No details are available about the event, we are left with secondary content of the song, that is, undertaking of go-between job by the barber. The chiefs and kings had to avail the services of the Brahmin and barber for the job of go-between. The lines of the song belonging to Bala category are as follows:

Naura re naura
Barber, O barber
Baisal re naura
You are sitting there, O barber
Kahere naura aguwa bhele
Why did you agree to be a go-between
Nayo ke chhoṛae, baba ke chhoṛae
You left your parents
Kahere re naura aguwa bhele
Why did you agree to be a go-between

It is through go-between that marriage negotiation proceeds and is settled. Below is one song belonging to Jatra category in which it is stated that one person, Puransae by name, was the go-between. When this marriage was celebrated, it is stated that about 900 persons were engaged to carry and manage the articles and other things of the marriage. The grandeur of the marriage can be perceived by the involvement of the persons only. The lines of the song are as follows:

Agua bhele Puransae
Puransae you became the go-between
Nau sae bharia thakala jaela
Nine hundred load-carriers were all exhausted

Nau sae bharia tore sopena
The nine hundred load-carriers were under your charge
Nau sae bharia thakala jaela
Nine hundred load carriers were all exhausted

As stated in the song, Puransae the go-between is blamed for the exhaustion of the load-carriers who was the incharge of them. It may be that he may not have allowed for rest on the way and so the result was exhaustion.

The grandeur of the marriage as celebrated by the chiefs and kings can be perceived by just seeing the magnitude of persons and animals involved. A vivid description is found in the song below which relates to the marriage of Dripnath Sahdeo, who later became the king of Chhotanagpur in the Nagbansi dynasty. There were no roads and no modern means of transport during those days, therefore, the bride and bridegroom were carried by the people engaged in *bet beggar* (without wages and food) all through the route. The area being hilly and forest clad, the marriage party had to pass through great difficulty only after clearing the route from trees, shrubs and even stones. The song belonging to Bala category describes how the valley is being cleared to enable the palanquin to pass. The lines of the song are as follows:

Icha ko toṅgori baba
The hill covered with Icha bush, O father
Sampela ghaṭ re
And the serpentine valley
Jahajo nahin re baba chalae
The palanquin would not pass, father
Dair ke kaṭaṭ jamu
I will go on chopping the branches
Daira ke fekat jamu
Pass on throwing away the branches
Dhela ke pasaṭ jamu
I will thrash to pieces the lump of clay
Pakhena ke kuchaṭ jamu
I will pass on crushing the stones
Tabe junu jahajo mora chalae
Then only palanquin mine may pass

The path, as mentioned is hilly, serpentine covered with the Icha bush. Moreover, the ground is not plain but rocky. In spite of these difficulties, the marriage party is determined to cross the valley with caravan.

King Dripnath Sahdeo married a princess of Keonjhar estate, now in Orissa, which was celebrated at Biru Keshelpur at the bride's maternal uncle's home. The song below which belongs to Jadur category relates to this marriage and goes on as under:

Hare babu lal babu re
O lat, the prince
Duyo bhai lale-lale
Both the *lal* brothers
Keoṇjhari ka rani baṛa sundar
The princess of Keonjhar is most beautiful
Palkot biha jaela
The Palkot is going to marry her
Boṛ bhai hathi nupare
The elder brother is on elephant back
Chhoṭ bhaiya ghoṛa nupare
The younger brother is on horse
Keoṇjhari ka rani baṛa sundar
The princess of Keonjhar is most beautiful
Palkot biha jaela
The Palkot is going to marry her

How the caravan of marriage party is slowly proceeding towards the river bank of Deonadi on way to Biru Keshelpur has been described in the following Bala category of song which runs as follows:

Chimṭi ka chail baba
Like the pace of ant, father
Bakula ko paiṇkh re
Also flying like crane
Dubraja nutaral bagicha
The prince is proceeding towards the garden

Seo bharia chail gelaiṇ Deonadi tira re
The load carriers have passed on to the river bank of Deonadi
Dubraja nutaral bagicha
The prince is proceeding towards the garden

The marriage caravan is proceeding with riding of horses and elephants towards the Deonadi river on way to Biru Keshelpur, with speed and beauty like flying cranes, while the load bearers are crawling like ants. The marriage party, before crossing the river took rest in the grove nearby and the load-bearers on the river banks.

The bearers of the load were usually engaged on *bet-beggar*, basis, that is, without payment of wages and food. The condition of the bearers became pitiable when the journey is long and arduous. The song below which belongs to Jatra category describes one such journey in which the queen of Manisae is carried on a palanquin. During the course of the journey, the carriers were all exhausted. The tiredness, as is believed by the Mundas, is associated with the character and nature of the person who is being carried. The work becomes light and easier when the personality of the one being carried was impressive and charming. The carriers of the queen, as stated in the song, became exhausted because she was having bad qualities in her personality. The lines of the song are as follows :

Guṭu hatu toṇgori tare
At the foothill of the hillock of Gutu hatu
Bharia tora thakala jaela
Bearers yours were all tired
Hae rani papi rani
O, the immoral queen
Bharia tora thakala jaela
Bearers yours were all tired

The bride and bridegroom would sit in the palanquin which is to be carried by the people engaged for the purpose. The song below relates to an episode in which the marriage party while returning was attacked by enemies. It was drizzling and the palanquin carriers were having great difficulty in travelling. The lines of the Jatra category of song are as follows:

Jhimir jhiṭa bijli
It was drizzling with flash of lightning
Dekhu ho Baroya raja
Be careful, O Baroya king
Nawa kaneya doli me
The just married bride is in the palanquin
Dekhu ho Baroya raja
Be careful, O Baroya king

The king of Baroya is requested to be extra cautious for it is drizzling and the enemies are likely to attack.

It was not only the bride and bridegroom who only were to be carried, but the food, camping materials, dress and ornaments of the ladies and articles to be used during dance known as *mergarai* were also carried. On their return journey, the bearers had to carry materials of dowry also. The following song which belongs to Jatra category describes this:

Haere Sonahatu raja
The king of Sonahatu
Haere sona me bharala jaela
How he is going loaded with gold
Haere kaneya ka lobhe
For the attraction of the bride
Haere sona me bharala jaela
How he is going loaded with gold

In this song, the king is not returning with dowry but is carrying a basketful of gold as bride-price to be given to the bride's parent as the existing practice among the Mundas.

Death

The Mundas have not only recorded events that relate to birth and marriage of the chiefs and kings but also of their death. The following Bala song mentions one such event which is related to the death of the Nagbansi king of Palkot. How the death of the king is being mourned by the king's relatives and courtiers, has been described in the following lines:

Itai bor baṇgela
So big a bungalow
Raja kahaṇ gel
Where did the king go
Haere, kuṭure-kuṭure rani kaṇdae
Alas, the queen is sobbing without break
Sukhala patai uṛi gel
The dried up leaf was blown off
Taisana raja uṛi gel
Similarly the king flew away
Haere, kuṭure-kuṭure rani kaṇdae
Alas, the queen is sobbing without break

The death of an old person has been perceived like dried up leaf which is blown away with a gust of wind. The soul of the king who was very old, left the body like falling of dried up leaf. The vacuum that is created after death, leaves behind immense impact on the relatives of the deceased, and particularly on the near and dear one's. The composer and singer of this song shares the grief with the queen who was heartbroken at the death of the king.

It is not only the death of a human being which is mourned, the following song records the mourning of the king and his courtiers at the death of the court's elephant. The elephant served the king during war, hunting and marriage. Its death is greatly mourned. The song belongs to Jatra category and the lines are as follows:

Kekara hathi re bhaiya
Whose elephant, brother
Hathi binu Palikoto suna bhel
Without the elephant, Palkot looks gloomy and deserted
Raja kera hathi re bhaiya
The king's elephant, brother
Hathi binu Palikoto suna bhel
Without the elephant, Palkot looks gloomy and deserted

The British Period

It is the British period that is remembered most for the immense changes it brought about in the region in the area of economy, society, culture, administration and politics. The British introduced new administrative system, rules and laws, new means of transport and communication system, through the introduction of rail, air and road transport, telegraph, new economic order through the introduction of money economy and established trade and market centres, followed by the introduction of new educational and judicial systems, etc. All these new systems had great impact and repercussion on the existing system of the people which affected their whole way of life—their thinking, practice and behavioural relationship. A glimpse of the situation that existed during those days as understood and perceived by the people, is found in their songs.

The socio-economic and political system of the people began deteriorating under the economic bondage of the Mughals. As found in the ethno-history of the Mundas, there were already incidents of revolt in many parts of the region due to what is said to be forcible settlement of outsiders on the tribal land through ejection and occupation. The British did nothing to ameliorate the tribal situation but added fire in the already worsened situation by siding with the local rajas, *jagirdars, zamindars* and moneylenders. The system of administration through middlemen, that is, through local rajas, *jagirdars* and *zamindars* brought havoc to the situation. It is observed that Britishers tried to bring about peace and good government through force and by establishment of police *thanas,* courts and new administrative divisions. The feudalistic system of *zamindari* and *jagirdari* was a great help to them. The Mundas have composed a good number of songs which describe the inhuman situation of their forefathers during the period.

Mundas have also composed few songs on the British ways of administration, their works, activities, and their relations with common man, etc. Whatever has been described through songs, may not represent the true picture of the situation, but it certainly indicates their angle and level of looking at the things and understanding of the situation. Mundas were not passive observers but were actively involved in the real drama of life in which they were dragged upon to play. The song represents an outcome of the experience of the people from empirical situation.

Grabbing of land, its measurement and establishment of courts were the three milestone events for the Mundas which shook their conviction and conscience on uprightness and morality from the very root upon which their traditions and socio-cultural set-up was established.

Rakhaldas Haldar was assigned the task of measurement of land of the Mundas which have been recorded in unforgettable memory in the following *Jatra* song, the lines of which are as follows:

> *Rakhal babu upa̭r bhelaiṇ*
> Rakhal babu came to the scene
> *Sat sae Sonpur napayo bhel, lekore*
> Seven hundred (villages) of Sonpur parganas were put under measurement
> *Rakhal babu upa̭r bhelain*
> Rakhal babu came to the scene
> *Keyari-keyari pathal gaṛae*
> Stones were laid at every plot

The purpose of the first measurement of land was not at all understood by the Mundas. They came to know it only when the result was made known to them. Through this measurement '*Dikus*' were implanted on the land of the Mundas. A new category of land in the possession of the '*Dikus*' were recorded. The song belonging to Jadur category below has rightly described the position of the Mundas when their lands were measured. The lines of the song are as follows:

1. *Chario kona, chario dharti soṇge jana do*
   The land of all four directions were measured
   Chario kona, chario dharti partal jana do
   The land of all four directions were traversed upon

2. *Chario kona soṇge jana, jetae kako ṭorana*
   All directions were measured but no one understood
   Chario kona partal jana, jetae kako bujhao jan
   All directions were traversed upon but no one perceived

3. *Chario kona soṇge jana, diku ko ṭorana*
   All directions were measured, *Diku* understood it
   Chario kona partal jana, raja ko bujhao jan
   All directions were measured, kings only perceived it

4 *Ḍiku ko ṭorana*
The *Dikus* understood it
Bakas ko ol keda
They wrote *bakas*
Raja ko bujhao jan, khuṇtkaṭi soṇge jan
The kings perceived, the *khuntkati* was measured

5. *Chario kona soṇge jan, amin ko ruaṛ jan*
Amin returned when measurement to all directions were over
Chario kona partal jan, Deputy ko nachur jan
All directions were traversed upon, the deputies have arrived

6. *Amin ko ruaṛ len office duar te*
Amin returned to their office
Deputy ko nachur len, settlement aṇka te
The deputies arrived to assess the settlement

The following *Baroya* category of song also describes how *amins* and surveyors revolutionized the area. The lines of the song are as follows:

Kahaṇ se ale amin babu re
From where did you come, O *amin*
Duniya ke hilo-hilo karae
You revolutionized the world
Purbe se ale amin babu re
You came from the east O, *amin* babu
Duniya ke hilo-hilo karae
You revolutionized the world

Family holding of land were reduced to uneconomic level due to land settlement besides parcelling out of good quality of land to non-tribal people. This was a great economic loss to the family. After the land settlement when outsiders firmly got settled, a reverse economic trend set in the tribal region. The value of money which can get everything on earth attained so much height that grain and other local products of the tribals became almost valueless. The demand of money was greater than grain. The following Bala category of song vividly describes the post-settlement-situation in Munda region. The lines of the song are as follows:

> *Eke kose jaṇgal, duyo kose jaṇgal bhitarege nayo*
> Inside a *kos* or two in the forest, mother
> *Duyo bhaiya bahina kaṇdae ge nayo*
> Brother and sister both are weeping, mother
> *Pani bhitare lili jhaṇḍa gaṛae ge nayo*
> Blue flag was pitched in the water pool, mother
> *Budi pokela, saṇḍi karakel*
> The she pokela and the *Karakel* villages
> *Hulsubu, Mahugaon, Rampa, Jaṛia, Jagira Bhela*
> Hulsud, Mahugaon, Rampa and Jaria became *jagir* villages
> *Basia, palkoto nakala bhela*
> Basia aed Palkot were put under record
> *Basia, Palkoto nakala bhela ge nayo*
> Basia and Palkot were put under record, mother
> *Goṇdli, maṛua sasata bhela*
> Gondli and millet became cheap
> *Goṇdli, maṛua sasata bhela ge nayo*
> Gondli and millet became cheap, mother
> *Eko anni, du anni, chau anni, atho anni, rupaiya, loṭo sasata bhelaiṇ ge nayo-nayo*
> The money of all denominations have become cheap, mother

The people could not understand the purpose of the land measurement as stated in the previous pages. They, therefore, did not tell the correct figure of land in their possession and so went unrecorded in their names and were instead recorded as *bakast,* that is, unclaimed land and these were recorded in the names of *jagirdars.* When this fact was realized by the Mundas, they became greatly disturbed and called upon meetings to decide the course of action to be taken. The following Bala category of song mentions this in these lines:

> *Chupe, chupe, chupe rahure-2*
> Keep mum, dear

Raja pati lili singara kar ganapatia
Kings, chiefs and courtiers are all decorated in blue
Jama karu re
Give a call, dear
Gaon kera, Munḍa, Pahaṇ aur Mahto
Munda, Pahan and Mahto of the village
Paṇcho re bhaiya
Five brothers of the *panch*
Raja, pati lili siṇgara kar ganpatia
Kings chiefs and courtiers are all decorated in blue

When the Mundas understood the fact of the settlement operation, it was too late but they tried their best to bring the actual position before the authorities. The Mundas also held a number of meetings in almost all affected villages to decide the course of action. The resentment against the settlement operation was in the form of revolt. One such revolt was led by Ganapati. There are few songs which reflect the situation of post-settlement operation. The following song belonging to Jadur category gives a picture of a distressed and panicky couple in these lines:

1. *Gaṛha ho doṛha ko or keda*
   Chain was drawn all through the ditches and ravines
   Gatim ho oko telaṇg seno mulina
   Where shall we go away my dear

2. *Assaṃ disum apasul bugina*
   It is good to earn livelihood in Assam
   Assaṃ telaṇg seno mulina
   We shall go away to Assam

3. *Assaṃ telaṇg seno re, haga hon jetae baṇko jan*
   If we go to Assam, there are no one of our brethren
   Gidi kuṛd tuyue jojoma
   Vulture, kite and jackal may eat us up

So, even if they did decide to go to Assam, they were afraid of going there for there will be no known person, all will be strangers. The social and community life among the rural Mundas was so strong that they would not like to leave it.

Perceiving the problem, the British authorities issued notices to the Mundas to see the Deputy Commissioner to get one's record corrected. The following Jatra song mentions how this news spread among the people and how they are rushing to see the officer. The lines of the song are as follows:

> *Dauru, dauru re Basia pargana, dauru*
> Rush out Basia pargana
> *Dauru re raja beta ho*
> Hurry up, O prince
> *Ranchi jhili-mili, dunia jhaka-maka*
> The glittering Ranchi and to the shining world
> *Zila saheb bolae*
> The District Officer has given a call

As the records could not be corrected by the Deputy Commissioner also, cases were filed in the court for redressal of the claims. Under this situation, a few courts were established in the region. At Chatra, the first such court was established. Earlier, when there were no courts in the region, the Mundas had to go to Calcutta for the purpose. How the officials of the court and *thanas* were busy in swindling the tribals in the name of court fee, etc, has been described in the following Bala category of song, the lines of which are as follows:

> *Maharani ko nane jojo pichhora*
> The queen has fine beautiful dress
> *Sona rupa ker chaṇdowa diyae*
> Gold and silver necklaces are being offered
> *Sikilment uṛi gela*
> Settlement operation is over
> *Ranchi sahare lal chaprasi, ukil, daroga*
> Ranchi is crowded with red turbaned policemen, pleaders and *darogas*
> *Sona rupa ker chandowa diyae*
> Gold and silver necklaces are being offered

In the court, cases were purchased like commodities with money and the policemen, the *daroga* of the police *thanas* and court pleaders were collecting gold and silver from the people engaged in court cases. This very fact has been indicated in the above song.

People rushed to the district office for getting correction on the records and on being disappointed, they filed cases against the *jagirdars* or moneylenders in whose names lands were recorded. The following Bala category of song mentions how the village chief, *parha* chief, etc, are fighting court cases. The lines of the song are as follows:

Khudishing raja
The king Khudising
Khudising raja ge nayo
The king Khudising, mother
Ukil, mokhtar, Deputy Commissioner
Pleader, Magistrate's assistants and Deputy Commissioner
Raja saṇge go laṛai lagae
Are fighting against the king

The song below belonging to Jadur category, relates to revision settlement which took place between the thirties and forties of this century and post revision situation. The people are filing court cases to get back their land. Many cases remained unattended due to non-availability of suitable pleader to take it up to the court. As stated in the song below, a person, Sonasing by name, however agreed to take up the case, but asks them to get the original record of right, locally known as *'patta'*. The lines of the song are as under:

1. *Kuṛa purti barogaon, tola ṭoyạd tạm seno tana*
The land of Kura Purti and nearby 12 villages, are being taken away
Mạr tạm upạr len me Sona siṇg munda
Please take up our case, O Sonasing Munda

2. *Upạr doiṇg upạr lena, paṭṭa tạm bano jaṇa*
I will take up, but I don't have the original record
Mạr dolabu uruṇgeya sida reya paṭṭa-2
Let us obtain the original record

As stated above, people were very much enthusiastic of getting back their land and were optimistic with the help of the court. The chances of recovery or winning the case, however, was bleak and this was a great frustration for them. But when a case was won, one in a rare of rare cases, it was a matter of great joy and rejoice involving the village as a whole. There was one such instance which is related to Sirka and Nachal *dari* plots of land, where people won the case. How the people celebrated the occasion has been mentioned in the following Bala category of song, the lines of which are as follows:

Sirka loyoṇg siyu koṛa ko
The plough boys of Sirka plot of land
Kaṛba reko mudạm keda
Put up rings on the handle of the plough
Nachạl daṛi da: au kuṛi ko
The water fetching girl from Nachal dari
Biṇḍa reko ḍaṇḍiḍ keda
Ornamented the pot pad with ear spikes
Kaṛba reko mudạm kedare
Put up rings on the handle of the plough, dear
Sekej ken, sekej ken
Ringing *sekej* and *sekej*
Biṇḍa reko ḍaṇḍiḍ kedare
Ornamented the potpad with ear spikes, dear
Rolob ken, rolob ken
Sounding *rolob* and *rolob*

It is at this time when everything was fast changing, the two friends sum up the whole situation in the following lines. The song belongs to Jadur category and the lines are as follows:

1. *Jau leka suku do gatim*
The happiness as usual, friend
Karem nameya gatim
You won't get anywhere, friend
Jau leka napae do saṇgaiṇg
The peace as usual friend
Karem chinae
You will see nowhere

2. *Hatu-hatu re gatim ko diguar janaya, gatim*
There are watchmen at every village, friend
Disum-disum re saṇgaiṇg ko koṭowar jan
There are reporters at every land

3. *Aṛi pichidya gatim dibua janaya, gatim*
Every inch of land have been priced
Kuṇḍi pichidya saṇgaiṇg dokara jan
Every plot of land has been put up on sale

There was happiness and peace everywhere when the land was not out for sale into the market. Now there are watchmen and reporters everywhere who supply regular reports to the authorities regarding ownership of land.

The history of Chhotanagpur is full of records of the people's valient opposition against the taking away of *khuntkati* lands by the *Dikus*. The collective opposition was initially very peaceful as the people had full trust on the uprightness and method of justice of the white rulers but as soon as the truth surfaced, it took the form of revolt. And in the name of law and order, all the revolts were ruthlessly curbed by the British forces. People who died during several such revolts, their names are found in the songs of the Mundas with praise and admiration. The British administration with its police and military forces had a telling time to curb these revolts. The movement of the forces as seen by the Mundas are recorded in songs which throw sufficient light on the situation that prevailed at that time. The song below belonging to the Bala category states how, like speed of the train, the police forces were deployed in trouble prone areas. The lines of the song are as follows :

Kahaṇ kera daroga, kahaṇ kera sipahia
Daroga and police from which place
Kahaṇ kera rele gari gudu kate awae
The train of which place coming whizzing
Hare Bunḍu kera sipahia, Tamaṛ kera ho daroga
The police from Bundu and *daroga* from Tamar
Hare rele gaṛi gudo kate awae
The train is coming whizzing

During one such revolt, a *zaminder* was killed by the Mundas and they carried him to the police *thana* like a pig on a pole to show and narrate the atrocities of the *zamindar*. He was killed with the same gun with which he used to kill the people. This event has been recorded in the Bala category of song, the lines of which are as follows:

Gora palṭan, kala palṭan
The white and the black military
Laṛai je lagae
Are fighting the battle
Gora palṭan laṛai je lagae
The white military are fighting
Kala palṭan laṛai je lagae
The black military are fighting
Naraṭi me lai gelaiṇ
It hit on the throat
Karajua feik gelaiṇ
The lever was thrown away
Banduka ke dharalaiṇ
They caught hold of the gun
Simdega chalan karalaiṇ
And sent it away to Simdega
Puchhalaiṇ jachhalaiṇ
Enquired and checked
Bano thana chali gelaiṇ
Proceeded to Bano police station
Naseta ke kine lelaiṇ
Purchased some breakfast on the way
Saṇdika ke dharalaiṇ
They took the road
Pabuḍa buchi ḍaṛi me gor dhowalaiṇ
Washed their feet on the stream at Pabuda
Sondaṛi Muṇgatoli
And Sondari Mungatoli

The song states that after killing the *zamindar* they carried him to Simdega, now a district headquarters. From there they carried him to Bano police station. On the way, they purchased breakfast and after drinking water from the stream at Pabuda, took rest at Soṇdari Mungatoli.

There were many great heroes who sacrificed their lives while fighting with the *jagirdars* and *zamindars*. Mention may be made of Singrae and Bindrae who are remembered by the Mundas in their songs and stories.

Birsa has been the legendary hero of the tribals of Chhotanagpur for his valour to oppose the mighty combined forces of the Britishers and the '*Dikus*'. He is remembered through numerous songs and stories and has become immortal among the people. The following Bala category of song describes his methods and strategies of fighting. The lines of the song are as follows:

Birsa ka laṛai baba
The battle of Birsa
Birsa ka laṛai re
The battle of Birsa, dear
Birsa ka laṛai baba tir balua re
The battle of Birsa was with bows, arrows and axes
Baṇdhalaiṇ chhaṇdhalaiṇ, Birsa ke lei gelaiṇ
Hand-cuffing him, he was taken away
Par ṭapu kala pani bais delaiṇ
On the island at Kalapani, he was put up there
Birsa ka laṛai baba
The battle of Birsa
Birsa ka laṛai baba tir balua re
The battle of Birsa was with bows, arrows and axes

The movement of military force during the revolt of Birsa, has been recorded in the following Bala category of song, the lines of which are as follows:

Ranchi ka saheb, Doraṇḍa ka paleṭaṇ
The officer of Ranchi with military of Doranda
Saheb sato sae ghoṛa lele awae
The officer is coming with seven hundred horses
Saheb biso sae ghoṛa lele awae
The officer is coming with twenty hundred horses
Saheb niṇdiyo ḍaṇḍe, jatera ḍaṇḍe, bich tambu thokae
The saheb encamped in the middle of the Ind Jatra field

Saheb sato sae ghoṛa lele awae
The officer is coming with seven hundred horses
Saheb biso sae ghoṛa lele awae
The officer is coming with twenty hundred horses

Ways of British Administration

The British administrative officers had to visit the rural areas for inspection, camping on the way at number of villages to assess the situation or to see the condition of the people by themselves. The two songs below give a vivid description of the scene of camp of the British officer. The lines of one Racha category of song is as follows:

Jhibir-jhibir pani bariasae
It is drizzling
Beech ḍanḍe tambu thokae
Encamped in the middle of the field
Bapa re hakim re
How brave is the judge
Beech ḍanḍe tambu thokae
Has encamped in the middle of the field

The lines of another song which belongs to Bala category is as follows:

Haṭia ka uthal saheb, gaṇjena me ḍera re
Departing from Hatia, the officer encamped at Ganjna village
Maṇgla chaṇwar dolae
Tuft of hair is being waved in honour of him
Maṇgla sato siṇgara sajae
The place is decorated beautifully in honour of him
Nayo ke baro jori
Twelve times salute to the mother
Baba ke tero jori
Thirteen times salute to the father
Maṇgla chaṇwar dolae
Tuft of hair is being waved in honour of him

Mangla sato singara sajae
The place is decorated beautifully in honour of him

The song describes how the British officer when he was out on tour was attended by his men. The Mundas had never witnessed such beautiful scenes worth remembering. Routine of such tours or visits were later on made regular. To avoid inconvenience and wasting of labour, money and time during such tours, permanent bungalows better known as *Dak* bungalows at suitable places were built. When the officer was camping in such bungalow, the scene was not less beautiful than camping on the field without having the bungalow. One such scene has been described in the following Bala category of song, the lines of which are as follows:

Chhoṭe moṭe toṅgori bangela moe banaloṇ
On a hillock, I constructed a bungalow
Hare, baṅgela aṅgena jhabaṛa jhoboṛa
The bungalow and courtyard have been decorated beautifully
Hakim mokhtaṛ maiuka diyae
The judge and attendants are allowing everybody a chance to meet
Munshi peshkaṛ pesh karae
Munshi and *peshkar* are presenting the case to the judge
Baṅgela duare joṛi baṇduk, joṛi police diyae
At the door of the bungalow, a pair of armed policemen have been posted
Hare baṅgela aṅgena jhabaṛa jhoboṛa
The bungalow and the courtyard have been decorated beautifully

For better administration, not only courts, police stations and bungalows were setup at suitable places but they also setup a network of communication, by way of roads, railways and telegraphs to link all the areas with the headquarters so as to be well informed in time and take action promptly when needed. There are few songs which mention this aspect of British administration. The following Racha category of song has mentioned this in these lines:

Hare rele chalae re-2
They opened the rail lines

Baṅgela bhitạre rele chalae re
They introduced train in Bengal
Bapare hakim, bapare saheb re
All praise to judge and officer
Baṅgela bhitạre rele chalae re-2
They introduced train in Bengal

Another thing which the Britishers did was the construction of overbridges and dams. The following Bala category of song mentions how train lines are being laid down. The lines of the song are as follows :

Chaibasa se uthạl saheb
Departing from Chaibasa
Koenara nadi pool baṇdhae re
Constructing over-bridge on the river Koenara
Gori, gori re company saheb
The white officers of the company
Tor raij me chauwani delaiṇ re
Got four annas as wage in your land
Dharti upạre gaṛha moe koraloṇ
I dug up a ditch on the earth
Gaṛha upạre rogoṛi moe ḍisaloṇ
I put stone pebbles on the ditch
Ruguṛi upạre kath moe disaloṇ
On stone pebbles I laid wooden slippers
Kath upạre pahiya moe disaloṇ
I put up rail on the wooden slippers
Pahiya upạre rela moe chalaloṇ
I drove train on the rail
Rẹla upạre manoa sawari lelaiṇ
People are travelling on the train
Gori, goṛi re company saheb
The white officers of the company
Tor raij me chauwani delaiṇ re
Got four annas as wage in your land

The song not only mentions how the train lines are laid down but it also mentions the rate of payment to construction workers in those days.

Reference of Rono-Rono saheb, that is, Major James Rennel, the Surveyor General of Bengal has also been made in the following Bala category of song which states that he constructed dams for irrigation as well as for fishiculture. The lines of the song are as follows:

> *Rono Rono saheb, Rono Rono saheb gẹ nayo*
> The Rono Rono saheb, mother
> *Pahar upare bandh je bandhae-2*
> Constructing dams on the mountain
> *Rangaini ko ḍaṇḍe pain je chalae*
> Opened canal through the field of Rangaini
> *Ropi delaiṇ dhatia kụmni*
> Laid down a big fish trap
> *Bajhi gelaiṇ chhalki re machhri*
> The flying fish got trapped on it
> *Lei gelaiṇ Haṭia re bazar*
> Carried them to Hatia market
> *Lei gelaiṇ raja re sipahia*
> The policemen of the king took away all the fishes

Besides the construction of dams and canals and laying down the fish trap on it, the song also indicates that when the fishes were trapped, the policemen of the king took away all the fishes, of course, without paying the price. Such incidents were very common. The *zamindars, jagirdars* and policemen were the real administrators of the land during British days. They could do anything which they wanted.

The following Jadur category of song mentions this in these lines:

1. *Jo suku jo lenạ re*
   The pumpkin bore fruits
   Ba malạn ba lena
   The bean too blossomed

2. *Miyad gi jo lena re*
   It bore fruit but one
   Baria gi baha lena
   There were only two flowers

3. *Alo sipahiạm gode ya*
Spare it, O policemen
Alo darogạm chagaṛeya
Don't pluck, it, O daroga

The fruits, vegetables, animals and fowls were usually taken away by the policemen without asking the owner.

Once in Dodma village, the best of cattle were driven away either by the *jagirdar* or *zamindar* or by the policemen resulting in the scarcity of cowdung in the village. This has been mentioned in the following Jadur category of song, the lines of which are as follows:

1. *Dodoma sahạr re dadaya*
In Dodoma town, brother
Gurijo kare namoa
Even cowdung is not available

2. *Dadaya gại gohạr, bhainsa gohạr re*
In the cattleshed of cow and buffalo
Gurijo kare namoa
Even cowdung is not available

3. *Dadaya jhanḍi toleme*
Pitch flags, O brother
Dadaya dhacha toleme
Fasten tuft of straws, brother
Dodoma sahạr re dadaya
In Dodoma town, brother
Gurijo kare namoa
Even cowdung is not available

Cowdung is used as fertilizer as well as firecake. So when policemen drove away most of the cattle of the village, whatever cowdung was available from few of the cattle, people had to claim it when the same was found in one's own field, by raising a sign of such claim on it.

During British days the practice of forced labour, better known as *bet beggar* was so rampant that able-bodied persons had to live in constant fear from the policemen or from the king's people who would forcibly take them for work and that too, without any payment.

The following song mentions how people were gripped with constant fear. The song belongs to Racha category and the lines are as follows:

> *Dolaṇg cha saking*
> Let us proceed, namesake mine
> *Janta ḍiṛi gaṇjao te*
> To arrange slate stone one upon the other
> *Kaiṇg sena sakiṇg*
> I shall not go, namesake mine
> *Diku ko totola*
> Dikus may handcuff us
> *Raja ko banḍera*
> The king may put us in mortgage

The *zamindar* or *jagirdar* would send their men to every household asking people to come at work. They would not spare even the old, disabled and children. If somebody expresses his reluctance, he is severely beaten (*Kurshnama*, 1982:135-36).

It was during British administration that cash payment against labour work began, As the people were deprived and uprooted from their land, they were forced to work as labourers. During those days avenues of job too were very bleak till the time tea gardens were not opened in the north-eastern region of the country and construction works, as mentioned in previous pages were not taken up. Earning of money was very difficult. The following Bala category of song mentions how difficult it was to earn the money. The lines of the song are as follows:

> *Chhoṭi chauani chalae*
> Small coin of annas four was circulated
> *Diya baṛo chauani chalae*
> The big coin of annas four was circulated
> *Sona hole badalae*
> If I had gold, I would have exchanged it
> *Rupa hole badalae*
> If I had silver, I would have exchanged it
> *Jiwa kaese badalae*
> How shall I exchange my life

Chhoṭo chauani chalae
Small coin of annas four was circulated
Baro chauani chalae
The big coin of annas four was circulated

It was during British rule that the Second World War was fought in which a good number of Mundas had joined the military service. The following Racha song mentions how the military are proceeding towards the battle front. The lines of the song are as follows:

Noko teko seno tana re
Where are they going
Palṭa̱n ko jham-jham re, palṭa̱n ko jham-jham
The military are marching together in rows
Larai teko seno tana re
Going for the battle
Palṭa̱n ko jham-jham re, palṭa̱n ko jham jham
The military are marching together in rows

The British officers like the kings and chiefs had great interest in hunting. It is during this period that large-scale deforestation and hunting of wild animals and birds were undertaken as a game. The Mundas have recorded it in their songs.

The record is also found in Munda songs about the Sepoy Mutiny and in this case, the name of Gangaram is particularly taken along with the name of the Thakur of Barkagarh and the name of Bisnath Sahdeo. They were the only Dikus who raised arms against the Britishers.

With all those unprecedented events that took place during British rule and the works and things that were left behind by them in India, the Mundas remember them as in the song below which belongs to Bala category as a token of good deeds, the lines are as follows:

Ranchi ka laṭ saheb chalala bilayat re
The Governor of Ranchi returned to Britain
Tisa̱n-tisa̱n rail gaṛi chalalaiṇ re
Did run train from station to station
Office-office radio chalalaiṇ re
At every office installed radio
Chali gelaiṇ bilayat re

They returned to Britain
Office-office radio chalalain re
At every office installed radio

It is during the rule of Mughals and Britishers that the Mundas came face to face with alien culture and tradition and it is during this period, for the first time, that they classified human being as *horo*, that is, man and *Dikus*, that is non-*horo* or exploiters. The latter category of people ransacked the whole fabric of the lives of the Mundas reducing it to shambles that sowed the seeds of cultural crisis among them. It is observed that in spite of all repressive measures adopted by the administration and their associates, that is, the *Dikus*, the culture of the Mundas, instead of decay, withstood the onslaught and regenerated itself by adopting new elements from outside. And this is the secret of survival of the Mundas and several other tribal people of this region. The folklore of the Mundas, that is, myths, legends, folk tales, music and dances all got enriched during this period in respect of motif, theme, rhyme and style. The associated folklore materials such as decorative ornaments, musical instruments as well as their use and handling became most refined and attained the level of perfection, the alternative of which could not be innovated even today.

The relations of the Mundas with the *Dikus* was too bitter as the latter could see the former as enemies. For the Mundas they were parasites and exploiters who lived on others' wealth and had no human qualities whatsoever. This was the clash of two civilizations—one represented by the *Dikus* and the other by the Mundas, that is, the tribal people. The period is marked for the struggle of survival, security, dignity and peaceful living for the Mundas which are well remembered through their songs.

Events that Made History

While we have a good number of songs which record political situation, administrative system and socio-economic condition of the tribals, people also remember events which, of course, are unrelated to any of the events of historical value. But such events of importance have become part of the tradition of the people. A few of such songs related to such an event have been taken for example.

In the Bala category of songs, mention of a big gathering of

Parha chiefs—the clan heads of the Munda tribe has been made. It was a historical meeting which is stated to have continued day and night for weeks. The lines of the song are as follows:

1. *Diṇyankel bagicha re*
   In the grove of Dinyankel village
   Kili-kili ga ko sala tana re
   Searching the history of each clan
   Jati-jati ga ko khojaṛ tana re
   The ethnic history is being traced
   Diṇyankel bagicha re
   In the grove of Dinyankel village

2. *Sala doko sala tana, piti doko piti tana*
   They are searching and investigating
   Jati-jati ga ko sala taha re
   Tracing the ethnic history
   Kili-kili-gako khojaṛ taṇa re
   Investigating the history of each clan

The historical meeting was held at Dinyankel village in Ranchi district sometime before independence. Before this, each *parha* or group of *parhas* had several meetings, but this was the only meeting of its kind where several thousand Mundas intensively discussed the history of each clan as well as the history of the tribe.

An event is also recorded in the history of the people which is in no way related to socio-cultural or political content. The event occurred in early part of 20th century. The song which is based on this event, belongs to Bala category and the lines are as follows:

Chhotanagpur Manisae jaṇgaḷ ekela bhela
In Chhotanagpur Manisae forest was rocked
Baṛa hiṇsa siṇh bagh ulaṭi, manusa ke nuksana karae
A great ferocious lion has turned up and killed the people
Jato saiṇya Ram ke kahi debe, bandukayo lei lanạb re
Tell Ram that he should bring gun with him
Naraṭi me laig gelaiṇ, bhuiṇye lapasi gelaiṇ re
Shot in the neck that made it fall on the ground

Bandhalaiṇ chhandalaiṇ, Beṛa Irgi utaralaiṇ
Fastening they carried it to Bera Irgi village
Chameṛa ke chhoṛalaiṇ, Bano thana lei gelaiṇ
After skinning they took it to Bano police station
Simdega chalan bhelain re
And exported further to Simdega the sub-divisional headquarters
Ram ke talab mailae, daso sae rupaiya
Ram got the reward of ten hundred rupees
Ram ke talab milae biso sae rupaiya
Ram got reward of twenty hundred rupees

The lion or tiger was the talk of the day of the people everywhere who had created panic among the people of the region. It is stated that its area of kill was too extensive and people had the belief that it was not an animal but a man turned animal through some magic power. The rumour was that it was a witch or a black magician who turned himself or herself as tiger at will. This conviction of the people was based on the event of the kill which it did on the same day at two different places of considerable distances from each other—say 60 to 70 miles apart. The government had announced a reward to anybody who would kill the animal. At last the tiger was shot dead by a Munda and this gave a great relief to the people. He was suitably rewarded by the government. The song gives detailed narration after the killing of the tiger.

17

DEGENERATION OF MUSICAL CULTURE

The Post-Independence Period

The political independence of India was expected to bring about a great change in the political situation with the change in administrative system and liquidation of feudalistic autocratic rulers. The structural change in administration was supposed to bring a corresponding change in the attitudes and behaviours of the persons manning the administration towards the common man. This change was expected because of the adoption of the democratic system of administration and ideology which made the common man its ultimate authority. In this system of administration, the representatives who form the government, are elected by the people through common adult franchise for a fixed period. Though in Munda songs, we do not get the organizational details of the system, how people are exercising their voting rights, has, however been described vividly. Under this system, different political parties who lay bare their plans, policies and programmes before the people for socio-economic development of the nation are formed to fight elections. Jharkhand party was one of the political parties in Bihar state and Jaipal Singh, a Munda was its president. The following two songs which belong to Bala category describe how people are casting their votes. The lines of one of the songs are as follows :

Jaipal Singh agua
Jaipal Singh, the leader
Paul Dayal secretary Munḍa ko nagin
Paul Dayal was the secretary, for the Mundas
Disum cha na ko repej tana
They are fighting for the country

Da: leka mayom lingi tana
They are shedding blood like water
Nelanabu hariyara tin bokosa
We have seen the green tin box
Nelanabu sim chhapa, urij chhapa do
We have also seen the symbol of cock and bullock
Tola-tola, mauja-mauja, thana-thana, zila-zila
In hamlets, villages, police stations and districts
Vote giya ko saju tana
People are casting their votes

The Jharkhand party fought many elections with the symbol of cock whose leader was Jaipal Singh and secretary Paul Dayal. The other party was Congress with the symbol of bullock. The last 20 to 25 years of this century have brought about tremendous changes in all spheres of life of the tribals along with changes in the physical and natural environment which have had serious repercussions in the whole set-up of tribal culture economy, philosophy and values.

Environmental Degradation

The alien intrusion in the tribal land and society began with the Mughals, who brought land as commodity of use for the first time along with the use of currency, the Britishers, while confirming the Mughal systems, brought modernization in all spheres of public life. The Mughals as well as the Britishers, both paved the way for large-scale immigration of people in the region under the exclusive domain of tribal people. These people, with the connivance of the *jagirdars*, *zamindars* and moneylenders settled by the Mughals and Britishers, were successful in dislodging and unsettling the tribals from their lands and forest.

Ever since the alien rulers and people entered into the Chhotanagpur plateau which was then covered with dense forest, deforestation in large-scale continued unabettedly till today. This has brought about great changes in the economy of the tribal people on the one hand, and in the climate and weather condition of the plateau, on the other. One phenomenon clearly detected is that the duration of rainy season as well as quantity of rains have considerably been reduced resulting in the lengthening of dry weather and depletion of water resources. This has adversely affected the plant life and other biological species. A good number of them have already become extinct.

Impact of Outsiders and Migration on Economic Life

The tribal people of Chhotanagpur are basically agriculturists and are fully dependent on monsoon for cultivation. With uncertain monsoon, agricultural operations have become unfruitful, resulting in increase of near poverty population every year. During the period of foreign rule, the presence of *jagirdars*, *zamindars* and moneylenders added fire to the situation when they evicted the tribals from their lands and further exploited them through various ways. But since opportunities for alternate source of livelihood based on non-agricultural occupations, such labour and services were available outside the region only, people sustained their lives through these means and methods, though reluctantly. The tribals had to earn their livelihood through labour during 17th and 18th century in the tea gardens of Assam and Tripura and in the agricultural fields of West Bengal. The First and Second World Wars created opportunities for the people of the region in military service, for the first time. Local jobs were not available and people had to move out to distant places in search of work. The trend continues till today. Till the 1970s, it was the military service which attracted most youths of the region that required little or no education. The acquaintance with foreign style and standard of living developed foreign taste among the youths. The job of service was better than the traditional occupation of agriculture as it provided a perennial source of income in cash which could purchase for them what they liked. The money economy occupied the first place in life. It relieved the people from total dependency on forest and agriculture for livelihood and made them drawn away from nature that ensued attitudinal change of the people towards nature.

Changes in the Mentality of the Tribals

The elements of modernism or modernization were introduced in the region during British rule. A materialistic mentality was enthused among the mind of the people as everything on earth was commercialized. Schools were set up to educate the people on this ideology and to train them for its practice. Natural resources were extravagantly exploited and number of industries were established in the tribal region. It destroyed and polluted the environment and in the mean time brought a hoard of outsiders to the region to run these industries and institutions. The locals were found unfit for these jobs, even for manual works, labourers were imported from outside. The trend still continues even after the independence of India as there is no reservation of jobs for tribal people in such private organizations. Even in government jobs where bribery and manipulation is rampant, the tribals are merely silent spectators. This has resulted in outmigration of tribal people to other states like Assam, West Bengal, Tripura, Andaman and Nicobar islands, in the east; and Delhi, Punjab, Haryana, Gujarat and Maharashtra, in the west. One important trend with respect to tribal migration today is the migration of female workforce. The unmarried girls, of the age group of 10 to 15 as maidservants in elite and affluent houses in metropolitan cities like Delhi and Calcutta who offer jobs to them with meagre salaries and facilities. They help in all household chores from baby sitting to everything. The outmigration of tribal workforce—males and females, has very seriously affected the society and traditional economy, that is, agriculture, and culture adversely. The tribal people have already suffered a lot due to this, besides modernization. The workforce is not available in villages today and the agriculture has been totally neglected.

There are schools in almost every village due to the private efforts of the people and not due to the government, and every family wants to get their children educated. Nowadays studying even in rural village environment, is a full time job and whole day affair. During earlier days, children while studying were also associated in agricultural operations and many other household works, and thus, a link was maintained with the traditional and modern. Now parents expect best results from their wards. The value of money and time are now considered great and since most of the schools are privately run, there is no free education, except in few *Balvadis* of the government, and since, agriculture has been pushed down to the lowest grade occupation, children are not given training in various chores of the occupation. Further, since children are not allowed to associate themselves in traditional occupation, like agriculture, they are drawn away from the nature and knowledge associated with it. The result is that the children are unaware of the importance and value of nature as science laboratory. Moreover, they develop aloofness towards agriculture and other traditional occupation.

The school-going children, thus keep themselves isolated or rather are kept so by the parents themselves for fear of poor performance in school which would defeat their aspiration of a good modern life. The grandparents and parents have no role to play in making the children's life, for they are not prepared and initiated into one's society and community. The role is now played by the teachers and books. The children are expected to learn the good things from the teachers and not from parents and the books are supposed to be the storehouse of knowledge which the students must acquire. Though, nowadays most of the teachers belong to the region itself, they themselves have developed disinterest in the knowledge that exist in their own society and culture since they were trained in the system that does not fit in the existing system. Since the knowledge of the community cannot provide the knowledge that is demanded by the modern world for which every member of the tribe has aspiration, it is looked upon as obsolete. The philosophy, values, etiquettes and morals that the society has inherited such as respect to the old and elders, honesty, truthfulness, fellow-feelings and compassion, etc., have no practical value in life. Instead the same values are taught in the schools by the teachers and learnt from books. The result is that the parents and society have no role in imparting moral education and discipline to children. The children learn and imbibe such values and practices which are foreign and unconducive to existing culture and society. Today children are being prepared or cultured in test-tube environment and they become misfit to their own society and culture. There is lack of empathy among youths resulting in the spread of social pathology and vices. Since the modern education gives emphasis in the preparation and development of a unidirectional individual personality and not on a wholistic man resulting in the disregard of common ideology lack of ability to accept the views of others even in matters of common interest. The going away from each other in different directions has resulted in disunity in the society. The quality of humility, trustworthiness, loyalty and honesty is no more there among the literate and educated tribals today. The parents and grandparents stand no ideals or models for today's youths and are unworthy of their respect. This has developed an ambience of drift from one's society and culture among the youths.

The tribal society today, is not getting the services of the youths they are preparing under modern education system. The society and the village lack leadership where it is needed urgently. The economy, society and culture has degenerated to the extent that its regeneration looks distant, though its attempt is already in the offing. The folklore traditions is the worst area of disregard by the community people themselves. The regular performance of traditional music and dance in village *akhra* have long been discontinued. When the craze for modern education was at its peak, singing and dancing were forbidden in the villages so as to put minimum disturbance to school-going children in their study. Even if the dances were performed during some auspicious occasion, the children were prohibited to participate stating that this is the symbol of backwardness.

Revival— A Distant Hope

Now, when the air of its revival is blowing in full speed, and *Akasvani* and *Doordarshan* provide enough time for folk music and dance in their broadcast and telecast and dance troupes are exported to various foreign countries, the youths have started participating in such dance activities. But the music and dance as is being performed today do not conform to the traditional forms and style at all. Further, there is a total lack of aesthetics in it, though it is labelled as tribal and traditional.

The position of music and dance today is that the traditional dance ground better known as *akhra* have already been reduced to personal property in most of the villages as music and dance are no longer performed. The traditional dress and ornaments too, are no longer in use and the knowledge of making traditional dress, decoration, ornament and music have already been forgotten by the people. Changes in dress, decoration and ornament is not due to change in taste of the people but it was done deliberately by the people themselves due to influence of modern education and impact of Christianity and Hinduization. The tribals who were influenced by the above three factors, denounced the practice and performance of music and dance. The performers were branded as backward, uncivilized and the traditional dress and ornament are symbols of such status. Though all the musical instruments that were in use earlier during dance are still in use, but the technique of its handling and traditional *tala*, that is, the knowledge of producing traditional musical sound have already been lost into oblivion except in *paika* dance. The sound of musical instruments played during dance is just a jumbled one with no tune and *tala*. So also is the case with dance. It lacks style and aesthetics, as steps and paces are not taken in a measured way as in traditional dance. So far as song is concerned, very few songs are composed these days and that too by the professionals and not by amateurists as earlier. However, whenever any dance is organized, traditional songs are sung, but because of lack of practice, it has lost the original melody. In short, the music and dance of the Mundas today have lost all vitality and beauty besides forms and styles and cannot be termed traditional, but since they are performed by the tribals, they are called tribal dance.

The musical culture that has been described in this treatise is no longer in existence. The valleys, dales and fields no longer resound with sounds of music. The melodious sound of *dumang* has already died out. Everywhere there exists an erie silence because the throat is sealed, the *mandar* has broken into pieces and the grass has overgrown in the *akhra*—the traditional dance ground and so, the musical culture of the Mundas is dead. But in future professionals in the area may emerge and then it will get a new life and direction.

BIBLIOGRAPHY

A. Van Exam, S.J., 1982, "The Religious System of the Munda Tribe." Collectanea Instituti, *Anthropos,* Vol. 128.

Annual Review of Anthropology, 1979 Vol. 20, No. 3 (September) pp. 585-86.

Annual Review of Anthropology, 1971, Vol. 7.

Anonymous, 1943, "An Indian Riddle Book, Chhotanagpur, 'Munda'." *Man in India, Vol.* 23, p. 288.

Anonymous, 1963-64, *Adibasi,* p. 182.

Anonymous, 1974, *The Hill of Fluits, A Life, Love and Poetry of Tribal India: A Portrait of the Santals.* London, George Allen & Unwin.

Anonymous, 1956, Brochure of Cultural Research Institute, West Bengal.

Anthropologist, 1968, *VOA* (Voice of America Broadcasting Service), Higgin Bothams (P) Limited.

Ashley Montague, 1961, *Man in Process,* A Mentor Book.

Badlock, C.R., 1975, *Levi-Strauss: Structuralism and Sociological Theory,* Hutchinson.

Bahl D. Van, *Symbol for Commumicbtion.* The Hague: Mouton Publishers.

Ben, Amos, Den and Kenneth Goldsmith, 1975, *Folklore: Performances and Communication* (eds.), The Hague: Mouton Publisher.

Bhaduri, B.N., 1942, "Hindu Influence on Munda Songs", In J.P. Mills *et al.,* (eds), *Essays in Anthropology, presented to S.C. Roy,* pp. 256-60.

Blackburn, Robin (ed.), 1972, *Ideology in Social Science: Readings in Critical Social Theory.*

Boas, Fanz, 1911, *The Mind of Primitive Man.* Macmillan, New York.

Boissevain, J. and Clyde Mitchel (eds.), *Network Analysis: Studies in Human Interaction,* The Hague: Mouton Publisher.

Bhatnagar, Manju, Oral Traditions and Society in Rajasthan: A Sociological Study of Folksong in a Selected Linguistic Region, Rajasthan, 1964-72. Doctoral Dissertation.

Bottomore, T.B., 1971, *Sociology: A Guide to Problem and Literature,* Revised edition.

Bowra, C.M., 1962, *Primitive Songs, V.* Vecidden. Field and Nicolsion, London.

Bright, William, 1963, "Language and Music, Areas for Co-operation", *Ethnomusicology,* 7(1), pp. 26-32.

Collins, Orvis and Jume M. Collins, 1972, *Interaction and Social Structure,* The Hague: Mouton Publisher.

Cuper A., *Anthropologists and Anthropology—The British School,* 1922-72.

Das, Amal Kumar. 1995, "A Systematic Analysis of the Social System of the Munda Community", *Bulletin of the Cultural Research Institute,* West Bengal, Vol. 4, p. 9.

Das, Nityanand, 1954 "Karam Festival in Munda Village." *Vanyajati,* Vol. 2, p. 22.

Davies, John Booth, *The Psychology of Music,* Stanford University Press.

Deva, Indira, 1978, "Must Folk Culture Die", *Eastern Anthropologist,* Vol. 37, No. 4, (Oct-Dec.), Special Issue.

Deva, Indira, 1956, "Modern Social Forces in Indian Folk Song." *Diogames,* p. 15.

Deva, Indira, *Folklore Studies : A Trend Report,* (In a Survey Research in Sociology and Social Anthropology). Bombay : Popular Prakashan.

D. Groot, Adrian D., *Methodology : Foundation of Inference and Research in the Behavioural Sciences.* The Hague : Mouton Publisher.

Donn, V. Hart, 1964, *Riddle in Filipino Folklore : An Anthropological Analysis.* Syracuse University Press.

Dorson, Richard, M. (ed.), *Folksong in the Modern World.* The Hague : Mouton Publisher.

Dorson, Richard, M. (ed.), *Folklore and Traditional History.* The Hague: Mounton Publisher.

Douglas, Mary, 1973, *Rules and Meanings, The Anthropology of Every Day Knowledge.* Penguin Modern Sociology Reading.

Douglas, Mary, 1973, *Natural Symbols Exploration in Cosmology,* Penguin Books.

Duncan, Hugh Dalziel, 1964, *Symbols and Social Theory.* Oxford University Press.

Dundes, Allen (ed.), *Analytical Essays in Folkloristics.* The Hague : Mouton Publisher.

Dundes, Allen (ed.), *Vario Folklorica.* The Thague : Mouton Publisher.

Finnegan, R., 1969, *Attitude to the Study of Oral Literature in British Social Anthropology,* pp. 59-89.

Firth, R., 1959, *Man and Culture,* Routledge and Kegan Paul.

Fishman, Joshua A., (ed.), 1972 *Reading in Sociology of Language.* The Hague : Mouton Publishers.

Fox Robin, 1967, *Kinship and Marriage in Anthropological Perspective* Penguin Books.

Francis, L.K. Hsu, 1972, *Psychological Anthropology.*

Fuchs, Stephen, 1965, *Rebellion Prophets : A Study of Messianic Movements in Indian Religions.* Asia Publishing House, Bombay.

Ganguli, Satya K., 1958, "A Few Munda and Oraon Folksongs", *Indian Folklore,* Vol. 1, No. 4.

Ganguli, Satya K., 1962, "A Munda Spring Festival", *Indian Folklore,* Vol. 3, No. 1.

Greene, John C., 1963, *Darwin and Modern Worldview, the Rockwell Lectures,* Rice University. A Mentor Book.

Hadon, T.C., 1921, "The Marriage (Munda)." *Man in India,* Vol. 1.

Hammond, Peter B., 1971, *An Introduction to Cultural and Social Anthropology.* New York : The MacMillan Company.

Handoo, Jawaharlal, 1982, "Theory and Problem of meaning in Folklore". In *International Journal of Asian Studies,* Vol. II, No. 1.

Harold D. Lasswell, Daniel Larner, Ithiel D. Sola Pool, 1952, *The*

Comparative Study of Symbols : An Introduction, Stanford University Press.

Hassan Wahid, U.I., 1957, "Economic of Exchange among the Munda." *Bulletin of the Deptt. of Anthropology,* Bihar University, Vol. 1.

Helmost, G.C., 1970, Research Concept in Human Behaviour.

Herskovits, Melvills, 1955, 1969, *Cultural-Anthropology,* Oxford University Press.

Herskovits, Melvills, 1974, *The Economic Life of Primitive People,* New Delhi : Eurasia Publishing House (Pvt.) Ltd.

Hillary Mansion, 1974, *British Social Anthorpology and Language : A History of Separate Development,* Oxford : Clarendon Press.

Hoffmann, John, 1907, "Mundari Poetry, Music and Dances", *Journal of the Royal Asiatic Society of Bengal,* Vol. 2.

Honingmann, John J., 1977, *Understanding Culture,* Oxford and IBH Publishing Company, Indian Edition.

Horstman, Monika Thiel, 1978, "Indian Traditional Christian Folksongs", *Man in India,* Vol. 58, No. 2 (April-June).

Hymes, Dell, 1964, *Language in Culture and Society : A Reader in Language and Anthropology,* Allied Publishers Private Limited.

Jason, Heda and Demitri, Segal (ed.), *Pattern in Oral Literature.* The Hague : Mouton Publishers.

Jellinhauss, T., 1871, "Sagen Sitten and Gebralcha Der Munda Kohlin Chhotanagpur." *Deitschrift fur Ethnologie,* Vol. 3.

Jenet L. Dolgin, David S. Kemmitzer and David M. Sneider (eds.), 1977, *Symbolic Anthropology : A Reading in the Study of Symbols and Meanings.* New York : Columbia University Press.

Jension, Heda, 1969, "A Multi-dimensional Approach in Oral Literature." *Current Anthropology.* X(U), Part-II.

Judith Lynne, Hanna, *To Dance is Human : A Theory of Non-verbal Communication.*

Kala Rani, 1959, "Coming of Age among Munda Girls." *Bulletin of the Deptt. of Anthropology,* Bihar University, Vol. 1.

Kluckhohn, C., 1962, *Culture and Behaviour.*

Kongas, Maranda, Elli and Pierre, Maranda, *Structural Model in Folklore and Transformal Essays,* The Hague : Mouton Publishers.

Lane, Michael (ed.), 1970, *Structuralism : A Reader*. London : Cape.

Lerrain, Jorge, 1979, *The Concept of Ideology,* BI Publications.

Lewis, I.M., 1979, *Social Anthropology in Perspective,* Penguin Books.

Loflin Marvin and James Silverberg (eds.). *Discourse and Inference in Cognitive Anthropology: An Approach to Psyschic Unity and Enculturation.* The Hague: Mouton Publisher.

Lomax, Alan *et al.,* 1968, *Folksong Style and Culture,* Washington (DC): American Association for the Advancement of Science.

Maletinsku, Eliazar M., 1976, "Structural Typological Study of Folklore". *Social Science* (USSR Academy of Sciences, Moscow), No. 3.

Mann, R.S., 1981, *Nature, Man-Spirit Complex in Tribal India.* New Delhi : Concept Publishing Company.

Maranda, P., *Soviet Structural Folkloristics.* The Hague : Mouton Publishers.

Maranda, P., *Mythology. Penguin Modern Sociology Readings.* Penguin Education.

Martin, Roderick, 1978, *The Sociology of Power.* New Delhi.

Mauric Freedman, *Social and Cultural Anthropology.* pp. 59-62 (Music).

Mccormack, William C. and Stephen A. Wuurm (eds.), *Approaches to Languages Anthropological Issues.* The Hague : Mouton Publisher.

Mccormack, W.C. and S.A. Wuurm, 1978, *Language and Thought.* Chicago: Aldine Publishing Company.

Meriam Alan P., 1964, *The Anthropology of Music.* Evaston North Western University Press.

Mitchel Rev. and J. Murrey, 1875, "Munda Kohl Wedding Songs from the German of the Rev. Jellinghauss." *Indian Antiquary,* Vol. 4.

Mitra, S.C., 1916, "Demon Cult in Mundari Children's Games". *Journal of Asiatic Society of Bengal,* Vol. 12.

Mukherjee, Radhakamal, 1979, *Society and Community.* Ajmer : Sachin Publication.

Mundri, Lal Sing, 1956, "A Munda Birth." *Man in India,* Vol. 36, No. 1.

Mundri, Lal Sing, 1956, "A Comparative Analysis of the Economics of the Munda Culture." *Vanyajati*, Vol. 4.

Pandey, Mithila Sharan, 1963, *The Historical Geography and Topography of Bihar*, Delhi : Motilal Banarasi Dass.

Parkinson, G.H.R. (ed.), 1968, *The Theory of Meaning*. Oxford University Press.

Parmer, Shyam, *Folk Music and Mass Media.*

Patnaik, Nityanand, 1955, "The Socio-political Organization of the Munda—A Study of Acculturation", *Vanyajati*, Vol. 3.

Patterson, Anyo, 1977, *Anthropology of Dance*. Royce Bloomington, Indiana University.

Ponette, S.J. (ed.), 1978, *The Munda World*. Hoffman Commemoration Volume, Ranchi : Catholic Press.

Prasad, Dineshwar, 1970, *Lok Sahitya aur Sanskriti*. Allahabad: Lok Bharati Prakashan.

Prasad, Dineshwar, 1955, "A Comparative Analysis of the Economic Aspect of the Munda Culture." *Vanyajati*, Vol. 3.

Prasad, Narmadeshwar, 1961, *Land and People of Tribal Bihar*, Ranchi: Bihar Tribal Research Institute.

Prasad, Onkar, 1978, "Contemporary Indian Music: A classification with special reference to the field of Benaras", *Man in India*, Vol. 58, No. 3.

Rev. Oakley F.S. and Tara Dutt Gairola, 1935, *Himalayan Folklore*. Allahabad.

Richard Feinberg, 1979, "Sneider's Symbolic Culture Theory: An Appraisal with CA Comments." In *Current Anthropology*, (Sept.) Vol. 20, No. 3: 541.

Riseley, H.M., 1891, *Tribes and Castes of Bengal*. Vol. II, Calcutta.

Roy, Mrinal, 1957, "Parha at Work": Bulletin of the Department of Anthropology. Bihar University, Vol. 1.

Roy, Manjushree, 1965, "Leisure—Its Utilization in a Munda Village". *Bulletin of the Cultural Research Institute*, West Bengal, Vol. 4.

Roy, Ramesh Chandra, 1930, "Aboriginal Village Organization in India." *Journal of the Bihar and Orissa Research Society*, Vol. 16.

Roy, S.C., 1907 "Cosmogony and Traditional History." *The Indian World* (December).

Roy, S.C., 1912, *The Munda and Their Country*. Calcutta: City Book Society.

Roy, S.C., 1914, "Magic and Witchcraft on the Chotanagpur Plateau (Oraon and Munda)." *Journal of the Asiatic Society of Bengal*, Vol. 10.

Roy, S.C., 1916, "The Divine Myth of the Mundas." *Journal of the Bihar and Orissa Research Society*, Vol. 2.

Roy, S.C., 1946, "Theory of Rent among the Mundas of Chotanagpur." *Man in India*, Vol. 26, No. 3-4.

Sachchidananda, 1957, "Crime and Punishment in a Munda Village." *Man in India*, Vol. 37, No. 2.

Sachchidananda, 1957, "Social Structure of a Chotanagpur Village". *Bulletin of the Department of Anthropology*. Bihar University.

Sachchidananda, 1959, *Culture Change among the Munda and the Oraon*. Ranchi: Bihar Tribal Research Institute.

Sachchidananda, 1960, "Culture Change in Tribal Bihar: Munda and Oraon", *Bulletin of Bihar Tribal Research Institute*. Ranchi, Vol. 2, No. 2.

Sachchidananda, 1965, *Profile of Tribal Culture in Bihar*, Calcutta: K.L. Mukhopadhyay.

Sachchidananda, 1979, *The Changing Munda*. New Delhi: Concept Publishing Company.

Sahu, L.N., 1955, "Munda Songs." *Vanyajati*, Vol. 3.

Sahu, R.K., 1955, "A Review of Munda Songs" *Vanyajati*, Vol. 3, No. 1.

Siegel, Bernard J. (ed.), 1959, 1962 1965, 1970, *Biennial Review of Anthropology*. Stanford University Press, Stanford (California).

Siegel and Beals, Alan R. (eds.), 1967, 1969, *Biennial Review of Anthropology*.

Singh, Ram Bhujawan, 1978, "Munda Ke Jaher." *Vanyajati*, Vol. 58, No. 3.

Singh, Suresh, 1966, *Dust-storm and Hanging Mist: Story of Birsa Munda and his Movement*. Calcutta: K.L. Mukhopadhyay.

Spencer, Dorothy M., 1959, The Munda Theory of Legal Punishment. *Bulletin of the Bihar Tribal Research Institute*, Ranchi, Vol. 1, No. 1.

Spiro M. (ed.), 1968, *Context and Meaning in Cultural Anthropology, The Rise of Anthropological Theory*. London : Routledge and Kegan Paul.

Srivastava, L.R.N., 1955, "The Munda Gods." *Orissa Tribal Research Institute Journal*. Cuttack, Inaugural Number, Vol. 1, No. 1.

Srivastava, L.R.N., 1955, "Munda Eschatology". *Bulletin of the Department of Anthropology*. Bihar University, No. 1.

Stephen, A. Tylor, 1969, "Cognitive Anthropology, Some Munda Songs." *Indian Folklore*, Vol. 1. No. 3.

Stephen, A. Tylor, "Funeral rites of the Mundas on the Ranchi Plateau", *Anthropos*, Vol. 50.

Fr. Toppo, Mathias, 1978, *Adibasi Lok Nrit*. Ranchi: St. Albert College.

Fr. Toppo, Mathias, 1978, *Mandar ka Sumdhur Tal*. Ranchi: St. Albert College.

Fr. Topno M., 1978, "Spirits in the Life and Belief of the Mundas." *Sevartham*.

Trigunayat, Jagdish, 1966, "Munda Geet aur Unmen Prem Pukar." *Vanyajati*, Vol. 4, No. 2.

Trigunayat, Jagdish, 1966, "Munda Geet our Unmen Prem Pukar." *Vanyajati*, Vol. 4, No.2.

Topno, Sem, 1982, *Kurshinama: Mundaon ka Nrijati Itihas*, Anthropological Survey of India, Calcutta.

Upadhyay, K. D., 1957, *Lok Sahitya ki Bhumika*, Allahabad.

Ved Prakash, Vatuk, 1979, *Studies in Indian Folk Traditions*. Delhi: Manohar Publishers.

Vidyarthi, L.P., 1955, "Land and Labour among the Mundas of Bihar." *Journal of the Bombay Research Society*, Vol. 41, No. 3.

Vogt, Vilmos, 1969, "Towards Balancing of Folklore Structuralism". *Acta Ethnographica* (Budapest), Vol. 18.

Vogt, Vilmos, Music in the Making. *International Journal of Social Sciences*. Vol. 94.

Vogt, Vilmos, 1967, Music. *Encyclopaedia of the Social Sciences*. (a) Vol. III, (b) Vol. XI, New York: The Macmillan Comp. Sixth Printing.

Vogt, Vilmos, 1979, "Music." *Current Anthropology,* Vol. 20, No. 3: 585-86.

V. Gordon Chide, 1956, *Man Makes Himself,* London: Watts and Co.

Wallace, Anthony F.C., 1970, *Religion: An Anthropological View.* New York: Random House.

William, Thomas R., *Psychological Anthropology.* The Hague: Mouton Publishers.

Worsley, Peter, 1970, *Introducing Sociology.* Penguin Books.

Yamadu, Rynji, 1955, "A General Survey of the Tribal Structures among the Mundas." *The Japanese Journal of Ethnology,* Vol. 20, No. 384.

Yamadu, Rynji, 1958, "The Myth of the Origin of the Cosmos among the Mundas". Notes from the Joint Meetings of the Japanese Anthropological Society and the Japanese Ethnological 12th.

Yamadu, Rynji, 1959, "The Concept of the Spirit of the Dead as Evidenced in Funeral among the Munda." *The Japanese Journal of Ethnology,* Vol. 23, 3-4.

INDEX